Catholic Bishops of Great Britain

A reference to Roman Catholic bishops from 1850 to 2015

— CHRIS LARSEN —

WITH A FOREWORD BY
HIS EMINENCE
CARDINAL CORMAC MURPHY-O'CONNOR

Sacristy
Press

Sacristy Press
PO Box 612, Durham, DH1 9HT

www.sacristy.co.uk

First published in 2016 by Sacristy Press, Durham

Sacristy Limited, registered in England & Wales, number 7565667

British Library Cataloguing-in-Publication Data
A catalogue record for the book is available from the British Library

ISBN 978-1-910519-25-7

ACKNOWLEDGEMENTS

- PIUS IX, Apostolic Letter: *Universalis ecclesiae* in BECK **AA** (ed.), Rt Rev. George Andrew, The English Catholics 1850–1950, London: Burns Oates, 1950, pp107–115. Reproduced by kind permission of Bloomsbury Publishing plc.
- LEO XIII, Apostolic Letter: *Ex supremo apostolatus apice*, Edinburgh: J Miller and Sons, 1878, (SM/6/28/2). Reproduced by kind permission of Scottish Catholic Archives: Historical Collection at University of Aberdeen.

With grateful thanks to the following bishops for the use of their personal coats of arms:

- His Eminence Vincent Cardinal Nichols, archbishop of Westminster.
- Rt Rev. C. P. Richard Moth, bishop of Arundel and Brighton.
- Most Rev. Bernard Longley, archbishop of Birmingham.
- Rt Rev. Alan Williams **SM**, bishop of Brentwood (diocesan arms).
- Most Rev. George Stack, archbishop of Cardiff (archdiocesan arms).
- Rt Rev. Declan Lang, bishop of Clifton.
- Rt Rev. Alan Hopes, bishop of East Anglia.
- Rt Rev. Ralph Heskett **CSsR**, bishop of Hallam.
- Rt Rev. Séamus Cunningham, bishop of Hexham and Newcastle (plus diocesan arms).
- Rt Rev. Michael Campbell **OSA**, bishop of Lancaster.
- Rt Rev. Marcus Stock, bishop of Leeds.
- Most Rev. Malcolm McMahon **OP**, archbishop of Liverpool (plus arch-diocesan arms).
- Rt Rev. Thomas Burns **SM**, bishop of Menevia.
- Rt Rev. Terence Drainey, bishop of Middlesbrough.
- Rt Rev. Peter Doyle, bishop of Northampton.
- Rt Rev. Patrick McKinney, bishop of Nottingham.

- Rt Rev. Mark O'Toole, bishop of Plymouth.
- Rt Rev. Philip Egan, bishop of Portsmouth.
- Rt Rev. John Arnold, bishop of Salford.
- Rt Rev. Mark Davies, bishop of Shrewsbury (diocesan arms).
- Most Rev. Peter Smith, archbishop of Southwark (plus archdiocesan arms).
- Rt Rev. Peter Brignall, bishop of Wrexham.

- Most Rev. Leo Cushley, archbishop of St Andrews and Edinburgh.
- Rt Rev. Dom. Hugh Gilbert **OSB**, bishop of Aberdeen.
- Rt Rev. Brian McGee, bishop of Argyll and the Isles (diocesan arms).
- Rt Rev. Stephen Robson, bishop of Dunkeld.
- Rt Rev. William Nolan, bishop of Galloway.
- Most Rev. Philip Tartaglia, archbishop of Glasgow.
- Rt Rev. Joseph Toal, bishop of Motherwell (diocesan arms).
- Rt Rev. John Keenan, bishop of Paisley (diocesan arms).

- His Excellency Most Rev. Antonio Mennini, apostolic nuncio to Great Britain.
- Rev. Stephen Sharkey, chancellor to the Bishopric of the Forces.
- Most Rev. Hlib Lonchyna **MSU**, Bishop of Ukrainian Eparchy of the Holy Family of London.
- Most Rev. Paul Chomnycky **OSBM**, Apostolic Exarch for Ukrainians in Stamford (CT), USA.
- Rev. Mgr Keith Newton, ordinary for Personal Ordinariate of Our Lady of Walsingham.

Also, grateful thanks to the following:

- His Eminence Cormac Cardinal Murphy-O'Connor, retired Cardinal archbishop of Westminster.
- His Excellency Most Rev. Giovanni Angelo Becciu, sostituto at Vatican Secretariat of State.

- Mr David Cheney, webmaster of "Catholic-Hierarchy".
- Mr Robert Finnigan, archivist of Diocese of Leeds.
- Rev. Vincent Flynn, Archdiocese of Southwark.
- Rev. Simon Gillespie, Diocese of Nottingham.
- Mr Brian Plumb, assistant archivist of Archdiocese of Liverpool.
- Mr Peter Sims-Coomber, archivist of Archdiocese of Cardiff.

FOREWORD

We read in the Gospels that Jesus called his earliest collaborators, the Twelve Apostles, and commissioned them to preach his Word and shepherd his people. Ever since those early days of the Church, the ministry of the Apostles has been handed on from generation to generation, so that the Good News may be heard in every place and time. The bishops of the Church, successors of the Apostles, are the guardians of this task. Together, they ensure that the Gospel continues to be proclaimed.

In our own country, this lineage of bishops has continued since at least St Augustine, sent by Pope St Gregory the Great in 597 AD. Although bishops could not be appointed during the penal times of the Reformation, Rome still continued to provide for the spiritual welfare of the people of our lands. However, in 1850 the Hierarchy was restored in England and Wales, and with it the full complement of bishops, able to publically undertake the functions of governing, teaching and sanctifying the people of God. Nor should we forget the Restoration of the Hierarchy in Scotland, which happened a few years later in 1878. Since then, around three hundred good and holy priests have been raised to the episcopacy in England, Wales and Scotland; for that we give thanks to God. Each has been given to the Church for a particular reason. They have been men of their time and place, and have left their mark on the lives of the people they were called to serve.

Their names are to be found in so many local places: in parish histories, on foundation stones, in portraits and in so many memories and retold stories. This book gathers much of that information together, bringing into one volume the briefest details of those many shepherds who have worked among the flock in these lands. Their names continue to live on, and we give thanks to God for the foundations they laid and the work they did: we continue to reap a rich harvest today from their sowing.

It is a tribute to so many Catholics in every part of our country that the faith has continued to burn so brightly over so many years. May the Church continue to be blessed with holy bishops, and may this book serve as an inspiration for all who follow in the footsteps of such illustrious men.

With my prayers and blessing to all who read this work.

His Eminence CORMAC Cardinal MURPHY-O'CONNOR
Cardinal-Priest of Santa Maria sopra Minerva
Retired Cardinal archbishop of Westminster
Chiswick, London, April 2015

PREFACE

This biographical history attempts to catalogue the significant events of all Catholic diocesan bishops who have been in office since the Restoration of the Catholic Hierarchy in England and Wales in 1850. There are further chapters relating to the diocesan bishops of Scotland, since the Restoration of the Catholic Hierarchy there in 1878. The work has developed over a number of years into a comprehensive reference guide to around 300 men, ordained in the episcopal order, who have given their life in service to the local Catholic Church.

Each diocese is taken in turn, first giving a brief description of the history of that territory, details of the province to which it belongs, as well as a definition of its geographical location. There follows a concise biographical list of all diocesan and auxiliary bishops who have ministered in that see, including the bishops' full names, any known qualifications, place and date of birth, places and dates of presbyteral and episcopal ordination, translation and retirement, followed by date and place of death and subsequent burial if appropriate. At the end of each individual entry, the last known address for that bishop is given, whether he died in office, abroad or in retirement. The last entry of each chapter shows the current bishop along with any of his auxiliaries.

Diocesan or episcopal coats of arms have been included, used with permission by those bishops mentioned in the Acknowledgements (above). These images have been obtained from a variety of sources, resulting in inferior reproduction quality in a small number of cases.

In addition, all Popes since 1800, the papal nuncios, bishops to the armed forces, the Ukrainian bishops and the Ordinary of Our Lady of Walsingham are treated in a similar way. A translation is given of the primary Letters Apostolic, "*Universalis ecclesiae*" and "*Ex supremo apostolatus apice*", which re-established the Catholic Hierarchy of bishops and dioceses in this country.

In the second half of the book, there is a quick-reference guide to the hierarchies in England and Wales and Scotland at the present time, followed by a more complete address list of all living bishops, including those who are now retired or living and working abroad. A full chronological list of all significant bishop events then follows along with indexes of titular sees and cardinal titles.

It is hoped that this reference book may be of particular use to diocesan archivists and church historians, but will equally appeal to all those interested in the general history and origins of the Catholic dioceses of Great Britain. The author has drawn on a wide variety of sources in an effort to organize and present the information as completely, concisely and consistently as possible. Although most of the facts and figures listed here may indeed be found in other publications and on various websites, this book brings it all together into one place of reference. The author would like to thank those diocesan secretaries and archivists who have provided invaluable assistance over the years with countless bits and pieces of information.

As this book records the episcopal milestones of the last two hundred years, it also stands as a respectful testament to those bishops who have gone before us marked with the sign of faith who continue to inspire and encourage their living successors in the Catholic Church in Britain today.

CHRIS LARSEN
Gateshead, December 2015

CONTENTS

UNIVERSALIS ECCLESIAE

THE POWER OF GOVERNING THE UNIVERSAL CHURCH, CONFIDED by Our Lord Jesus Christ to the Roman Pontiff in the person of St Peter, Prince of the Apostles, has preserved in the Apostolic See, during the whole course of centuries, that admirable solicitude with which she watches over the good of the Catholic religion in all the earth, and zealously provides for its advancing progress. Thus is fulfilled the design of her Divine Founder, who in establishing a Head, assured, in His profound wisdom, the safety of the Church even to the consummation of the world. The effect of this Pontifical solicitude was felt by the noble realm of England as well as by other nations. History attests that from the first ages of the Church, the Christian religion was introduced into Great Britain, where it flourished until the middle of the fifth century, when not only public affairs, but religion also, fell into the most deplorable condition after the invasion of the Angli and the Saxons. But Our most holy predecessor, Gregory the Great, quickly sent to that island the monk Augustine and his companions, and after raising him and many others to the episcopal dignity, and adding a considerable number of monks who were priests, he converted the Anglo-Saxons to the Christian religion, and succeeded, by their means, in re-establishing and extending the Catholic Faith in Britain, which then began to be called England. To come, however, to things more recent, nothing more evident can be found in the history of the Anglican schism, which was consummated in the sixteenth century, than the action and ever constant solicitude of the Roman Pontiffs, Our predecessors, in succouring and sustaining, by every possible means, the Catholic religion, exposed in that kingdom to the greatest perils and reduced to extremities.

It was for this purpose, not to mention other matters, that the Supreme Pontiffs, and those acting by their orders and with their approbation, exerted themselves that England should never want for men dedicated to the support of Catholicism, and that Catholic youths of good dispositions should be sent to the continent, there to be carefully educated, and instructed above all in the ecclesiastical sciences, in order that when they had received holy orders, they should return to their country, to sustain their compatriots with the ministry of the word and sacraments, and to defend and propagate the true faith.

But the zeal of Our predecessors will be seen more clearly in their exertions to provide the English Catholics with pastors clothed with episcopal character, after a furious and implacable tempest had deprived them of the presence and pastoral zeal of bishops. First of all, the Letters Apostolic of Gregory XV, commencing with the words *Ecclesia romana*, and dated 23 March 1623, prove that the Supreme Pontiff, as soon as ever it was possible, deputed to the government of English and Scottish Catholics, William Bishop, consecrated Bishop of *Chalcedon*, with ample faculties and with the proper power of Ordinaries. After the death of Bishop, Urban VIII renewed this mission, by his Letters Apostolic of 4 February 1625, directed to Richard Smith, on whom he conferred the bishopric of *Chalcedon*, and all the powers accorded to Bishop. More favourable days seemed dawning for the Catholic religion at the commencement of the reign of James II. Innocent XI was quick to use the opportunity, and, in 1685, deputed John Leyburne, Bishop of *Adrumetum*, as Vicar Apostolic over all the Kingdom of England. Afterwards, by Letters Apostolic of 30 January 1688, commencing *Super cathedram*, he added to him three other Vicars Apostolic, bishops *in partibus*, so that all England, by the care of the Apostolic Nuncio there resident, namely Ferdinand, Archbishop of *Amasia*, was divided by this Pope into four districts, the London, the Western, the Central and the Northern, which then began to be governed by Vicars Apostolic, fortified with the necessary faculties and with the proper power of Ordinaries. To aid them in fulfilling the duties of so grave a charge, the Vicars received rules which were either derived from the decisions of Benedict XIV in his Constitution of 30 May 1750, commencing with the words *Apostolicum ministerium*, or from the decisions of other Pontiffs, Our predecessors, or from those of Our Congregation for the Propagation of the Faith. This partition of all England into four Apostolic vicariates lasted until the time of Gregory XVI, who, considering the increase then obtained by the Catholic religion in that Kingdom, made a new ecclesiastical division of the country. And by his Letters Apostolic of 3 July 1840, commencing *Muneris apostolici*, he doubled the number of the Vicars Apostolic, confiding the spiritual government of England to eight Vicars Apostolic of the London district, the Western and Eastern, the Central, and the districts of Wales, Lancashire, Yorkshire and the Northern.

The little already said, many other matters being passed by in silence, proves clearly that Our predecessors exerted themselves strenuously to use every means which their authority offered them, to console and restore the Church in England after her immense misfortunes. Having therefore before Our eyes this fair example of Our predecessors, and being desirous to imitate them and fulfil the duties of the Supreme Apostolate, and being moreover urged on by the affection of Our heart for that portion of the Lord's vineyard, We determined, from the very beginning of Our Pontificate, to follow up a work so well commenced, and to apply Ourselves seriously to favour the daily development of the Church in that Kingdom. Wherefore, considering the whole actual condition of Catholicism in England, reflecting on the considerable number of the Catholics, a number every day augmenting, and remarking how from day to day the obstacles become removed which chiefly opposed the propagation of the Catholic religion, We perceived that the time had arrived for restoring in England the ordinary form of ecclesiastical government, as freely constituted in other nations, where no particular cause necessitates the ministry of Vicars Apostolic.

We thought that considering the progress of time and of events, it was no longer necessary that English Catholics should be governed by Vicars Apostolic, but that, on the contrary, the changes already produced, demanded the form of ordinary episcopal government. This opinion was strengthened by the desires which were expressed by common accord by the Vicars Apostolic of England, and by great numbers of clergy and laymen distinguished for their virtues and for their rank, as well as by an immense majority among English Catholics.

In maturing this Our design We have not omitted to implore the aid of God, who is supremely great and good, that in the deliberation of so important a matter, it might be vouchsafed to Us to know and to do, that which would tend to the greater advantage of the Church. Moreover We implored the aid of the Mother of God, the most Holy Virgin Mary, and of the Saints who glorified England with their virtue, that they might obtain for Us, by intercession with God, a happy termination of this undertaking. We then confided the affair entirely to Our Venerable brothers the Cardinals of the Holy Roman Church who form Our Congregation of the Propaganda. Their decision was wholly conformable to Our desire, and We resolved to approve it and put it into execution. Therefore having weighed with the most scrupulous attention everything regarding this matter, We, of Our mere motion, of Our certain knowledge and by the plenitude of Our Apostolic authority, have decreed, and decree, the re-establishment within the kingdom of England, according to the common rules of the Church, of the Hierarchy of bishops ordinary, who shall take their names from the Sees which We by these present letters erect in the several districts of the Vicars Apostolic.

To commence with the London District, it shall form two sees, one, the See of Westminster, which We raise to the dignity of Metropolitan, or Archiepiscopal, the other, the See of Southwark, which, as also the other sees now created, We make suffragan to Westminster. The Diocese of Westminster shall comprehend that portion of the said district which extends to the banks of the Thames, and contains the counties of Middlesex, Essex and Hertford. The Diocese of Southwark will contain the portion lying to the south of the Thames, comprising the counties of Berkshire, Southampton, Surrey, Sussex and Kent, with the islands of Wight, Jersey, Guernsey and others adjacent. The Northern District shall be one Diocese only, taking its name from the city of Hexham, and the limits of the Diocese shall be the same as those of the District. The District of York similarly shall form one Diocese, whose bishop shall have his see at Beverley. In the Lancashire District shall be two bishops, one of whom, the Bishop of Liverpool, shall have for his Diocese, along with the Isle of Man, the Hundreds of Lonsdale, Amounderness, and West Derby; and the other, who will reside at Salford, and whose see will take its name from that city, shall have for his Diocese the Hundreds of Salford, Blackburn and Leyland*. Cheshire, although part of the Lancashire District, We adjoin to another Diocese. In the District of Wales there shall be two episcopal sees, namely Shrewsbury and Menevia united with Newport. The Diocese of Shrewsbury will consist of the counties lying in the northern part of the Welsh District, the counties namely of Anglesey, Caernarfon, Denbigh, Flint, Merioneth and Montgomery, to which We add Cheshire, taken from the Lancashire District, and Shropshire, taken from the Central District. To the Bishop of Newport and Menevia We assign for Diocese the southern part of the District of Wales, namely Brecknockshire, Cardiganshire, Carmarthenshire, Glamorganshire, Pembrokeshire and Radnorshire, and also the English counties of Monmouth and Hereford.

In the Western District We constitute the two episcopal Sees of Clifton and Plymouth, assigning to the Bishop of Clifton, for his Diocese, Gloucestershire, Somersetshire and Wiltshire. The Diocese of Plymouth shall comprise Devonshire, Dorsetshire and Cornwall. The Central District, from which We have already detached Shropshire, shall have two episcopal sees, at Nottingham and Birmingham. To Nottingham We assign for its Diocese Nottinghamshire, Derbyshire and Leicestershire, besides the counties of Lincoln and Rutland, which We separate from the Eastern District. Birmingham Diocese shall have Staffordshire, Warwickshire, Worcestershire and Oxfordshire. In the Eastern District will be but one bishopric, taking its name from Northampton, and it will comprise for its Diocese the former Eastern District, excepting the counties of Rutland and Lincoln, which We have already assigned to Nottingham. Thus in the very flourishing kingdom of England there will be one single Ecclesiastical Province, consisting of one Archbishop or Metropolitan, with twelve Suffragan Bishops, whose zeal and pastoral labours will, We hope, through the grace of God, ever produce fresh increase of Catholicism.

And therefore We desire at present to reserve it to Us and Our successors to divide this province still further and to augment the number of Dioceses, as necessity may arise, and in general to establish freely new boundaries of the same, according as it may seem fitting in the Lord's sight.

We command, meanwhile, the aforesaid archbishop and bishops, to send, at the appointed times, to the Congregation of the Propaganda, reports of the state of their churches, and to be diligent in informing Propaganda of everything which they shall think profitable for the spiritual good of their flocks. We will continue, in effect, to use the ministry of this Congregation in everything which concerns the churches in England. But in the sacred government of clergy and people, and in all that regards the pastoral office, the English archbishop and bishops will from the present time enjoy the rights and faculties which are or can be used, according to the general dispositions of the sacred canons and apostolic constitutions, by the Catholic archbishops and bishops of other nations, and they will be equally bound by the obligations, by which other archbishops and bishops are bound according to the common discipline of the Church.

With regard to whatever now prevails or is in vigour, either in the ancient form of the English churches, or in the subsequent state of the missions, by virtue of special constitutions, privileges or peculiar customs, seeing that the circumstances are no longer the same, none of these things shall for the future import either right or obligation. And, that no doubt concerning this matter may remain, We, in the plenitude of Our Apostolic authority, suppress and entirely abrogate all the obligatory and juridical force of these peculiar constitutions, privileges and customs, whatever may be their antiquity. The archbishop and bishops of England shall accordingly possess the integral power of regulating all the things which pertain to the carrying out of the common law of the Church, or which are left to the authority of bishops by the general discipline of the Church. We, however, will certainly not omit to assist them with Our Apostolic authority, and even with gladness will second their demands in everything which may seem to Us conducive to the greater glory of God and the salvation of souls. In decreeing, by these Our Letters, the restoration of the ordinary Hierarchy of Bishops and the resumption of the common law of the Church, We had it principally in view to provide for the prosperity and increase of the Catholic religion in the kingdom of England, but at the same time We desired to grant the prayers as well of Our Venerable Brothers, who govern the church in that kingdom as Vicars Apostolic of the Holy See, as also of very many beloved children of the Catholic clergy and people, from whom We received most urgent solicitations in this behalf. Their forefathers made often times similar demands to Our predecessors multiplied the number of vicars and of districts from time to time, not with the design of subjecting perpetually the

Catholic Church in England to an extraordinary form of government, but rather with the intention that while they provided, according to circumstances, for its increase, they at the same time might prepare the way for the future restoration of the ordinary Hierarchy.

And therefore We, to whom the accomplishment of this great work has been vouchsafed by God's infinite goodness, do hereby expressly declare that it is far from Our mind and intention to cause the prelates of England, now invested with the name and rights of Bishops Ordinary, to be in any manner deprived of the advantages which they previously enjoyed under the title of Vicars Apostolic. For reason forbids that Our decrees, wherewith We grant the prayers of English Catholics for the good of religion, should turn out to the detriment of the vicars. Furthermore, We rely with firmest confidence upon the hope that Our beloved children in Christ, who during such a variety of times have never failed in sustaining by their alms and donations the Catholic Church in England and the prelates who governed it as Vicars Apostolic, will display even greater liberality towards the bishops themselves, now bound by a more stable bond to the English churches, the splendour of Divine worship, the sustentation of the clergy, the relief of the poor, and other ecclesiastical purposes.

Finally, raising Our eyes to the hills from whence cometh Our help, We beseech God supremely good and great, with all prayer and supplication, with thanksgiving, that He, by the virtue of His Divine aid, may confirm the things by Us decreed for the welfare of the Church, and may grant the strength of His grace to those to whom appertains the execution of Our decree, to the end that they may feed the flock of God committed to their charge, and apply their zeal more and more to propagate the greater glory of His name. And, to obtain more abundant aids from heavenly grace, We lastly invoke, as intercessors with God, the most holy Mother of God, the holy apostles Peter and Paul, with the other celestial Patrons of England, and by name We invoke also Saint Gregory the Great, that, since to Us, notwithstanding the insufficiency of Our merits, was granted the renewal of episcopal sees in England, as he in his day established them to the great advantage of the Church, so the restoration of episcopal Dioceses, effected by Us in that Kingdom, may prove for the benefit of the Catholic religion.

We decree that these Our Apostolic Letters can never at any time be charged with the fault of omission or addition, or with defect of Our intention, or with any other defect, any that they can never be impugned in any way, but shall always be held valid and firm, and shall obtain effect in all things, and ought to be inviolably observed, notwithstanding general Apostolic edicts, and special sanctions of Synodal, Provincial and Universal Councils, and notwithstanding the rights and privileges of the ancient English Sees, and missions, and Apostolic vicariates subsequently constituted, and of the rights of any churches or pious institutes whatsoever, even although ratified by oath, or by Apostolic, or any other confirmation, and notwithstanding anything whatever to the contrary. For We expressly abrogate all such things, as far as they contradict this Our decree, even although special mention ought to be made, or although some other particular formality ought to be observed in their abrogation. We decree moreover that whatever may be done to the contrary, knowingly or ignorantly, by any person, in the name of any authority whatsoever shall be null and void. We decree also that copies, even printed, of these Our Letters, when subscribed by a Public Notary and confirmed by the seal of an Ecclesiastical Dignitary, shall have the same authenticity and credit, as would be given to the expression of Our will by the exhibition of the original Diploma itself.

Given at Rome at St Peter's, under the Fisherman's ring, the twenty-ninth day of September, one thousand eight hundred and fifty, in the fifth year of Our Pontificate.

x *His Holiness* **POPE BL. PIUS IX**

NOTES

*   By a re-script of the Letters Apostolic (*Universalis ecclesiae*) of POPE BL. PIUS IX, dated 27 June 1851, the Hundred of Leyland in the County of Lancashire was transferred from the Diocese of Salford to the Diocese of Liverpool, following a petition from Rt Rev. George Brown, first Bishop of Liverpool, thus correcting a geographical error inherent in the original document.

EX SUPREMO APOSTOLATUS APICE

FROM THE HIGHEST SUMMIT OF THE APOSTLESHIP, TO WHICH without any merit of Ours but by disposition of the divine goodness We have recently been raised, the Roman Pontiffs, Our predecessors, never ceased to watch as from a mountain-top the various portions of the Lord's field, in order that they might perceive what, as years rolled on, would be most conducive to the estate, beauty, and stability of all the churches. Hence, as far as was given them from on high, they were exceedingly solicitous, not only to erect and plant episcopal sees in every land, but also to recall to new life such as had through evil times ceased to exist. For, inasmuch as the Holy Ghost has placed bishops to rule the Church of God, whensoever the state of most holy religion in any region is such as to admit of the ordinary episcopal government to be either established or restored therein, it certainly is not beseeming to deprive it of those benefits which naturally flow from this divinely established institution.

Wherefore, Our immediate predecessor, Pius IX, of sacred memory, so lately called away to Our sorrow and the regret of all, even from the beginning of his Pontificate, when it was apparent that the missions in the most noble and flourishing kingdom of England had made such progress that the form of Church government which exists in other Catholic nations could be restored therein, restored to the English their ordinary bishops by an Apostolic Letter, dated 1st October 1850 (sic), and beginning *Universalis ecclesiae*; and as, not long after, he perceived that the illustrious countries of Holland and Brabant could enjoy the same salutary arrangement, he there also, without delay, restored the episcopal Hierarchy by another Apostolic Letter, dated 4th March 1853, beginning *Ex qua die*. The wisdom of these measures—to say nothing of the Restoration of the Patriarchate of Jerusalem—has been amply proved by the result, which, through the divine grace has fully realised the hopes of this Holy See; since it is known and evident to all how great an increase the Catholic Church has received in both these places through the Restoration of the episcopal Hierarchy.

The loving heart of the Pontiff could ill brook that Scotland could not as yet have the same good fortune. And this grief of his paternal heart was the keener, inasmuch as the great progress made by the Catholic Church in Scotland in days gone by was well known. And, indeed, whoever is even slightly conversant with Church history must have known that the light of the Gospel shone upon the Scots at an early date; for, to say nothing of what tradition has handed down of more ancient Apostolic missions to the said kingdom, it is recounted that towards the end of the fourth century, St Ninian—who, as Venerable Bede attests, had been taught the faith and the mysteries of the truth at Rome—and in the fifth century, St Palladius, a deacon of the Roman Church, having been both invested with the sacred mitre, preached the faith of Christ therein; and that St Columba, abbot, who landed there in the sixth century, built a monastery, from which many others sprang. And, although from the middle of the eighth to the eleventh, historical documents concerning the ecclesiastical state of Scotland are almost entirely awanting, still it has been handed down that there were many bishops in the country, although some of them had no fixed sees. But after Malcolm III came into possession of the sovereign power in the year 1057, through his exertions at the exhortation of his sainted spouse, Margaret, the Christian religion, which, either through the inroads of foreign peoples, or through various political vicissitudes had suffered heavy losses, began to be restored and spread; and the still existing remains of churches, monasteries, and other religious buildings bear a brilliant witness to the piety of the ancient Scots. But, to come more directly to Our subject, it is known that, in the fifteenth century, the episcopal sees had so increased as to number thirteen, to wit St Andrew's, Glasgow, Dunkeld, Aberdeen, Moray, Brechin, Dunblane, Ross, Caithness, Whithorn, Lismore, Sodor or the Isles, and Orkney—all which were immediately subject to the Apostolic See. It is also known—and the Scots are justly proud of the fact—that the Roman Pontiffs taking the Kingdom of Scotland under their special protection, regarded the above-named churches with special favour; hence, whilst they themselves acted as metropolitans of Scotland, they more than once decreed that their privileges and immunities, granted them in past times by the Roman Church, mother and teacher of all the churches, should be preserved intact; so that, as was decreed by Honorius III of holy memory, the Scottish Church should be like a favourite daughter, immediately subject to the Apostolic See without any intermediary. But whereas up to his time, Scotland was without a metropolitan, Sixtus IV reflecting on the expense and difficulties which the Scots had to undergo in coming to the Roman metropolis, by an Apostolic Letter of the 17th August 1472, beginning *Triumphans pastor aeternus* raised the

See of St Andrew's, which, owing to its remote origin and the veneration due to the apostle, patron of the kingdom, had naturally obtained the first place—to be the metropolitan and archiepiscopal see of the whole kingdom, the other sees being subjected to it as suffragans. This also was done in the case of the see of Glasgow in the year 1491, which, being withdrawn from the Ecclesiastical province of St Andrew's, was, by Innocent VIII, raised to the dignity of a metropolitan see, and had some of the above sees assigned to it as suffragans.

Whilst the Scottish Church thus constituted was in a flourishing condition, it was reduced to a pitiable state of utter ruin by the outbreak of heresy in the sixteenth century. Yet never did the anxious care, solicitude, and watchfulness of the Supreme Pontiffs, Our predecessors, fail the Scots to keep them strong in faith, as is clearly seen from many evidences. For, moved with compassion for that people, and seeing the wide havoc wrought by the storm, now by repeatedly sending missionaries from various families of religious, again by Apostolic legations and by every kind of assistance, they laboured strenuously to succour religion thus laid low. By their means, in this citadel of the Catholic world, besides the Urban College, a special college was opened for chosen youths of the Scottish nation, in which they should be trained in sacred knowledge, and prepared for the priesthood, in order, thereafter, to exercise its sacred functions in their native land, and to bring spiritual aid to their fellow-countrymen. And as that beloved portion of the Lord's flock was bereft of its pastors, Gregory XV, of happy memory, as soon as he had it in his power, sent William, ordained Bishop of *Chalcedon*, and furnished with ample faculties, even those which by proper right belong to ordinaries, to both England and Scotland, in order to assume the pastoral charge of those scattered sheep; as may be seen in the Apostolic Letter, beginning *Ecclesia romana*, dated 23rd March 1623, to restore the orthodox faith in the said regions, and to procure the salvation of the English and Scots, Urban VIII granted ample faculties to Francis Barberini, Cardinal of Holy Roman Church, as is shown by his letter, *Inter gravissimas* in form of a brief, dated 18th May 1630, to the same intent also is another letter of the same Pontiff, beginning *Multa sunt*, written to the Queen of France on the 12th day of February, 1633, for the purpose of recommending to her good offices the faithful and the said church, reduced to a most sad state.

Again, in order to provide in the best manner possible for the spiritual government of the Scots, in 1694, Pope Innocent XII deputed, as his vicar-apostolic, Thomas Nicholson, who was created and consecrated Bishop of *Peristachium*, committing to his care all the kingdom and the islands adjacent. And not long thereafter, when one vicar-apostolic was no longer sufficient for the cultivation of the whole of the said vineyard of the Lord, Benedict XIII hastened to give the aforesaid bishop a colleague, which he was able to effect in the year 1727. Thus it came to pass that the whole of the kingdom of Scotland was divided into two apostolic vicariates, one of which embraced the southern, the other the northern portion. But the division which had appeared sufficient for the government of the number of Catholics then existing, when through the Lord's blessing their numbers daily increased, was no longer suitable. Hence this Apostolic See perceived the necessity of providing additional help for watching over and spreading religion in Scotland, by the institution of a third vicariate. Wherefore, Leo XII of happy memory, by an Apostolic Letter of 13th February 1827, beginning: *Quanti laetitia affecti simus*, divided Scotland into three districts or apostolic vicariates, namely, the Eastern, Western, and Northern. It is known to all what a rich harvest, through the zeal of the new bishops and the anxious care of Our Congregation de Propaganda Fide has been gathered in by the Catholic Church in the said kingdom. Whence it is sufficiently cleat that this Holy See, through that solicitude which it bears for all the churches, has used every endeavour to recruit and strengthen day by day the Scottish nation suffering from the sad calamities of bygone times.

But Pius IX, of happy memory, had exceedingly at heart the Restoration of the illustrious Scottish Church to its pristine beauty and comeliness. For the bright example of his predecessors urged him on, they having, as it were, smoothed the way for the advancement of the work. And in truth, having on the one hand considered attentively the whole state of the Catholic religion in Scotland, and the daily increase of the number of the faithful, of sacred workers, churches, missions, and religious houses, and like institutions, as well as the sufficiency of temporal means; on the other hand, being aware that owing to the liberty which the renowned British Government grants to Catholics, any impediment there might be in the way of giving back to the Scots the ordinary rule of bishops was lessening day by day, the said Pontiff was persuaded that the Restoration of the episcopal Hierarchy should be no longer deferred. Meanwhile the vicars apostolic themselves, and very many of the clergy and laity, men conspicuous by noble birth and virtue besought him earnestly to delay no longer to satisfy their earnest wishes in this matter. This humble request was again laid before him when a chosen band from every rank in the said country, having at their head Our venerable brother, John Strain, Bishop of *Abila Lysaniae, in partibus infidelium*, and Vicar Apostolic of the Eastern District, came to this city to congratulate him on the fiftieth anniversary of his episcopal consecration. When the matter was in this position, the said Pius IX entrusted it, as its importance demanded, for full discussion to Our venerable brethren Cardinals of Holy Roman Church of the Congregation de Propaganda Fide, and their opinion confirmed him more and more in the resolution he had formed. But whilst he rejoiced that he had come to the completion of a work long and greatly wished for, he was called by a just Judge to receive the crown of justice.

What, therefore, Our predecessor was hindered by death from bringing to a conclusion, God, who is plentiful in mercy and glorious in all his works has granted Us to effect, so that We might, as it were, inaugurate with a happy omen Our Pontificate, which in these calamitous times, We have received with trembling. Wherefore, after having acquired a full knowledge of the entire matter, We have willingly deemed that what had been decreed by the lately-deceased Pius IX should be put in execution. Therefore, raising up Our eyes to the Father of Light, from whom cometh every best gift and every perfect gift, We have invoked the aid of divine grace, praying also for the help of the Blessed Virgin Mary, conceived without stain; of Blessed Joseph her spouse and Patron of the Universal Church; of the Blessed Apostles Peter and Paul, of Andrew and of the other saints whom the Scots venerate as patrons, in order that they by their suffrages before God might aid Us to bring the said matter to a prosperous issue.

Having therefore premised these things, by an act of Our own will, with certain knowledge, and acting in virtue of the Apostolic authority which We possess over the whole Church, to the greater glory of Almighty God, and the exaltation of the Catholic faith, We ordain and decree that in the kingdom of Scotland, according to what is prescribed by the canon laws, the Hierarchy of ordinary bishops, who shall be named from the sees which by this Our constitution We erect, shall be revived and shall constitute an ecclesiastical province. Moreover, We ordain that, for the present, six sees shall be erected and these We will to be founded, to wit, St Andrew's with the addition of the title of Edinburgh, Glasgow, Aberdeen, Dunkeld, Whithorn or Galloway, likewise Argyll and the Isles.

Recalling to mind the illustrious past in the history of the Church of St Andrew's, and taking into account the existing capital of the said kingdom, and weighing other considerations as well, calling up, as it were, from the grave, the said renowned see, We cannot but raise it or restore it with the addition of the title of Edinburgh to the rank of the metropolitan or archiepiscopal dignity, to which it had formerly been raised by Our predecessor, Sixtus IV, of venerable memory, and assign to it as by these presents, by virtue of Our Apostolic authority, We do assign, add and give unto it—four of the above named sees as suffragans—namely, Aberdeen, Dunkeld, Whithorn or Galloway, Argyll and the Isles. As regards the see of Glasgow, considering the antiquity, importance, and nobility of that city, and especially in view of the highly flourishing state of religion therein, and the archiepiscopal pre-eminence conferred upon it by Innocent VIII, We have thought it altogether fitting to decree to give to its bishop the name and insignia of an archbishop, as also, by these presents, We give, in such manner, however, that until it shall have been otherwise ordained by Us or Our successors, he shall not receive, beyond the prerogative of the name and honour, any right proper to a true archbishop and metropolitan. We will also and ordain that the Archbishop of Glasgow, as long as he shall be without suffragans, shall be present with the other bishops in the provincial synod of Scotland.

Now in the aforesaid archiepiscopal or metropolitan see of St Andrew's and Edinburgh shall be included the counties of Edinburgh, Linlithgow, Haddington, Berwick, Selkirk, Peebles, Roxburgh, and the southern part of Fife, which lies to the right of the River Eden; also the County of Stirling, saving the territories of Baldernock and East Kilpatrick.

In the Archdiocese of Glasgow shall be included the counties of Lanark, Renfrew, Dumbarton, the territories of Baldernock and East Kilpatrick, situated in the County of Stirling, the northern portion of the County of Ayr, which is separated from the southern portion of the same by the Lugton Water flowing into the River Garnock; also the islands of Great and Little Cumbrae.

In the Diocese of Aberdeen shall be contained the counties of Aberdeen, Kincardine, Banff, Elgin or Moray, Nairn, Ross (except Lewis in the Hebrides), Cromarty, Sutherland, Caithness, the Orkney and Shetland Islands; finally that portion of the County of Inverness which lies to the north of a straight line drawn from the most northerly point of Loch Luing to the eastern boundary of the said County of Inverness, where the counties of Aberdeen and Banff join.

In the Diocese of Dunkeld shall be included the counties of Perth, Forfar, Clackmannan, Kinross, and the northern portion of the County of Fife lying to the left of the River Eden; also those portions of the County of Stirling which are disjoined from it and are surrounded by the counties of Perth and Clackmannan.

The Diocese of Whithorn or Galloway shall contain the counties of Dumfries, Kirkcudbright, Wigtown, and that portion of Ayr which stretches southwards to the left of the Lugton Water flowing into the River Garnock.

Finally, the Diocese of Argyll and the Isles shall embrace the County of Argyll, the Islands of Bute and Arran, the Hebrides, and the southern portion of the County of Inverness which stretches from Loch Luing to the eastern boundary of the said County according to the line above described.

Thus, therefore, in the kingdom of Scotland, besides the honorary archbishopric of Glasgow there shall be one only ecclesiastical province, consisting of one archbishop or metropolitan and four suffragan bishops.

We doubt not but what the new prelates, following in the footsteps of their predecessors who by their virtues rendered the Church of Scotland illustrious, will use every endeavour to make the name of the Catholic religion in their country shine with still greater brightness, and to promote the salvation of souls and the increase of the Divine worship in the best manner possible. Wherefore, We from now declare that We reserve to Ourselves and to Our successors in the Apostolic

See, to divide when needful the aforesaid dioceses into others, to increase their number, to change their boundaries, and to freely execute whatever else may seem to Us in the Lord most conducive to the propagation of the orthodox faith in the same.

And as We see clearly that it will be of great benefit to the said churches, We will and ordain that their prelates shall never fail to transmit to Our Congregation de Propaganda Fide, which hitherto has bestowed special and assiduous care upon the said region, reports upon their sees and flocks committed to their care; and shall inform Us through the said congregation concerning whatever they may deem it necessary or useful to decree in fulfilment of their pastoral duty, and for the increase of their churches. Let them remember, moreover, that they are bound to send in this report, as well as to visit the tombs of the Holy Apostles every four years, as is enacted in the constitution of Sixtus V, of sacred memory, dated 20th December 1585, beginning *Romanus pontifex*. In all other matters, likewise, which belong to the same pastoral office, the above-named archbishops and bishops shall enjoy all the rights and faculties which the Catholic bishops of other nations by virtue of the common law of the canons and Apostolic constitutions do enjoy or can now or hereafter enjoy; and shall be bound by the same obligations which, through the same common and general discipline of the Catholic Church, bind other bishops. Whatever, therefore, either owing to the ancient state of the churches in Scotland, or in the subsequent condition of the missions by special constitutions or privileges or particular customs may have been in force, now that the circumstances are changed, shall not henceforward have any power to convey any right or to impose any obligation. And for this end, in order that no doubt may arise in future on this head, We, by the plenitude of Our Apostolic authority deprive the said special statutes, ordinances, and privileges of whatever kind, and customs, at however a remote or immemorial time they may have been introduced, and are now in force, of all power of inducing any obligation or conveying any right.

Wherefore it shall be in the power of the Scottish prelates to decree whatever is requisite for the execution of the common law and whatever is competent to the episcopal authority according to the common discipline of the Church. Let them feel assured that We shall willingly lend them the aid of Our Apostolic authority in whatever may seem conducive towards increasing the glory of God's name and helping on the spiritual welfare of souls. And as an earnest of this Our goodwill towards the beloved daughter of the Holy See, the Church of Scotland, We will and declare that the bishops when they have been invested with the name and rights of ordinary bishops, must by no means be deprived of those advantages and more ample faculties which they formerly enjoyed along with the title of Vicars of Ourselves and the Holy See. For it is not right that they should suffer any loss from what, in compliance with the wishes of the Scottish Catholics, has been decreed by Us for the greater good of religion in their country. And whereas the condition of Scotland is such that adequate means for the support of the clergy and the various needs of each church are wanting, We have a certain hope that Our beloved sons in Christ, to whose earnest wish for the Restoration of the episcopal Hierarchy We have acceded, will continue to aid those Pastors whom We shall place over them with sill more ample alms and offerings, whereby they may be able to provide for the Restoration of the episcopal sees, the splendour of the churches and of the Divine worship, the support of the clergy and the poor, and the other needs of the Church.

But now We turn with most humble prayer to Him in whom it hath pleased God the Father in the dispensation of the fullness of time to restore all things, beseeching Him who has begun the good work to perfect it, confirm it, and strengthen it, and to give, to all those whose duty it is to execute the things which We have decreed, the light and strength of heavenly grace, so that the episcopal Hierarchy restored by Us in the kingdom of Scotland may be for the greater good of Catholic religion. For this end, also, We invoke as intercessors with Our Saviour, Jesus Christ, His most blessed Mother, blessed Joseph, his reputed Father, the blessed Apostles, Peter and Paul; likewise St Andrew, whom Scotland venerates with special devotion, and the rest of the Saints, and especially St Margaret, Queen of Scotland, the glory and pillar of the kingdom, that they may benignantly favour that Church now rising again from its ashes.

Finally We decree this Our letter can never at any time be charged with the fault of omission or addition, or with any defect of Our intention or with any other defect, but shall always be held valid and firm, and shall obtain effect in all things, and shall be inviolably observed. Notwithstanding Apostolic edicts and general or special sanctions published in synodal, provincial, and Universal councils, and notwithstanding the rights and privileges of the ancient sees of Scotland, and of the missions and apostolic vicariates afterwards constituted therein, and notwith-standing the rights and privileges of all churches or pious institutes whatsoever, even although ratified by oath, or by Apostolic or any other confirmation, and all things to the contrary notwithstanding, We expressly abrogate all these things in so far as they contradict the foregoing although for their abrogation they would require special mention or any other formality, however particular. We decree, moreover, that whatever be done to the contrary knowingly or ignorantly by any person in the name of any authority whatsoever shall be null and void. We will also that copies, even printed, of this letter, when subscribed by a public notary, and stamped with the seal of an ecclesiastical dignitary, shall have the same credit as would be given to the expression of Our will by the exhibition of this diploma itself.

Let no man therefore dare to infringe or rashly gainsay this page of Our erection, constitution, restoration, institution, assignation, addition, attribution, decree, mandate, and will. If anyone should presume to attempt this, let him know that he shall incur indignation of Almighty God and of His Blessed Apostles Peter and Paul.

Given at Rome at St Peter's in the year of the Lord's Incarnation one thousand eight hundred and seventy-eight, the fourth of the nones of March, in the first year of Our Pontificate (4 March 1878).

x *His Holiness* POPE LEO XIII

THE UNIVERSAL CHURCH

ROMAN PONTIFFS SINCE 1800

CCL.   † x *His Holiness* POPE PIUS VII (**BARNABA NICCOLÒ MARIA LUIGI GREGORIO CHIARAMONTI OSB**): born 14 August 1742 at Cesena (Forli-Cesena), Italy • professed (Order of Saint Benedict) 20 August 1758 at Cesena (Forli-Cesena), Italy • ordained priest (Order of Saint Benedict) 21 September 1765 at Cesena (Forli-Cesena), Italy • ordained Bishop of Tivoli 21 December 1782 at Tivoli (Roma), Italy • translated 14 February 1785 to Diocese of Imola • elevated 14 February 1785 to Cardinal-Priest of San Callisto • elected Pope 14 March 1800 at Rome, Italy • installed 21 March 1800 at Rome, Italy • resigned 8 March 1816 as Bishop of Imola • died 20 August 1823 at the Apostolic Palace, Rome, Italy aged 81 • buried at St Peter's Basilica, Vatican City.

CCLI.   † x *His Holiness* POPE LEO XII (**ANNIBALE SERMATTEI DELLA GENGA**): born 22 August 1760 at Castello della Genga (Ancona), Italy • ordained priest (Rome) 4 June 1783 at Rome, Italy • entered diplomatic service to the Holy See 1794 at Rome, Italy • ordained titular Archbishop of *Tyrus* and appointed Apostolic Nuncio to Germany 24 February 1794 at Rome, Italy • translated 8 March 1816 to Diocese of Senigallia • appointed *Archbishop ad personam* 8 March 1816 at Rome, Italy • elevated 8 March 1816 to Cardinal-Priest of Santa Maria in Trastevere • resigned 10 September 1816 as Bishop of Senigallia • appointed 9 May 1820 Prefect of the Roman Curia • appointed 10 February 1821 Archpriest of the Basilica of St Mary Major • elected Pope 28 September 1823 at Rome, Italy • installed 5 October 1823 at Rome, Italy • died 10 February 1829 at the Apostolic Palace, Rome, Italy aged 68 • buried at St Peter's Basilica, Vatican City.

CCLII.   † x *His Holiness* POPE PIUS VIII (**FRANCESCO SAVERIO MARIA FELICE CASTIGLIONI**): born 20 November 1761 at Cingoli

(Macerata), Italy • ordained priest (Cingoli) 17 December 1785 at Cingoli (Macerata), Italy • ordained Bishop of Montalto (delle Marche) 17 August 1800 at Rome, Italy • translated 8 March 1816 to Diocese of Cesena • elevated 8 March 1816 to Cardinal-Priest of Santa Maria in Traspontina • elevated 13 August 1821 to Cardinal-Bishop of Frascati and appointed Prefect of the Roman Curia • elected Pope 31 March 1829 at Rome, Italy • installed 5 April 1829 at Rome, Italy • died 30 November 1830 at the Apostolic Palace, Rome, Italy aged 69 • buried at St Peter's Basilica, Vatican City.

CCLIII. † x *His Holiness* **POPE GREGORY XVI (BARTOLOMEO ALBERTO MAURO CAPPELLARI OSB):** born 18 September 1765 at Belluno (Belluno), Italy • professed (Order of Saint Benedict) 1786 at Murano (Venezia), Italy • ordained priest (Order of Saint Benedict) 1787 at Murano (Venezia), Italy • elevated 21 March 1825 to Cardinal-Priest *in pectore* • elevated 13 March 1826 to Cardinal-Priest of San Callisto • appointed 1 October 1826 Prefect of the Congregation for the Doctrine of the Faith at Rome, Italy • elected Pope 2 February 1831 at Rome, Italy • ordained Bishop of Rome and installed 6 February 1831 at Rome, Italy • died 1 June 1846 at the Apostolic Palace, Rome, Italy aged 80 • buried at St Peter's Basilica, Vatican City.

CCLIV. † x *His Holiness* **POPE BL. PIUS IX (GIOVANNI MARIA MASTAI-FERRETTI):** born 13 May 1792 at Senigallia (Ancona), Italy • ordained priest (Senigallia) 10 April 1819 at Senigallia (Ancona), Italy • ordained Archbishop of Spoleto 3 June 1827 at Spoleto (Perugia), Italy • translated 17 December 1832 to Archdiocese of Imola • appointed *Archbishop ad personam* 17 December 1832 at Rome, Italy • elevated 23 December 1839 to Cardinal-Priest *in pectore* • elevated 14 December 1840 to Cardinal-Priest of Santi Marcellino e Pietro • elected Pope 16 June 1846 at Rome, Italy • installed 21 June 1846 at Rome, Italy • convoked First Vatican Council 8 December 1869 to 20 October 1870 at Rome, Italy • died 7 February 1878 at the Apostolic Palace, Rome, Italy aged 85 • buried at St Peter's Basilica, Vatican City • reinterred 13 July 1881 at St Lawrence's Basilica (outside the walls), Rome, Italy • beatified 3 September 2000 at Vatican City.

CCLV. † x *His Holiness* **POPE LEO XIII (VINCENZO GIOACCHINO RAFFAELE LUIGI PECCI):** born 2 March 1810 at Carpineto Romano

(Roma), Italy • ordained priest (Anagni) 31 December 1837 at Rome, Italy • entered diplomatic service to the Holy See 1843 at Rome, Italy • ordained titular Archbishop of *Tamiathis* and appointed Apostolic Nuncio to Belgium 19 February 1843 at Rome, Italy • translated 18 January 1846 to Archdiocese of Perugia • appointed *Archbishop ad personam* 18 January 1846 at Rome, Italy • elevated 19 December 1853 to Cardinal-Priest of San Crisogono • appointed Council Father at First Vatican Council 8 December 1869 to 20 October 1870 • elected Pope 20 February 1878 at Rome, Italy • installed 3 March 1878 at Rome, Italy • died 20 July 1903 at the Apostolic Palace, Rome, Italy aged 93 • buried at the Basilica of St John Lateran, Rome, Italy.

CCLVI. † x *His Holiness* POPE ST PIUS X (GIUSEPPE MELCHIORRE SARTO): born 2 June 1835 at Riese Pio X (Treviso), Italy • ordained priest (Treviso) 18 September 1858 at Treviso (Treviso), Italy • ordained Bishop of Mantova 20 November 1884 at Mantua (Mantua), Italy • elevated 12 June 1893 to Cardinal-Priest of San Bernardo alle Terme • translated 15 June 1893 to Patriarch Archdiocese of Venice • elected Pope 4 August 1903 at Rome, Italy • installed 9 August 1903 at Rome, Italy • died 20 August 1914 at the Apostolic Palace, Rome, Italy aged 79 • buried at St Peter's Basilica, Vatican City • beatified 3 June 1951 at Vatican City • canonised 29 May 1954 at Vatican City.

CCLVII. † x *His Holiness* POPE BENEDICT XV (GIACOMO PAOLO GIOVANNI-BATTISTA DELLA CHIESA): born 21 November 1854 at Pegli (Genova), Italy • ordained priest (Rome) 21 December 1878 at Rome, Italy • ordained Archbishop of Bologna 22 December 1907 at Rome, Italy • elevated 25 May 1914 to Cardinal-Priest of Santi Quattro Coronati • elected Pope 3 September 1914 at Rome, Italy • installed 6 September 1914 at Rome, Italy • died 22 January 1922 at the Apostolic Palace, Rome, Italy aged 67 • buried at St Peter's Basilica, Vatican City.

CCLVIII. † x *His Holiness* POPE PIUS XI (AMBROGIO DAMIANO ACHILLE RATTI): born 31 May 1857 at Desio (Monza e Brianza), Italy • ordained priest (Milano) 27 December 1879 at Rome, Italy • entered diplomatic service to the Holy See 1912 at Rome, Italy • ordained titular Archbishop of *Naupactus* and appointed Apostolic Nuncio to Poland 28 October 1919 at Rome, Italy • translated 29 April 1921 to titular Archbishop of *Adana* • translated 13 June 1921 to Archdiocese of Milan • elevated 13

June 1921 to Cardinal-Priest of Santi Silvestro e Martino ai Monti • elected Pope 6 February 1922 at Rome, Italy • installed 12 February 1922 at Rome, Italy • died 10 February 1939 at the Apostolic Palace, Vatican City aged 81 • buried at St Peter's Basilica, Vatican City.

CCLIX.   † x *His Holiness* POPE VEN. PIUS XII (EUGENIO MARIA GIUSEPPE GIOVANNI PACELLI): born 2 March 1876 at Rome, Italy • ordained priest (Rome) 2 April 1899 at Rome, Italy • entered diplomatic service to the Holy See 1917 at Rome, Italy • ordained titular Archbishop of *Sardes* and appointed Apostolic Nuncio to Germany 13 May 1917 at Rome, Italy • elevated 16 December 1929 to Cardinal-Priest of Santi Giovanni e Paolo • appointed Secretary of the Secretariat of State 9 February 1930 at Vatican City • appointed Camerlengo of the Apostolic Chamber 1 April 1935 at Vatican City • elected Pope 2 March 1939 at Vatican City • installed 12 March 1939 at Vatican City • died 9 October 1958 at Castel Gandolfo (Roma), Italy aged 82 • buried at St Peter's Basilica, Vatican City • proclaimed *Venerable* 19 December 2009 at Vatican City.

CCLX.   † x *His Holiness* POPE ST JOHN XXIII (ANGELO GIUSEPPE RONCALLI): born 25 November 1881 at Sotto il Monte Giovanni XXIII (Bergamo), Italy • ordained priest (Bergamo) 10 August 1904 at Bergamo (Bergamo), Italy • entered diplomatic service to the Holy See 1925 at Rome, Italy • ordained titular Archbishop of *Areopolis* and appointed Apostolic Official to Bulgaria 19 March 1925 at Rome, Italy • appointed 16 October 1931 Apostolic Delegate to Bulgaria • translated 30 November 1934 to titular Archbishop of *Mesembria* • appointed 12 January 1935 Apostolic Delegate to Greece and Turkey • appointed 23 December 1944 Apostolic Nuncio to France • elevated 12 January 1953 to Cardinal-Priest of Santa Prisca • translated 15 January 1953 to Patriarch Archdiocese of Venice • elected Pope 28 October 1958 at Vatican City • installed 4 November 1958 at Vatican City • convoked Second Vatican Council 11 October 1962 to 8 December 1962 • died 3 June 1963 at the Apostolic Palace, Vatican City aged 81 • buried at St Peter's Basilica, Vatican City • beatified 3 September 2000 at Vatican City • canonised 27 April 2014 at Vatican City.

CCLXI.   † x *His Holiness* POPE BL. PAUL VI (GIOVANNI-BATTISTA ENRICO ANTONIO MARIA MONTINI): born 26 September 1897 at Concesio (Brescia), Italy • ordained priest (Brescia) 29 May 1920 at Brescia (Brescia), Italy • ordained Archbishop of Milan 12 December 1954 at Milan (Milano), Italy • elevated 15 December 1958 to Cardinal-Priest of Santi Silvestro e Martino ai Monti • appointed Council Father at Second Vatican Council 11 October 1962 to 8 December 1962 • elected Pope 21 June 1963 at Vatican City • installed 30 June 1963 at Vatican City • convoked Second Vatican Council 29 September 1963 to 8 December 1965 • died 6 August 1978 at Castel Gandolfo (Roma), Italy aged 80 • buried at St Peter's Basilica, Vatican City • beatified 19 October 2014 at Vatican City.

CCLXII.   † x *His Holiness* POPE JOHN PAUL I (**ALBINO LUCIANI**): born 17 October 1912 at Forno di Canale (Belluno), Italy • ordained priest (Belluno e Feltre) 7 July 1935 at Belluno (Belluno), Italy • ordained Bishop of Vittorio Veneto 27 December 1958 at Vittorio Veneto (Treviso), Italy • appointed Council Father at Second Vatican Council 11 October 1962 to 8 December 1965 • translated 15 December 1969 to Patriarch Archdiocese of Venice • elevated 5 March 1973 to Cardinal-Priest of San Marco • elected Pope 26 August 1978 at Vatican City • installed 3 September 1978 at Vatican City • died 28 September 1978 at the Apostolic Palace, Vatican City aged 65 • buried at St Peter's Basilica, Vatican City.

CCLXIII.   † x *His Holiness* POPE ST JOHN PAUL II (**KAROL JÓZEF WOJTYŁA**): born 18 May 1920 at Wadowice (Wadowice), Poland • ordained priest (Kraków) 1 November 1946 at Kraków (Kraków), Poland • ordained titular Bishop of *Ombi* and appointed auxiliary Bishop of Kraków 28 September 1958 at Kraków (Kraków), Poland • appointed Council Father at Second Vatican Council 11 October 1962 to 8 December 1965 • translated 13 January 1964 to Archdiocese of Kraków • elevated 26 June 1967 to Cardinal-Priest of San Cesario in Palatio • elected Pope 16 October 1978 at Vatican City • installed 22 October 1978 at Vatican City • died 2 April 2005 at the Apostolic Palace, Vatican City aged 84 • buried at St Peter's Basilica, Vatican City • beatified 1 May 2011 at Vatican City • canonised 27 April 2014 at Vatican City.

CCLXIV.   ® x *His Holiness* POPE BENEDICT XVI (**JOSEPH ALOISIUS RATZINGER**): born 16 April 1927 at Marktl am Inn (Bavaria), Germany • ordained priest (München und Freising) 29 June 1951 at Freising (Bavaria), Germany • ordained Archbishop of München und Freising

28 May 1977 at Munich (Bavaria), Germany • elevated 27 June 1977 to Cardinal-Priest of Santa Maria Consolatrice al Tiburtino • appointed 25 November 1981 Prefect of the Congregation for the Doctrine of the Faith at Vatican City • resigned 15 February 1982 as Archbishop of München und Freising • elevated 5 April 1993 to Cardinal-Bishop of Velletri Segni • elevated 30 November 2002 to Cardinal-Bishop of Ostia and appointed Dean of the College of Cardinals • elected Pope 19 April 2005 at Vatican City • installed 24 April 2005 at Vatican City • resigned 28 February 2013 as Pope and retired to Vatican City. • *Monastero "Mater Ecclesiae", 00120 VATICAN CITY*

CCLXV. x *His Holiness* POPE FRANCIS (JORGE MARIO BERGOGLIO SJ): born 17 December 1936 at Buenos Aires (Buenos Aires), Argentina • professed (Society of Jesus) 12 March 1960 at San Miguel (Corrientes), Argentina • ordained priest (Society of Jesus) 13 December 1969 at San Miguel (Corrientes), Argentina • ordained titular Bishop of *Auca* and appointed auxiliary Bishop of Buenos Aires 27 June 1992 at Buenos Aires (Buenos Aires), Argentina • translated 3 June 1997 to coadjutor Archbishop of Buenos Aires • succeeded 28 February 1998 as Archbishop of Buenos Aires • elevated 21 February 2001 to Cardinal-Priest of San Roberto Bellarmino • elected Pope 13 March 2013 at Vatican City • installed 19 March 2013 at Vatican City.

PONTIFICAL MOTTOS

† POPE PIUS VII (1800–1823): *Aquila rapax*

† POPE LEO XII (1823–1829): *n/a*

† POPE PIUS VIII (1829–1830): *Vir religiosus*

† POPE GREGORY XVI (1831–1846): *De balneis Etruriae*

† POPE BL. PIUS IX (1846–1878): *Crux de cruce*

† POPE LEO XIII (1878–1903): *Lumen in Caelo*

† POPE ST PIUS X (1903–1914): *Instaurare omnia in Christo*

† POPE BENEDICT XV (1914–1922): *In te, Domine, speravi; non confundar in aeternum*

† POPE PIUS XI (1922–1939): *Pax Christi in regno Christi*

† POPE VEN. PIUS XII (1939–1958): *Opus iustitiae pax*

† POPE ST JOHN XXIII (1958–1963): *Oboedientia et pax*

† POPE BL. PAUL VI (1963–1978): *In nomine Domini*

† POPE JOHN PAUL I (1978): *Humilitas*

† POPE ST JOHN PAUL II (1978–2005): *Totus tuus*

® POPE BENEDICT XVI (2005–2013): *Cooperatores veritatis*

POPE FRANCIS (2013–): *Miserando atque eligendo*

HIS HOLINESS POPE FRANCIS

Bishop of Rome

Vicar of Jesus Christ

Successor of St Peter, Prince of the Apostles

Supreme Pastor of the Universal Church

Primate of Italy

*Archbishop and Metropolitan
of the Roman Province*

Sovereign of the State of the Vatican City

Servant of the Servants of God

x *His Holiness* POPE FRANCIS (**JORGE MARIO BERGOGLIO SJ**): born 17 December 1936 at Buenos Aires (Buenos Aires), Argentina • professed (Society of Jesus) 12 March 1960 at San Miguel (Corrientes), Argentina • ordained priest (Society of Jesus) 13 December 1969 at San Miguel (Corrientes), Argentina • ordained titular Bishop of *Auca* and appointed auxiliary Bishop of Buenos Aires 27 June 1992 at Buenos Aires (Buenos Aires), Argentina • translated 3 June 1997 to coadjutor Archbishop of Buenos Aires • succeeded 28 February 1998 as Archbishop of Buenos Aires • elevated 21 February 2001 to Cardinal-Priest of San Roberto Bellarmino • elected Pope 13 March 2013 at Vatican City • installed 19 March 2013 at Vatican City.

Now gloriously reigning

HIS HOLINESS POPE BENEDICT XVI

Pope Emeritus

® x *His Holiness* POPE BENEDICT XVI (JOSEPH ALOISIUS RATZINGER):
born 16 April 1927 at Marktl am Inn (Bavaria), Germany • ordained priest (München
und Freising) 29 June 1951 at Freising (Bavaria), Germany • ordained Archbishop
of München und Freising 28 May 1977 at Munich (Bavaria), Germany • elevated
27 June 1977 to Cardinal-Priest of Santa Maria Consolatrice al Tiburtino •
appointed 25 November 1981 Prefect of the Congregation for the Doctrine of the
Faith at Vatican City • resigned 15 February 1982 as Archbishop of München und
Freising • elevated 5 April 1993 to Cardinal-Bishop of Velletri Segni • elevated 30
November 2002 to Cardinal-Bishop of Ostia and appointed Dean of the College
of Cardinals • elected Pope 19 April 2005 at Vatican City • installed 24 April 2005
at Vatican City • resigned 28 February 2013 as Pope and retired to Vatican City.
• *Monastero "Mater Ecclesiae, 00120 VATICAN CITY*

NATIONAL JURISDICTIONS

PROLOGUE

By Letters Apostolic (*Universalis ecclesiae*) of POPE BL. PIUS IX, dated 29 September 1850, the English and Welsh Hierarchy was restored and the Metropolitan See fixed at Westminster. At first, the Hierarchy comprised the Archdiocese of Westminster with twelve suffragan sees: Beverley; Birmingham; Clifton; Hexham; Liverpool; Newport and Menevia; Northampton; Nottingham; Plymouth; Salford; Shrewsbury; and Southwark.

By Letters Apostolic (*Paterna caritas*) of POPE PIUS XI, dated 21 November 1938, the Apostolic Delegation was formed, with jurisdiction over Great Britain, Malta and Gibraltar (with Bermuda added later).

By Apostolic Decree (*Inexhausta caritate*) of POPE VEN. PIUS XII, dated 21 November 1953, the Bishopric of the Forces was established in Great Britain, coming into effect on 23 April 1954. The Bishopric covers the whole country and anywhere in the world that British military personnel are deployed.

By Papal Mandate of POPE VEN. PIUS XII, dated 10 June 1957, the Apostolic Exarchate was erected for the faithful of the Byzantine-Ukrainian Rite resident in England and Wales. It was extended to Scotland and Great Britain on 12 May 1968.

By Papal Mandate of POPE BL. PAUL VI, dated 12 May 1968, the episcopal see of the Apostolic Exarchate for Ukrainians in Great Britain was transferred from the Ukrainian Pro-Cathedral Church of Our Lady of Protection and St Theodore of Canterbury, City of London to the Ukrainian Cathedral Church of the Holy Family in Exile, Mayfair, London

By Letters Apostolic (*Quo amplius*) of POPE ST JOHN PAUL II, dated 16 January 1982, the Apostolic Delegation in Great Britain was raised to a Nunciature (without overseas territories) when papal ambassadors to Great Britain became known as Pro-Nuncios. From 1 January 1994, all papal representatives throughout the world became known as Nuncios.

By Apostolic Constitution (*Spirituali militum curae*) of POPE ST JOHN PAUL II, dated 21 April 1986, the canonical framework for Military Ordinariates was approved, equivalent in law to dioceses and which replaced Military Vicariates.

By Congregation for Bishops Decree (*Pro sollicitudine omnium ecclesiarum*), dated 24 October 1987, the Holy See ratified the Statutes of the Military Ordinariate of Great Britain, known in local usage as the Bishopric of the Forces. The episcopal see was fixed at the Cathedral Garrison Church of SS Michael and George, Aldershot, consecrated on 7 October 1893 (by the Anglican Bishop of Winchester and in the presence of Queen Victoria).

By Apostolic Constitution (*Anglicanorum coetibus*) of POPE BENEDICT XVI, dated 4 November 2009, the Personal Ordinariate of Our Lady of Walsingham was established, being implemented on 15 January 2011. The Ordinariate exists within the territory of England and Wales for those groups of Anglican clergy and faithful who have expressed their desire to enter into full and visible communion with the Catholic Church. The Ordinariate is placed under the patronage of Bl. **John Henry** Cardinal **Newman CO**.

By Papal Mandate of POPE BENEDICT XVI, dated 18 January 2013, the Ukrainian Apostolic Exarchate of Great Britain was elevated to the Ukrainian Eparchy of the Holy Family of London. The Apostolic Exarch was henceforth appointed as Bishop of the new Eparchy. The episcopal see remained at the Ukrainian Cathedral Church of the Holy Family in Exile, Mayfair, London.

In conclusion, twelve Popes have governed the Roman Catholic Church since the Restoration of the Hierarchy in England and Wales. Great Britain has had nine Apostolic Nuncios appointed since 1938 and five Ukrainian Apostolic Exarchs since 1957, the last of whom became the first Bishop of the Ukrainian Eparchy of the Holy Family of London in 2013. The Bishopric of the Forces in Great Britain has been led by seven bishops since it was formed in 1918. Finally, one episcopal Ordinary has been appointed to the Personal Ordinariate of Our Lady of Walsingham since 2011. Seven other British-born prelates are currently serving elsewhere in the world, either in diplomatic posts, as diocesan bishops or in other clerical appointments.

APOSTOLIC NUNCIATURE
TO GREAT BRITAIN

The Apostolic Delegation was formed by Letters Apostolic (*Paterna caritas*) of Pope Pius XI, dated 21 November 1938, with jurisdiction over Great Britain, Malta and Gibraltar (with Bermuda added later). The Apostolic Delegation was raised to a Nunciature (without overseas territories) by Letters Apostolic (*Quo amplius*) of Pope St John Paul II, dated 16 January 1982, when papal ambassadors to Great Britain became known as Pro-Nuncios. From 1 January 1994, all papal representatives throughout the world became known as Nuncios.

I. † His Excellency Most Rev. Dr WILLIAM GODFREY DD PhD:
    born 25 September 1889 at Kirkdale, Liverpool • ordained priest (Liverpool) 28 October 1916 at Rome, Italy • entered diplomatic service to
    the Holy See 1938 at Vatican City • ordained titular Archbishop of *Cius*
    and appointed Apostolic Delegate to Great Britain, Malta and Gibraltar
    21 December 1938 at Vatican City • translated 14 November 1953 to
    Archdiocese of Liverpool • translated 3 December 1956 to Archdiocese
    of Westminster • appointed 10 June 1957 to the Apostolic Exarchate
    for Ukrainians in England and Wales • elevated 15 December 1958 to
    Cardinal-Priest of Santi Nereo ed Achilleo • appointed Council Father
    at Second Vatican Council 11 October 1962 to 8 December 1962 • died 22
    January 1963 at Westminster, London aged 73 • buried at the Metropolitan
    Cathedral Church of the Most Precious Blood, Westminster, London.
    • *Archbishop's House, Ambrosden Avenue, LONDON SW1P 1QJ*

II. † His Excellency Most Rev. Dr **GERALD PATRICK ALOYSIUS
    O'HARA** DD STD JUD: born 4 May 1895 at Scranton (PA), USA •
    ordained priest (Philadelphia) 3 April 1920 at Philadelphia (PA), USA •
    ordained titular Bishop of *Heliopolis in Phoenicia* and appointed auxiliary
    Bishop of Philadelphia (PA), USA 21 May 1929 at Philadelphia (PA), USA •
    translated 16 November 1935 to Diocese of Savannah (GA), USA • translated
    5 January 1937 to renamed Diocese of Savannah-Atlanta (GA), USA •
    entered diplomatic service to the Holy See 1947 at Vatican City • appointed
    19 February 1947 Apostolic Nuncio to Romania • appointed 12 July 1950
    Archbishop ad personam at Vatican City • appointed 27 November 1951
    Apostolic Nuncio to Ireland • appointed 8 June 1954 Apostolic Delegate to
    Great Britain, Malta, Gibraltar and Bermuda • translated 2 July 1956 to newly
    restructured Diocese of Savannah (GA), USA • resigned 12 November 1959
    as Bishop of Savannah (GA), USA and appointed titular Archbishop of *Pessinus* • appointed Council Father at Second Vatican Council 11 October 1962
    to 8 December 1962 • died 16 July 1963 at Wimbledon, London aged 68 •
    buried at the Cathedral Church of SS Peter and Paul, Philadelphia (PA), USA.
    • *The Apostolic Nunciature, 54 Parkside, LONDON SW19 5NE*

III. † His Excellency Most Rev. Dr **IGINO EUGENE CARDINALE** DD
    JCD: born 14 October 1916 at Fondi (Latina), Italy • ordained priest (Naples)
    13 July 1941 at Naples (Napoli), Italy • entered diplomatic service to the Holy
    See 1946 at Vatican City • appointed Council Father at Second Vatican Council 29 September 1963 to 8 December 1965 • ordained titular Archbishop of

Nepte and appointed Apostolic Delegate to Great Britain, Malta, Gibraltar and Bermuda 20 October 1963 at Vatican City • appointed 19 April 1969 Apostolic Nuncio to Belgium and Luxembourg • appointed 10 November 1970 Apostolic Nuncio to the European Community • died 24 March 1983 at Brussels (Capitale), Belgium aged 66 • buried at Castel di Guido (Roma), Italy. • *Avenue des Franciscains 9, 1150 BRUXELLES (Capitale), Belgium*

IV. † His Excellency Most Rev. Dr **DOMENICO ENRICI** DD JCD: born 9 April 1909 at Cervasca (Cuneo), Italy • ordained priest (Cuneo) 29 June 1933 at Cuneo (Cuneo), Italy • entered diplomatic service to the Holy See 1938 at Vatican City • ordained titular Archbishop of *Ancusa* and appointed Apostolic Inter-nuncio to Indonesia 1 November 1955 at Vatican City • appointed 30 January 1958 Apostolic Nuncio to Haiti • appointed 5 January 1960 Apostolic Inter-nuncio to Japan • appointed Council Father at Second Vatican Council 11 October 1962 to 21 November 1964 • appointed 12 October 1962 Apostolic Delegate to Australia, New Zealand and Oceania • appointed 26 April 1969 Apostolic Delegate to Great Britain, Malta, Gibraltar and Bermuda • appointed 16 July 1973 official of State at the Roman Curia • resigned 1 December 1979 as official of State and retired to Cervasca (Cuneo), Italy • died 3 December 1997 at Cervasca (Cuneo), Italy aged 88 • buried at Cervasca (Cuneo), Italy. • *c/o Via Roma 7, 12100 CUNEO (Cuneo), Italy*

V. † His Excellency Most Rev. Dr **BRUNO BERNHARD HEIM** PhD JCD: born 5 March 1911 at Neuendorf (Solothurn), Switzerland • ordained priest (Basel) 29 June 1938 at Solothurn (Solothurn), Switzerland • entered diplomatic service to the Holy See 1947 at Vatican City • ordained titular Archbishop of *Xanthus* and appointed Apostolic Delegate to Scandinavia 10 December 1961 at Solothurn (Solothurn), Switzerland • appointed Council Father at Second Vatican Council 11 October 1962 to 8 December 1965 • appointed 16 February 1966 Apostolic Pro-Nuncio to Finland • appointed 7 May 1969 Apostolic Pro-Nuncio to Egypt • appointed 16 July 1973 Apostolic Delegate to Great Britain, Malta, Gibraltar and Bermuda • appointed 16 January 1982 Apostolic Pro-Nuncio to Great Britain (without overseas territories) • resigned 31 July 1985 as Apostolic Pro-Nuncio to Great Britain and retired to Olten (Solothurn), Switzerland • died 18 March 2003 at Olten (Solothurn), Switzerland aged 92 • buried at Neuendorf (Solothurn), Switzerland. • *c/o Baselstrasse 58, 4501 SOLOTHURN (Solothurn), Switzerland*

VI.   ® His Excellency Most Rev. Dr **LUIGI BARBARITO** GCVO DD JCD: born 19 April 1922 at Atripalda (Avellino), Italy • ordained priest (Avellino) 20 August 1944 at Avellino (Avellino), Italy • entered diplomatic service to the Holy See 1953 at Vatican City • ordained titular Archbishop of *Fiorentino* and appointed Apostolic Nuncio to Haiti 10 August 1969 at Vatican City • appointed 5 April 1975 Apostolic Pro-Nuncio to Senegal, Niger, Upper Volta, Mali, Mauritania, Guinea Bissau and Cape Verde Islands • appointed 10 June 1978 Apostolic Pro-Nuncio to Australia • appointed 21 January 1986 Apostolic Pro-Nuncio to Great Britain • appointed 1 January 1994 Apostolic Nuncio to Great Britain • retired 31 July 1997 to Rome, Italy thence to Pietradefusi (Avellino), Italy.
• *Suore Francescane, via Grottone 28, 83030 PIETRADEFUSI (Avellino), Italy*

VII.   ® His Excellency Most Rev. Dr **PABLO PUENTE BUCES** PhL STL JCD: born 16 June 1931 at Colindres (Cantabria), Spain • ordained priest (Santander) 2 April 1956 at Santander (Cantabria), Spain • entered diplomatic service to the Holy See 1962 at Vatican City • ordained titular Archbishop of *Macri* and appointed Apostolic Pro-Nuncio to Indonesia 25 May 1980 at Vatican City • appointed 15 March 1986 Apostolic Pro-Nuncio to Cape Verde, Mali and Senegal and Apostolic Delegate to Guinea-Bissau and Mauritania • appointed 31 July 1989 Apostolic Nuncio to Lebanon • appointed 25 May 1993 Apostolic Nuncio to Kuwait • appointed 31 July 1997 Apostolic Nuncio to Great Britain • resigned 23 October 2004 as Apostolic Nuncio to Great Britain and retired to Colindres (Cantabria), Spain.
• *La Parroquia de San Juan Bautista, 39750 COLINDRES (Cantabria), Spain*

VIII.   † His Excellency Most Rev. Dr **FAUSTINO SAINZ MUÑOZ** JCD STL LLD: born 5 June 1937 at Almadén (Ciudad Real), Spain • ordained priest (Madrid) 19 December 1964 at Madrid (Madrid), Spain • entered diplomatic service to the Holy See 1970 at Vatican City • ordained titular Archbishop of *Novaliciana* and appointed Apostolic Pro-Nuncio to Cuba 18 December 1988 at Vatican City • appointed 7 October 1992 Apostolic Nuncio to Democratic Republic of Congo • appointed 21 January 1999 Apostolic Nuncio to European Community • appointed 11 December 2004 Apostolic Nuncio to Great Britain • resigned 5 December 2010 as Apostolic Nuncio to Great Britain and retired to Madrid (Madrid), Spain • died 31 October 2012 at Madrid (Madrid), Spain aged 75 • buried at Madrid (Madrid), Spain.
• *c/o Sede del Arzobispado, Bailén 8, 28071 MADRID (Madrid), Spain*

IX.   His Excellency Most Rev. Dr **ANTONIO MENNINI** STD: born 2 September 1947 at Rome, Italy • ordained priest (Rome) 14 December 1974 at Rome, Italy • entered diplomatic service to the Holy See 1981 at Vatican City • ordained titular Archbishop of *Ferentium* and appointed Apostolic Nuncio to Bulgaria 12 September 2000 at Vatican City • appointed 6 November 2002 Apostolic Nuncio to Russian Federation • appointed 26 July 2008 Apostolic Nuncio to Uzbekistan • appointed 18 December 2010 Apostolic Nuncio to Great Britain. • *The Apostolic Nunciature, 54 Parkside, LONDON SW19 5NE*

BISHOPRIC OF THE FORCES IN GREAT BRITAIN

Before November 1917, the Archbishop of Westminster was Vicar Delegate to the Army and Royal Navy. He remained Vicar Delegate to the Royal Navy until 23 April 1954.

The Bishopric of the Forces was established by Apostolic Decree (*Inexhausta caritate*) of Pope Ven. Pius XII, dated 21 November 1953, which came into effect on 23 April 1954.

By Apostolic Constitution (*Spirituali militum curae*) of 21 April 1986, Pope St John Paul II approved the canonical framework for Military Ordinariates, equivalent in law to dioceses, which replaced Military Vicariates from 21 July 1986. By Congregation for Bishops Decree (*Pro sollicitudine omnium ecclesiarum*) of 24 October 1987, the Holy See ratified the Statutes of the Military Ordinariate of Great Britain, known in local usage as the Bishopric of the Forces. The episcopal see was fixed at the Cathedral Garrison Church of SS Michael and George, Aldershot (1986–), consecrated on 7 October 1893 (by the Anglican Bishop of Winchester and in the presence of Queen Victoria).

I. † Rt Rev. **WILLIAM LEWIS KEATINGE** CMG CBE: born 1 August 1869 at London • ordained priest (Southwark) 27 August 1893 at Rome, Italy • commissioned as military chaplain 1 May 1897 • ordained titular Bishop of *Metellopolis* and appointed Vicar Delegate to the Army and Royal Air Force 25 February 1918 at Rome, Italy • released from military service 31 December 1924 • died 21 February 1934 at Westminster, London aged 64 • buried at St Mary's Cemetery, Kensal Green, London.
    • *3 Ashley Gardens, LONDON SW1P 1QD*

II. † Rt Rev. **JAMES DEY** DSO RAChD: born 14 October 1869 at Walsall • ordained priest (Birmingham) 17 February 1894 at Oscott, Sutton Coldfield • commissioned as military chaplain 7 August 1903 • released from military service 17 October 1929 • ordained titular Bishop of *Sebastopolis in Armenia* and appointed Vicar Delegate to the Army and Royal Air Force 2 June 1935 at Oscott, Sutton Coldfield • died 8 June 1946 at Barton on Sea, New Milton aged 76 • buried at St Mary's College, Oscott, Sutton Coldfield.
    • *Fairfax House, Church Road East, FARNBOROUGH GU14 6QJ*

a. **APOSTOLIC ADMINISTRATOR:** † Rev. Mgr **JOHN MICHAEL CLARKE** CBE: born 20 December 1893 at Bootle, Liverpool • ordained priest (Saint Joseph's Missionary Society of Mill Hill) 2 December 1917 at Bootle, Liverpool • released from St Joseph's Missionary Society of Mill Hill 1 November 1920 • commissioned as military chaplain 10 December 1930 • incardinated 1944 into Archdiocese of Westminster at Westminster, London • appointed 8 June 1946 Apostolic Administrator of the Bishopric of the Forces in Great Britain until 23 April 1954 • released from military service 23 April 1954 and appointed chaplain to St Margaret's Chapel, Tichborne House, Alresford • appointed 1958 administrator of St Bede's Church, Croxley Green, Rickmansworth • retired 1960 to Dublin City (Dublin), Ireland • died 5 May 1963 at Dublin City (Dublin), Ireland aged 69 • buried at Deans Grange Cemetery, Dun Laoghaire (Dublin), Ireland.
    • *St Stephen's Green Club, 9 St Stephen's Green, DUBLIN 2, Ireland.*

III. † Most Rev. Dr **DAVID JAMES MATHEW** MA LittD LLD FSA FRSL: born 16 January 1902 at Lyme Regis • ordained priest (Cardiff) 25 May 1929 at Rome, Italy • ordained titular Bishop of *Aeliae* and appointed auxiliary Bishop of Westminster 21 December 1938 at the Metropolitan Cathedral Church of the Most Precious Blood, Westminster, London • translated 10 May

1946 to titular Archbishop of *Apamea in Bithynia* and appointed Apostolic Delegate to British East and West Africa • commissioned as military chaplain and translated 23 April 1954 to Military Vicar to HM Forces • appointed Council Father at Second Vatican Council 11 October 1962 to 8 December 1962 • released from military service and retired 29 March 1963 to Stonor Park, Henley-on-Thames • died 12 December 1975 at St John's Wood, London aged 73 • buried at the Abbey Church of St Gregory, Downside, Radstock.
• *Stonor Park, Stonor, HENLEY-ON-THAMES RG9 6HF*

IV.   † Rt Rev. **GERARD (JOCK) WILLIAM TICKLE**: born 2 November 1909 at Birkenhead • ordained priest (Shrewsbury) 28 October 1934 at Rome, Italy • commissioned as military chaplain 15 December 1941 • released from military service 24 August 1946 • ordained titular Bishop of *Bela* and appointed Military Vicar to HM Forces 30 November 1963 at Rome, Italy • appointed Council Father at Second Vatican Council 14 September 1964 to 8 December 1965 • released from military service and retired 8 January 1979 to Neston thence to Ruthin • died 14 September 1994 at Colwyn Bay aged 84 • buried at St Winefride's Church, Neston.
• *Ty Mair, 115 Mwrog Street, RUTHIN LL15 1LE*

V.   ® Rt Rev. **FRANCIS JOSEPH WALMSLEY** CBE: born 9 November 1926 at Woolwich, London • ordained priest (Southwark) 30 May 1953 at Wonersh, Guildford • commissioned as military chaplain 3 October 1960 • released from military service 8 January 1979 • ordained titular Bishop of *Tamalluma* and appointed Military Vicar to HM Forces 22 February 1979 at Aldershot • appointed 21 July 1986 Bishop in Ordinary to HM Forces • resigned 7 March 1998 as titular Bishop of *Tamalluma* • released from military service and retired 24 May 2002 to Kiln Green, Reading.
• *St John's Convent, Linden Hill Lane, Kiln Green, READING RG10 9XP*

VI.   Rt Rev. **THOMAS MATTHEW BURNS** SM BA BD KC*HS: born 3 June 1944 at Belfast (Antrim), Ireland • professed (Society of Mary) 12 September 1965 at Paignton • ordained priest (Society of Mary) 16 December 1971 at Paignton • commissioned as military chaplain 8 September 1986 • ordained Bishop in Ordinary to HM Forces 18 June 2002 at Aldershot • released from military service 16 October 2008 • translated 1 December 2008 to Diocese of Menevia.
• *Bryn Rhos, 79 Walter Road, SWANSEA SA1 4PS*

VII.   Rt Rev. **CHARLES PHILLIP RICHARD MOTH** MA JCL KCHS:
born 8 July 1958 at Chingola (Copperbelt), Zambia • ordained priest
(Southwark) 3 July 1982 at Wonersh, Guildford • commissioned as military
chaplain 1 April 1988 • released from military service 25 July 2009 •
ordained Bishop in Ordinary to HM Forces 29 September 2009 at the
Metropolitan Cathedral Church of the Most Precious Blood, Westminster,
London • translated 21 March 2015 to Diocese of Arundel and Brighton.
• *High Oaks, Old Brighton Road, Pease Pottage, CRAWLEY RH11 9AJ*

VIII.   SEDE VACANTE:
• *Bishop's House, 26 The Crescent, FARNBOROUGH GU14 7AS*

APOSTOLIC EXARCHATE FOR UKRAINIANS IN GREAT BRITAIN

(Magnae Britanniae)

The Apostolic Exarchate was erected on 10 June 1957 for the faithful of the Byzantine-Ukrainian Rite resident in England and Wales. It was extended to Scotland and Great Britain on 12 May 1968.

The episcopal see was fixed at the Ukrainian Pro-Cathedral Church of Our Lady of Protection and St Theodore of Canterbury, City of London (1957–1968), consecrated on 5 December 1948, then at the Ukrainian Cathedral Church of the Holy Family in Exile, Mayfair, London (1968–), consecrated on 29 June 1968.

I.   † + *His Eminence* **Cardinal** Dr **WILLIAM GODFREY** DD PhD:
       born 25 September 1889 at Kirkdale, Liverpool • ordained priest (Liv-
       erpool) 28 October 1916 at Rome, Italy • entered diplomatic service to
       the Holy See 1938 at Vatican City • ordained titular Archbishop of *Cius*
       and appointed Apostolic Delegate to Great Britain, Malta and Gibraltar
       21 December 1938 at Rome, Italy • translated 14 November 1953 to
       Archdiocese of Liverpool • translated 3 December 1956 to Archdiocese
       of Westminster • appointed 10 June 1957 to the Apostolic Exarchate
       for Ukrainians in England and Wales • elevated 15 December 1958 to
       Cardinal-Priest of Santi Nereo ed Achilleo • appointed Council Father
       at Second Vatican Council 11 October 1962 to 8 December 1962 • died 22
       January 1963 at Westminster, London aged 73 • buried at the Metropolitan
       Cathedral Church of the Most Precious Blood, Westminster, London.
       • *Archbishop's House, Ambrosden Avenue, LONDON SW1P 1QJ*

       a.   Most Rev. Dr **AUGUSTINE EUGENE HORNYAK** OSBM
             STD JCB: see **II.** below.

II.   † Most Rev. Dr **AUGUSTINE EUGENE HORNYAK** OSBM
       STD JCB: born 7 October 1919 at Kucura (Backa), Serbia • ordained
       priest (Philadelphia-Ukrainian) 25 March 1945 at Rome, Italy • professed
       (Basilian Order of St Josaphat) 19 June 1956 at Mundare (AB), Canada •
       ordained titular Bishop of *Hermonthis* and appointed auxiliary Bishop of
       the Apostolic Exarchate for Ukrainians in England and Wales 26 October
       1961 at Philadelphia (PA), USA • appointed Council Father at Second
       Vatican Council 11 October 1962 to 8 December 1965 • translated 18
       April 1963 to the Apostolic Exarchate for Ukrainians in England and
       Wales • translated 12 May 1968 to the Apostolic Exarchate for Ukrain-
       ians in Great Britain • resigned 29 September 1987 as Apostolic Exarch
       for Ukrainians in Great Britain and retired to Acton, London • died 16
       November 2003 at Acton, London aged 84 • buried at Kucura (Backa), Serbia.
       • *14 Newburgh Road, LONDON W3 6DQ*

       a.   **APOSTOLIC ADMINISTRATOR:** † Most Rev. Dr **MICHEL
             HRYNCHYSHYN** CSsR: born 18 February 1929 at Buchanan
             (SK), Canada • professed (Congregation of the Most Holy Redeemer)
             28 July 1946 at Yorkton (SK), Canada • ordained priest (Congrega-
             tion of the Most Holy Redeemer) 25 May 1952 at Toronto (ON),
             Canada • ordained titular Bishop of *Zygris* and appointed Bishop

of the Apostolic Exarchate for Ukrainians in France, Benelux and Switzerland 30 January 1983 at Rome, Italy • appointed 29 September 1987 Apostolic Administrator of the Apostolic Exarchate for Ukrainians in Great Britain until 24 June 1989 • appointed 16 December 1996 Apostolic Administrator of the Apostolic Exarchate for Ukrainians in Germany and Scandinavia until 20 November 2000 • retired 21 July 2012 to Vincennes (Val-de-Marne), France • died 12 November 2012 at Vincennes (Val-de-Marne), France aged 83 • buried at Holy Family Cemetery, Winnipeg (MB), Canada.
• *chez L'Évêché, 27 Avenue Foch, 94300 VINCENNES, France*

III.   † Most Rev. Dr **MICHAEL KUCHMIAK** CSsR DD: born 5 February 1923 at Obertyn (pov. Horodenka), Ukraine • professed (Congregation of the Most Holy Redeemer) 3 October 1948 at Mercato San Severino (Salerno), Italy • ordained priest (Congregation of the Most Holy Redeemer) 13 May 1956 at Meadowvale (ON), Canada • ordained titular Bishop of *Agathopolis* and appointed auxiliary Bishop of the Apostolic Exarchate for Ukrainians in Philadelphia (PA), USA 27 April 1988 at Philadelphia (PA), USA • translated 24 June 1989 to the Apostolic Exarchate for Ukrainians in Great Britain • retired 11 June 2002 to Newark (NJ), USA thence to Yorkton (SK), Canada • died 26 August 2008 at Saskatoon (SK), Canada aged 85 • buried at Holy Family Cemetery, Winnipeg (MB), Canada.
• *St John's Parish, 719 Sandford Avenue, NEWARK NJ 07106, USA*

IV.   Most Rev. **PAUL PATRICK CHOMNYCKY** OSBM BEcon STB: born 19 May 1954 at Vancouver (BC), Canada • professed (Basilian Order of St Josaphat) 1 November 1982 at Glen Cove (NY), USA • ordained priest (Basilian Order of St Josaphat) 1 October 1988 at Vancouver (BC), Canada • ordained titular Bishop of *Buffada* and appointed Bishop of the Apostolic Exarchate for Ukrainians in Great Britain 11 June 2002 at Edmonton (AB), Canada • translated 20 February 2006 to the Apostolic Exarchate for Ukrainians in Stamford (CT), USA.
• *Chancery Office, 14 Peveril Road, STAMFORD CT 06902, USA*

a.   **APOSTOLIC ADMINISTRATOR:** ® Rev. Mgr Dr **BOHDAN BENJAMIN LYSYKANYCH** DLitt PhD: born 2 January 1943 at Bielefield (Nord Rhein-Westfalia), Germany • ordained priest (Salford) 4 April 1982 at Rochdale • appointed 21 February 2006 Apostolic Administrator of the Apostolic Exarchate for Ukrainians in Great Britain until 2 June 2009 • appointed 2 June 2009 parish priest of All Saints' Ukrainian Church, Oldham. • *All Saints' Presbytery, Chadderton Way, OLDHAM OL9 6DH*

b.   **APOSTOLIC ADMINISTRATOR:** Most Rev. Dr **HLIB BORYS SVIATOSLAV LONCHYNA** MSU DLitt: see **I.** below.

UKRAINIAN EPARCHY OF THE HOLY FAMILY OF LONDON

(Eparchia Sanctae Familiae Londiniensis)

The Apostolic Exarchate was erected on 10 June 1957 for the faithful of the Byzantine-Ukrainian Rite resident in England and Wales. It was extended to Scotland and Great Britain on 12 May 1968. The Apostolic Exarchate was elevated on 18 January 2013 to the Eparchy of the Holy Family of London with the previous Exarch appointed as first Bishop of the new eparchy.

The episcopal see was fixed at the Ukrainian Pro-Cathedral Church of Our Lady of Protection and St Theodore of Canterbury, City of London (1957–1968), consecrated on 5 December 1948, then at the Ukrainian Cathedral Church of the Holy Family in Exile, Mayfair, London (1968–), consecrated on 29 June 1968.

I.	Most Rev. Dr **HLIB BORYS SVIATOSLAV LONCHYNA** MSU DLitt: born 23 February 1954 at Steubenville (OH), USA • professed (Order of Ukrainian Studite Monks) 19 December 1976 at Grottaferrata (Roma), Italy • ordained priest (Order of Ukrainian Studite Monks) 3 July 1977 at Grottaferrata (Roma), Italy • ordained titular Bishop of *Bareta* and appointed auxiliary Bishop of the Ukrainian Archeparchy of Lviv 27 February 2002 at Lviv (Lviv), Ukraine • translated 6 December 2004 to auxiliary Bishop of the Ukrainian Archeparchy of Kyiv-Halyč (Kiev), Ukraine • appointed 2 June 2009 Apostolic Administrator of the Apostolic Exarchate for Ukrainians in Great Britain until 14 June 2011 • translated 14 June 2011 to the Apostolic Exarchate for Ukrainians in Great Britain • appointed 18 January 2013 Bishop of the Ukrainian Eparchy of the Holy Family of London. • *Ukrainian Catholic Cathedral, 22 Binney Street, LONDON W1K 5BQ*

PERSONAL ORDINARIATE OF OUR LADY OF WALSINGHAM

(Dominae Nostrae Valsinghamensis in Anglia et Cambria)

The Personal Ordinariate of Our Lady of Walsingham was established in accordance with the provisions of the Apostolic Constitution (*Anglicanorum coetibus*) of Pope Benedict XVI, dated 4 November 2009, which came into effect on 15 January 2011.

The Ordinariate exists within the territory of England and Wales for those groups of Anglican clergy and faithful who have expressed their desire to enter into full and visible communion with the Catholic Church. The Ordinariate is placed under the patronage of Bl. **John Henry** Cardinal **Newman CO**.

I. *CE* Rev. Mgr **KEITH NEWTON** ProtAp BD PGCE AKC : born 10 April 1952 at Liverpool • ordained Church of England deacon (Chelmsford) 29 June 1975 at Chelmsford • ordained Church of England priest (Chelmsford) 27 June 1976 at Chelmsford • ordained Bishop Suffragan of Richborough (Provincial Episcopal Visitor) 9 March 2002 at Chelmsford • resigned 31 December 2010 as Bishop Suffragan of Richborough and Church of England priest • received into Catholic Church 1 January 2011 at the Metropolitan Cathedral Church of the Most Precious Blood, Westminster, London • ordained priest (Our Lady of Walsingham) 15 January 2011 at the Metropolitan Cathedral Church of the Most Precious Blood, Westminster, London • appointed 15 January 2011 as ordinary for Personal Ordinariate of Our Lady of Walsingham. • *24 Golden Square, LONDON W1F 9JR*

BRITISH BISHOPS AROUND THE WORLD

I.   Rt Rev. Dr **KURT RICHARD BURNETTE** JCL PhD: born 7 November 1955 at Fakenham • ordained priest (Van Nuys (Ruthenian)) 26 April 1989 at Sherman Oaks (CA), USA • incardinated 18 December 2009 into Eparchy of Holy Protection of Mary of Phoenix (Ruthenian) at Sherman Oaks (CA), USA • ordained Bishop of Passaic (Ruthenian) 4 December 2013 at Passaic (NJ), USA.
     • *445 Lackawanna Avenue, WOODLAND PARK NJ 07424, USA*

II. Rt Rev. **PATRICK JAMES DUNN** BSc MTh: born 5 February 1950 at London • ordained priest (Auckland) 24 April 1976 at Remuera (Auckland), New Zealand • ordained titular Bishop of *Fesseë* and appointed auxiliary Bishop of Auckland 25 July 1994 at Auckland (Auckland), New Zealand • translated 19 December 1994 to Diocese of Auckland.
     • *Pompallier Diocesan Centre, 30 New Street, Ponsonby, AUCKLAND 1011, New Zealand*

III. Rev. Mgr **HARRY ENTWISTLE** BSc DipTh: born 31 May 1940 at Chorley • ordained Church of England deacon (Blackburn) 22 September 1963 at Blackburn • ordained Church of England priest (Blackburn) 20 September 1964 at Blackburn • received into Catholic Church 10 June 2012 at Guildford (WA), Australia • ordained priest (Our Lady of the Southern Cross) 15 June 2012 at Perth (WA), Australia • appointed 15 June 2012 as ordinary for Personal Ordinariate of Our Lady of the Southern Cross, Australia.
     • *Our Lady of the Southern Cross, 40a Mary Street, HIGHGATE WA 6003, Australia*

IV. ℞ His Excellency Most Rev. Dr **MICHAEL LOUIS FITZGERALD** **MAfr** BA STD: born 17 August 1937 at Walsall • professed (Missionaries of Africa (White Fathers)) 7 September 1956 at s'Heerenberg (Gelderland), Netherlands • ordained priest (Missionaries of Africa (White Fathers)) 3

February 1961 at Whetstone, London • appointed 22 January 1987 Secretary of the Pontifical Council for Inter-religious Dialogue at Vatican City • ordained titular Bishop of *Nepte* 6 January 1992 at Vatican City • appointed titular Archbishop of *Nepte* and President of the Pontifical Council for Inter-religious Dialogue 1 October 2002 at Vatican City • appointed 15 February 2006 Apostolic Nuncio to Egypt • retired 23 October 2012 to Rome, Italy. • *c/o Padri Bianchi, via Aurelia 269, 00165 ROME, Italy.*

V.   His Excellency Most Rev. Dr **PAUL RICHARD GALLAGHER** STL JCD: born 23 January 1954 at Liverpool • ordained priest (Liverpool) 31 July 1977 at the Metropolitan Cathedral Church of Christ the King, Liverpool • entered diplomatic service to the Holy See 1 May 1984 at Vatican City • ordained titular Archbishop of *Hodelm* and appointed Apostolic Nuncio to Burundi 13 March 2004 at Rome, Italy • appointed 19 February 2009 Apostolic Nuncio to Guatemala • appointed 11 December 2012 Apostolic Nuncio to Australia • appointed Secretary of the Secretariat of State 8 November 2014 at Vatican City. • *Palazzo Apostolico Vaticano, 00120 VATICAN CITY.*

VI.   Rt Rev. **RALPH HESKETT** CSsR: born 3 March 1953 at Sunderland • professed (Congregation of the Most Holy Redeemer) 28 August 1971 at Kinnoul, Perth • ordained priest (Congregation of the Most Holy Redeemer) 10 July 1976 at Sunderland • ordained Bishop of Gibraltar 10 July 2010 at Gibraltar • translated 20 May 2014 to Diocese of Hallam. • *Bishop's House, 75 Norfolk Road, SHEFFIELD S2 2SZ*

VII. Rev. Mgr **MICHAEL BERNARD McPARTLAND** SMA: born 29 September 1939 at Middlesbrough • professed (Society of African Missions) 27 September 1974 at New Barnet, Barnet • ordained priest (Society of African Missions) 14 May 1978 at Grove Hill, Middlesbrough • appointed 31 July 2002 Apostolic Prefect of Falkland Islands and Superior *missio sui iuris* of Saint Helena, Ascension and Tristan da Cunha. • *St Mary's Church, 12 Ross Road, STANLEY FIQQ 1ZZ, Falkland Islands*

VIII. Most Rev. **ARTHUR ROCHE** STB STL: born 6 March 1950 at Batley Carr, Dewsbury • ordained priest (Leeds) 19 July 1975 at Batley Carr, Dewsbury • ordained titular Bishop of *Rusticiana* and appointed auxiliary Bishop of Westminster 10 May 2001 at the Metropolitan Cathedral Church of the Most Precious Blood, Westminster, London

• translated 16 July 2002 to coadjutor Bishop of Leeds • succeeded 7 April 2004 as Bishop of Leeds • appointed 26 June 2012 secretary of the Congregation for Divine Worship and Discipline of the Sacraments • appointed 26 June 2012 *Archbishop ad personam* at Vatican City. • *Palazzo delle Congregazioni, Piazza Pio XII 10, 00193 ROMA, Italy*

ENGLAND AND WALES SINCE 1850

PROLOGUE

By Letters Apostolic (*Universalis ecclesiae*) of POPE BL. PIUS IX, dated 29 September 1850, the English and Welsh Hierarchy was restored and the Metropolitan See fixed at Westminster. At first, the Hierarchy comprised the Archdiocese of Westminster with twelve suffragan sees: Beverley; Birmingham; Clifton; Hexham; Liverpool; Newport and Menevia; Northampton; Nottingham; Plymouth; Salford; Shrewsbury; and Southwark.

By a re-script of the Letters Apostolic (*Universalis ecclesiae*) of POPE BL. PIUS IX, dated 27 June 1851, the Hundred of Leyland in the County of Lancashire was transferred from the Diocese of Salford to the Diocese of Liverpool, following a petition from Rt Rev. George Brown, first Bishop of Liverpool, and thus correcting a geographical error inherent in the original document.

By Papal Mandate of POPE BL. PIUS IX, dated 25 March 1858, the episcopal see of the Diocese of Plymouth was transferred from the Pro-Cathedral Chapel of the Blessed Virgin Mary and St John the Evangelist, Stonehouse, Plymouth, to the Cathedral Church of SS Mary and Boniface, Plymouth.

By Apostolic Decree (*Decretum de propaganda fide*) of POPE BL. PIUS IX, dated 23 May 1861, the Diocese of Hexham was renamed the Diocese of Hexham and Newcastle, with the episcopal see fixed at the Cathedral Church of St Mary, Newcastle upon Tyne, and remained a suffragan see within the Province of Westminster.

By Papal Mandate of POPE BL. PIUS IX, dated 1 June 1864, the episcopal see of the Diocese of Beverley was transferred from the Pro-Cathedral Church of St George, York, to the Pro-Cathedral Church of St Wilfrid, York.

By Papal Mandate of POPE BL. PIUS IX, dated 2 July 1869, the episcopal see of the Archdiocese of Westminster was transferred from the Pro-Cathedral Church of St Mary Moorfields, City of London, to the Pro-Cathedral Church of Our Lady of Victories, South Kensington, London.

By Apostolic Decree (*Quae ex hac*) of POPE LEO XIII, dated 20 December 1878, the Diocese of Leeds and the Diocese of Middlesbrough were formed by division of the Diocese of Beverley. The Diocese of Leeds comprised the West

Riding of Yorkshire while the Diocese of Middlesbrough comprised the North and East Ridings of Yorkshire, with the episcopal sees fixed at the Cathedral Church of St Anne, Cookridge Street, Leeds, and the Cathedral Church of Our Lady of Perpetual Succour, Sussex Street, Middlesbrough, respectively. Both dioceses became suffragan sees within the Province of Westminster.

By Apostolic Brief of POPE LEO XIII, dated 19 May 1882, the Diocese of Portsmouth was formed by division of the Diocese of Southwark, comprising the counties of Hampshire, Berkshire (south of the River Thames), Oxfordshire (south of the River Thames), with the islands of Wight, Jersey, Guernsey and others adjacent, with the episcopal see fixed at the Cathedral Church of St John the Evangelist, Portsmouth. The diocese became a suffragan see within the Province of Westminster.

By Apostolic Brief (*De animarum salute*) of POPE LEO XIII, dated 4 March 1895, the whole Principality of Wales except Glamorgan and Monmouthshire was made into a separate Vicariate of Wales by division of the Diocese of Newport and the Diocese of Shrewsbury, with the episcopal see fixed at the Cathedral Church of Our Lady of Sorrows, Wrexham. The Vicariate remained a suffragan see within the Province of Westminster.

By the same Apostolic Brief (*De animarum salute*) of POPE LEO XIII, dated 4 March 1895, the Diocese of Newport and Menevia was renamed the Diocese of Newport comprising Glamorgan, Monmouthshire and Herefordshire, with the episcopal see fixed at the Priory Church of St Michael and All Angels, Belmont, Hereford. The Diocese remained a suffragan see within the Province of Westminster.

By Apostolic Decree of POPE LEO XIII, dated 12 May 1898, the Vicariate of Wales was renamed as the Diocese of Menevia, with the episcopal see remaining at the Cathedral Church of Our Lady of Sorrows, Wrexham. The Diocese remained a suffragan see within the Province of Westminster.

By Papal Mandate of POPE ST PIUS X, dated 24 December 1903, the episcopal see of the Archdiocese of Westminster was transferred again from the Pro-Cathedral Church of Our Lady of Victories, South Kensington, London, to the Metropolitan Cathedral Church of the Most Precious Blood, Westminster, London.

By Papal Mandate of POPE ST PIUS X, dated 16 June 1904, the episcopal see of the Diocese of Leeds was transferred from the Cathedral Church of St Anne, Cookridge Street, Leeds, to the Cathedral Church of St Anne, Great George Street, Leeds.

By Letters Apostolic (*Si qua est*) of POPE ST PIUS X, dated 28 October 1911, the Province of Westminster was divided into three new metropolitan provinces of Westminster, Birmingham and Liverpool, reserving certain special privileges to the Archbishop of Westminster. The Province of Westminster then comprised the Archdiocese of Westminster with the suffragan sees of Northampton, Nottingham, Portsmouth and Southwark. The Province of Birmingham then comprised the Archdiocese of Birmingham with the suffragan sees of Clifton, Newport, Menevia, Plymouth and Shrewsbury. The Province of Liverpool then comprised the Archdiocese of Liverpool with the suffragan sees of Hexham and Newcastle, Leeds, Middlesbrough and Salford.

By Letters Apostolic (*Cambria celtica*) of POPE BENEDICT XV, dated 7 February 1916, the Province of Birmingham was divided further into two new metropolitan provinces of Birmingham and Cardiff. The Province of Birmingham then comprised the Archdiocese of Birmingham with the suffragan sees of Clifton, Plymouth and Shrewsbury. The Province of Cardiff then comprised the Archdiocese of Cardiff (renamed from the Diocese of Newport) with the suffragan see of Menevia.

By Apostolic Consistory of POPE BENEDICT XV, dated 22 March 1917, the Diocese of Essex was formed by division of the Archdiocese of Westminster, comprising the entire County of Essex.

By a Bull (*Universalis ecclesiae procuratio*) of POPE BENEDICT XV, dated 20 July 1917, the Diocese of Essex was renamed Brentwood, with the episcopal see fixed at the Cathedral Church of the Sacred Heart and St Helen, Brentwood. The Diocese of Brentwood became a suffragan see within the Province of Westminster.

By Papal Mandate of POPE BENEDICT XV, dated 12 March 1920, the episcopal see of the Archdiocese of Cardiff was transferred from the Priory Church of St Michael and All Angels, Belmont, Hereford to the Metropolitan Cathedral Church of St David, Cardiff. The episcopal see of the Diocese of Menevia remained at the Cathedral Church of Our Lady of Sorrows, Wrexham.

By Apostolic Constitution (*Universalis ecclesiae solicitudo*) of POPE PIUS XI, dated 22 November 1924, the Diocese of Lancaster was formed by division of the Diocese of Hexham and Newcastle and the Archdiocese of Liverpool, comprising the counties of Cumberland and Westmorland and the Hundreds of Amounderness and Lonsdale in the County of Lancashire (north of the River Ribble), with the episcopal see fixed at the Cathedral Church of St Peter, Lancaster. The Diocese of Lancaster became a suffragan see within the Province of Liverpool.

By Papal Mandate of POPE ST JOHN XXIII, dated 26 October 1958, the episcopal see of the Archdiocese of Liverpool was transferred from the Pro-Cathedral Church of St Nicholas, Liverpool, to the Pro-Cathedral Pontifical Crypt of Christ the King, Liverpool.

By Letters Apostolic (*Romanorum pontificum*) of POPE BL. PAUL VI, dated 28 May 1965, the Province of Westminster was divided further into two new metropolitan provinces of Westminster and Southwark. The Province of Westminster then comprised the Archdiocese of Westminster with the suffragan sees of Brentwood, Northampton and Nottingham. The Province of Southwark then comprised the Archdiocese of Southwark with the suffragan sees of Arundel and Brighton, Portsmouth and Plymouth (thus transferred from the Province of Birmingham).

By the same Letters Apostolic (*Romanorum pontificum*) of POPE BL. PAUL VI, dated 28 May 1965, the Diocese of Arundel and Brighton was formed by division of the Archdiocese of Southwark, comprising the counties of East Sussex, West Sussex and the part of Surrey (south of the River Thames) lying outside the Greater London boroughs, with the episcopal see fixed at the Cathedral Church of Our Lady and St Philip Howard, Arundel. The Diocese of Arundel and Brighton became a suffragan see within the Province of Southwark.

By Papal Mandate of POPE BL. PAUL VI, dated 14 May 1967, the episcopal see of the Archdiocese of Liverpool was transferred again from the Pro-Cathedral Pontifical Crypt of Christ the King, Liverpool to the Metropolitan Cathedral Church of Christ the King, Liverpool.

By Papal Mandate of POPE BL. PAUL VI, dated 29 June 1973, the episcopal see of the Diocese of Clifton was transferred from the Pro-Cathedral Church of the Twelve Apostles, Clifton, Bristol to the Cathedral Church of SS Peter and Paul, Clifton, Bristol.

By Apostolic Decree (*Quod ecumenicum*) of POPE BL. PAUL VI, dated 13 March 1976, the Diocese of East Anglia was formed by division of the Diocese of Northampton, comprising the counties of Norfolk, Suffolk and Cambridgeshire, with the episcopal see fixed at the Cathedral Church of St John the Baptist, Norwich. The Diocese of East Anglia became a suffragan see within the Province of Westminster.

By a Bull (*Qui arcano dei*) of POPE ST JOHN PAUL II, dated 30 May 1980, the Diocese of Hallam was formed by division of the Diocese of Leeds and the Diocese of Nottingham, comprising the County of South Yorkshire, parts of the High Peak and Chesterfield districts of Derbyshire and the district of Bassetlaw in Nottinghamshire, with the episcopal see fixed at the Cathedral Church of St Marie, Sheffield. The Diocese of Hallam became a suffragan see within the Province of Liverpool.

By Apostolic Brief of POPE ST JOHN PAUL II, dated 2 May 1982, two parishes in the City of York (south of the River Ouse) were transferred from the Diocese of Leeds to the Diocese of Middlesbrough to unite the city within one diocese.

By Papal Mandate of POPE ST JOHN PAUL II, dated 20 December 1986, the episcopal see of the Diocese of Middlesbrough was transferred from the Cathedral Church of Our Lady of Perpetual Succour, Sussex Street, Middlesbrough, to the Cathedral Church of St Mary, Coulby Newham, Middlesbrough.

By Apostolic Decree (*Fiducia freti*) of POPE ST JOHN PAUL II, dated 12 February 1987, the Diocese of Wrexham was formed by division of the Diocese of Menevia, comprising the counties of Anglesey, Caernarfon, Denbigh, Flint, Merioneth, Montgomery and Wrexham, with the episcopal see fixed at the Cathedral Church of Our Lady of Sorrows, Wrexham. The Diocese of Wrexham became a suffragan see within the Province of Cardiff.

By the same Apostolic Decree (*Fiducia freti*) of POPE ST JOHN PAUL II, dated 12 February 1987, the episcopal see of the Diocese of Menevia was transferred from the Cathedral Church of Our Lady of Sorrows, Wrexham, to the Cathedral Church of St Joseph, Swansea, and the former County of West Glamorgan was transferred from the Archdiocese of Cardiff to the Diocese of Menevia.

By Apostolic Brief of POPE ST JOHN PAUL II, dated 1988, the parish of Dunsop Bridge in Lancashire was transferred from the Diocese of Leeds to the Diocese of Salford.

By Apostolic Brief (*Fines dioecesium*) of POPE ST JOHN PAUL II, dated 7 November 2003, the parish of Howden in East Yorkshire was transferred from the Diocese of Middlesbrough to the Diocese of Leeds, being implemented on 1 February 2004.

Today, the Hierarchy in England and Wales now comprises five metropolitan Archdioceses and provinces with a further seventeen suffragan sees. The Province of Westminster comprises the Archdiocese of Westminster with the suffragan sees of Brentwood, East Anglia, Northampton and Nottingham. The Province of Birmingham comprises the Archdiocese of Birmingham with the suffragan sees of Clifton and Shrewsbury. The Province of Liverpool comprises the Archdiocese of Liverpool with the suffragan sees of Hallam, Hexham and Newcastle, Lancaster, Leeds, Middlesbrough and Salford. The Province of Cardiff comprises the Archdiocese of Cardiff with the suffragan sees of Menevia and Wrexham. The Province of Southwark comprises the Archdiocese of Southwark with the suffragan sees of Arundel and Brighton, Plymouth and Portsmouth.

Since the Restoration of the Hierarchy in England and Wales, there have been 165 diocesan bishops, including eleven cardinals, who have carried out their ministry in this country, assisted by a further forty-seven who remained as auxiliary Bishops. Of these 212 bishops, there have been twenty-six who were (or are) members of religious orders, including one cardinal and six assistant bishops; another forty-two auxiliary Bishops went on to become diocesan bishops and a further twenty-five were ordained as coadjutor Bishops, four of whom failed to succeed as the following diocesan bishop.

In conclusion, twelve Popes have governed the Roman Catholic Church since the Restoration of the Hierarchy in England and Wales. Great Britain has had nine

Apostolic Nuncios appointed since 1938 and five Ukrainian Exarchs appointed since 1957. Finally, the Bishopric of the Forces in Great Britain has been led by seven bishops since it was formed in 1918.

A variety of religious orders has been represented in the Catholic Hierarchy of England and Wales. These have included ten Benedictines (**OSB**), two each from the Order of Friars Minor (**OFM**), Oratorians (**CO**), Redemptorists (**CSsR**) and Marists (**SM**), and one each from the Order of St Francis (**OSF**), the Society of African Missions (**SMA**), Assumptionists (**AA**), Mill Hill Missionaries (**MHM**), Passionists (**CP**), Dominicans (**OP**), Picpus Fathers (**SS.CC**) and Augustinians (**OSA**).

ARCHDIOCESE OF WESTMINSTER

FORTIS UT MORS DILECTIO

(Archidioecesis Vestmonasteriensis)

By Letters Apostolic (*Universalis ecclesiae*) of Pope Bl. Pius IX, dated 29 September 1850, the Archdiocese of Westminster was formed, with the episcopal see fixed at the Pro-Cathedral Church of St Mary Moorfields, City of London (1850–1869), opened in 1820 and rebuilt in 1899, then at the Pro-Cathedral Church of Our Lady of Victories, South Kensington, London (1869–1903), opened on 2 July 1869 and consecrated on 14 May 1901, then at the Metropolitan Cathedral Church of the Most Precious Blood, Westminster, London (1903–), opened on 26 June 1903 and consecrated on 28 June 1910.

At first, the Metropolitan Archdiocese of Westminster comprised the cities of London and Westminster with the counties of Middlesex, Essex and Hertfordshire.

By Letters Apostolic (*Si qua est*) of Pope St Pius X, dated 28 October 1911, the Province of Westminster was divided into three new provinces of Birmingham, Liverpool and Westminster, with the Archdiocese of Westminster remaining as the primary metropolitan Archdiocese and province and certain special privileges being reserved by the Archbishop of Westminster.

By Apostolic Consistory of Pope Benedict XV, dated 22 March 1917, the Diocese of Essex was formed by division of the Archdiocese of Westminster, taking the

County of Essex from the Archdiocese of Westminster. By a Bull (*Universalis ecclesiae procuratio*) of Pope Benedict XV, dated 20 July 1917, the Diocese of Essex was renamed Brentwood.

The Province of Westminster comprises the Archdiocese of Westminster with the suffragan sees of Brentwood, East Anglia, Northampton and Nottingham. The Archdiocese today comprises those Greater London boroughs north of the River Thames and west of the River Lea, the district of Spelthorne in Surrey, and the County of Hertfordshire.

I. † + *His Eminence* **Cardinal** Dr **NICHOLAS PATRICK STEPHEN WISEMAN** DD: born 3 August 1802 at Seville (Sevilla), Spain • ordained priest (Northern District) 19 March 1825 at Rome, Italy • ordained titular Bishop of *Milopotamos* and appointed coadjutor Vicar Apostolic for the Midland District 8 June 1840 at Rome, Italy • translated 3 July 1840 to coadjutor Vicar Apostolic of the Central District • translated 29 August 1847 to coadjutor Vicar Apostolic of the London District • succeeded 18 February 1849 as Vicar Apostolic of the London District • translated 29 September 1850 to Archbishop and Metropolitan of newly raised and restored Archdiocese and Province of Westminster • appointed 29 September 1850 Apostolic Administrator of Diocese of Southwark until 4 July 1851 • elevated 30 September 1850 to Cardinal-Priest of Santa Pudenziana • died 15 February 1865 at Portman Square, London aged 62 • buried at St Mary's Cemetery, Kensal Green, London • reinterred 15 February 1907 at the Metropolitan Cathedral Church of the Most Precious Blood, Westminster, London. • *Archbishop's House, 8 York Place, LONDON W1H 6LA*

a. † Most Rev. Dr **GEORGE ERRINGTON** DD: born 14 September 1804 at Clints Hall, Marske, Richmond • ordained priest (Northern District) 22 December 1827 at Rome, Italy • ordained Bishop of restored Diocese of Plymouth 25 July 1851 at Salford • translated 30 March 1855 to titular Archbishop of *Trapezus* and appointed coadjutor Archbishop of Westminster • appointed 22 October 1855 Apostolic Administrator of the Diocese of Clifton until 15 February 1857 • resigned 2 July 1862 as coadjutor Archbishop of Westminster • appointed 1 September 1865 parish priest of St Mary's Church, Douglas, Isle of Man • nominated 27 January 1868 Apostolic Delegate in Scotland but declined the appointment 12 August 1868 • appointed Council Father at First Vatican Council 8 December 1869 to 20 October 1870 • retired 1

September 1874 to Prior Park, Bath • died 19 January 1886 at Prior Park, Bath aged 81 • buried at Prior Park College chapel, Bath.
• *Prior Park College, Ralph Allan Drive, BATH BA2 5AH*

II.   † *CE* + *His Eminence* **Cardinal** Dr **HENRY EDWARD MANNING** MA DTh: born 15 July 1808 at Totteridge, London • ordained Church of England deacon (Oxford) 23 December 1832 at Oxford • ordained Church of England priest (Chichester) 9 June 1833 at Lincoln's Inn, London • received into Catholic Church 6 April 1851 at Mayfair, London • ordained priest (Westminster) 14 June 1851 at Mayfair, London • ordained Archbishop of Westminster 8 June 1865 at Moorfields, City of London • appointed 1 October 1867 Apostolic Visitor to Scotland • appointed Council Father at First Vatican Council 8 December 1869 to 20 October 1870 • elevated 31 March 1875 to Cardinal-Priest of Santi Andrea e Gregorio Magno al Monte Celio • died 14 January 1892 at Westminster, London aged 83 • buried at St Mary's Cemetery, Kensal Green, London • reinterred 15 February 1907 at the Metropolitan Cathedral Church of the Most Precious Blood, Westminster, London.
• *Archbishop's House, 22 Carlisle Place, LONDON SW1P 1JA*

a.   † Rt Rev. Dr **WILLIAM WEATHERS** DD: born 12 November 1814 at London • ordained priest (London District) 1838 at Old Hall Green, Ware • ordained titular Bishop of *Amycla* and appointed auxiliary Bishop of Westminster 28 October 1872 at Salford • died 4 March 1895 at Isleworth aged 80 • buried at St Edmund's College, Old Hall Green, Ware.
• *Nazareth House, Richmond Road, ISLEWORTH TW7 7BP*

b.   † *CE* Rt Rev. **JAMES LAIRD PATTERSON** MA: born 16 November 1822 at Marylebone, London • ordained Church of England deacon (Oxford) 21 December 1844 at Oxford • ordained Church of England priest (Oxford) 21 December 1845 at Oxford • received into Catholic Church 30 March 1850 at Jerusalem, Israel • ordained priest (Westminster) 1855 at Moorfields, City of London • ordained titular Bishop of *Emmaüs* and appointed auxiliary Bishop of Westminster 10 May 1880 at Rome, Italy • died 2 December 1902 at Chelsea, London aged 80 • buried at St Edmund's College, Old Hall Green, Ware.
• *St Mary's Rectory, Draycott Terrace, LONDON SW3 2QR*

III. † + *His Eminence* Cardinal Dr **HERBERT ALFRED HENRY VAUGHAN** DD: born 15 April 1832 at Gloucester • ordained priest (Westminster) 28 October 1854 at Lucca (Lucca), Italy • ordained Bishop of Salford 28 October 1872 at Salford • translated 29 March 1892 to Archdiocese of Westminster • elevated 16 January 1893 to Cardinal-Priest of Santi Andrea e Gregorio Magno al Monte Celio • died 19 June 1903 at Mill Hill, London aged 71 • buried at Mill Hill, London • reinterred 14 March 2005 at the Metropolitan Cathedral Church of the Most Precious Blood, Westminster, London.
• *Archbishop's House, 22 Carlisle Place, LONDON SW1P 1JA*

  a. † Rt Rev. **ROBERT BRINDLE** DSO: born 4 November 1837 at Everton, Liverpool • ordained priest (Plymouth) 27 December 1862 at Lisbon (Lisboa), Portugal • commissioned as military chaplain 12 January 1874 • ordained titular Bishop of *Hermopolis Maior* and appointed auxiliary Bishop of Westminster 12 March 1899 at Rome, Italy • released from military service 5 July 1899 • translated 6 December 1901 to Diocese of Nottingham • appointed 1 June 1915 titular Bishop of *Tacapae* and retired to Spinkhill, Sheffield • died 27 June 1916 at Spinkhill, Sheffield aged 78 • buried at the Cathedral Church of St Barnabas, Nottingham.
  • *Mount St Mary's College, Spinkhill, SHEFFIELD S21 3YL*

  b. † *CE* Rt Rev. **ALGERNON CHARLES STANLEY** MA: born 16 September 1843 at Winnington, Northwich • ordained Church of England deacon (Worcester) 21 December 1866 at Worcester • ordained Church of England priest (Worcester) 7 June 1868 at Coventry • received into Catholic Church 1879 at London • ordained priest (Westminster) 18 December 1880 at Rome, Italy • ordained titular Bishop of *Emmaüs* and appointed auxiliary Bishop of Westminster 15 March 1903 at Rome, Italy • died 23 April 1928 at Rome, Italy aged 84 • buried at Rome, Italy.
  • *1 via Giulia, 00186 ROME, Italy*

IV. † + *His Eminence* Cardinal **FRANCIS ALPHONSUS BOURNE**: born 23 March 1861 at Clapham, London • ordained priest (Southwark) 11 June 1884 at Clapham, London • ordained titular Bishop of *Epiphania in Cilicia* and appointed coadjutor Bishop of Southwark 1 May 1896 at the Cathedral Church of St George, Southwark, London • succeeded 9 April 1897 as Bishop of Southwark • translated 11 September

1903 to Archdiocese of Westminster • elevated 27 November 1911 to
Cardinal-Priest of Santa Pudenziana • Archdiocese of Westminster
restructured 22 March 1917 • died 1 January 1935 at Westminster,
London aged 73 • buried at St Edmund's College, Old Hall Green, Ware.
• *Archbishop's House, Ambrosden Avenue, LONDON SW1P 1QJ*

a. † Rt Rev. **PATRICK FENTON**: born 19 August 1837 at Soho,
London • ordained priest (Westminster) 22 September 1866 at Old Hall
Green, Ware • ordained titular Bishop of *Amycla* and appointed auxil-
iary Bishop of Westminster 1 May 1904 at the Metropolitan Cathedral
Church of the Most Precious Blood, Westminster, London • retired
10 April 1917 to Bexhill-on-Sea • died 22 August 1918 at Bexhill-on-
Sea aged 81 • buried at St Edmund's College, Old Hall Green, Ware.
• *30 Morpeth Mansions, Morpeth Terrace, LONDON SW1P 1ET*

b. † Rt Rev. Dr **WILLIAM ANTONY JOHNSON** DD: born 20
August 1832 at Somers Town, London • ordained priest (Westmin-
ster) 19 December 1857 at Rome, Italy • ordained titular Bishop of
Arindela and appointed auxiliary Bishop of Westminster 1 May 1906
at the Metropolitan Cathedral Church of the Most Precious Blood,
Westminster, London • died 27 March 1909 at Westminster, London
aged 76 • buried at St Edmund's College, Old Hall Green, Ware.
• *Archbishop's House, Ambrosden Avenue, LONDON SW1P 1QJ*

c. † Most Rev. **JOSEPH BUTT**: born 27 March 1869 at Richmond
• ordained priest (Southwark) 18 July 1897 at Wonersh, Guildford
• ordained titular Bishop of *Cambysopolis* and appointed auxiliary
Bishop of Westminster 24 February 1911 at the Metropolitan Cathedral
Church of the Most Precious Blood, Westminster, London • appointed
23 April 1938 titular Archbishop of *Nicopsis* and retired to Downside,
Radstock • died 23 August 1944 at Downside, Radstock aged 75 •
buried at the Abbey Church of St Gregory, Downside, Radstock.
• *Downside Abbey, Stratton-on-the-Fosse, RADSTOCK BA3 4RH*

d. † Rt Rev. Dr **MANUEL JOHN BIDWELL** CBE DD BSc: born
29 June 1872 at Palma de Mallorca (Islas Baleares), Spain • ordained
priest (Westminster) 8 May 1898 at Rome, Italy • ordained titular
Bishop of *Miletopolis* and appointed auxiliary Bishop of Westminster
8 December 1917 at the Metropolitan Cathedral Church of the

Most Precious Blood, Westminster, London • died 11 July 1930 at Chelsea, London aged 58 • buried at St Vincent's Hospital, Pinner. • *St Mary's Rectory, Draycott Terrace, LONDON SW3 2QR*

e.   † Most Rev. **EDWARD MYERS**: born 8 September 1875 at Walmgate, York • ordained priest (Westminster) 7 December 1902 at Oscott, Sutton Coldfield • ordained titular Bishop of *Lamus* and appointed auxiliary Bishop of Westminster 25 July 1932 at the Metropolitan Cathedral Church of the Most Precious Blood, Westminster, London • appointed 20 May 1951 titular Archbishop of *Beroea* and appointed coadjutor Archbishop of Westminster *sedi datus sine jure successionis* • died 13 September 1956 at Chelsea, London aged 81 • buried at St Edmund's College, Old Hall Green, Ware. • *St Mary's Rectory, Draycott Terrace, LONDON SW3 2QR*

V.   † + *His Eminence* **Cardinal** Dr **ARTHUR HINSLEY** DD PhD: born 25 August 1865 at Carlton, Selby • ordained priest (Leeds) 23 December 1893 at Rome, Italy • incardinated 1904 into Diocese of Southwark at Southwark, London • ordained titular Bishop of *Sebastopolis in Armenia* 30 November 1926 at Rome, Italy • appointed 9 January 1930 titular Archbishop of *Sardes* and appointed Apostolic Delegate to West Africa • translated 29 April 1935 to Archdiocese of Westminster • elevated 16 December 1937 to Cardinal-Priest of Santa Susanna • died 17 March 1943 at Hare Street, Buntingford aged 77 • buried at the Metropolitan Cathedral Church of the Most Precious Blood, Westminster, London. • *Archbishop's House, Ambrosden Avenue, LONDON SW1P 1QJ*

a.   † Most Rev. Dr **DAVID JAMES MATHEW** MA LittD LLD FSA FRSL: born 16 January 1902 at Lyme Regis • ordained priest (Cardiff) 25 May 1929 at Rome, Italy • ordained titular Bishop of *Aeliae* and appointed auxiliary Bishop of Westminster 21 December 1938 at the Metropolitan Cathedral Church of the Most Precious Blood, Westminster, London • translated 10 May 1946 to titular Archbishop of *Apamea in Bithynia* and appointed Apostolic Delegate to British East and West Africa • translated 23 April 1954 to Military Vicar to HM Forces • appointed Council Father at Second Vatican Council 11 October 1962 to 8 December 1962 • retired 29 March 1963 to Stonor Park, Henley-on-Thames • died 12 December 1975 at St John's Wood, London, aged 73 •

buried at the Abbey Church of St Gregory, Downside, Radstock.
• *Stonor Park, Stonor, HENLEY-ON-THAMES RG9 6HF*

VI.   † + *His Eminence* Cardinal Dr **BERNARD WILLIAM GRIFFIN** DD
JCD: born 21 February 1899 at Cannon Hill, Birmingham • ordained priest
(Birmingham) 1 November 1924 at Rome, Italy • ordained titular Bishop of
Appia and appointed auxiliary Bishop of Birmingham 30 June 1938 at the
Metropolitan Cathedral Church of St Chad, Birmingham • translated 18
December 1943 to Archdiocese of Westminster • elevated 18 February 1946
to Cardinal-Priest of Santi Andrea e Gregorio Magno al Monte Celio •
died 20 August 1956 at Polzeath, Wadebridge, aged 57 • buried at the Metro-
politan Cathedral Church of the Most Precious Blood, Westminster, London.
• *Archbishop's House, Ambrosden Avenue, LONDON SW1P 1QJ*

a.   † Rt Rev. **GEORGE LAURENCE CRAVEN.** MC: born 1
February 1884 at Wednesbury • ordained priest (Westminster)
29 June 1912 at the Metropolitan Cathedral Church of the Most
Precious Blood, Westminster, London • ordained titular Bishop
of *Sebastopolis in Armenia* and appointed auxiliary Bishop of
Westminster 25 July 1947 at the Metropolitan Cathedral Church
of the Most Precious Blood, Westminster, London • appointed
Council Father at Second Vatican Council 11 October 1962 to 8
December 1962 • died 15 March 1967 at Marylebone, London,
aged 83 • buried at St Edmund's College, Old Hall Green, Ware.
• *St James's Church, 22 George Street, LONDON W1U 3QY*

VII.   † + *His Eminence* Cardinal Dr **WILLIAM GODFREY** DD PhD:
born 25 September 1889 at Kirkdale, Liverpool • ordained priest (Liverpool) 28 October 1916 at Rome, Italy • entered diplomatic service to
the Holy See 1938 at Vatican City • ordained titular Archbishop of *Cius*
and appointed Apostolic Delegate to Great Britain, Malta and Gibraltar
21 December 1938 at Rome, Italy • translated 14 November 1953 to
Archdiocese of Liverpool • translated 3 December 1956 to Archdiocese
of Westminster • appointed 10 June 1957 to the Apostolic Exarchate
for Ukrainians in England and Wales • elevated 15 December 1958 to
Cardinal-Priest of Santi Nereo ed Achilleo • appointed Council Father
at Second Vatican Council 11 October 1962 to 8 December 1962 • died 22
January 1963 at Westminster, London, aged 73 • buried at the Metropolitan

Cathedral Church of the Most Precious Blood, Westminster, London.
• *Archbishop's House, Ambrosden Avenue, LONDON SW1P 1QJ*

a.　† Rt Rev. **DAVID JOHN CASHMAN** STL: born 27 December 1912 at Bristol • ordained priest (Birmingham) 24 December 1938 at Rome, Italy • ordained titular Bishop of *Cantanus* and appointed auxiliary Bishop of Westminster 27 May 1958 at the Metropolitan Cathedral Church of the Most Precious Blood, Westminster, London • appointed Council Father at Second Vatican Council 11 October 1962 to 8 December 1965 • translated 28 May 1965 to newly erected Diocese of Arundel and Brighton • died 14 March 1971 at Arundel aged 58 • buried at the Cathedral Churchyard of Our Lady and St Philip Howard, Arundel. • *St Joseph's Hall, Greyfriars Lane, Storrington, PULBOROUGH RH20 4HE*

VIII.　† + *His Eminence* **Cardinal** Dr **JOHN CARMEL HEENAN** DD PhD: born 26 January 1905 at Ilford • ordained priest (Brentwood) 6 July 1930 at Ilford • ordained Bishop of Leeds 12 March 1951 at Leeds • translated 7 May 1957 to Archdiocese of Liverpool • appointed Council Father at Second Vatican Council 11 October 1962 to 8 December 1965 • translated 2 September 1963 to Archdiocese of Westminster • elevated 22 February 1965 to Cardinal-Priest of San Silvestro in Capite • died 7 November 1975 at Westminster, London, aged 70 • buried at the Metropolitan Cathedral Church of the Most Precious Blood, Westminster, London. • *Archbishop's House, Ambrosden Avenue, LONDON SW1P 1QJ*

a.　† Rt Rev. **PATRICK JOSEPH CASEY**: born 20 November 1913 at Stoke Newington, London • ordained priest (Westminster) 3 September 1939 at the Metropolitan Cathedral Church of the Most Precious Blood, Westminster, London • ordained titular Bishop of *Sufar* and appointed auxiliary Bishop of Westminster 2 February 1966 at the Metropolitan Cathedral Church of the Most Precious Blood, Westminster, London • translated 28 November 1969 to Diocese of Brentwood • resigned 11 December 1979 as Bishop of Brentwood and appointed parish priest of Holy Redeemer and St Thomas More Church, Chelsea, London • retired 25 September 1989 to Leigh-on-Sea • died 26 January 1999 at Leigh-on-Sea aged 85 •

buried at the Cathedral Church of SS Mary and Helen, Brentwood.
• *7 Cliffsea Grove, LEIGH-ON-SEA SS9 1NG*

b.   † *CE* Rt Rev. Dr Dom. **BASIL EDWARD CHRISTOPHER BUTLER** OSB MA LLD: born 7 May 1902 at Reading • ordained Church of England deacon (Oxford) 19 September 1926 at Christ Church, Oxford • received into Catholic Church 1928 at Downside, Radstock • professed (Order of Saint Benedict) 1929 at Downside, Radstock • ordained priest (Order of Saint Benedict) 10 June 1933 at Downside, Radstock • elected 12 September 1946 Abbot of the Abbey Church of St Gregory, Downside, Radstock • ordained titular Bishop of *Nova Barbara* and appointed auxiliary Bishop of Westminster 21 December 1966 at the Metropolitan Cathedral Church of the Most Precious Blood, Westminster, London • retired 21 September 1977 to Old Hall Green, Ware • died 20 September 1986 at St John's Wood, London, aged 84 • buried at the Abbey Church of St Gregory, Downside, Radstock.
• *St Edmund's College, Old Hall Green, WARE SG11 1DS*

c.   † Rt Rev. **VICTOR GUAZZELLI**: born 19 March 1920 at Stepney, London • ordained priest (Westminster) 17 March 1945 at Lisbon (Lisboa), Portugal • ordained titular Bishop of *Lindisfarna* and appointed auxiliary Bishop of Westminster 23 May 1970 at the Metropolitan Cathedral Church of the Most Precious Blood, Westminster, London • retired 21 December 1996 to Westminster, London • died 1 June 2004 at Vauxhall, London aged 84 • buried at St Mary's Cemetery, Kensal Green, London.
• *Cathedral Clergy House, 42 Francis Street, LONDON SW1P 1QW*

d.   † Rt Rev. **GERALD THOMAS MAHON** MHM MA: born 4 May 1922 at Fulham, London • ordained priest (Saint Joseph's Missionary Society of Mill Hill) 14 July 1946 at Mill Hill, London • ordained titular Bishop of *Eanach Dúin* and appointed auxiliary Bishop of Westminster 23 May 1970 at the Metropolitan Cathedral Church of the Most Precious Blood, Westminster, London • died 29 January 1992 at Littlehampton aged 69 • buried at Mill Hill, London.
• *34 Whitehall Gardens, LONDON W3 9RD*

IX.   † + *His Eminence* **Cardinal** Dom. **GEORGE BASIL HUME** OSB MA
STL OM: born 2 March 1923 at Newcastle upon Tyne • professed (Order of
Saint Benedict) 23 September 1942 at Ampleforth, York • ordained priest
(Order of Saint Benedict) 23 July 1950 at Ampleforth, York • elected 17
April 1963 Abbot of the Abbey Church of St Laurence, Ampleforth, York
• ordained Archbishop of Westminster 25 March 1976 at the Metropolitan
Cathedral Church of the Most Precious Blood, Westminster, London •
elevated 24 May 1976 to Cardinal-Priest of San Silvestro in Capite • died 17
June 1999 at St John's Wood, London, aged 76 • buried at the Metropolitan
Cathedral Church of the Most Precious Blood, Westminster, London.
• *Archbishop's House, Ambrosden Avenue, LONDON SW1P 1QJ*

a.   † Rt Rev. **PHILIP JAMES BENEDICT HARVEY** OBE:
born 6 March 1915 at Richmond • ordained priest (Westminster)
3 June 1939 at the Metropolitan Cathedral Church of the Most
Precious Blood, Westminster, London • ordained titular Bishop of
Bahanna and appointed auxiliary Bishop of Westminster 25 April
1977 at the Metropolitan Cathedral Church of the Most Precious
Blood, Westminster, London • retired 3 July 1990 to Whitton,
Twickenham • died 2 February 2003 at Whitton, Twickenham
aged 87 • buried at St Mary's Cemetery, Kensal Green, London.
• *Nazareth House, 162 East End Road, LONDON N2 0RU*

b.   ® Rt Rev. Dr **DAVID EVERY KONSTANT** MA PGCE DD
LLD: born 16 June 1930 at Blackheath, London • ordained priest
(Westminster) 12 June 1954 at the Metropolitan Cathedral Church
of the Most Precious Blood, Westminster, London • ordained titular
Bishop of *Betagbarar* and appointed auxiliary Bishop of Westminster
25 April 1977 at the Metropolitan Cathedral Church of the Most
Precious Blood, Westminster, London • translated 25 September
1985 to Diocese of Leeds • retired 7 April 2004 to Headingley, Leeds.
• *Ashlea, 62 Headingley Lane, LEEDS LS6 2BU*

c.   † Rt Rev. Dr **JAMES JOSEPH O'BRIEN** DLitt: born 5 August
1930 at Wood Green, London • ordained priest (Westminster)
12 June 1954 at the Metropolitan Cathedral Church of the Most
Precious Blood, Westminster, London • ordained titular Bishop
of *Manaccenser* and appointed auxiliary Bishop of Westminster 21 September 1977 at the Metropolitan Cathedral Church

of the Most Precious Blood, Westminster, London • retired 30 June 2005 to London Colney, St Albans • died 11 April 2007 at London Colney, St Albans aged 76 • cremated and interred at Our Lady of Lourdes Church, New Southgate, London. • *Gate House Lodge, Shenley Lane, London Colney, ST ALBANS AL2 1AG*

d.   ® Rt Rev. **JOHN PATRICK CROWLEY**: born 23 June 1941 at Newbury • ordained priest (Westminster) 12 June 1965 at the Metropolitan Cathedral Church of the Most Precious Blood, Westminster, London • ordained titular Bishop of *Thala* and appointed auxiliary Bishop of Westminster 8 December 1986 at the Metropolitan Cathedral Church of the Most Precious Blood, Westminster, London • translated 18 January 1993 to Diocese of Middlesbrough • retired 3 May 2007 to Wanstead, London thence to Harpenden. • *1 Kirkwick Avenue, HARPENDEN AL5 2QH*

e.   Rt Rev. VINCENT GERARD NICHOLS PhL MA MEd STL: see **XI.** below.

f.   ® Rt Rev. **PATRICK O'DONOGHUE**: born 4 May 1934 at Mourne Abbey (Cork), Ireland • ordained priest (Westminster) 25 May 1967 at Analeentha, Mourne Abbey (Cork), Ireland • ordained titular Bishop of *Tulana* and appointed auxiliary Bishop of Westminster 29 June 1993 at the Metropolitan Cathedral Church of the Most Precious Blood, Westminster, London • translated 4 July 2001 to Diocese of Lancaster • retired 1 May 2009 to Bantry (Cork), Ireland • appointed 3 July 2009 assistant priest of St Finbarr's parish, Bantry (Cork), Ireland • retired 2 April 2013 to Mallow (Cork), Ireland. • *Nazareth House, Drommahane, MALLOW (Cork), Ireland*

X.   ® + *His Eminence* Cardinal Dr **CORMAC MURPHY-O'CONNOR** STL PhL DD: born 24 August 1932 at Reading • ordained priest (Portsmouth) 28 October 1956 at Rome, Italy • ordained Bishop of Arundel and Brighton 21 December 1977 at Arundel • translated 22 March 2000 to Archdiocese of Westminster • elevated 21 February 2001 to Cardinal-Priest of Santa Maria sopra Minerva • retired 3 April 2009 to Chiswick, London. • *St Edward's, 7 Dukes Avenue, LONDON W4 2AA* a.　Rt Rev. **ARTHUR ROCHE** STB STL: born 6 March 1950 at Batley Carr, Dewsbury • ordained priest (Leeds) 19 July 1975 at Batley Carr, Dewsbury • ordained titular Bishop of *Rusticiana* and appointed auxiliary Bishop of Westminster 10 May 2001 at the Metropolitan Cathedral Church of the Most Precious Blood, Westminster, London • translated 16 July 2002 to coadjutor Bishop of Leeds • succeeded 7 April 2004 as Bishop of Leeds • appointed 26 June 2012 secretary of the Congregation for Divine Worship and Discipline of the Sacraments • appointed 26 June 2012 *Archbishop ad personam* at Vatican City. • *Palazzo delle Congregazioni, Piazza Pio XII 10, 00193 ROME, Italy*

b.　Rt Rev. **GEORGE STACK** BEd KCHS: born 9 May 1946 at Cork City (Cork), Ireland • ordained priest (Westminster) 21 May 1972 at Poplar, London • ordained titular Bishop of *Gemellae in Numidia* and appointed auxiliary Bishop of Westminster 10 May 2001 at the Metropolitan Cathedral Church of the Most Precious Blood, Westminster, London • translated 19 April 2011 to Archdiocese of Cardiff. • *Archbishop's House, 43 Cathedral Road, CARDIFF CF11 9HD*

c.　*CE* Rt Rev. **ALAN STEPHEN HOPES** BD AKC: born 14 March 1944 at Oxford • ordained Church of England deacon (London) 21 May 1967 at St Paul's Cathedral, City of London • ordained Church of England priest (London) 9 June 1968 at St Paul's Cathedral, City of London • received into Catholic Church 8 December 1994 at Kensington, London • ordained priest (Westminster) 4 December 1995 at the Metropolitan Cathedral Church of the Most Precious Blood, Westminster, London • ordained titular Bishop of *Cuncacestre* and appointed auxiliary Bishop of Westminster 24 January 2003 at the Metropolitan Cathedral Church of the Most Precious Blood, Westminster, London • translated 11 June 2013 to Diocese of East Anglia. • *The White House, 21 Upgate, Poringland, NORWICH NR14 7SH*

d.　Rt Rev. Dr **BERNARD LONGLEY** MA STL DD: born 5 April 1955 at City of Manchester • ordained priest (Arundel and Brighton) 12 December 1981 at Wonersh, Guildford • ordained titular Bishop of *Zarna* and appointed auxiliary Bishop of Westminster 24 January 2003 at the Metropolitan Cathedral Church of the Most Precious Blood, Westminster, London

• translated 1 October 2009 to Archdiocese of Birmingham.
• *Archbishop's House, 8 Shadwell Street, BIRMINGHAM B4 6EY*

e. Rt Rev. Dr **JOHN STANLEY KENNETH ARNOLD** LLB
MA JCD: born 12 June 1953 at Sheffield • professed (Institute
of Charity) 19 March 1978 at Wonersh, Guildford • ordained
priest (Westminster) 16 July 1983 at the Metropolitan Cathedral
Church of the Most Precious Blood, Westminster, London •
ordained titular Bishop of *Lindisfarna* and appointed auxiliary
Bishop of Westminster 2 February 2006 at the Metropolitan
Cathedral Church of the Most Precious Blood, Westminster,
London • translated 30 September 2014 to Diocese of Salford.
• *Wardley Hall, Wardley Hall Road, Worsley, MANCHESTER M28
2ND*

XI. + *His Eminence* **Cardinal** Dr **VINCENT GERARD NICHOLS** PhL
MA MEd STL DLitt: born 8 November 1945 at Crosby, Liverpool • ordained
priest (Liverpool) 21 December 1969 at Rome, Italy • ordained titular Bishop
of *Othona* and appointed auxiliary Bishop of Westminster 24 January 1992 at
the Metropolitan Cathedral Church of the Most Precious Blood, Westminster,
London • translated 29 March 2000 to Archdiocese of Birmingham • translated
21 May 2009 to Archdiocese of Westminster • elevated 22 February 2014 to
Cardinal-Priest of Santissimo Redentore e Sant'Alfonso in Via Merulana.
• *Archbishop's House, Ambrosden Avenue, LONDON SW1P 1QJ*

a. Rt Rev. **JOHN FRANCIS SHERRINGTON** BA MA STL: born
5 January 1958 at Leicester • ordained priest (Nottingham) 13 June
1987 at Leicester • ordained titular Bishop of *Hilta* and appointed auxiliary Bishop of Westminster 14 September 2011 at the Metropolitan
Cathedral Church of the Most Precious Blood, Westminster, London.
• *81 Parkway, WELWYN GARDEN CITY AL8 6JF*

b. Rt Rev. **NICHOLAS GILBERT ERSKINE HUDSON**
BA MA STL: born 14 February 1959 at Hammersmith, London •
ordained priest (Southwark) 19 July 1986 at Wimbledon, London
• ordained titular Bishop of *Sanctus Germanus* and appointed
auxiliary Bishop of Westminster 4 June 2014 at the Metropolitan
Cathedral Church of the Most Precious Blood, Westminster, London.
• *Flat 5, 8 Morpeth Terrace, LONDON SW1P 1EQ*

c.   Rt Rev. **PAUL McALEENAN**: born 15 July 1951 at Belfast (Antrim), Ireland • ordained priest (Westminster) 8 June 1985 at the Metropolitan Cathedral Church of the Most Precious Blood, Westminster, London • ordained titular Bishop of *Mercia* and appointed auxiliary Bishop of Westminster 25 January 2016 at the Metropolitan Cathedral Church of the Most Precious Blood, Westminster, London. • *c/o Archbishop's House, Ambrosden Avenue, LONDON SW1P 1QJ*

d.   CE Rt Rev. Dr **JOHN WILSON** BA STB STL PhD: born 4 July 1968 at Sheffield • received into Catholic Church 23 February 1985 at Sheffield • ordained priest (Leeds) 29 July 1995 at Halifax • ordained titular Bishop of *Lindisfarna* and appointed auxiliary Bishop of Westminster 25 January 2016 at the Metropolitan Cathedral Church of the Most Precious Blood, Westminster, London. • *c/o Archbishop's House, Ambrosden Avenue, LONDON SW1P 1QJ*

DIOCESE OF ARUNDEL AND BRIGHTON

PAX ET GAUDIUM IN DOMINO

(Dioecesis Arundeliensis-Brichtelmestunensis)

By Letters Apostolic (*Romanorum pontificum*) of Pope Bl. Paul VI, dated 28 May 1965, the Diocese of Arundel and Brighton was formed by division of the Diocese of Southwark, with the episcopal see fixed at the Cathedral Church of Our Lady and St Philip Howard, Arundel (1965–), consecrated on 14 May 1952.

By the same Letters Apostolic (*Romanorum pontificum*) of Pope Bl. Paul VI, dated 28 May 1965, the Province of Westminster was divided further into two new provinces of Southwark and Westminster, with the Diocese of Arundel and Brighton being made part of the newly erected Province of Southwark. The episcopal see remained at the Cathedral Church of Our Lady and St Philip Howard, Arundel (1965–).

At first, the Diocese of Arundel and Brighton comprised the County of Sussex and the part of Surrey (south of the River Thames) lying outside the Greater London boroughs (1965).

The Diocese today comprises the counties of East Sussex, West Sussex and the part of Surrey (south of the River Thames) lying outside the Greater London boroughs (1965) and the City of Brighton and Hove.

I.   † Rt Rev. **DAVID JOHN CASHMAN** STL: born 27 December 1912 at Bristol • ordained priest (Birmingham) 24 December 1938 at Rome, Italy • ordained titular Bishop of *Cantanus* and appointed auxiliary Bishop of Westminster 27 May 1958 at the Metropolitan Cathedral Church of the Most Precious Blood, Westminster, London • appointed Council Father at Second Vatican Council 11 October 1962 to 8 December 1965 • translated 28 May 1965 to newly erected Diocese of Arundel and Brighton • died 14 March 1971 at Arundel aged 58 • buried at the Cathedral Churchyard of Our Lady and St Philip Howard, Arundel. • *St Joseph's Hall, Greyfriars Lane, Storrington, PULBOROUGH RH20 4HE*

    a.   ® Rt Rev. **MICHAEL GEORGE BOWEN** STL PhL: see **II.** below.

II.   ® Rt Rev. **MICHAEL GEORGE BOWEN** STL PhL: born 23 April 1930 at Gibraltar • ordained priest (Southwark) 6 July 1958 at Rome, Italy • incardinated 28 May 1965 into Diocese of Arundel and Brighton at Storrington, Pulborough • ordained titular Bishop of *Lamsorti* and appointed coadjutor Bishop of Arundel and Brighton 27 June 1970 at Arundel • succeeded 14 March 1971 as Bishop of Arundel and Brighton • translated 23 April 1977 to Archdiocese of Southwark • retired 6 November 2003 to Blackheath, London. • *54 Parkside, Vanbrugh Fields, LONDON SE3 7QF*

III. ® Rt Rev. CORMAC MURPHY-O'CONNOR STL PhL: born 24 August 1932 at Reading • ordained priest (Portsmouth) 28 October 1956 at Rome, Italy • ordained Bishop of Arundel and Brighton 21 December 1977 at Arundel • translated 22 March 2000 to Archdiocese of Westminster • elevated 21 February 2001 to Cardinal-Priest of Santa Maria sopra Minerva • retired 3 April 2009 to Chiswick, London. • *St Edward's, 7 Dukes Avenue, LONDON W4 2AA*

IV.   ® Rt Rev. **KIERAN THOMAS CONRY** PhB STL: born 1 February 1951 at Coventry • ordained priest (Birmingham) 19 July 1975 at Coventry • ordained Bishop of Arundel and Brighton 9 June 2001 at Arundel • resigned 4 October 2014 as Bishop of Arundel and Brighton and retired to Pease Pottage, Crawley. • *c/o High Oaks, Old Brighton Road, Pease Pottage, CRAWLEY RH11 9AJ*

    a.   **APOSTOLIC ADMINISTRATOR:** Most Rev. Dr **PETER DAVID GREGORY SMITH** LLB JCD: born 21 October

1943 at Battersea, London • ordained priest (Southwark) 5 July 1972 at Wonersh, Guildford • ordained Bishop of East Anglia 27 May 1995 at Norwich • translated 26 October 2001 to Archdiocese of Cardiff • translated 30 April 2010 to Archdiocese of Southwark • appointed 4 October 2014 Apostolic Administrator of the Diocese of Arundel and Brighton until 28 May 2015.
• *Archbishop's House, 150 St George's Road, LONDON SE1 6HX*

V.   Rt Rev. **CHARLES PHILLIP RICHARD MOTH** MA JCL KCHS: born 8 July 1958 at Chingola (Copperbelt), Zambia • ordained priest (Southwark) 3 July 1982 at Wonersh, Guildford • commissioned as military chaplain 1 April 1988 • released from military service 25 July 2009 • ordained Bishop in Ordinary to HM Forces 29 September 2009 at the Metropolitan Cathedral Church of the Most Precious Blood, Westminster, London • translated 21 March 2015 to Diocese of Arundel and Brighton.
• *High Oaks, Old Brighton Road, Pease Pottage, CRAWLEY RH11 9AJ*

DIOCESE OF BEVERLEY

(Dioecesis Beverlacensis)

By Letters Apostolic (*Universalis ecclesiae*) of Pope Bl. Pius IX, dated 29 September 1850, the Diocese of Beverley was formed, with the episcopal see fixed at the Pro-Cathedral Church of St George, York (1850–1864), consecrated on 16 April 1991, then at the Pro-Cathedral Church of St Wilfrid, York (1864–1878), consecrated on 14 July 1945.

The Diocese of Beverley was an original suffragan see within the Province of Westminster. At first, the Diocese of Beverley comprised the entire County of Yorkshire.

By Apostolic Decree (*Quae ex hac*) of Pope Leo XIII, dated 20 December 1878, the Diocese of Leeds was formed by division of the Diocese of Beverley, with the episcopal see fixed at the Cathedral Church of St Anne, Cookridge Street, Leeds (1878–1904), opened in October 1838 and demolished after 1901, then at the Cathedral Church of St Anne, Great George Street, Leeds (1904–), opened in 1904 and consecrated on 19 July 1924.

By the same Apostolic Decree (*Quae ex hac*) of Pope Leo XIII, dated 20 December 1878, the Diocese of Middlesbrough was formed by division of the Diocese of Beverley, with the episcopal see fixed at the Cathedral Church of Our Lady of

Perpetual Succour, Sussex Street, Middlesbrough (1878–1986), consecrated on 6 September 1911 and destroyed by fire on 30 May 2000, then at the Cathedral Church of St Mary, Coulby Newham, Middlesbrough (1986–), opened and consecrated on 15 May 1986.

I. † Rt Rev. Dr **JOHN BRIGGS** DD: born 20 May 1788 at Barton-upon-Irwell, Manchester • ordained priest (Northern District) 19 July 1814 at Ushaw, Durham • ordained titular Bishop of *Trachis* and appointed coadjutor Vicar Apostolic for the Northern District 29 June 1833 at Ushaw, Durham • succeeded 28 January 1836 as Vicar Apostolic for the Northern District • translated 3 July 1840 to Vicar Apostolic for the Yorkshire District • translated 29 September 1850 to restored Diocese of Beverley • retired 7 November 1860 to Fulford, York • died 4 January 1861 at Fulford, York, aged 72 • buried at St Leonard's chapel, Hazlewood, Tadcaster. • *Fulford Park House, Main Street, Fulford, YORK YO10 4PQ*

II. † Rt Rev. **ROBERT CORNTHWAITE**: born 9 May 1818 at Preston • ordained priest (Northern District) 9 November 1845 at Rome, Italy • ordained Bishop of Beverley 10 November 1861 at Moorfields, City of London • appointed Council Father at First Vatican Council 8 December 1869 to 20 October 1870 • translated 20 December 1878 to newly erected Diocese of Leeds • appointed 20 December 1878 Apostolic Administrator of Diocese of Middlesbrough until 18 December 1879 • died 16 June 1890 at Leeds aged 72 • buried at the Church of Mary Immaculate, Sicklinghall, Wetherby. • *Springfield House, Hyde Street, LEEDS LS2 9LH*

DIOCESE OF BIRMINGHAM

(Dioecesis Birminghamiensis)

By Letters Apostolic (*Universalis ecclesiae*) of Pope Bl. Pius IX, dated 29 September 1850, the Diocese of Birmingham was formed, with the episcopal see fixed at the Cathedral Church of St Chad, Birmingham (1850–1911), consecrated on 21 June 1841.

The Diocese of Birmingham was an original suffragan see within the Province of Westminster. At first, the Diocese of Birmingham comprised the counties of Oxfordshire (north of the River Thames), Staffordshire, Warwickshire and Worcestershire.

I.   † Most Rev. Dom. **WILLIAM BERNARD ULLATHORNE** OSB:
born 7 May 1806 at Pocklington, York • professed (Order of Saint Benedict)
5 April 1825 at Downside, Radstock • ordained priest (Order of Saint
Benedict) 24 September 1831 at Ushaw, Durham • ordained titular Bishop
of *Hetalonia* and appointed Vicar Apostolic for the Western District 21 June
1846 at Coventry • translated 28 July 1848 to Vicar Apostolic for the Central
District • translated 29 September 1850 to restored Diocese of Birmingham
• appointed 29 September 1850 Apostolic Administrator of the Diocese of
Nottingham until 22 June 1851 • appointed Council Father at First Vatican
Council 8 December 1869 to 20 October 1870 • appointed 17 February 1888
titular Archbishop of *Cabasa* and retired to Oscott, Sutton Coldfield • died 21
March 1889 at Oscott, Sutton Coldfield, aged 82 • buried at Aston Hall, Stone.
• *Oscott College, Chester Road, SUTTON COLDFIELD B73 5AA*

a.   † Rt Rev. **EDWARD ILSLEY**: see **II.** below.

II.   † Rt Rev. **EDWARD ILSLEY**: born 11 May 1838 at Appleyard Court,
Stafford • ordained priest (Birmingham) 29 June 1861 at the Cathedral
Church of St Chad, Birmingham • ordained titular Bishop of *Fesseë* and
appointed auxiliary Bishop of Birmingham 4 December 1879 at the
Cathedral Church of St Chad, Birmingham • translated 17 February
1888 to Diocese of Birmingham • appointed 28 October 1911 Arch-
bishop and Metropolitan of newly raised Archdiocese and Province of
Birmingham • appointed 15 January 1921 titular Archbishop of *Macra*
and retired to Harvington Hall, Kidderminster thence to Oscott, Sutton
Coldfield • died 1 December 1926 at Oscott, Sutton Coldfield, aged 88 •
buried at the Metropolitan Cathedral Church of St Chad, Birmingham.
• *Oscott College, Chester Road, SUTTON COLDFIELD B73 5AA*

ARCHDIOCESE OF BIRMINGHAM

(Archidioecesis Birminghamiensis)

By Letters Apostolic (*Si qua est*) of Pope St Pius X, dated 28 October 1911, the Province of Westminster was divided into three new provinces of Birmingham, Liverpool and Westminster, with the Diocese of Birmingham being raised to a metropolitan Archdiocese and province. The episcopal see remained at the Metropolitan Cathedral Church and Minor Basilica (11 June 1941) of St Chad, Birmingham (1911–).

The Province of Birmingham comprises the Archdiocese of Birmingham with the suffragan sees of Clifton and Shrewsbury. The Archdiocese today comprises the counties of Oxfordshire (north of the River Thames), Staffordshire, Warwickshire and Worcestershire and the unitary authorities of Birmingham, Coventry, Dudley, Sandwell, Solihull, Stoke-on-Trent, Walsall and Wolverhampton.

I. † Most Rev. **EDWARD ILSLEY**: born 11 May 1838 at Appleyard Court, Stafford • ordained priest (Birmingham) 29 June 1861 at the Cathedral Church of St Chad, Birmingham • ordained titular Bishop of *Fesseë* and appointed auxiliary Bishop of Birmingham 4 December 1879 at the Cathedral Church of St Chad, Birmingham • translated 17 February 1888 to Diocese of Birmingham • appointed 28 October 1911 Archbishop and Metropolitan of newly raised Archdiocese and Province of Birmingham • appointed 15 January 1921 titular Archbishop of *Macra* and retired to Harvington Hall, Kidderminster thence to Oscott, Sutton Coldfield • died 1 December 1926 at Oscott, Sutton Coldfield, aged 88 • buried at the Metropolitan Cathedral Church of St Chad, Birmingham. • *Oscott College, Chester Road, SUTTON COLDFIELD B73 5AA*

a. † Rt Rev. Dr **JOHN McINTYRE** DD: see **II.** below.

II. † Most Rev. Dr **JOHN McINTYRE** DD: born 1 January 1855 at Snow Hill, Birmingham • ordained priest (Birmingham) 22 May 1880 at Rome, Italy • ordained titular Bishop of *Lamus* and appointed auxiliary Bishop of Birmingham 30 July 1912 at the Metropolitan Cathedral Church of St Chad, Birmingham • appointed 24 August 1917 titular Archbishop of *Oxyrynchus* and appointed auxiliary Bishop of Birmingham • translated 16 June 1921 to Archdiocese of Birmingham • appointed 16 November 1928 titular Archbishop of *Odessus* and retired to Edgbaston, Birmingham • died 21 November 1934 at Edgbaston, Birmingham, aged 79 • buried at the Metropolitan Cathedral Church of St Chad, Birmingham. • *Oscott College, Chester Road, SUTTON COLDFIELD B73 5AA*

a. † Rt Rev. **MICHAEL FRANCIS GLANCEY**: born 25 October 1854 at Wolverhampton • ordained priest (Birmingham) 22 December 1877 at Olton, Solihull • ordained titular Bishop of *Flaviopolis* and appointed auxiliary Bishop of Birmingham 29 September 1924 at the Metropolitan Cathedral Church of St Chad, Birmingham • died 16 October 1925 at Edgbaston, Birmingham aged 70 • buried at St Mary's College, Oscott, Sutton Coldfield. • *Archbishop's House, 6 Norfolk Road, Edgbaston, BIRMINGHAM B15 3QD*

b. † Rt Rev. Dr **JOHN PATRICK BARRETT** BA DD PhD: born 31 October 1878 at Liverpool • ordained priest (Liverpool) 9 June 1906

at Upholland, Skelmersdale • ordained titular Bishop of *Assus* and appointed auxiliary Bishop of Birmingham 22 February 1927 at the Metropolitan Cathedral Church of St Chad, Birmingham • translated 7 June 1929 to Diocese of Plymouth • died 2 November 1946 at Torquay aged 68 • buried at the Abbey Church of St Mary, Buckfastleigh.
• *Stoodley Knowle Convent, Ansteys Cove Road, TORQUAY TQ1 2JB*

III.   † Most Rev. **THOMAS LEIGHTON WILLIAMS** MA: born 20 March 1877 at Handsworth, Birmingham • ordained priest (Birmingham) 24 August 1900 at Oscott, Sutton Coldfield • ordained Archbishop of Birmingham 25 July 1929 at the Metropolitan Cathedral Church of St Chad, Birmingham • died 1 April 1946 at Edgbaston, Birmingham, aged 69 • buried at St Mary's College, Oscott, Sutton Coldfield.
• *Archbishop's House, 6 Norfolk Road, Edgbaston, BIRMINGHAM B15 3QD*

a.   † Rt Rev. Dr BERNARD WILLIAM GRIFFIN DD JCD: born 21 February 1899 at Cannon Hill, Birmingham • ordained priest (Birmingham) 1 November 1924 at Rome, Italy • ordained titular Bishop of *Appia* and appointed auxiliary Bishop of Birmingham 30 June 1938 at the Metropolitan Cathedral Church of St Chad, Birmingham • translated 18 December 1943 to Archdiocese of Westminster • elevated 18 February 1946 to Cardinal-Priest of Santi Andrea e Gregorio Magno al Monte Celio • died 20 August 1956 at Polzeath, Wadebridge, aged 57 • buried at the Metropolitan Cathedral Church of the Most Precious Blood, Westminster, London.
• *Archbishop's House, Ambrosden Avenue, LONDON SW1P 1QJ*

b.   † Rt Rev. **HUMPHREY PENDERELL BRIGHT**: born 27 January 1903 at Brentwood • ordained priest (Birmingham) 2 June 1928 at Oscott, Sutton Coldfield • commissioned as military chaplain 26 January 1939 • released from military service 31 August 1944 • ordained titular Bishop of *Soli* and appointed auxiliary Bishop of Birmingham 28 October 1944 at the Metropolitan Cathedral Church of St Chad, Birmingham • appointed Council Father at Second Vatican Council 11 October 1962 to 4 December 1963 • died 26 March 1964 at Tunstall, Stoke-on-Trent, aged 61 • buried at St Mary's College, Oscott, Sutton Coldfield.
• *Presbytery, 13 Queen's Avenue, STOKE-ON-TRENT ST6 6EE*

IV. † Most Rev. Dr **JOSEPH MASTERSON** DD PhD JCD: born 29 January 1899 at Manchester • ordained priest (Salford) 27 July 1924 at Rome, Italy • ordained Archbishop of Birmingham 19 March 1947 at the Metropolitan Cathedral Church of St Chad, Birmingham • died 30 November 1953 at Edgbaston, Birmingham, aged 54 • buried at St Mary's College, Oscott, Sutton Coldfield. • *Archbishop's House, 6 Norfolk Road, Edgbaston, BIRMINGHAM B15 3QD*

V. † Most Rev. Dr **FRANCIS EDWARD JOSEPH GRIMSHAW** DD: born 6 October 1901 at Bridgwater • ordained priest (Clifton) 27 February 1926 at Bristol • ordained Bishop of Plymouth 25 July 1947 at Plymouth • translated 11 May 1954 to Archdiocese of Birmingham • appointed Council Father at Second Vatican Council 11 October 1962 to 21 November 1964 • died 22 March 1965 at Edgbaston, Birmingham, aged 63 • buried at St Mary's College, Oscott, Sutton Coldfield. • *Archbishop's House, 6 Norfolk Road, Edgbaston, BIRMINGHAM B15 3QD*

    a. † Rt Rev. **JOSEPH FRANCIS CLEARY**: born 4 September 1912 at Dublin City (Dublin), Ireland • ordained priest (Birmingham) 29 June 1939 at Oscott, Sutton Coldfield • ordained titular Bishop of *Cresima* and appointed auxiliary Bishop of Birmingham 25 January 1965 at the Metropolitan Cathedral Church of St Chad, Birmingham • appointed Council Father at Second Vatican Council 14 September 1965 to 8 December 1965 • retired 4 September 1987 to Wolverhampton • died 25 February 1991 at Wolverhampton aged 78 • buried at Banbury. • *The Presbytery, Snow Hill, WOLVERHAMPTON WV2 4AD*

VI. † Most Rev. Dr **GEORGE PATRICK DWYER** DD PhD BA: born 25 September 1908 at Miles Platting, Manchester • ordained priest (Salford) 1 November 1932 at Rome, Italy • ordained Bishop of Leeds 24 September 1957 at Leeds • appointed Council Father at Second Vatican Council 11 October 1962 to 8 December 1965 • translated 21 December 1965 to Archdiocese of Birmingham • retired 1 September 1981 to Selly Park, Birmingham • died 17 September 1987 at Selly Park, Birmingham aged 78 • buried at St Mary's College, Oscott, Sutton Coldfield. • *St Paul's Convent, 94 Selly Park Road, Selly Park, BIRMINGHAM B29 7LL*

    a. † Rt Rev. **ANTHONY JOSEPH EMERY**: born 17 May 1918 at Burton-on-Trent • enlisted as military soldier 1940 • released from military service 1945 • ordained priest (Birmingham) 30 May 1953 at Oscott, Sutton Coldfield • ordained titular Bishop of *Tamallula* and appointed auxiliary Bishop of Birmingham 4 March 1968 at the Metropolitan Cathedral Church of St Chad, Birmingham • translated 5 November 1976 to Diocese of Portsmouth • died 5 April 1988 at Portsmouth aged 69 • buried at Milton Cemetery, Portsmouth. • *Bishop's House, Edinburgh Road, PORTSMOUTH PO1 3HG*

b.   ® Rt Rev. **PATRICK LEO McCARTIE**: born 5 September 1925 at West Hartlepool • ordained priest (Birmingham) 17 July 1949 at Trent Vale, Stoke-on-Trent • ordained titular Bishop of *Elmhama* and appointed auxiliary Bishop of Birmingham 20 May 1977 at the Metropolitan Cathedral Church of St Chad, Birmingham • translated 19 March 1990 to Diocese of Northampton • retired 29 March 2001 to Aston, Stone thence to Harborne, Birmingham. • *Little Sisters of the Poor, 71 Queens Park Road, BIRMINGHAM B32 2LB*

VII.   † Most Rev. Dr **MAURICE NOËL LÉON COUVE DE MURVILLE** MA MPhil STL DD: born 27 June 1929 at Saint Germain en Laye (Yvelines), France • ordained priest (Southwark) 29 June 1957 at Leatherhead • incardinated 28 May 1965 into Diocese of Arundel and Brighton at Storrington, Pulborough • ordained Archbishop of Birmingham 25 March 1982 at the Metropolitan Cathedral Church of St Chad, Birmingham • retired 12 June 1999 to Seaford thence to Horsham • died 3 November 2007 at Storrington, Pulborough, aged 78 • buried at St Mary's College, Oscott, Sutton Coldfield. • *53 North Parade, HORSHAM RH12 2DE*

a.   ® Rt Rev. Dr **ROGER FRANCIS CRISPIAN HOLLIS** MA STL LLD: born 17 November 1936 at Bristol • ordained priest (Clifton) 11 July 1965 at Rome, Italy • ordained titular Bishop of *Cincari* and appointed auxiliary Bishop of Birmingham 5 May 1987 at the Metropolitan Cathedral Church of St Chad, Birmingham • translated 27 January 1989 to Diocese of Portsmouth • retired 11 July 2012 to Mells, Frome. • *Stable House, Fairview, Mells, FROME BA11 3PP*

b.   ® Rt Rev. **PHILIP PARGETER**: born 13 June 1933 at Wolverhampton • ordained priest (Birmingham) 21

February 1959 at Oscott, Sutton Coldfield • ordained titular Bishop of *Valentiniana* and appointed auxiliary Bishop of Birmingham 21 February 1990 at the Metropolitan Cathedral Church of St Chad, Birmingham • retired 31 July 2009 to Sutton Coldfield.
• *Grove House, 90 College Road, SUTTON COLDFIELD B73 5AH*

c. ® Rt Rev. **TERENCE JOHN BRAIN**: born 19 December 1938 at Coventry • ordained priest (Birmingham) 22 February 1964 at the Metropolitan Cathedral Church of St Chad, Birmingham • ordained titular Bishop of *Amudarsa* and appointed auxiliary Bishop of Birmingham 25 April 1991 at the Metropolitan Cathedral Church of St Chad, Birmingham • translated 7 October 1997 to Diocese of Salford • retired 30 September 2014 to Middleton, Manchester.
• *106 Crow Hill South, Middleton, MANCHESTER M24 1JU*

VIII. Most Rev. Dr VINCENT GERARD NICHOLS PhL MA MEd STL DLitt: born 8 November 1945 at Crosby, Liverpool • ordained priest (Liverpool) 21 December 1969 at Rome, Italy • ordained titular Bishop of *Othona* and appointed auxiliary Bishop of Westminster 24 January 1992 at the Metropolitan Cathedral Church of the Most Precious Blood, Westminster, London • translated 29 March 2000 to Archdiocese of Birmingham • translated 21 May 2009 to Archdiocese of Westminster • elevated 22 February 2014 to Cardinal-Priest of Santissimo Redentore e Sant'Alfonso in Via Merulana.
• *Archbishop's House, Ambrosden Avenue, LONDON SW1P 1QJ*

a. Rt Rev. **DAVID CHRISTOPHER McGOUGH** LSS STL: born 20 November 1944 at Tunstall, Stoke-on-Trent • ordained priest (Birmingham) 14 March 1970 at Tunstall, Stoke-on-Trent • ordained titular Bishop of *Chunavia* and appointed auxiliary Bishop of Birmingham 8 December 2005 at the Metropolitan Cathedral Church of St Chad, Birmingham.
• *The Rocks, 106 Draycott Road, Tean, STOKE-ON-TRENT ST10 4JF*

b. **APOSTOLIC ADMINISTRATOR**: Rt Rev. Dr **LEONARD WILLIAM KENNEY** CP KCHS Fil.Kand STL PhD: born 7 May 1946 at Newcastle upon Tyne • professed (Congregation of the Passion of Jesus Christ) 1 September 1963 at Broadway • ordained priest (Congregation of the Passion of Jesus Christ) 29 June 1969 at the Metropolitan Cathedral Church of St Chad,

Birmingham • ordained titular Bishop of *Midica* and appointed auxiliary Bishop of Stockholm 24 August 1987 at Stockholm (Stockholm), Sweden • translated 17 October 2006 to auxiliary Bishop of Birmingham • appointed 22 May 2009 Apostolic Administrator of the Archdiocese of Birmingham until 8 December 2009.
• *St Hugh's House, 27 Hensington Road, WOODSTOCK OX20 1JH*

IX. Most Rev. Dr **BERNARD LONGLEY** MA STL DD: born 5 April 1955 at City of Manchester • ordained priest (Arundel and Brighton) 12 December 1981 at Wonersh, Guildford • ordained titular Bishop of *Zarna* and appointed auxiliary Bishop of Westminster 24 January 2003 at the Metropolitan Cathedral Church of the Most Precious Blood, Westminster, London • translated 1 October 2009 to Archdiocese of Birmingham.
• *Archbishop's House, 8 Shadwell Street, BIRMINGHAM B4 6EY*

a. Rt Rev. **ROBERT BYRNE** CO BD AKC: born 22 September 1956 at Urmston, Manchester • professed (Congregation of the Oratory) 30 September 1982 at Edgbaston, Birmingham • ordained priest (Congregation of the Oratory) 5 January 1985 at Edgbaston, Birmingham • ordained titular Bishop of *Cuncacestre* and appointed auxiliary Bishop of Birmingham 13 May 2014 at the Metropolitan Cathedral Church of St Chad, Birmingham.
• *Oscott College, Chester Road, SUTTON COLDFIELD B73 5AA*

DIOCESE OF BRENTWOOD

(Dioecesis Brentvoodensis)

By Apostolic Consistory of Pope Benedict XV, dated 22 March 1917, the Diocese of Essex was formed by division of the Archdiocese of Westminster, comprising the entire County of Essex. By a Bull (*Universalis ecclesiae procuratio*) of Pope Benedict XV, dated 20 July 1917, the Diocese of Essex was renamed Brentwood, with the episcopal see fixed at the Cathedral Church of the Sacred Heart and St Helen, Brentwood (1917–1991), consecrated on 15 June 1869, which was enlarged in 1974 then rebuilt and rededicated on 31 May 1991 as the Cathedral Church of SS Mary and Helen, Brentwood (1991–).

Since 22 March 1917, the Diocese of Brentwood has been a suffragan see within the Province of Westminster. At first, the Diocese of Brentwood comprised the entire County of Essex.

The diocese today comprises the County of Essex, the unitary authorities of Southend-on-Sea and Thurrock and those Greater London boroughs east of the River Lea.

a.   APOSTOLIC ADMINISTRATOR: † Rt Rev. **BERNARD FRAN-
CIS NICHOLAS WARD**: see **I.** below.

I.   † Rt Rev. **BERNARD FRANCIS NICHOLAS WARD**: born 4
February 1857 at Old Hall Green, Ware • ordained priest (Westminster) 8
October 1882 at Old Hall Green, Ware • appointed 22 March 1917 Apostolic
Administrator of the newly erected Diocese of Essex until 20 July 1917 •
ordained titular Bishop of *Lydda* 10 April 1917 at the Metropolitan Cathedral
Church of the Most Precious Blood, Westminster, London • translated
20 July 1917 to renamed Diocese of Brentwood • died 21 January 1920 at
Brentwood aged 62 • buried at St Edmund's College, Old Hall Green, Ware.
• *Bishop's House, Queens Road, BRENTWOOD CM14 4HE*

II.   † Rt Rev. **ARTHUR HENRY DOUBLEDAY** BA: born 16
October 1865 at Pietermaritzburg (Natal), South Africa • ordained
priest (Southwark) 22 December 1888 at the Cathedral Church of St
George, Southwark, London • ordained Bishop of Brentwood 23
June 1920 at the Cathedral Church of St George, Southwark, London
• died 23 January 1951 at Brentwood aged 85 • buried at the Cathe-
dral Church Cemetery of the Sacred Heart and St Helen, Brentwood.
• *Bishop's House, Queens Road, BRENTWOOD CM14 4HE*

a.   † Rt Rev. Dr **GEORGE ANDREW BECK** AA BA LLD: see
III. below.

III.   † Rt Rev. Dr **GEORGE ANDREW BECK** AA BA LLD: born 28
May 1904 at Streatham, London • ordained priest (Augustinians of the
Assumption) 24 July 1927 at Louvain (Flemish Brabant), Belgium • ordained
titular Bishop of *Tigias* and appointed coadjutor Bishop of Brentwood
21 September 1948 at the Metropolitan Cathedral Church of the Most
Precious Blood, Westminster, London • succeeded 23 January 1951 as
Bishop of Brentwood • translated 28 November 1955 to Diocese of Salford • appointed Council Father at Second Vatican Council 11 October
1962 to 8 December 1965 • translated 29 January 1964 to Archdiocese
of Liverpool • retired 11 February 1976 to Upholland, Skelmersdale •
died 13 September 1978 at Mossley Hill, Liverpool, aged 74 • buried
at the Metropolitan Cathedral Crypt of Christ the King, Liverpool.
• *St Joseph's College, College Road, Upholland, SKELMERSDALE WN8 0PY*

IV.   † Rt Rev. Dr **BERNARD PATRICK WALL** DD: born 15 March 1894 at
        Tonbridge • ordained priest (Southwark) 14 July 1918 at Wonersh, Guildford
        • ordained Bishop of Brentwood 18 January 1956 at Brompton Oratory, Kens-
        ington, London • appointed Council Father at Second Vatican Council 11
        October 1962 to 8 December 1965 • appointed 15 April 1969 titular Bishop of
        Othona and retired to South Woodford, London • died 18 June 1976 at South
        Woodford, London, aged 82 • buried at St John's College, Wonersh, Guildford.
        • *18 Bressey Grove, LONDON E18 2HP*

V.   † Rt Rev. **PATRICK JOSEPH CASEY**: born 20 November 1913 at
        Stoke Newington, London • ordained priest (Westminster) 3 September
        1939 at the Metropolitan Cathedral Church of the Most Precious Blood,
        Westminster, London • ordained titular Bishop of *Sufar* and appointed aux-
        iliary Bishop of Westminster 2 February 1966 at the Metropolitan Cathedral
        Church of the Most Precious Blood, Westminster, London • translated 28
        November 1969 to Diocese of Brentwood • resigned 11 December 1979 as
        Bishop of Brentwood and appointed parish priest of Holy Redeemer and
        St Thomas More Church, Chelsea, London • retired 25 September 1989
        to Leigh-on-Sea • died 26 January 1999 at Leigh-on-Sea aged 85 • buried
        at the Cathedral Church Cemetery of SS Mary and Helen, Brentwood.
        • *7 Cliffsea Grove, LEIGH-ON-SEA SS9 1NG*

VI.   ® Rt Rev. Dr **THOMAS McMAHON** DUniv: born 17 June
        1936 at Dorking • ordained priest (Brentwood) 28 November
        1959 at Wonersh, Guildford • ordained Bishop of Brentwood 17
        July 1980 at Brentwood • retired 14 April 2014 and re-appointed
        parish priest of Our Lady and St Joseph Church, Stock, Ingatestone.
        • *Bishop's House, Stock Road, Stock, INGATESTONE CM4 9BU*

VII.   Rt Rev. Dr **ALAN WILLIAMS** SM MA PhD: born 15 March 1951 at
        Oldham • professed (Society of Mary) 8 September 1976 at Whitechapel,
        London • ordained priest (Society of Mary) 30 April 1983 at Whitechapel,
        London • ordained Bishop of Brentwood 1 July 2014 at Brentwood.
        • *Cathedral House, Ingrave Road, BRENTWOOD CM15 8AT*

ARCHDIOCESE OF CARDIFF

(Archidioecesis Cardiffensis)

By Letters Apostolic (*Cambria celtica*) of Pope Benedict XV, dated 7 February 1916, the Province of Birmingham was divided further into two new metropolitan provinces of Birmingham and Cardiff, with the Diocese of Newport being renamed the Archdiocese of Cardiff and raised to a metropolitan Archdiocese and province. The episcopal see was fixed at the Priory Church of St Michael and All Angels, Belmont, Hereford (1916–1920), consecrated on 4 September 1860 then at the Metropolitan Cathedral Church of St David, Cardiff (1920–), which was destroyed by fire bombs on 3 March 1941, rebuilt and consecrated on 4 February 1959.

By Apostolic Decree (*Fiducia freti*) of Pope St John Paul II, dated 12 February 1987, the Diocese of Wrexham was formed by division of the Diocese of Menevia, with the episcopal see fixed at the Cathedral Church of Our Lady of Sorrows, Wrexham (1987–).

By the same Apostolic Decree (*Fiducia freti*) of Pope St John Paul II, dated 12 February 1987, the episcopal see of the Diocese of Menevia was transferred from the Cathedral Church of Our Lady of Sorrows, Wrexham (1895–1987) to the Cathedral Church of St Joseph, Swansea (1987-) and the former County of West Glamorgan was transferred from the Archdiocese of Cardiff to the Diocese of Menevia. The Diocese of Menevia and the Diocese of Wrexham remained suffragan sees within the Province of Cardiff.

The Archdiocese today comprises the City and County of Cardiff, the counties of Monmouthshire and Herefordshire and the unitary authorities of Blaenau Gwent, Bridgend, Caerphilly, Merthyr Tydfil, Newport City, Rhonnda Cynon Taff, Torfaen and the Vale of Glamorgan.

I. † Most Rev. Dom. **JAMES ROMANUS BILSBORROW** OSB: born 27 August 1862 at Walton-le-Dale, Preston • professed (Order of Saint Benedict) 25 January 1884 at Belmont, Hereford • ordained priest (Order of Saint Benedict) 23 June 1889 at Douai (Nord), France • ordained Bishop of Port-Louis, Mauritius 24 February 1911 at Upper Woolhampton, Reading • translated 7 February 1916 to Archbishop and Metropolitan of newly raised Archdiocese and Province of Cardiff • resigned 1 September 1920 as Archbishop of Cardiff • appointed 16 December 1920 titular Archbishop of *Cius* and retired to Upper Woolhampton, Reading thence to St Pierre de Moka, Mauritius • died 19 June 1931 at Belle Rose, Mauritius, aged 68 • buried at the Cathedral Church of St Louis, Port-Louis, Mauritius.
    • *Douai Abbey, Upper Woolhampton, READING RG7 5TQ*

II. † Most Rev. **FRANCIS EDWARD JOSEPH MOSTYN**: born 6 August 1860 at Talacre, Holywell • ordained priest (Shrewsbury) 14 September 1884 at Ushaw, Durham • ordained titular Bishop of *Ascalon* and appointed Vicar Apostolic for the Welsh District 14 September 1895 at Birkenhead • translated 12 May 1898 to newly erected Diocese of Menevia • translated 7 March 1921 to Archdiocese of Cardiff • appointed 7 March 1921 Apostolic Administrator of the Diocese of Menevia until 8 September 1926 • died 25 October 1939 at Cardiff aged 79 • buried at Cathays Cemetery, Cardiff.
    • *Archbishop's House, 24 Newport Road, CARDIFF CF24 0DB*

III. † Most Rev. Dr **MICHAEL JOSEPH McGRATH** MA DD LLD: born 24 March 1882 at Kilkenny City (Kilkenny), Ireland • ordained priest (Clifton) 12 July 1908 at Clifton, Bristol • ordained Bishop of Menevia 24 September 1935 at Wrexham • translated 20 June 1940 to Archdiocese of Cardiff • died 28 February 1961 at Cardiff aged 78 • buried at the Abbey Church of St Joseph, Llantarnam, Cwmbran.
    • *Archbishop's House, 24 Newport Road, CARDIFF CF24 0DB*

IV.   † Most Rev. Dr **JOHN ALOYSIUS MURPHY** DD: born 21 December 1905 at Birkenhead • ordained priest (Shrewsbury) 21 March 1931 at Lisbon (Lisboa), Portugal • ordained titular Bishop of *Appia* and appointed coadjutor Bishop of Shrewsbury 25 February 1948 at Chester • succeeded 3 June 1949 as Bishop of Shrewsbury • translated 26 August 1961 to Archdiocese of Cardiff • appointed Council Father at Second Vatican Council 11 October 1962 to 8 December 1965 • retired 25 March 1983 to Malpas, Newport • died 18 November 1995 at Malpas, Newport, aged 89 • buried at the Abbey Church of St Joseph, Llantarnam, Cwmbran.
• *St Joseph's Hospital, Harding Avenue, NEWPORT NP20 6ZE*

a.   ® Rt Rev. **DANIEL JOSEPH MULLINS** BA: born 10 July 1929 at Kilfinane (Limerick), Ireland • ordained priest (Cardiff) 12 April 1953 at Oscott, Sutton Coldfield • ordained titular Bishop of *Sidnacestre* and appointed auxiliary Bishop of Cardiff 1 April 1970 at the Metropolitan Cathedral Church of St David, Cardiff • translated 12 February 1987 to newly restructured Diocese of Menevia • retired 12 June 2001 to Kidwelly.
• *8 Rhodfa'r Gwendraeth, KIDWELLY SA17 4SR*

V.   † Most Rev. Friar **JOHN ALOYSIUS WARD** OFM Cap.: born 24 January 1929 at Leeds • professed (Order of Friars Minor Capuchin) 25 January 1950 at Peckham, London • ordained priest (Order of Friars Minor Capuchin) 7 June 1953 at Peckham, London • ordained coadjutor Bishop of Menevia 1 October 1980 at Wrexham • succeeded 5 February 1981 as Bishop of Menevia • translated 25 March 1983 to Archdiocese of Cardiff • retired 26 October 2001 to Ystradowen, Cowbridge • died 27 March 2007 at Ystradowen, Cowbridge, aged 78 • buried at the Abbey Church of St Joseph, Llantarnam, Cwmbran.
• *11 Badgers Brook Drive, Ystradowen, COWBRIDGE CF71 7TX*

VI.   Most Rev. Dr **PETER DAVID GREGORY SMITH** LLB JCD: born 21 October 1943 at Battersea, London • ordained priest (Southwark) 5 July 1972 at Wonersh, Guildford • ordained Bishop of East Anglia 27 May 1995 at Norwich • translated 26 October 2001 to Archdiocese of Cardiff • translated 30 April 2010 to Archdiocese of Southwark • appointed 4 October 2014 Apostolic Administrator of the Diocese of Arundel and Brighton until 28 May 2015.
• *Archbishop's House, 150 St George's Road, LONDON SE1 6HX*

VII.   Most Rev. **GEORGE STACK** BEd KCHS: born 9 May 1946 at Cork City (Cork), Ireland • ordained priest (Westminster) 21 May 1972 at Poplar, London • ordained titular Bishop of *Gemellae in Numidia* and appointed auxiliary Bishop of Westminster 10 May 2001 at the Metropolitan Cathedral Church of the Most Precious Blood, Westminster, London • translated 19 April 2011 to Archdiocese of Cardiff. • *Archbishop's House, 43 Cathedral Road, CARDIFF CF11 9HD*

DIOCESE OF CLIFTON

(Dioecesis Cliftoniensis)

By Letters Apostolic (*Universalis ecclesiae*) of Pope Bl. Pius IX, dated 29 September 1850, the Diocese of Clifton was formed, with the episcopal see fixed at the Pro-Cathedral Church of the Twelve Apostles, Clifton, Bristol (1850–1973), consecrated on 21 September 1848, then at the Cathedral Church of SS Peter and Paul, Clifton, Bristol (1973–), consecrated on 29 June 1973.

The Diocese of Clifton was an original suffragan see within the Province of Westminster. At first, the Diocese of Clifton comprised the City and County of Bristol and the counties of Gloucestershire, Somerset and Wiltshire.

By Letters Apostolic (*Si qua est*) of Pope St Pius X, dated 28 October 1911, the Province of Westminster was divided into three new provinces of Birmingham, Liverpool and Westminster, with the Diocese of Clifton being made part of the Province of Birmingham. The episcopal see remained at the Pro-Cathedral Church of the Twelve Apostles, Clifton, Bristol (1850–1973), then at the Cathedral Church of SS Peter and Paul, Clifton, Bristol (1973–).

The Diocese today comprises the City and County of Bristol, the counties of Gloucestershire, Wiltshire and Somerset, and the unitary authorities of Bath and North East Somerset, North Somerset, South Gloucestershire and Swindon.

I. † Rt Rev. **JOSEPH WILLIAM FRANCIS HENDREN** OSF: born 19 October 1791 at Birmingham • professed (Order of Saint Francis) 2 August 1806 at Abergavenny • ordained priest (Order of Saint Francis) 28 September 1815 at Wolverhampton • ordained titular Bishop of *Verinopolis* and appointed Vicar Apostolic for the Western District 10 September 1848 at Bristol • translated 29 September 1850 to restored Diocese of Clifton • appointed 29 September 1850 Apostolic Administrator of Diocese of Plymouth until 22 June 1851 • translated 22 June 1851 to restored Diocese of Nottingham • appointed 23 February 1853 titular Bishop of *Martyropolis* and retired to Birmingham thence to Taunton • died 14 November 1866 at Taunton aged 75 • buried at the Franciscan Convent, Taunton • reinterred 4 October 1997 at St George's Church, Taunton. • *Franciscan Convent, Billet Street, TAUNTON TA1 3NN*

II. † Rt Rev. Dom. **THOMAS LAWRENCE BURGESS** OSB: born 1 October 1791 at Clayton Green, Chorley • professed (Order of Saint Benedict) 13 October 1807 at Ampleforth, York • ordained priest (Order of Saint Benedict) 1814 at Ushaw, Durham • ordained Bishop of Clifton 27 July 1851 at the Cathedral Church of St George, Southwark, London • died 27 November 1854 at Westbury-on-Trym, Bristol aged 63 • buried at the Pro-Cathedral Church of the Twelve Apostles, Clifton, Bristol • reinterred 4 March 1973 at Holy Souls Chapel Crypt, Arnos Vale, Bristol. • *Prior Park College, Ralph Allan Drive, BATH BA2 5AH*

a. **APOSTOLIC ADMINISTRATOR:** † Most Rev. Dr **GEORGE ERRINGTON** DD: born 14 September 1804 at Clints Hall, Marske, Richmond • ordained priest (Northern District) 22 December 1827 at Rome, Italy • ordained Bishop of restored Diocese of Plymouth 25 July 1851 at Salford • translated 30 March 1855 to titular Archbishop of *Trapezus* and appointed coadjutor Archbishop of Westminster • appointed 22 October 1855 Apostolic Administrator of the Diocese of Clifton until 15 February 1857 • resigned 2 July 1862 as coadjutor Archbishop of Westminster • appointed 1 September 1865 parish priest of St Mary's Church, Douglas, Isle of Man • nominated 27 January 1868 Apostolic Delegate in Scotland but declined the appointment 12 August 1868 • appointed Council Father at First Vatican Council 8 December 1869 to 20 October 1870 • retired 1 September 1874 to Prior Park, Bath • died 19 January 1886 at Prior

Park, Bath, aged 81 • buried at Prior Park College chapel, Bath.
• *Prior Park College, Ralph Allan Drive, BATH BA2 5AH*

III. † Rt Rev. Dr **WILLIAM HUGH JOSEPH CLIFFORD** DD: born 24 December 1823 at Irnham, Grantham • ordained priest (Western District) 25 August 1850 at Clifton, Bristol • ordained Bishop of Clifton 15 February 1857 at Rome, Italy • appointed Council Father at First Vatican Council 8 December 1869 to 20 October 1870 • died 14 August 1893 at Prior Park, Bath, aged 69 • buried at Prior Park College chapel, Bath. • *22 Meridian Place, BRISTOL BS8 1JL*

IV. † *CE* Rt Rev. **WILLIAM ROBERT BERNARD BROWNLOW** MA: born 4 July 1830 at Wilmslow • ordained Church of England deacon (Lichfield) 18 December 1853 at Lichfield • ordained Church of England priest (Lichfield) 18 May 1856 at St Paul's Cathedral, City of London • received into Catholic Church 1 November 1863 at Edgbaston, Birmingham • ordained priest (Plymouth) 22 December 1866 at Rome, Italy • ordained Bishop of Clifton 1 May 1894 at Clifton, Bristol • died 9 November 1901 at Clifton, Bristol, aged 71 • buried at Holy Souls Chapel Crypt, Arnos Vale, Bristol. • *22 Meridian Place, BRISTOL BS8 1JL*

V. † Rt Rev. Dr **GEORGE CROMPTON AMBROSE BURTON** DD: born 7 June 1852 at Hull • ordained priest (Hexham and Newcastle) 31 May 1890 at Rome, Italy • ordained Bishop of Clifton 1 May 1902 at Clifton, Bristol • died 8 February 1931 at Leigh Woods, Bristol, aged 78 • buried at Holy Souls Chapel Crypt, Arnos Vale, Bristol. • *St Ambrose, North Road, Leigh Woods, BRISTOL BS8 3PW*

VI. † Rt Rev. **WILLIAM LEE** MBE: born 27 September 1875 at Mitchelstown (Cork), Ireland • ordained priest (Clifton) 2 March 1901 at Oscott, Sutton Coldfield • ordained Bishop of Clifton 26 January 1932 at Clifton, Bristol • died 21 September 1948 at Leigh Woods, Bristol, aged 72 • buried at Holy Souls Cemetery, Arnos Vale, Bristol. • *St Ambrose, North Road, Leigh Woods, BRISTOL BS8 3PW*

VII. † Rt Rev. Dr **JOSEPH EDWARD RUDDERHAM** MA DD: born 17 June 1899 at Norwich • ordained priest (Northampton) 31 October 1926 at Rome, Italy • ordained Bishop of Clifton 25 July 1949 at Clifton, Bristol • appointed Council Father at Second Vatican Council 11

October 1962 to 8 December 1965 • retired 31 August 1974 to Charlton Kings, Cheltenham • died 24 February 1979 at Charlton Kings, Cheltenham, aged 79 • buried at Holy Souls Cemetery, Arnos Vale, Bristol. • *Nazareth House, London Road, Charlton Kings, CHELTENHAM GL52 6YJ*

a.   † Rt Rev. Dr **MERVYN ALBAN NEWMAN ALEXANDER** DD: see **VIII.** below.

VIII.   † Rt Rev. Dr **MERVYN ALBAN NEWMAN ALEXANDER** DD LLD: born 29 June 1925 at Highbury, London • ordained priest (Clifton) 18 July 1948 at Rome, Italy • ordained titular Bishop of *Pinhel* and appointed auxiliary Bishop of Clifton 25 April 1972 at Clifton, Bristol • translated 20 December 1974 to Diocese of Clifton • retired 28 March 2001 and appointed parish priest of St Joseph's Church, Weston-super-Mare • retired 20 February 2008 to Clifton Down, Bristol • died 14 August 2010 at Clifton Down, Bristol, aged 85 • buried at the Cathedral Churchyard of SS Peter and Paul, Clifton, Bristol. • *St Angela's, 5 Litfield Place, Clifton Down, BRISTOL BS8 3LU*

IX.   Rt Rev. **DECLAN RONAN LANG** BA: born 15 April 1950 at Cowes • ordained priest (Portsmouth) 7 June 1975 at Portsmouth • ordained Bishop of Clifton 28 March 2001 at Clifton, Bristol. • *St Ambrose, North Road, Leigh Woods, BRISTOL BS8 3PW*

DIOCESE OF EAST ANGLIA

(Dioecesis Angliae Orientalis)

By Apostolic Decree (*Quod ecumenicum*) of Pope Bl. Paul VI, dated 13 March 1976, the Diocese of East Anglia was formed by division of the Diocese of Northampton, with the episcopal see fixed at the Cathedral Church of St John the Baptist, Norwich (1976–), consecrated on 26 June 1957.

Since 13 March 1976, the Diocese of East Anglia has been a suffragan see within the Province of Westminster. At first, the Diocese of East Anglia comprised the counties of Norfolk, Suffolk and Cambridgeshire.

The Diocese today comprises the counties of Norfolk, Suffolk and Cambridgeshire and the unitary authority of Peterborough.

I. † Rt Rev. Dr **ALAN CHARLES CLARK** DD: born 9 August 1919 at Bickley, Bromley • ordained priest (Southwark) 11 February 1945 at Bromley • ordained titular Bishop of *Elmhama* and appointed auxiliary Bishop of Northampton 13 May 1969 at Northampton • translated 2 June 1976 to newly erected Diocese of East Anglia • retired 27 May 1995 to Poringland, Norwich thence to Norwich • died 16 July 2002 at Norwich aged 82 • buried at the Catholic National Shrine of Our Lady of Walsingham, Houghton St Giles, Walsingham.
• *Oakwood House, Watton Road, NORWICH NR4 7TP*

II. Rt Rev. Dr **PETER DAVID GREGORY SMITH** LLB JCD: born 21 October 1943 at Battersea, London • ordained priest (Southwark) 5 July 1972 at Wonersh, Guildford • ordained Bishop of East Anglia 27 May 1995 at Norwich • translated 26 October 2001 to Archdiocese of Cardiff • translated 30 April 2010 to Archdiocese of Southwark • appointed 4 October 2014 Apostolic Administrator of the Diocese of Arundel and Brighton until 28 May 2015.
• *Archbishop's House, 150 St George's Road, LONDON SE1 6HX*

III. † Rt Rev. **MICHAEL CHARLES EVANS** MTh: born 10 August 1951 at Camberwell, London • ordained priest (Southwark) 22 June 1975 at Wonersh, Guildford • ordained Bishop of East Anglia 19 March 2003 at Norwich • died 11 July 2011 at Norwich aged 59 • cremated and interred at the Cathedral Church of St John the Baptist, Norwich.
• *The White House, 21 Upgate, Poringland, NORWICH NR14 7SH*

IV. *CE* Rt Rev. **ALAN STEPHEN HOPES** BD AKC: born 14 March 1944 at Oxford • ordained Church of England deacon (London) 21 May 1967 at St Paul's Cathedral, City of London • ordained Church of England priest (London) 9 June 1968 at St Paul's Cathedral, City of London • received into Catholic Church 8 December 1994 at Kensington, London • ordained priest (Westminster) 4 December 1995 at the Metropolitan Cathedral Church of the Most Precious Blood, Westminster, London • ordained titular Bishop of *Cuncacestre* and appointed auxiliary Bishop of Westminster 24 January 2003 at the Metropolitan Cathedral Church of the Most Precious Blood, Westminster, London • translated 11 June 2013 to Diocese of East Anglia.
• *The White House, 21 Upgate, Poringland, NORWICH NR14 7SH*

DIOCESE OF HALLAM

(*Dioecesis Hallamensis*)

By a Bull (*Qui arcano dei*) of Pope St John Paul II, dated 30 May 1980, the Diocese of Hallam was formed by division of the Diocese of Leeds and the Diocese of Nottingham, with the episcopal see fixed at the Cathedral Church of St Marie, Sheffield (1980–) consecrated on 1 June 1889.

Since 30 May 1980, the Diocese of Hallam has been a suffragan see within the Province of Liverpool. At first, the Diocese of Hallam comprised the County of South Yorkshire, parts of the districts of High Peak and Chesterfield in Derbyshire, and the district of Bassetlaw in Nottinghamshire.

The diocese today comprises the unitary authorities of Sheffield City, Barnsley, Doncaster and Rotherham and parts of the districts of High Peak and Chesterfield in Derbyshire, and the district of Bassetlaw in Nottinghamshire.

I.   † Rt Rev. Dr **GERALD MOVERLEY** JCD LLD: born 19 April 1922 at Bradford • ordained priest (Leeds) 28 April 1946 at Leeds • ordained titular Bishop of *Tinis in Proconsulari* and appointed auxiliary Bishop of Leeds 25 January 1968 at Sheffield • translated 30 May 1980 to newly erected Diocese of Hallam • retired 8 July 1996 to Sheffield • died 14 December 1996 at Sheffield aged 74 • buried at the Cathedral Church of St Marie, Sheffield. • *Quarters, Carsick Hill Way, SHEFFIELD S10 3LT*

II.   ® Rt Rev. **JOHN ANTHONY RAWSTHORNE**: born 12 November 1936 at Crosby, Liverpool • ordained priest (Liverpool) 16 June 1962 at Upholland, Skelmersdale • ordained titular Bishop of *Rotdon* and appointed auxiliary Bishop of Liverpool 16 December 1981 at the Metropolitan Cathedral Church of Christ the King, Liverpool • translated 3 July 1997 to Diocese of Hallam • retired 20 May 2014 to Widnes • *St Michael's Church, St Michael's Road, WIDNES WA8 8TF*

III.   Rt Rev. **RALPH HESKETT** CSsR: born 3 March 1953 at Sunderland • professed (Congregation of the Most Holy Redeemer) 28 August 1971 at Kinnoul, Perth • ordained priest (Congregation of the Most Holy Redeemer) 10 July 1976 at Sunderland • ordained Bishop of Gibraltar 10 July 2010 at Gibraltar • translated 20 May 2014 to Diocese of Hallam. • *Bishop's House, 75 Norfolk Road, SHEFFIELD S2 2SZ*

DIOCESE OF HEXHAM

(Dioecesis Hagulstadensis)

By Letters Apostolic (*Universalis ecclesiae*) of Pope Bl. Pius IX, dated 29 September 1850, the Diocese of Hexham was formed, with the episcopal see fixed at the Cathedral Church of St Mary, Newcastle upon Tyne (1850–), consecrated on 21 August 1860.

The Diocese of Hexham was an original suffragan see within the Province of Westminster. At first, the Diocese of Hexham comprised the counties of Northumberland, Durham, Cumberland and Westmorland.

I.   † Rt Rev. **WILLIAM HOGARTH**: born 25 March 1786 at Dodding Green, Kendal • ordained priest (Northern District) 20 December 1809 at Ushaw, Durham • ordained titular Bishop of *Samosata* and appointed Vicar Apostolic for the Northern District 24 August 1848 at Ushaw, Durham • translated 29 September 1850 to restored Diocese of Hexham • translated 23 May 1861 to renamed Diocese of Hexham and Newcastle • died 29 January 1866 at Darlington aged 79 • buried at St Cuthbert's College, Ushaw, Durham. • *St Augustine's Presbytery, 30 Coniscliffe Road, DARLINGTON DL3 7RG*

DIOCESE OF HEXHAM AND NEWCASTLE

(Dioecesis Hagulstadensis et Novacastrensis)

By Apostolic Decree (*Decretum de propaganda fide*) of Pope Bl. Pius IX, dated 23 May 1861, the Diocese of Hexham was renamed Hexham and Newcastle, with the episcopal see remaining at the Cathedral Church of St Mary, Newcastle upon Tyne (1850–).

By Letters Apostolic (*Si qua est*) of Pope St Pius X, dated 28 October 1911, the Province of Westminster was divided into three new provinces of Birmingham, Liverpool and Westminster, with the Diocese of Hexham and Newcastle being made part of the Province of Liverpool. The episcopal see remained at the Cathedral Church of St Mary, Newcastle upon Tyne (1850–).

By Apostolic Constitution (*Universalis ecclesiae solicitudo*) of Pope Pius XI, dated 22 November 1924, the Diocese of Lancaster was formed by division of the Diocese of Hexham and Newcastle and the Archdiocese of Liverpool, taking the counties of Cumberland and Westmorland from the Diocese of Hexham and Newcastle.

The Diocese today comprises the counties of Northumberland and Durham and the unitary authorities of Newcastle upon Tyne, Darlington, Gateshead, Hartlepool, North Tyneside, South Tyneside and Stockton-on-Tees (north of the River Tees).

I.   † Rt Rev. **WILLIAM HOGARTH**: born 25 March 1786 at Dodding Green, Kendal • ordained priest (Northern District) 20 December 1809 at Ushaw, Durham • ordained titular Bishop of *Samosata* and appointed Vicar Apostolic for the Northern District 24 August 1848 at Ushaw, Durham • translated 29 September 1850 to restored Diocese of Hexham • translated 23 May 1861 to renamed Diocese of Hexham and Newcastle • died 29 January 1866 at Darlington aged 79 • buried at St Cuthbert's College, Ushaw, Durham.
• *St Augustine's Presbytery, 30 Coniscliffe Road, DARLINGTON DL3 7RG*

II. † Rt Rev. Dr **JAMES CHADWICK** DD: born 24 April 1813 at Drogheda (Louth), Ireland • ordained priest (Northern District) 17 December 1837 at Ushaw, Durham • ordained Bishop of Hexham and Newcastle 28 October 1866 at Ushaw, Durham • appointed Council Father at First Vatican Council 8 December 1869 to 20 October 1870 • died 14 May 1882 at Newcastle upon Tyne aged 69 • buried at St Cuthbert's College, Ushaw, Durham.
• *72 Rye Hill, NEWCASTLE UPON TYNE NE4 7LH*

III. † Rt Rev. Dr **JOHN WILLIAM BEWICK** DD: born 20 April 1824 at Minsteracres, Consett • ordained priest (Northern District) 27 May 1850 at Ushaw, Durham • ordained Bishop of Hexham and Newcastle 18 October 1882 at Newcastle upon Tyne • died 29 October 1886 at Tynemouth, North Shields aged 62 • buried at Ashburton Cemetery, Gosforth, Newcastle upon Tyne.
• *Bishop's House, Front Street, Tynemouth, NORTH SHIELDS NE30 4DZ*

IV. † Most Rev. Dr **HENRY O'CALLAGHAN** DD: born 29 March 1827 at London • ordained priest (Westminster) 15 March 1851 at Old Hall Green, Ware • ordained Bishop of Hexham and Newcastle 18 January 1888 at Rome, Italy • resigned 27 September 1889 as Bishop of Hexham and Newcastle and appointed titular Archbishop of *Nicosia* and retired to Rome, Italy • died 11 October 1904 at Florence (Firenze), Italy aged 79 • buried at San Miniato, Florence (Firenze), Italy.
• *never took up residence in the diocese*

   a.   † Rt Rev. **THOMAS WILLIAM WILKINSON** BA: see **V.** below.

V.   † Rt Rev. **THOMAS WILLIAM WILKINSON** BA: born 5 April 1825 at Harperley, Stanley • received into Catholic Church 29 December 1846 at Leeds • ordained priest (Northern District) 23 December 1848 at Ushaw,

Durham • ordained titular Bishop of *Cisamus* and appointed auxiliary Bishop of Hexham and Newcastle 25 July 1888 at Ushaw, Durham • translated 28 December 1889 to Diocese of Hexham and Newcastle • died 17 April 1909 at Ushaw, Durham aged 84 • buried at St Cuthbert's College, Ushaw, Durham. • *Ushaw College, DURHAM DH7 9RH*

a. † Rt Rev. Dr **RICHARD PRESTON** DD: born 12 December 1856 at St Leonard's Gate, Lancaster • ordained priest (Liverpool) 7 June 1884 at Rome, Italy • ordained titular Bishop of *Phocaea* and appointed auxiliary Bishop of Hexham and Newcastle 25 July 1900 at Ushaw, Durham • resigned 22 December 1904 as auxiliary Bishop of Hexham and Newcastle and retired to Southfield, Lancaster • died 9 February 1905 at Southfield, Lancaster aged 48 • buried at St Cuthbert's College, Ushaw, Durham. • *Southfield, South Road, LANCASTER LA1 4XD*

b. † Rt Rev. **RICHARD COLLINS**: see **VI.** below.

VI. † Rt Rev. **RICHARD COLLINS**: born 5 April 1857 at Newbury • ordained priest (Hexham and Newcastle) 30 May 1885 at Ushaw, Durham • ordained titular Bishop of *Selinus* and appointed auxiliary Bishop of Hexham and Newcastle 29 June 1905 at Newcastle upon Tyne • translated 21 June 1909 to Diocese of Hexham and Newcastle • died 9 February 1924 at Newcastle upon Tyne aged 66 • buried at St Cuthbert's College, Ushaw, Durham. • *St Mary's Cathedral, Clayton Street West, NEWCASTLE UPON TYNE NE1 5HH*

VII. † Rt Rev. **JOSEPH THORMAN**: born 6 August 1871 at Gateshead • ordained priest (Hexham and Newcastle) 27 September 1896 at Ushaw, Durham • ordained Bishop of newly restructured Diocese of Hexham and Newcastle 27 January 1925 at Newcastle upon Tyne • died 7 October 1936 at Newcastle upon Tyne aged 65 • buried at St Cuthbert's College, Ushaw, Durham. • *Bishop's House, Front Street, Tynemouth, NORTH SHIELDS NE30 4DZ*

VIII. † Rt Rev. **JOSEPH McCORMACK**: born 17 May 1887 at Broadway • ordained priest (Hexham and Newcastle) 11 August 1912 at Ushaw, Durham • ordained Bishop of Hexham and Newcastle 4 February 1937 at Newcastle upon Tyne • died 2 March 1958 at Newcastle

upon Tyne aged 70 • buried at St Cuthbert's College, Ushaw, Durham.
• *Bishop's House, 800 West Road, NEWCASTLE UPON TYNE NE5 2BJ*

a.   † Rt Rev. **JAMES CUNNINGHAM** JCL: see **IX.** below.

IX.   † Rt Rev. **JAMES CUNNINGHAM** JCL: born 15 August 1910 at
Rusholme, Manchester • ordained priest (Salford) 22 May 1937 at Uphol-
land, Skelmersdale • ordained titular Bishop of *Ios* and appointed auxiliary
Bishop of Hexham and Newcastle 12 November 1957 at Newcastle upon
Tyne • translated 1 July 1958 to Diocese of Hexham and Newcastle •
appointed Council Father at Second Vatican Council 11 October 1962 to 8
December 1965 • resigned 16 May 1974 as Bishop of Hexham and Newcastle
and retired to Newcastle upon Tyne • died 10 July 1974 at Newcastle
upon Tyne aged 63 • buried at St Cuthbert's College, Ushaw, Durham.
• *Bishop's House, 800 West Road, NEWCASTLE UPON TYNE NE5 2BJ*

a.   † Rt Rev. **HUGH LINDSAY**: see **X.** below.

X.   † Rt Rev. **HUGH LINDSAY**: born 20 June 1927 at Jesmond, Newcastle upon Tyne • ordained priest (Hexham and Newcastle) 19 July
1953 at Newcastle upon Tyne • ordained titular Bishop of *Cuncacestre*
and appointed auxiliary Bishop of Hexham and Newcastle 11 December
1969 at Newcastle upon Tyne • translated 12 December 1974 to Diocese of Hexham and Newcastle • resigned 11 January 1992 as Bishop
of Hexham and Newcastle and retired to Allithwaite, Grange-over-
Sands • died 19 January 2009 at Allithwaite, Grange-over-Sands, aged
81 • buried at the Cathedral Crypt of St Mary, Newcastle upon Tyne.
• *Boarbank Hall, Allithwaite, GRANGE-OVER-SANDS LA11 7NH*

a.   † Rt Rev. Dr **OWEN FRANCIS SWINDLEHURST**
PhL STL JCD: born 10 May 1928 at Newburn, Newcastle upon
Tyne • ordained priest (Hexham and Newcastle) 11 July 1954
at Rome, Italy • ordained titular Bishop of *Cuncacestre* and
appointed auxiliary Bishop of Hexham and Newcastle 25 July
1977 at Newcastle upon Tyne • died 28 August 1995 at Sunderland
aged 67 • buried at Our Lady Immaculate Church, Washington.
• *Oaklea, Tunstall Road, SUNDERLAND SR2 7JR*

XI. † Rt Rev. Dom. **MICHAEL AMBROSE GRIFFITHS** OSB KC*HS BSc MA: born 4 December 1928 at Twickenham • professed (Order of Saint Benedict) 25 September 1951 at Ampleforth, York • ordained priest (Order of Saint Benedict) 21 July 1957 at Ampleforth, York • elected 7 April 1976 Abbot of the Abbey Church of St Laurence, Ampleforth, York • resigned 5 April 1984 as Abbot of the Abbey Church of St Laurence, Ampleforth, York and appointed titular Abbot of *Westminster* and parish priest of St Mary's Church, Leyland • ordained Bishop of Hexham and Newcastle 20 March 1992 at Newcastle upon Tyne • retired 26 March 2004 to Leyland • died 14 June 2011 at Leyland aged 82 • buried at the Abbey Church of St Laurence, Ampleforth, York. • *St Mary's Priory, Broadfield Walk, LEYLAND PR25 1PD*

XII. † Rt Rev. Dr **KEVIN JOHN DUNN** STL JCD: born 9 July 1950 at Clayton, Newcastle • ordained priest (Birmingham) 17 January 1976 at Clayton, Newcastle • ordained Bishop of Hexham and Newcastle 25 May 2004 at Newcastle upon Tyne • died 1 March 2008 at Newcastle upon Tyne aged 57 • buried at the Cathedral Crypt of St Mary, Newcastle upon Tyne. • *Bishop's House, 800 West Road, NEWCASTLE UPON TYNE NE5 2BJ*

XIII. Rt Rev. **SÉAMUS CUNNINGHAM**: born 7 July 1942 at Castle-bar (Mayo), Ireland • ordained priest (Hexham and Newcastle) 12 June 1966 at Waterford City (Waterford), Ireland • ordained Bishop of Hexham and Newcastle 20 March 2009 at Newcastle upon Tyne. • *Bishop's House, 800 West Road, NEWCASTLE UPON TYNE NE5 2BJ*

DIOCESE OF LANCASTER

(Dioecesis Lancastrensis)

By Apostolic Constitution (*Universalis ecclesiae solicitudo*) of Pope Pius XI, dated 22 November 1924, the Diocese of Lancaster was formed by division of the Diocese of Hexham and Newcastle and the Archdiocese of Liverpool, with the episcopal see fixed at the Cathedral Church of St Peter, Lancaster (1924–), consecrated on 4 October 1859.

Since 22 November 1924, the Diocese of Lancaster has been a suffragan see within the Province of Liverpool. At first, the Diocese of Lancaster comprised the counties of Cumberland and Westmorland with the Hundreds of Amounderness and Lonsdale in the County of Lancashire.

The Diocese today comprises the County of Cumbria and the Hundreds of Amounderness and Lonsdale in the County of Lancashire (north of the River Ribble).

I.   † Rt Rev. Dom. **THOMAS WULSTAN PEARSON** OSB BA: born 4 January 1870 at Preston • professed (Order of Saint Benedict) 12 December 1890 at Belmont, Hereford • ordained priest (Order of Saint Benedict) 26 September 1897 at Downside, Radstock • ordained Bishop of newly erected Diocese of Lancaster 24 February 1925 at Lancaster • died 1 December 1938 at Preston aged 68 • buried at the Cathedral Church of St Peter, Lancaster.
• *Bishop's House, Cannon Hill, LANCASTER LA1 5NG*

II.   † Rt Rev. Dr **THOMAS EDWARD FLYNN** PhD MA: born 6 January 1880 at Portsmouth • ordained priest (Liverpool) 13 June 1908 at Upholland, Skelmersdale • ordained Bishop of Lancaster 24 July 1939 at Lancaster • died 4 November 1961 at Lancaster aged 81 • buried at the Cathedral Church of St Peter, Lancaster.
• *Bishop's House, Cannon Hill, LANCASTER LA1 5NG*

a.   † Rt Rev. Dr **THOMAS BERNARD PEARSON** PhD: born 18 January 1907 at Preston • ordained priest (Lancaster) 1 November 1933 at Rome, Italy • ordained titular Bishop of *Sinda* and appointed auxiliary Bishop of Lancaster 25 July 1949 at Lancaster • appointed Council Father at Second Vatican Council 11 October 1962 to 8 December 1965 • retired 31 October 1983 to Carlisle • died 17 November 1987 at Carlisle aged 80 • buried at the Cathedral Church of St Peter, Lancaster.
• *Howard Lodge, 90 Warwick Road, CARLISLE CA1 1JU*

III. † Rt Rev. Dr **BRIAN CHARLES FOLEY** STL DLitt: born 25 May 1910 at Ilford • ordained priest (Brentwood) 25 July 1937 at Rome, Italy • ordained Bishop of Lancaster 13 June 1962 at Lancaster • appointed Council Father at Second Vatican Council 11 October 1962 to 8 December 1965 • retired 22 May 1985 to Lancaster • died 23 December 1999 at Lancaster aged 89 • buried at the Cathedral Church of St Peter, Lancaster.
• *Nazareth House, Ashton Road, LANCASTER LA1 5AQ*

a.   † Rt Rev. **JOHN (JACK) BREWER** STL JCL PhL: see **IV.** below.

IV.   † Rt Rev. **JOHN (JACK) BREWER** STL JCL PhL: born 24 November 1929 at Burnage, Manchester • ordained priest (Shrewsbury) 8 July 1956 at Rome, Italy • ordained titular Bishop of *Britonia* and appointed auxiliary Bishop of Shrewsbury 28 July 1971 at Stockport • translated 15

November 1983 to coadjutor Bishop of Lancaster • succeeded 22 May 1985 as Bishop of Lancaster • died 10 June 2000 at Allithwaite, Grange-over-Sands aged 70 • buried at the Cathedral Churchyard of St Peter, Lancaster.
• *Bishop's House, Cannon Hill, LANCASTER LA1 5NG*

V.   ® Rt Rev. **PATRICK O'DONOGHUE**: born 4 May 1934 at Mourne Abbey (Cork), Ireland • ordained priest (Westminster) 25 May 1967 at Ana-leentha, Mourne Abbey (Cork), Ireland • ordained titular Bishop of *Tulana* and appointed auxiliary Bishop of Westminster 29 June 1993 at the Metro-politan Cathedral Church of the Most Precious Blood, Westminster, London • translated 4 July 2001 to Diocese of Lancaster • retired 1 May 2009 to Bantry (Cork), Ireland • appointed 3 July 2009 assistant priest of St Finbarr's parish, Bantry (Cork), Ireland • retired 2 April 2013 to Mallow (Cork), Ireland.
• *Nazareth House, Drommahane, MALLOW (Cork), Ireland*

  a.   Rt Rev. **MICHAEL GREGORY CAMPBELL** OSA BA STL MA: see **VI.** below.

VI.   Rt Rev. **MICHAEL GREGORY CAMPBELL** OSA BA STL MA: born 2 October 1941 at Larne (Antrim), Ireland • professed (Order of Saint Augustine) 17 September 1966 at Clare, Sudbury • ordained priest (Order of Saint Augustine) 16 September 1971 at Carlisle • ordained coadjutor Bishop of Lancaster 31 March 2008 at Lancaster • succeeded 1 May 2009 as Bishop of Lancaster.
• *The Pastoral Centre, Balmoral Road, LANCASTER LA1 3BT*

DIOCESE OF LEEDS

(Dioecesis Loidensis)

By Apostolic Decree (*Quae ex hac*) of Pope Leo XIII, dated 20 December 1878, the Diocese of Leeds was formed by division of the Diocese of Beverley, with the episcopal see fixed at the Cathedral Church of St Anne, Cookridge Street, Leeds (1878–1904), opened in October 1838 and demolished after 1901, then at the Cathedral Church of St Anne, Great George Street, Leeds (1904–), opened in 1904 and consecrated on 19 July 1924.

From 20 December 1878, the Diocese of Leeds was a suffragan See within the Province of Westminster. At first, the Diocese of Leeds comprised the County of the West Riding of Yorkshire.

By Letters Apostolic (*Si qua est*) of Pope St Pius X, dated 28 October 1911, the Province of Westminster was divided into three new provinces of Birmingham, Liverpool and Westminster, with the Diocese of Leeds being made part of the Province of Liverpool. The episcopal see remained at the Cathedral Church of St Anne, Great George Street, Leeds (1904–).

By a Bull (*Qui arcano dei*) of Pope St John Paul II, dated 30 May 1980, the Diocese of Hallam was formed by division of the Diocese of Leeds and the Diocese of Nottingham, taking the County of South Yorkshire from the Diocese of Leeds.

The Diocese today comprises the counties of North Yorkshire (south of the River Ure and River Ouse excluding the City of York) and East Riding of Yorkshire (south of the River Ouse including the parish of Howden and Goole) and the unitary authorities of Bradford, Calderdale (except the parish of Todmorden), Kirklees, Leeds and Wakefield. In addition, the Diocese comprises the parish of Barnoldswick (in the Pendle district of Lancashire) and the parish of Uppermill (in Oldham Metropolitan District).

I. † Rt Rev. **ROBERT CORNTHWAITE**: born 9 May 1818 at Preston • ordained priest (Northern District) 9 November 1845 at Rome, Italy • ordained Bishop of Beverley 10 November 1861 at Moorfields, City of London • appointed Council Father at First Vatican Council 8 December 1869 to 20 October 1870 • translated 20 December 1878 to newly erected Diocese of Leeds • appointed 20 December 1878 Apostolic Administrator of Diocese of Middlesbrough until 18 December 1879 • died 16 June 1890 at Leeds aged 72 • buried at the Church of Mary Immaculate, Sicklinghall, Wetherby. • *Springfield House, Hyde Street, LEEDS LS2 9LH*

a. † Rt Rev. **WILLIAM GORDON**: see **II.** below.

II. † Rt Rev. **WILLIAM GORDON**: born 24 September 1831 at Thirsk • ordained priest (Beverley) 10 February 1859 at York • ordained titular Bishop of *Arcadiopolis in Asia* and appointed coadjutor Bishop of Leeds 24 February 1890 at Leeds • succeeded 16 June 1890 as Bishop of Leeds • died 7 June 1911 at Leeds aged 79 • buried at Killingbeck Cemetery, Leeds. • *Springfield House, Hyde Street, LEEDS LS2 9LH*

a. † Rt Rev. Dr **JOSEPH ROBERT COWGILL** DD: see **III.** below.

III. † Rt Rev. Dr **JOSEPH ROBERT COWGILL** DD: born 23 February 1860 at Broughton in Craven, Skipton • ordained priest (Leeds) 19 May 1883 at Rome, Italy • ordained titular Bishop of *Olena* and appointed coadjutor Bishop of Leeds 30 November 1905 at Leeds • succeeded 7 June 1911 as Bishop of Leeds • died 12 May 1936 at Leeds aged 76 • buried at Killingbeck Cemetery, Leeds. • *Springfield House, Hyde Street, LEEDS LS2 9LH*

IV. † *CE* Rt Rev. Dr **HENRY JOHN POSKITT** MA DD JCD: born 6 September 1888 at Birkin, Selby • ordained Church of England deacon (Ripon) 1911 at Ripon • ordained Church of England priest (Ripon) 1912 at Ripon • received into Catholic Church 25 September 1915 at Ampleforth, York • ordained priest (Middlesbrough) 15 July 1917 at Rome, Italy • ordained Bishop of Leeds 21 September 1936 at Leeds • died 19 February 1950 at Leeds aged 61 • buried at St Edward's Church, Clifford, Wetherby. • *Bishop's House, Weetwood Lane, LEEDS*

V.   † Rt Rev. Dr JOHN CARMEL HEENAN DD PhD: born 26 January 1905 at Ilford • ordained priest (Brentwood) 6 July 1930 at Ilford • ordained Bishop of Leeds 12 March 1951 at Leeds • translated 7 May 1957 to Archdiocese of Liverpool • appointed Council Father at Second Vatican Council 11 October 1962 to 8 December 1965 • translated 2 September 1963 to Archdiocese of Westminster • elevated 22 February 1965 to Cardinal-Priest of San Silvestro in Capite • died 7 November 1975 at Westminster, London aged 70 • buried at the Metropolitan Cathedral Church of the Most Precious Blood, Westminster, London. • *Archbishop's House, Ambrosden Avenue, LONDON SW1P 1QJ*

VI.   † Rt Rev. Dr **GEORGE PATRICK DWYER** DD PhD BA: born 25 September 1908 at Miles Platting, Manchester • ordained priest (Salford) 1 November 1932 at Rome, Italy • ordained Bishop of Leeds 24 September 1957 at Leeds • appointed Council Father at Second Vatican Council 11 October 1962 to 8 December 1965 • translated 21 December 1965 to Archdiocese of Birmingham • retired 1 September 1981 to Selly Park, Birmingham • died 17 September 1987 at Selly Park, Birmingham aged 78 • buried at St Mary's College, Oscott, Sutton Coldfield. • *St Paul's Convent, 94 Selly Park Road, Selly Park, BIRMINGHAM B29 7LL*

VII.   † *CE* Rt Rev. Dr **WILLIAM GORDON WHEELER** MA DD: born 5 May 1910 at Dobcross, Oldham • ordained Church of England deacon (Chichester) 21 December 1933 at Chichester • ordained Church of England priest (Derby) 23 December 1934 at Derby • received into Catholic Church 18 September 1936 at Downside, Radstock • ordained priest (Westminster) 31 March 1940 at the Metropolitan Cathedral Church of the Most Precious Blood, Westminster, London • ordained titular Bishop of *Theudalis* and appointed coadjutor Bishop of Middlesbrough 19 March 1964 at Middlesbrough • appointed Council Father at Second Vatican Council 14 September 1964 to 8 December 1965 • translated 3 May 1966 to Diocese of Leeds • Diocese of Leeds restructured 30 May 1980 • retired 10 September 1985 to Headingley, Leeds • died 20 February 1998 at

Headingley, Leeds aged 87 • buried at St Edward's Church, Clifford, Wetherby.
• *Mount St Joseph's, Shire Oak Road, LEEDS LS6 2DE*

a.   † Rt Rev. Dr **GERALD MOVERLEY** JCD LLD: born 19
April 1922 at Bradford • ordained priest (Leeds) 28 April 1946
at Leeds • ordained titular Bishop of *Tinis in Proconsulari* and
appointed auxiliary Bishop of Leeds 25 January 1968 at Sheffield
• translated 30 May 1980 to newly erected Diocese of Hallam •
retired 8 July 1996 to Sheffield • died 14 December 1996 at Sheffield
aged 74 • buried at the Cathedral Church of St Marie, Sheffield.
• *Quarters, Carsick Hill Way, SHEFFIELD S10 3LT*

VIII.   ® Rt Rev. Dr **DAVID EVERY KONSTANT** MA PGCE DD LLD: born
16 June 1930 at Blackheath, London • ordained priest (Westminster) 12 June
1954 at the Metropolitan Cathedral Church of the Most Precious Blood,
Westminster, London • ordained titular Bishop of *Betagbarar* and appointed
auxiliary Bishop of Westminster 25 April 1977 at the Metropolitan Cathedral
Church of the Most Precious Blood, Westminster, London • translated 25 September 1985 to Diocese of Leeds • retired 7 April 2004 to Headingley, Leeds.
• *Ashlea, 62 Headingley Lane, LEEDS LS6 2BU*

a.   Rt Rev. **ARTHUR ROCHE** STB STL: see **IX.** below.

IX.   Most Rev. **ARTHUR ROCHE** STB STL: born 6 March 1950 at
Batley Carr, Dewsbury • ordained priest (Leeds) 19 July 1975 at Batley
Carr, Dewsbury • ordained titular Bishop of *Rusticiana* and appointed
auxiliary Bishop of Westminster 10 May 2001 at the Metropolitan
Cathedral Church of the Most Precious Blood, Westminster, London
• translated 16 July 2002 to coadjutor Bishop of Leeds • succeeded 7
April 2004 as Bishop of Leeds • appointed 26 June 2012 secretary of
the Congregation for Divine Worship and Discipline of the Sacraments
• appointed 26 June 2012 *Archbishop ad personam* at Vatican City.
• *Palazzo delle Congregazioni, Piazza Pio XII 10, 00193 ROMA, Italy*

X.   CE Rt Rev. **MARCUS NIGEL STOCK** MA STL: born 27 August
1961 at London • ordained priest (Birmingham) 13 August 1988 at Caversham, Reading • ordained Bishop of Leeds 13 November 2014 at Leeds.
• *Bishop's House, 13 North Grange Road, LEEDS LS6 2BR*

DIOCESE OF LIVERPOOL

(Dioecesis Liverpolitanus)

By Letters Apostolic (*Universalis ecclesiae*) of Pope Bl. Pius IX, dated 29 September 1850, the Diocese of Liverpool was formed, with the episcopal see fixed at the Pro-Cathedral Church of St Nicholas, Liverpool (1850–1958), consecrated in 1815 and closed in 1972.

The Diocese of Liverpool was an original suffragan see within the Province of Westminster. At first, the Diocese of Liverpool comprised the Hundreds of Amounderness, Lonsdale and West Derby in the County of Lancashire, with the Isle of Man. By a re-script of Pope Bl. Pius IX, dated 27 June 1851, the Hundred of Leyland in the County of Lancashire was transferred from the Diocese of Salford to the Diocese of Liverpool.

I.   † Rt Rev. Dr **GEORGE HILARY BROWN** DD: born 13 January 1786 at Clifton-in-the-Fylde, Preston • ordained priest (Northern District) 13 June 1810 at Ushaw, Durham • ordained titular Bishop of *Bugia* and appointed Vicar Apostolic for the Lancashire district 24 August 1840 at Vauxhall, Liverpool • appointed 22 April 1842 titular Bishop of *Tlos* • translated 29 September 1850 to restored Diocese of Liverpool • appointed 29 September 1850 Apostolic Administrator of the Diocese of Salford until 25 July 1851 • died 25 January 1856 at Litherland, Liverpool, aged 70 • buried at St Oswald's Church, Old Swan, Liverpool.
• *17 Catharine Street, LIVERPOOL L8 7NH*

a.   † Rt Rev. Dr **ALEXANDER GOSS** DD: see **II.** below.

II.   † Rt Rev. Dr **ALEXANDER GOSS** DD: born 5 July 1814 at Ormskirk • ordained priest (Lancashire district) 4 July 1841 at Rome, Italy • ordained titular Bishop of *Gerrha* and appointed coadjutor Bishop of Liverpool 25 September 1853 at the Pro-Cathedral Church of St Nicholas, Liverpool • succeeded 25 January 1856 as Bishop of Liverpool • died 3 October 1872 at St Edward's College, Everton, Liverpool, aged 58 • buried at Ford Cemetery, Litherland, Liverpool.
• *St Edward's College, St Domingo Road, LIVERPOOL L5 0RR*

III. † Rt Rev. **BERNARD O'REILLY**: born 10 January 1824 at Ballybeg (Meath), Ireland • ordained priest (Lancashire district) 9 May 1847 at Ushaw, Durham • ordained Bishop of Liverpool 19 March 1873 at St Vincent de Paul Church, Liverpool • died 9 April 1894 at St Edward's College, Everton, Liverpool,aged 70 • buried at Upholland, Skelmersdale.
• *St Edward's College, St Domingo Road, LIVERPOOL L5 0RR*

IV.   † Rt Rev. Dr **THOMAS WHITESIDE** DD: born 17 April 1857 at Lancaster • ordained priest (Liverpool) 30 May 1885 at Rome, Italy • ordained Bishop of Liverpool 15 August 1894 at the Pro-Cathedral Church of St Nicholas, Liverpool • appointed 28 October 1911 Archbishop and Metropolitan of newly raised Archdiocese and Province of Liverpool • died 28 January 1921 at Princes Park, Liverpool aged 63 • buried at Ford Cemetery, Litherland, Liverpool • reinterred 8 September 1936 at the Metropolitan Cathedral Crypt of Christ the King, Liverpool.
• *St Edward's College, St Domingo Road, LIVERPOOL L5 0RR*

ARCHDIOCESE OF LIVERPOOL

NON NISI TE

(Archidioecesis Liverpolitanus)

By Letters Apostolic (*Si qua est*) of Pope St Pius X, dated 28 October 1911, the Province of Westminster was divided into three new provinces of Birmingham, Liverpool and Westminster, with the Diocese of Liverpool being raised to a metropolitan Archdiocese and province. The episcopal see remained at the Pro-Cathedral Church of St Nicholas, Liverpool (1850–1958), consecrated in 1815 and closed in 1972, then at the Pro-Cathedral Pontifical Crypt of Christ the King, Liverpool (1958–1967), consecrated on 14 May 1967, then at the Metropolitan Cathedral Church of Christ the King, Liverpool (1967-), consecrated on 14 May 1967.

By Apostolic Constitution (*Universalis ecclesiae solicitudo*) of Pope Pius XI, dated 22 November 1924, the Diocese of Lancaster was formed by division of the Diocese of Hexham and Newcastle and the Archdiocese of Liverpool, taking the Hundreds of Amounderness and Lonsdale in the County of Lancashire from the Archdiocese of Liverpool.

The Province of Liverpool comprises the Archdiocese of Liverpool with the suffragan sees of Hallam, Hexham and Newcastle, Lancaster, Leeds, Middlesbrough and Salford. The Archdiocese today comprises the Hundreds of Leyland and West Derby in the County of Lancashire (south of the River Ribble), with the Isle of Man.

I. † Most Rev. Dr **THOMAS WHITESIDE** DD: born 17 April 1857 at Lancaster • ordained priest (Liverpool) 30 May 1885 at Rome, Italy • ordained Bishop of Liverpool 15 August 1894 at the Pro-Cathedral Church of St Nicholas, Liverpool • appointed 28 October 1911 Archbishop and Metropolitan of newly raised Archdiocese and Province of Liverpool • died 28 January 1921 at Princes Park, Liverpool aged 63 • buried at Ford Cemetery, Litherland, Liverpool • reinterred 8 September 1936 at the Metropolitan Cathedral Crypt of Christ the King, Liverpool. • *Archbishop's House, 5 Belvidere Road, Princes Park, LIVERPOOL L8 3TF*

II. † Most Rev. Dr **FREDERICK WILLIAM KEATING** DD: born 13 June 1859 at City of Birmingham • ordained priest (Birmingham) 20 October 1882 at Olton, Solihull • ordained Bishop of Northampton 25 February 1908 at the Cathedral Church of St Chad, Birmingham • translated 13 June 1921 to Archdiocese of Liverpool • died 7 February 1928 at Princes Park, Liverpool aged 68 • buried at Upholland, Skelmersdale. • *Archbishop's House, 5 Belvidere Road, Princes Park, LIVERPOOL L8 3TF*

a. † Rt Rev. **ROBERT DOBSON**: born 21 January 1867 at New Orleans (LA), USA • ordained priest (Liverpool) 23 May 1891 at Upholland, Skelmersdale • ordained titular Bishop of *Cynopolis in Arcadia* and appointed auxiliary Bishop of Liverpool 30 November 1922 at the Pro-Cathedral Church of St Nicholas, Liverpool • died 6 January 1942 at Sefton Park, Liverpool aged 74 • buried at Upholland, Skelmersdale. • *Norwood, Grassendale Park North, LIVERPOOL L19*

III. † Most Rev. Dr **RICHARD JOSEPH DOWNEY** DD PhD LLD: born 5 May 1881 at Kilkenny City (Kilkenny), Ireland • ordained priest (Liverpool) 25 May 1907 at Upholland, Skelmersdale • ordained Archbishop of Liverpool 21 September 1928 at the Pro-Cathedral Church of St Nicholas, Liverpool • died 16 June 1953 at Gateacre Grange, Liverpool aged 72 • buried at the Metropolitan Cathedral Crypt of Christ the King, Liverpool. • *Gateacre Grange, Rose Brow, LIVERPOOL L25 4RB*

a. † Rt Rev. Dr **JOSEPH FORMBY HALSALL** PhD JCD STL: born 15 February 1902 at Ainsdale, Southport • ordained priest (Liverpool) 19 April 1930 at Rome, Italy • ordained titular Bishop of *Zabi* and appointed auxiliary Bishop of Liverpool 21 September 1945 at the Pro-Cathedral Church of St Nicholas, Liverpool •

died 13 March 1958 at Allithwaite, Grange-over-Sands aged 56
• buried at SS Peter and Paul Church, Great Crosby, Liverpool.
• *SS Peter & Paul Church, 161 Liverpool Road, Crosby, LIVERPOOL
L23 5TE*

IV.   † Most Rev. Dr WILLIAM GODFREY DD PhD: born 25 September
1889 at Kirkdale, Liverpool • ordained priest (Liverpool) 28 October 1916 at
Rome, Italy • entered diplomatic service to the Holy See 1938 at Vatican City
• ordained titular Archbishop of *Cius* and appointed Apostolic Delegate to
Great Britain, Malta and Gibraltar 21 December 1938 at Rome, Italy • translated 14 November 1953 to Archdiocese of Liverpool • translated 3 December
1956 to Archdiocese of Westminster • appointed 10 June 1957 to the Apostolic Exarchate for Ukrainians in England and Wales • elevated 15 December
1958 to Cardinal-Priest of Santi Nereo ed Achilleo • appointed Council
Father at Second Vatican Council 11 October 1962 to 8 December 1962 • died
22 January 1963 at Westminster, London aged 73 • buried at the Metropolitan
Cathedral Church of the Most Precious Blood, Westminster, London.
• *Archbishop's House, Ambrosden Avenue, LONDON SW1P 1QJ*

V.   † Most Rev. Dr JOHN CARMEL HEENAN DD PhD: born 26
January 1905 at Ilford • ordained priest (Brentwood) 6 July 1930 at Ilford
• ordained Bishop of Leeds 12 March 1951 at Leeds • translated 7 May
1957 to Archdiocese of Liverpool • appointed Council Father at Second
Vatican Council 11 October 1962 to 8 December 1965 • translated 2
September 1963 to Archdiocese of Westminster • elevated 22 February
1965 to Cardinal-Priest of San Silvestro in Capite • died 7 Novem-
ber 1975 at Westminster, London aged 70 • buried at the Metropolitan
Cathedral Church of the Most Precious Blood, Westminster, London.
• *Archbishop's House, Ambrosden Avenue, LONDON SW1P 1QJ*

VI.   † Most Rev. Dr GEORGE ANDREW BECK AA BA LLD: born
28 May 1904 at Streatham, London • ordained priest (Augustinians of
the Assumption) 24 July 1927 at Louvain (Flemish Brabant), Belgium
• ordained titular Bishop of *Tigias* and appointed coadjutor Bishop of
Brentwood 21 September 1948 at the Metropolitan Cathedral Church of
the Most Precious Blood, Westminster, London • succeeded 23 January
1951 as Bishop of Brentwood • translated 28 November 1955 to Diocese of Salford • appointed Council Father at Second Vatican Council
11 October 1962 to 8 December 1965 • translated 29 January 1964 to

Archdiocese of Liverpool • retired 11 February 1976 to Upholland, Skelmersdale • died 13 September 1978 at Mossley Hill, Liverpool aged 74 • buried at the Metropolitan Cathedral Crypt of Christ the King, Liverpool. • *St Joseph's College, College Road, Upholland, SKELMERSDALE WN8 0PY*

a.   † Rt Rev. **AUGUSTINE HARRIS**: born 27 October 1917 at West Derby, Liverpool • ordained priest (Liverpool) 30 May 1942 at Upholland, Skelmersdale • ordained titular Bishop of *Socia* and appointed auxiliary Bishop of Liverpool 11 February 1966 at the Pro-Cathedral Pontifical Crypt of Christ the King, Liverpool • translated 20 November 1978 to Diocese of Middlesbrough • retired 3 November 1992 to Ince Blundell, Liverpool • died 30 August 2007 at Ince Blundell, Liverpool aged 89 • buried at the Cathedral Church of St Mary, Coulby Newham, Middlesbrough. • *Ince Blundell Hall, Back O'the Town Lane, LIVERPOOL L38 6JL*

b.   † Rt Rev. Dr **JOSEPH GRAY** JCD: born 20 October 1919 at Finternagh (Cavan), Ireland • ordained priest (Birmingham) 20 June 1943 at Cavan City (Cavan), Ireland • ordained titular Bishop of *Mercia* and appointed auxiliary Bishop of Liverpool 16 February 1969 at the Metropolitan Cathedral Church of Christ the King, Liverpool • translated 30 August 1980 to Diocese of Shrewsbury • retired 30 August 1995 to Birkenhead • died 7 May 1999 at Birkenhead aged 79 • buried at St Winefride's Church, Neston. • *Bishop's House, 99 Eleanor Road, BIRKENHEAD CH43 7QW*

VII.   † Most Rev. **DEREK JOHN HARFORD WORLOCK** CH: born 4 February 1920 at St John's Wood, London • ordained priest (Westminster) 3 June 1944 at Old Hall Green, Ware • appointed Council Father at Second Vatican Council 14 September 1965 to 8 December 1965 • ordained Bishop of Portsmouth 21 December 1965 at Portsmouth • translated 7 February 1976 to Archdiocese of Liverpool • died 8 February 1996 at Mossley Hill, Liverpool aged 76 • buried at the Metropolitan Cathedral of Christ the King, Liverpool. • *Lowood, Carnatic Road, LIVERPOOL L18 8BY*

a.   † Rt Rev. **ANTHONY HITCHEN**: born 23 May 1930 at Chorley • ordained priest (Liverpool) 17 July 1955 at Chorley • ordained titular Bishop of *Othona* and appointed auxiliary Bishop of Liverpool 3 July 1979 at the Metropolitan Cathedral Church

of Christ the King, Liverpool • died 10 April 1988 at Freshfield, Liverpool aged 57 • buried at St Gregory's Church, Chorley.
• *55 Victoria Road, Formby, LIVERPOOL L37 1LN*

b.   † Rt Rev. **KEVIN O'CONNOR** JCL: born 20 May 1929 at Kirkdale, Liverpool • ordained priest (Liverpool) 12 June 1954 at Upholland, Skelmersdale • ordained titular Bishop of *Glastonia* and appointed auxiliary Bishop of Liverpool 3 July 1979 at the Metropolitan Cathedral Church of Christ the King, Liverpool • died 5 May 1993 at Fleetwood aged 63 • buried at SS Peter and Paul Church, Great Crosby, Liverpool.
• *12 Richmond Close, Eccleston, ST HELENS WA10 5JE*

c.   ⓡ Rt Rev. **JOHN ANTHONY RAWSTHORNE**: born 12 November 1936 at Crosby, Liverpool • ordained priest (Liverpool) 16 June 1962 at Upholland, Skelmersdale • ordained titular Bishop of *Rotdon* and appointed auxiliary Bishop of Liverpool 16 December 1981 at the Metropolitan Cathedral Church of Christ the King, Liverpool • translated 3 July 1997 to Diocese of Hallam • retired 20 May 2014 to Widnes • appointed 5 September 2014 parish priest of St Michael's Church, Widnes.
• *St Michael's Church, St Michael's Road, WIDNES WA8 8TF*

d.   ⓡ Rt Rev. Dr **VINCENT MALONE** DD BSc PGCE DipEd FCollP: born 11 September 1931 at Old Swan, Liverpool • ordained priest (Liverpool) 18 September 1955 at Old Swan, Liverpool • ordained titular Bishop of *Abora* and appointed auxiliary Bishop of Liverpool 3 July 1989 at the Metropolitan Cathedral Church of Christ the King, Liverpool • retired 26 October 2006 to Old Swan, Liverpool.
• *17 West Oakhill Park, LIVERPOOL L13 4BN*

VIII.   ⓡ Most Rev. Dr **PATRICK ALTHAM KELLY** KC*HS DD LLD STL PhL: born 23 November 1938 at Morecambe • ordained priest (Lancaster) 18 February 1962 at Rome, Italy • ordained Bishop of Salford 3 April 1984 at Salford • translated 3 July 1996 to Archdiocese of Liverpool • resigned 27 February 2013 as Archbishop of Liverpool and retired to Southport.
• *St Marie's House, 27 Seabank Road, SOUTHPORT PR9 0EJ*

a.   **APOSTOLIC ADMINISTRATOR:** Rt Rev. **THOMAS ANTHONY WILLIAMS** KC*HS: born 10 February 1948 at

Vauxhall, Liverpool • ordained priest (Liverpool) 27 May 1972 at the Metropolitan Cathedral Church of Christ the King, Liverpool • ordained titular Bishop of *Mageó* and appointed auxiliary Bishop of Liverpool 27 May 2003 at the Metropolitan Cathedral Church of Christ the King, Liverpool • appointed 27 February 2013 Apostolic Administrator of the Archdiocese of Liverpool until 1 May 2014.
• *14 Hope Place, LIVERPOOL L1 9BG*

IX.   Most Rev. **MALCOLM PATRICK McMAHON** OP KC*HS BSc BD MTh: born 14 June 1949 at Brixton, London • professed (Order of Preachers) 16 December 1977 at Haverstock Hill, London • ordained priest (Order of Preachers) 26 June 1982 at Haverstock Hill, London • ordained Bishop of Nottingham 8 December 2000 at Nottingham • translated 21 March 2014 to Archdiocese of Liverpool.
• *Archbishop's House, 19 Salisbury Road, LIVERPOOL L19 0PH*

DIOCESE OF MENEVIA

(Dioecesis Menevensis)

By Apostolic Brief (*De animarum salute*) of Pope Leo XIII, dated 4 March 1895, the whole Principality of Wales except Glamorgan and Monmouthshire was made a separate vicariate by division of the Diocese of Newport and the Diocese of Shrewsbury, with the episcopal see fixed at the Cathedral Church of Our Lady of Sorrows, Wrexham (1895–1987). The Vicariate remained a suffragan see within the Province of Westminster.

By the same Apostolic Brief (*De animarum salute*) of Pope Leo XIII, dated 4 March 1895, the Diocese of Newport and Menevia was renamed the Diocese of Newport, and comprised Glamorgan, Monmouthshire and Herefordshire, with the episcopal see fixed at the Priory Church of St Michael and All Angels, Belmont, Hereford (1859–1920). The Diocese remained a suffragan see within the Province of Westminster.

By a further decree of Pope Leo XIII, dated 12 May 1898, the Welsh Vicariate was renamed as the Diocese of Menevia, with the episcopal see remaining at the Cathedral Church of Our Lady of Sorrows, Wrexham (1895–1987). The Diocese remained a suffragan see within the Province of Westminster.

By Letters Apostolic (*Si qua est*) of Pope St Pius X, dated 28 October 1911, the Province of Westminster was divided into three new provinces of Birmingham, Liverpool and Westminster, with the Diocese of Newport and the Diocese of Menevia both being made part of the Province of Birmingham. The episcopal sees remained at the Priory Church of St Michael and All Angels, Belmont, Hereford (1859–1920) and the Cathedral Church of Our Lady of Sorrows, Wrexham (1895–1987) respectively.

By Letters Apostolic (*Cambria celtica*) of Pope Benedict XV, dated 7 February 1916, the Province of Birmingham was divided further into two new provinces of Birmingham and Cardiff, with the Diocese of Menevia being made part of the Province of Cardiff. The episcopal see remained at the Cathedral Church of Our Lady of Sorrows, Wrexham (1895–1987), consecrated on 7 November 1907, then at the Cathedral Church of St Joseph, Swansea (1987–), consecrated on 5 October 1919, which was reordered and rededicated as a cathedral church on 7 December 1988.

By Apostolic Decree (*Fiducia freti*) of Pope St John Paul II, dated 12 February 1987, the Diocese of Wrexham was formed by division of the Diocese of Menevia, taking the counties of Anglesey, Caernarfon, Denbigh, Flint, Merioneth, Montgomery and Wrexham from the newly restructured Diocese of Menevia.

By the same Apostolic Decree (*Fiducia freti*) of Pope St John Paul II, dated 12 February 1987, the episcopal see of the Diocese of Menevia was transferred from the Cathedral Church of Our Lady of Sorrows, Wrexham (1895–1987) to the Cathedral Church of St Joseph, Swansea (1987-) and the former County of West Glamorgan was transferred from the Archdiocese of Cardiff to the Diocese of Menevia. The Diocese of Menevia and the Diocese of Wrexham remained suffragan sees within the Province of Cardiff.

The diocese today comprises the City and County of Swansea, the counties of Brecknockshire, Cardiganshire, Carmarthenshire, Pembrokeshire and Radnorshire and the unitary authority of Neath Port Talbot.

I.   † Rt Rev. **FRANCIS EDWARD JOSEPH MOSTYN**: born 6 August 1860 at Talacre, Holywell • ordained priest (Shrewsbury) 14 September 1884 at Ushaw, Durham • ordained titular Bishop of *Ascalon* and appointed Vicar Apostolic for the Welsh District 14 September 1895 at Birkenhead • translated 12 May 1898 to newly erected Diocese of Menevia • translated 7 March 1921 to Archdiocese of Cardiff • appointed 7 March 1921 Apostolic Administrator of the Diocese of Menevia until 8 September 1926 • died 25 October 1939 at Cardiff aged 79 • buried at Cathays Cemetery, Cardiff. • *Archbishop's House, 24 Newport Road, CARDIFF CF24 0DB*

a.   APOSTOLIC ADMINISTRATOR: † Rt Rev. **FRANCIS EDWARD JOSEPH MOSTYN**: see **I.** above.

II.   † Rt Rev. **FRANCIS JOHN VAUGHAN**: born 5 May 1877 at Courtfield, Ross-on-Wye • ordained priest (Newport) 5 July 1903 at Ushaw, Durham • ordained Bishop of Menevia 8 September 1926 at the Metropolitan Cathedral Church of St David, Cardiff • died 13 March 1935 at Wrexham aged 57 • buried at Wrexham. • *Bishop's House, Sontley Road, WREXHAM LL13 7EW*

III.   † Rt Rev. Dr **MICHAEL JOSEPH McGRATH** MA DD LLD: born 24 March 1882 at Kilkenny City (Kilkenny), Ireland • ordained priest (Clifton) 12 July 1908 at Clifton, Bristol • ordained Bishop of Menevia 24 September 1935 at Wrexham • translated 20 June 1940 to Archdiocese of Cardiff • died 28 February 1961 at Cardiff aged 78 • buried at the Abbey Church of St Joseph, Llantarnam, Cwmbran. • *Archbishop's House, 24 Newport Road, CARDIFF CF24 0DB*

IV.   † Rt Rev. **DANIEL JOSEPH HANNON**: born 12 June 1884 at Rotherham • ordained priest (Newport) 22 September 1907 at Oscott, Sutton Coldfield • ordained Bishop of Menevia 1 May 1941 at Wrexham • died 26 April 1946 at Wrexham aged 61 • buried at Wrexham. • *Bishop's House, Sontley Road, WREXHAM LL13 7EW*

V.   † Rt Rev. **JOHN EDWARD PETIT** MA: born 22 June 1895 at Highgate, London • ordained priest (Brentwood) 9 May 1918 at Old Hall Green, Ware • ordained Bishop of Menevia 25 March 1947 at Llandudno • appointed Council Father at Second Vatican Council 11 October 1962 to 8 December 1965 • retired 16 June 1972 to Wrexham • died 3 June 1973 at Wrexham aged 77 • buried at Pantasaph, Holywell. • *Nazareth House, 2 Hillbury Road, WREXHAM LL13 7EU*

a.   † Rt Rev. Dr **LANGTON DOUGLAS FOX** MA DD: see **VI.** below.

VI.   † Rt Rev. Dr **LANGTON DOUGLAS FOX** MA DD: born 21 February 1917 at Golders Green, London • ordained priest (Southwark) 30 May 1942 at Wonersh, Guildford • appointed Council Father at Second Vatican Council 14 September 1965 to 8 December 1965 • ordained titular Bishop of *Maura*

and appointed auxiliary Bishop of Menevia 16 December 1965 at Wrexham
• translated 16 June 1972 to Diocese of Menevia • retired 5 February 1981
to Wrexham • died 26 July 1997 at Wrexham aged 80 • buried at Wrexham.
• *Nazareth House, 2 Hillbury Road, WREXHAM LL13 7EU*

    a.   † Rt Rev. Friar **JOHN ALOYSIUS WARD** OFM Cap.: see **VII.** below.

VII.   † Rt Rev. Friar **JOHN ALOYSIUS WARD** OFM Cap.: born 24 January 1929 at Leeds • professed (Order of Friars Minor Capuchin) 25 January 1950 at Peckham, London • ordained priest (Order of Friars Minor Capuchin) 7 June 1953 at Peckham, London • ordained coadjutor Bishop of Menevia 1 October 1980 at Wrexham • succeeded 5 February 1981 as Bishop of Menevia • translated 25 March 1983 to Archdiocese of Cardiff • retired 26 October 2001 to Ystradowen, Cowbridge • died 27 March 2007 at Ystradowen, Cowbridge aged 78 • buried at the Abbey Church of St Joseph, Llantarnam, Cwmbran.
• *11 Badgers Brook Drive, Ystradowen, COWBRIDGE CF71 7TX*

VIII.   † Rt Rev. **JAMES HANNIGAN**: born 15 July 1928 at Glenfinn (Donegal), Ireland • ordained priest (Menevia) 27 June 1954 at Paris (Paris), France • ordained Bishop of Menevia 23 November 1983 at Wrexham • translated 12 February 1987 to newly erected Diocese of Wrexham • died 4 March 1994 at Chester aged 65 • buried at Wrexham.
• *Bishop's House, Sontley Road, WREXHAM LL13 7EW*

IX.   ® Rt Rev. **DANIEL JOSEPH MULLINS** BA: born 10 July 1929 at Kilfinane (Limerick), Ireland • ordained priest (Cardiff) 12 April 1953 at Oscott, Sutton Coldfield • ordained titular Bishop of *Sidnacestre* and appointed auxiliary Bishop of Cardiff 1 April 1970 at the Metropolitan Cathedral Church of St David, Cardiff • translated 12 February 1987 to newly restructured Diocese of Menevia • retired 12 June 2001 to Kidwelly.
• *8 Rhodfa'r Gwendraeth, KIDWELLY SA17 4SR*

    a.   ® Rt Rev. Dom. **JOHN PETER MARK JABALÉ** OSB LèsL DipEd: see **X.** below.

X.   ® Rt Rev. Dom. **JOHN PETER MARK JABALÉ** OSB LèsL DipEd: born 16 October 1933 at Alexandria (Alexandria), Egypt • professed (Order of Saint Benedict) 29 September 1953 at Belmont, Hereford • ordained

priest (Order of Saint Benedict) 13 July 1958 at Belmont, Hereford •
elected 1 September 1993 Abbot of the Abbey Church of St Michael and
All Angels, Belmont, Hereford • ordained coadjutor Bishop of Menevia
7 December 2000 at Swansea • succeeded 12 June 2001 as Bishop of
Menevia • retired 16 October 2008 and appointed parish priest of Holy
Trinity Church, Chipping Norton • retired 2014 to Hendon, London.
• *14 Egerton Gardens, LONDON NW4 4BA*

XI.   Rt Rev. **THOMAS MATTHEW BURNS** SM BA BD KC*HS:
born 3 June 1944 at Belfast (Antrim), Ireland • professed (Society of Mary) 12 September 1965 at Paignton • ordained priest
(Society of Mary) 16 December 1971 at Paignton • commissioned as
military chaplain 8 September 1986 • ordained Bishop in Ordinary to
HM Forces 18 June 2002 at Aldershot • released from military service
16 October 2008 • translated 1 December 2008 to Diocese of Menevia.
• *Bryn Rhos, 79 Walter Road, SWANSEA SA1 4PS*

DIOCESE OF MIDDLESBROUGH

(Dioecesis Medioburgensis)

By Apostolic Decree (*Quae ex hac*) of Pope Leo XIII, dated 20 December 1878, the Diocese of Middlesbrough was formed by division of the Diocese of Beverley, with the episcopal see fixed at the Cathedral Church of Our Lady of Perpetual Succour, Sussex Street, Middlesbrough (1878–1986), consecrated on 6 September 1911 and destroyed by fire on 30 May 2000, then at the Cathedral Church of St Mary, Coulby Newham, Middlesbrough (1986–), opened and consecrated on 15 May 1986.

From 20 December 1878, the Diocese of Middlesbrough was a suffragan see within the Province of Westminster. At first, the Diocese of Middlesbrough comprised the counties of the North Riding of Yorkshire and the East Riding of Yorkshire.

By Letters Apostolic (*Si qua est*) of Pope St Pius X, dated 28 October 1911, the Province of Westminster was divided into three new Provinces of Birmingham, Liverpool and Westminster, with the Diocese of Middlesbrough being made part of the Province of Liverpool. The episcopal see remained at the Cathedral Church of Our Lady of Perpetual Succour, Sussex Street, Middlesbrough (1878–1986), then at the Cathedral Church of St Mary, Coulby Newham, Middlesbrough (1986–).

The Diocese today comprises the counties of North Yorkshire (north of the River Ure and River Ouse including the City of York) and East Riding of Yorkshire (north of the River Ouse but excluding the parish of Howden and Goole) and the unitary authorities of Kingston upon Hull, Middlesbrough, Redcar and Cleveland, Stockton-on-Tees (south of the River Tees) and the City of York.

a. **APOSTOLIC ADMINISTRATOR:** † Rt Rev. **ROBERT CORNTHWAITE**: born 9 May 1818 at Preston • ordained priest (Northern District) 9 November 1845 at Rome, Italy • ordained Bishop of Beverley 10 November 1861 at Moorfields, City of London • appointed Council Father at First Vatican Council 8 December 1869 to 20 October 1870 • translated 20 December 1878 to newly erected Diocese of Leeds • appointed 20 December 1878 Apostolic Administrator of Diocese of Middlesbrough until 18 December 1879 • died 16 June 1890 at Leeds aged 72 • buried at the Church of Mary Immaculate, Sicklinghall, Wetherby. • *Springfield House, Hyde Street, LEEDS LS2 9LH*

I. † Rt Rev. **RICHARD LACY**: born 16 January 1841 at Navan (Meath), Ireland, ordained priest (Beverley) 21 December 1867 at Rome, Italy • ordained Bishop of newly erected Diocese of Middlesbrough 18 December 1879 at Middlesbrough • died 11 April 1929 at Middlesbrough aged 88 • buried at St Joseph's Cemetery, North Ormesby, Middlesbrough • reinterred 7 June 2005 at the Cathedral Church of St Mary, Coulby Newham, Middlesbrough. • *Bishop's House (Grove Lea), Marton Road, MIDDLESBROUGH*

a. † Rt Rev. **THOMAS SHINE**: see II. below.

II. † Most Rev. **THOMAS SHINE**: born 11 February 1872 at Knocknaveigh (Tipperary), Ireland • ordained priest (Leeds) 29 June 1894 at Leeds • ordained titular Bishop of *Lamus* and appointed coadjutor Bishop of Middlesbrough 29 June 1921 at Middlesbrough • succeeded 11 April 1929 as Bishop of Middlesbrough • appointed 19 January 1955 *Archbishop ad personam* at Vatican City • died 22 November 1955 at Middlesbrough aged 83 • buried at St Joseph's Cemetery, North Ormesby, Middlesbrough • reinterred 7 June 2005 at the Cathedral Church of St Mary, Coulby Newham, Middlesbrough. • *Bishop's House, 16 Cambridge Road, MIDDLESBROUGH TS5 5NN*

a. † Rt Rev. **GEORGE BRUNNER** BA: see III. below.

III. † Rt Rev. **GEORGE BRUNNER** BA: born 21 August 1889 at Hull
• ordained priest (Middlesbrough) 9 April 1917 at Ushaw, Durham •
ordained titular Bishop of *Elis* and appointed auxiliary Bishop of Middlesbrough 25 July 1946 at Middlesbrough • translated 7 June 1956
to Diocese of Middlesbrough • appointed Council Father at Second
Vatican Council 11 October 1962 to 4 December 1963 • appointed 12
June 1967 titular Bishop of *Murustaga* and retired to Middlesbrough •
died 21 March 1969 at Middlesbrough aged 79 • buried at St Joseph's
Cemetery, North Ormesby, Middlesbrough • reinterred 7 June 2005 at
the Cathedral Church of St Mary, Coulby Newham, Middlesbrough.
• *Bishop's House, 16 Cambridge Road, MIDDLESBROUGH TS5 5NN*

a. † *CE* Rt Rev. Dr **WILLIAM GORDON WHEELER** MA DD:
born 5 May 1910 at Dobcross, Oldham • ordained Church of England
deacon (Chichester) 21 December 1933 at Chichester • ordained
Church of England priest (Derby) 23 December 1934 at Derby •
received into Catholic Church 18 September 1936 at Downside,
Radstock • ordained priest (Westminster) 31 March 1940 at the
Metropolitan Cathedral Church of the Most Precious Blood, Westminster, London • ordained titular Bishop of *Theudalis* and appointed
coadjutor Bishop of Middlesbrough 19 March 1964 at Middlesbrough
• appointed Council Father at Second Vatican Council 14 September
1964 to 8 December 1965 • translated 3 May 1966 to Diocese of Leeds
• Diocese of Leeds restructured 30 May 1980 • retired 10 September
1985 to Headingley, Leeds • died 20 February 1998 at Headingley,
Leeds aged 87 • buried at St Edward's Church, Clifford, Wetherby.
• *Mount St Joseph's, Shire Oak Road, LEEDS LS6 2DE*

b. † Rt Rev. **JOHN GERARD McCLEAN**: see **IV.** below.

IV. † Rt Rev. **JOHN GERARD McCLEAN**: born 24 September
1914 at Redcar • ordained priest (Middlesbrough) 22 March 1942 at
Ushaw, Durham • ordained titular Bishop of *Maxita* and appointed
coadjutor Bishop of Middlesbrough 24 February 1967 at Middlesbrough • succeeded 12 June 1967 as Bishop of Middlesbrough • died
27 August 1978 at Blackley, Manchester aged 63 • buried at St Joseph's
Cemetery, North Ormesby, Middlesbrough • reinterred 7 June 2005 at
the Cathedral Church of St Mary, Coulby Newham, Middlesbrough.
• *Bishop's House, 16 Cambridge Road, MIDDLESBROUGH TS5 5NN*

V.   † Rt Rev. **AUGUSTINE HARRIS**: born 27 October 1917 at West
      Derby, Liverpool • ordained priest (Liverpool) 30 May 1942 at Upholland,
      Skelmersdale • ordained titular Bishop of *Socia* and appointed auxiliary
      Bishop of Liverpool 11 February 1966 at the Pro-Cathedral Pontifical Crypt
      of Christ the King, Liverpool • translated 20 November 1978 to Diocese
      of Middlesbrough • retired 3 November 1992 to Ince Blundell, Liverpool
      • died 30 August 2007 at Ince Blundell, Liverpool aged 89 • buried at
      the Cathedral Church of St Mary, Coulby Newham, Middlesbrough.
      • *Ince Blundell Hall, Back O'the Town Lane, LIVERPOOL L38 6JL*

a.   † Rt Rev. **THOMAS KEVIN O'BRIEN**: born 18 February 1923
      at Cork City (Cork), Ireland • ordained priest (Leeds) 20 June 1948 at
      Dublin City (Dublin), Ireland • ordained titular Bishop of *Árd Carna*
      and appointed auxiliary Bishop of Middlesbrough 8 December 1981
      at Middlesbrough • retired 25 June 1998 to Hull thence to Headingley,
      Leeds • died 27 December 2004 at Headingley, Leeds aged 81 • buried
      at the Cathedral Church of St Mary, Coulby Newham, Middlesbrough.
      • *Mount St Joseph's, Shire Oak Road, LEEDS LS6 2DE*

VI.   ® Rt Rev. **JOHN PATRICK CROWLEY**: born 23 June 1941 at Newbury
      • ordained priest (Westminster) 12 June 1965 at the Metropolitan Cathedral
      Church of the Most Precious Blood, Westminster, London • ordained titular
      Bishop of *Thala* and appointed auxiliary Bishop of Westminster 8 December
      1986 at the Metropolitan Cathedral Church of the Most Precious Blood,
      Westminster, London • translated 18 January 1993 to Diocese of Middles-
      brough • retired 3 May 2007 to Wanstead, London thence to Harpenden.
      • *1 Kirkwick Avenue, HARPENDEN AL5 2QH*

VII. Rt Rev. **TERENCE PATRICK DRAINEY** STB: born 1
      August 1949 at Droylesden, Manchester • ordained priest (Sal-
      ford) 12 July 1975 at Fairfield, Manchester • ordained Bishop of
      Middlesbrough 25 January 2008 at Coulby Newham, Middlesbrough.
      • *Bishop's House, 16 Cambridge Road, MIDDLESBROUGH TS5 5NN*

DIOCESE OF NEWPORT (AND MENEVIA)

(Dioecesis Neoportensis et Menevensis)

By Letters Apostolic (*Universalis ecclesiae*) of Pope Bl. Pius IX, dated 29 September 1850, the Diocese of Newport and Menevia was formed, with the episcopal see fixed at the Priory Church of St Michael and All Angels, Belmont, Hereford (1859–1920), consecrated on 4 September 1860.

The Diocese of Newport and Menevia was an original suffragan see within the Province of Westminster. At first, the Diocese of Newport and Menevia comprised the counties of Brecknockshire, Cardiganshire, Carmarthenshire, Glamorgan, Pembrokeshire, Radnorshire with Monmouthshire and Herefordshire.

By Apostolic Brief (*De animarum salute*) of Pope Leo XIII, dated 4 March 1895, the whole Principality of Wales except Glamorgan and Monmouthshire was made a separate vicariate by division of the Diocese of Newport and the Diocese of Shrewsbury, with the episcopal see fixed at the Cathedral Church of Our Lady of Sorrows, Wrexham (1895–1987).

By the same Apostolic Brief (*De animarum salute*) of Pope Leo XIII, dated 4 March 1895, the Diocese of Newport and Menevia was renamed the Diocese of Newport, and comprised Glamorgan, Monmouthshire and Herefordshire, with the episcopal see fixed at the Priory Church of St Michael and All Angels, Belmont, Hereford (1859–1920).

By a further decree of Pope Leo XIII, dated 12 May 1898, the Welsh Vicariate was renamed as the Diocese of Menevia, with the episcopal see remaining at the Cathedral Church of Our Lady of Sorrows, Wrexham (1895–1987). The Diocese of Newport and the Diocese of Menevia both remained suffragan sees within the Province of Westminster.

By Letters Apostolic (*Si qua est*) of Pope St Pius X, dated 28 October 1911, the Province of Westminster was divided into three new provinces of Birmingham, Liverpool and Westminster, with the Diocese of Newport and the Diocese of Menevia both being made part of the Province of Birmingham. The episcopal sees remained at the Priory Church of St Michael and All Angels, Belmont, Hereford (1859–1920) and the Cathedral Church of Our Lady of Sorrows, Wrexham (1895–1987) respectively.

I.   † Rt Rev. Dom. **THOMAS JOSEPH BROWN** OSB DD: born 2 May 1798 at Bath • professed (Order of Saint Benedict) 28 October 1814 at Downside, Radstock • ordained priest (Order of Saint Benedict) 7 April 1823 at London • ordained titular Bishop of *Apollonia* and appointed Vicar Apostolic for the Welsh District 28 October 1840 at Bath • translated 29 September 1850 to restored Diocese of Newport and Menevia • appointed 29 September 1850 Apostolic Administrator of the Diocese of Shrewsbury until 27 July 1851 • died 12 April 1880 at Lower Bullingham, Hereford aged 81 • buried at the Abbey Church of St Michael and All Angels, Belmont, Hereford. • *Manor House, Lower Bullingham, HEREFORD HR2 6EG*

   a.   † Rt Rev. Dom. **JOHN EDWARD CUTHBERT HEDLEY** OSB: see **II.** below.

II.   † Rt Rev. Dom. **JOHN EDWARD CUTHBERT HEDLEY** OSB: born 15 April 1837 at Carlisle House, Morpeth • professed (Order of Saint Benedict) 1 January 1855 at Ampleforth, York • ordained priest (Order of Saint Benedict) 19 October 1862 at Ampleforth, York • ordained titular Bishop of *Caesaropolis* and appointed auxiliary Bishop of Newport and Menevia 29 September 1873 at Belmont, Hereford • translated 18 February 1881 to Diocese of Newport and Menevia • translated 4 March 1895 to renamed Diocese of Newport • died 11 November 1915 at Llanishen, Cardiff aged 78 • buried at Cathays Cemetery, Cardiff. • *Bishop's House, 96 Station Road, Llanishen, CARDIFF CF14 5UX*

DIOCESE OF NORTHAMPTON

(Dioecesis Nortantoniensis)

By Letters Apostolic (Universalis ecclesiae) of Pope Bl. Pius IX, dated 29 September 1850, the Diocese of Northampton was formed, with the episcopal see fixed at the Pro-Cathedral Priory Church of SS Felix and Andrew, Northampton (1850–1864), consecrated on 25 June 1844, which was extended and rededicated as the Cathedral Church of Our Lady Immaculate and St Thomas of Canterbury, Northampton (1864–), consecrated on 22 June 1960.

The Diocese of Northampton was an original suffragan see within the Province of Westminster. At first, the Diocese of Northampton comprised the counties of Bedfordshire, Berkshire (north of the River Thames), Buckinghamshire, Cambridgeshire, Huntingdonshire, Northamptonshire, Norfolk and Suffolk.

By Letters Apostolic (*Si qua est*) of Pope St Pius X, dated 28 October 1911, the Province of Westminster was divided into three new provinces of Birmingham, Liverpool and Westminster, with the Diocese of Northampton remaining part of the Province of Westminster. The episcopal see remained at the Cathedral Church of Our Lady Immaculate and St Thomas of Canterbury, Northampton (1864–).

By Apostolic Decree (*Quod ecumenicum*) of Pope Bl. Paul VI, dated 13 March 1976, the Diocese of East Anglia was formed by division of the Diocese of

Northampton, taking the counties of Cambridgeshire, Norfolk and Suffolk from the Diocese of Northampton.

The Diocese today comprises the counties of Bedfordshire, Buckinghamshire and Northamptonshire and the unitary authorities of Luton, Milton Keynes and Slough.

I.   † Rt Rev. **WILLIAM WAREING**: born 14 February 1791 at Lincoln's Inn Fields, London • ordained priest (Midland District) 28 September 1815 at Wolverhampton • ordained titular Bishop of *Areopolis* and appointed Vicar Apostolic for the Eastern District 21 September 1840 at Oscott, Sutton Coldfield • translated 29 September 1850 to restored Diocese of Northampton • appointed 11 February 1858 titular Bishop of *Rhithymna* and retired to Old Hall Convent, East Bergholt, Colchester • died 26 December 1865 at Old Hall Convent, East Bergholt, Colchester aged 74 • buried at Old Hall Convent, East Bergholt, Colchester. • *Old Hall, Rectory Hill, East Bergholt, COLCHESTER CO7 6TG*

II.   † Rt Rev. Dr **FRANCIS KERRIL AMHERST** DD: born 21 March 1819 at Marylebone, London • ordained priest (Central District) 6 June 1846 at Oscott, Sutton Coldfield • ordained Bishop of Northampton 4 July 1858 at Northampton • appointed Council Father at First Vatican Council 8 December 1869 to 20 October 1870 • resigned 2 April 1879 as Bishop of Northampton • appointed 2 April 1879 Apostolic Administrator of the Diocese of Northampton until 9 June 1880 • appointed 27 July 1880 titular Bishop of *Sozusa in Palaestina* and retired to Fieldgate House, Kenilworth • died 21 August 1882 at Fieldgate House, Kenilworth aged 63 • buried at the Cathedral Church of Our Lady and St Thomas, Northampton. • *Fieldgate House, Fieldgate Lane, KENILWORTH CV8 1BU*

a.   APOSTOLIC ADMINISTRATOR: † Rt Rev. Dr **FRANCIS KERRIL AMHERST** DD: see **II.** above.

III. † Rt Rev. **ARTHUR GRANGE RIDDELL**: born 15 September 1836 at York • ordained priest (Beverley) 24 September 1859 at Ushaw, Durham • ordained Bishop of Northampton 9 June 1880 at Northampton • died 15 September 1907 at Northampton aged 71 • buried at Kingsthorpe Cemetery, Northampton • reinterred 1964 at the Cathedral Church of Our Lady and St Thomas, Northampton. • *Bishop's House, Marriott Street, NORTHAMPTON NN2 6AW*

IV. † Rt Rev. Dr **FREDERICK WILLIAM KEATING** DD: born 13 June 1859 at City of Birmingham • ordained priest (Birmingham) 20 October 1882 at Olton, Solihull • ordained Bishop of Northampton 25 February 1908 at the Cathedral Church of St Chad, Birmingham • translated 13 June 1921 to Archdiocese of Liverpool • died 7 February 1928 at Princes Park, Liverpool aged 68 • buried at Upholland, Skelmersdale.
• *Archbishop's House, 5 Belvidere Road, Princes Park, LIVERPOOL L8 3TF*

V.   † Rt Rev. **DUDLEY CHARLES CARY-ELWES**: born 5 February 1868 at Nice (Alpes-Maritimes), France • ordained priest (Northampton) 30 May 1896 at Rome, Italy • ordained Bishop of Northampton 15 December 1921 at Northampton • died 1 May 1932 at Hampstead, London aged 64 • buried at Great Billing, Northampton.
• *Bishop's House, Marriott Street, NORTHAMPTON NN2 6AW*

VI. † Rt Rev. **LAURENCE WALTER YOUENS** SMA: born 14 December 1872 at High Wycombe • received into Catholic Church 1890 at High Wycombe • professed (Society of African Missionaries) at Wilton (Cork), Ireland • ordained priest (Society of African Missionaries) 30 June 1901 at Choubrah (Cairo), Egypt • incardinated 23 September 1904 into Diocese of Northampton at High Wycombe • ordained Bishop of Northampton 25 July 1933 at Northampton • died 14 November 1939 at Northampton aged 66 • buried at the Abbey Church of St Michael and All Angels, Belmont, Hereford.
• *Bishop's House, Marriott Street, NORTHAMPTON NN2 6AW*

VII. † Rt Rev. **THOMAS LEO PARKER** MA: born 21 December 1887 at Sutton Coldfield • ordained priest (Salford) 29 May 1915 at Ushaw, Durham • ordained Bishop of Northampton 11 February 1941 at Northampton • appointed Council Father at Second Vatican Council 11 October 1962 to 8 December 1965 • appointed 17 January 1967 titular Bishop of *Magarmel* and retired to Poringland, Norwich thence to Burnham, Slough • died 25 March 1975 at Kiln Green, Reading aged 87 • buried at the Cathedral Church of Our Lady and St Thomas, Northampton.
• *Fox Den, Dorney Wood Road, Burnham, SLOUGH SL1 8PS*

a.   † Rt Rev. **CHARLES ALEXANDER GRANT** MA JCL: see **VIII.** below.

VIII.   † Rt Rev. **CHARLES ALEXANDER GRANT** MA JCL: born 25 October 1906 at Cambridge • received into Catholic Church 1921 at Cambridge • ordained priest (Northampton) 16 June 1935 at Oscott, Sutton Coldfield • ordained titular Bishop of *Alinda* and appointed auxiliary Bishop of Northampton 25 April 1961 at Northampton • appointed Council Father at Second Vatican Council 11 October 1962 to 8 December 1965 • translated 25 March 1967 to Diocese of Northampton • Diocese of Northampton restructured 13 March 1976 • retired 29 September 1982 to Kiln Green, Reading • died 24 April 1989 at Kiln Green, Reading aged 82 • buried at Woburn Sands, Milton Keynes.
• *St John's Convent, Linden Hill Lane, Kiln Green, READING RG10 9XP*

a.   † Rt Rev. Dr **ALAN CHARLES CLARK** DD: born 9 August 1919 at Bickley, Bromley • ordained priest (Southwark) 11 February 1945 at Bromley • ordained titular Bishop of *Elmhama* and appointed auxiliary Bishop of Northampton 13 May 1969 at Northampton • translated 2 June 1976 to newly erected Diocese of East Anglia • retired 27 May 1995 to Poringland, Norwich thence to Norwich • died 16 July 2002 at Norwich aged 82 • buried at the Catholic National Shrine of Our Lady of Walsingham, Houghton St Giles, Walsingham.
• *Oakwood House, Watton Road, NORWICH NR4 7TP*

IX.   † Rt Rev. **FRANCIS GERARD THOMAS** STL: born 29 May 1930 at Stone • ordained priest (Birmingham) 5 June 1955 at Oscott, Sutton Coldfield • ordained Bishop of Northampton 29 September 1982 at Northampton • died 25 December 1988 at Beaconsfield aged 58 • buried at the Cathedral Church of Our Lady and St Thomas, Northampton.
• *Bishop's House, Marriott Street, NORTHAMPTON NN2 6AW*

X.   ® Rt Rev. **PATRICK LEO McCARTIE**: born 5 September 1925 at West Hartlepool • ordained priest (Birmingham) 17 July 1949 at Trent Vale, Stoke-on-Trent • ordained titular Bishop of *Elmhama* and appointed auxiliary Bishop of Birmingham 20 May 1977 at the Metropolitan Cathedral Church of St Chad, Birmingham • translated 19 March 1990 to Diocese of Northampton • retired 29 March 2001 to Aston, Stone thence to Harborne, Birmingham.
• *Little Sisters of the Poor, 71 Queen's Park Road, BIRMINGHAM B32 2LB*

XI.   ® Rt Rev. Dr **KEVIN JOHN PATRICK McDONALD** BA STL STD: born 18 August 1947 at Stoke-on-Trent • ordained priest

(Birmingham) 20 July 1974 at Rome, Italy • ordained Bishop of Northampton 2 May 2001 at Northampton • translated 8 December 2003 to Archdiocese of Southwark • resigned 4 December 2009 as Archbishop of Southwark and retired to Southwark, London. • *c/o Archbishop's House, 150 St George's Road, LONDON SE1 6HX*

XII.   Rt Rev. **PETER JOHN HAWORTH DOYLE**: born 3 May 1944 at Wilpshire, Blackburn • ordained priest (Portsmouth) 8 June 1968 at Portsmouth • ordained Bishop of Northampton 28 June 2005 at Northampton. • *Bishop's House, Marriott Street, NORTHAMPTON NN2 6AW*

DIOCESE OF NOTTINGHAM

(Dioecesis Nottinghamensis)

By Letters Apostolic (*Universalis ecclesiae*) of Pope Bl. Pius IX, dated 29 September 1850, the Diocese of Nottingham was formed, with the episcopal see fixed at the Cathedral Church of St Barnabas, Nottingham (1850–), consecrated on 27 August 1844.

The Diocese of Nottingham was an original suffragan see within the Province of Westminster. At first, the Diocese of Nottingham comprised the counties of Derbyshire, Leicestershire, Lincolnshire, Nottinghamshire and Rutland.

By Letters Apostolic (*Si qua est*) of Pope St Pius X, dated 28 October 1911, the Province of Westminster was divided into three new provinces of Birmingham, Liverpool and Westminster, with the Diocese of Nottingham remaining part of the Province of Westminster. The episcopal see remained at the Cathedral Church of St Barnabas, Nottingham (1850–).

By a Bull (*Qui arcano dei*) of Pope St John Paul II, dated 30 May 1980, the Diocese of Hallam was formed by division of the Diocese of Leeds and the Diocese of Nottingham, taking parts of the districts of High Peak and Chesterfield in Derbyshire, and the district of Bassetlaw in Nottinghamshire from the Diocese of Nottingham.

The Diocese today comprises the counties of Nottinghamshire (except the district of Bassetlaw), Derbyshire (except parts of the districts of High Peak and Chesterfield), Leicestershire, Lincolnshire and Rutland and the unitary authorities of Derby, Leicester, North East Lincolnshire, North Lincolnshire and Nottingham.

a.   **APOSTOLIC ADMINISTRATOR:** † Most Rev. Dom. **WILLIAM BERNARD ULLATHORNE** OSB: born 7 May 1806 at Pocklington, York • professed (Order of Saint Benedict) 5 April 1825 at Downside, Radstock • ordained priest (Order of Saint Benedict) 24 September 1831 at Ushaw, Durham • ordained titular Bishop of *Hetalonia* and appointed Vicar Apostolic for the Western District 21 June 1846 at Coventry • translated 28 July 1848 to Vicar Apostolic for the Central District • translated 29 September 1850 to restored Diocese of Birmingham • appointed 29 September 1850 Apostolic Administrator of the Diocese of Nottingham until 22 June 1851 • appointed Council Father at First Vatican Council 8 December 1869 to 20 October 1870 • appointed 17 February 1888 titular Archbishop of *Cabasa* and retired to Oscott, Sutton Coldfield • died 21 March 1889 at Oscott, Sutton Coldfield aged 82 • buried at Aston Hall, Stone. • *Oscott College, Chester Road, SUTTON COLDFIELD B73 5AA*

I.   † Rt Rev. **JOSEPH WILLIAM FRANCIS HENDREN** OSF: born 19 October 1791 at Birmingham • professed (Order of Saint Francis) 2 August 1806 at Abergavenny • ordained priest (Order of Saint Francis) 28 September 1815 at Wolverhampton • ordained titular Bishop of *Verinopolis* and appointed Vicar Apostolic for the Western District 10 September 1848 at Bristol • translated 29 September 1850 to restored Diocese of Clifton • appointed 29 September 1850 Apostolic Administrator of Diocese of Plymouth until 22 June 1851 • translated 22 June 1851 to restored Diocese of Nottingham • appointed 23 February 1853 titular Bishop of *Martyropolis* and retired to Birmingham thence to Taunton • died 14 November 1866 at Taunton aged 75 • buried at the Franciscan Convent, Taunton • reinterred 4 October 1997 at St George's Church, Taunton. • *Franciscan Convent, Billet Street, TAUNTON TA1 3NN*

II.   † Rt Rev. Dr **RICHARD BUTLER ROSKELL** DD: born 15 August 1817 at Gateacre, Liverpool • ordained priest (Lancashire District) 9 June 1840 at Rome, Italy • ordained Bishop of Nottingham 21 September 1853 at Nottingham • appointed Council Father at First Vatican

Council 8 December 1869 to 20 October 1870 • appointed 12 November 1874 titular Bishop of *Abdera* and retired to Glascoed, Wrexham thence to Whitewell, Clitheroe • died 27 January 1883 at Whitewell, Clitheroe aged 65 • buried at St Hubert's Church, Dunsop Bridge, Clitheroe. • *St Hubert's Presbytery, Trough Road, Dunsop Bridge, CLITHEROE BB7 3BG*

III.   † Most Rev. Dr **EDWARD GILPIN BAGSHAWE** CO DD: born 12 January 1829 at Holborn, London • professed (Confederation of Oratorians of Saint Philip Neri) 2 November 1849 at Strand, London • ordained priest (Confederation of Oratorians of Saint Philip Neri) 6 March 1852 at Strand, London • ordained Bishop of Nottingham 12 November 1874 at Brompton Oratory, London • resigned 25 November 1901 as Bishop of Nottingham • appointed 27 January 1902 titular Bishop of *Hypaepa* • appointed 17 January 1904 titular Archbishop of *Selucia in Isauria* and retired to Gunnersbury, London • died 6 February 1915 at Gunnersbury, London aged 86 • buried at Isleworth Cemetery • reinterred 16 December 1921 at the Cathedral Church of St Barnabas, Nottingham. • *Gunnersbury House, Gunnersbury Park, LONDON W3 8LQ*

IV.   † Rt Rev. **ROBERT BRINDLE** DSO: born 4 November 1837 at Everton, Liverpool • ordained priest (Plymouth) 27 December 1862 at Lisbon (Lisboa), Portugal • commissioned as military chaplain 12 January 1874 • ordained titular Bishop of *Hermopolis Maior* and appointed auxiliary Bishop of Westminster 12 March 1899 at Rome, Italy • released from military service 5 July 1899 • translated 6 December 1901 to Diocese of Nottingham • appointed 1 June 1915 titular Bishop of *Tacapae* and retired to Spinkhill, Sheffield • died 27 June 1916 at Spinkhill, Sheffield aged 78 • buried at the Cathedral Church of St Barnabas, Nottingham. • *Mount St Mary's College, Spinkhill, SHEFFIELD S21 3YL*

V.   † Rt Rev. **THOMAS DUNN**: born 28 July 1870 at Marylebone, London • ordained priest (Westminster) 2 February 1893 at South Kensington, London • ordained Bishop of Nottingham 25 February 1916 at Nottingham • died 21 September 1931 at Nottingham aged 61 • buried at the Cathedral Church of St Barnabas, Nottingham. • *Cathedral House, North Circus Street, NOTTINGHAM NG1 5AE*

VI.   † Rt Rev. Dr **JOHN FRANCIS McNULTY** MA DD: born 11 August 1879 at Collyhurst, Manchester • ordained priest (Salford)

16 April 1911 at Salford • ordained Bishop of Nottingham 11 June 1932 at Nottingham • died 8 June 1943 at Dollis Hill, London aged 63 • buried at the Cathedral Church of St Barnabas, Nottingham.
• *Bishop's House, 27 Cavendish Road East, NOTTINGHAM NG7 1BB*

VII.   † Rt Rev. Dr **EDWARD ELLIS** DD PhD: born 30 June 1899 at Radford, Nottingham • ordained priest (Nottingham) 15 October 1922 at Nottingham • ordained Bishop of Nottingham 1 May 1944 at Nottingham • appointed Council Father at Second Vatican Council 11 October 1962 to 8 December 1965 • retired 31 October 1974 to Nottingham • died 6 July 1979 at Nottingham aged 80 • buried at the Cathedral Church of St Barnabas, Nottingham.
• *Nazareth House, Priory Street, NOTTINGHAM NG7 1NY*

     a.   † Rt Rev. Dr **JAMES JOSEPH McGUINNESS** DD: see **VIII.** below.

VIII.   † Rt Rev. Dr **JAMES JOSEPH McGUINNESS** DD: born 2 October 1925 at Londonderry (Derry), Ireland • ordained priest (Nottingham) 3 June 1950 at Nottingham • ordained titular Bishop of *Sanctus Germanus* and appointed coadjutor Bishop of Nottingham 23 March 1972 at Nottingham • succeeded 31 October 1974 as Bishop of Nottingham • Diocese of Nottingham restructured 30 May 1980 • retired 8 December 2000 to Nottingham thence to Ednaston, Ashbourne • died 6 April 2007 at Ednaston, Ashbourne aged 81 • buried at the Cathedral Church of St Barnabas, Nottingham.
• *St Mary's Nursing Home, Ednaston, ASHBOURNE DE6 3BA*

IX.   Rt Rev. **MALCOLM PATRICK McMAHON** OP KC*HS BSc BD MTh: born 14 June 1949 at Brixton, London • professed (Order of Preachers) 16 December 1977 at Haverstock Hill, London • ordained priest (Order of Preachers) 26 June 1982 at Haverstock Hill, London • ordained Bishop of Nottingham 8 December 2000 at Nottingham • translated 21 March 2014 to Archdiocese of Liverpool.
• *Archbishop's House, 19 Salisbury Road, LIVERPOOL L19 0PH*

X.   Rt Rev. **PATRICK JOSEPH McKINNEY** STL: born 30 April 1954 at Balsall Heath, Birmingham • ordained priest (Birmingham) 29 July 1978 at Buncrana (Donegal), Ireland • ordained Bishop of Nottingham 3 July 2015 at Nottingham.
• *Bishop's House, 27 Cavendish Road East, NOTTINGHAM NG7 1BB*

DIOCESE OF PLYMOUTH

IN MANUS TUAS, DOMINE

(Dioecesis Plymuthensis)

By Letters Apostolic (*Universalis ecclesiae*) of Pope Bl. Pius IX, dated 29 September 1850, the Diocese of Plymouth was formed, with the episcopal see fixed at the Pro-Cathedral Chapel of the Blessed Virgin Mary and St John the Evangelist, Stonehouse, Plymouth (1850–1858), consecrated on 20 December 1807, then at the Cathedral Church of SS Mary and Boniface, Plymouth (1858–), consecrated on 22 September 1880.

The Diocese of Plymouth was an original suffragan see within the Province of Westminster. At first, the Diocese of Plymouth comprised the counties of Cornwall, Devon and Dorset, with the Isles of Scilly.

By Letters Apostolic (*Si qua est*) of Pope St Pius X, dated 28 October 1911, the Province of Westminster was divided into three new provinces of Birmingham, Liverpool and Westminster, with the Diocese of Plymouth being made part of the Province of Birmingham. The episcopal see remained at the Cathedral Church of SS Mary and Boniface, Plymouth (1858–).

By Letters Apostolic (*Romanorum pontificum*) of Pope Bl. Paul VI, dated 28 May 1965, the Province of Westminster was divided further into two new provinces of Southwark and Westminster, with the Diocese of Plymouth being made part of the newly erected Province of Southwark. The episcopal see remained at the Cathedral Church of SS Mary and Boniface, Plymouth (1858–).

The Diocese today comprises the counties of Cornwall, Devon and Dorset (including the Borough of Poole, but excluding the Boroughs of Bournemouth and Christchurch), with the Isles of Scilly, as well as the parish of Kinson and Ensbury Park in Bournemouth.

a.   **APOSTOLIC ADMINISTRATOR:** † Rt Rev. **JOSEPH WILLIAM FRANCIS HENDREN** OSF: born 19 October 1791 at Birmingham • professed (Order of Saint Francis) 2 August 1806 at Abergavenny • ordained priest (Order of Saint Francis) 28 September 1815 at Wolverhampton • ordained titular Bishop of *Verinopolis* and appointed Vicar Apostolic for the Western District 10 September 1848 at Bristol • translated 29 September 1850 to restored Diocese of Clifton • appointed 29 September 1850 Apostolic Administrator of Diocese of Plymouth until 22 June 1851 • translated to Birmingham 22 June 1851 to restored Diocese of Nottingham • appointed 23 February 1853 titular Bishop of *Martyropolis* and retired to Birmingham thence to Taunton • died 14 November 1866 at Taunton aged 75 • buried at the Franciscan Convent, Taunton • reinterred 4 October 1997 at St George's Church, Taunton. • *Franciscan Convent, Billet Street, TAUNTON TA1 3NN*

I.   † Rt Rev. Dr **GEORGE ERRINGTON** DD: born 14 September 1804 at Clints Hall, Marske, Richmond • ordained priest (Northern District) 22 December 1827 at Rome, Italy • ordained Bishop of restored Diocese of Plymouth 25 July 1851 at Salford • translated 30 March 1855 to titular Archbishop of *Trapezus* and appointed coadjutor Archbishop of Westminster • appointed 22 October 1855 Apostolic Administrator of the Diocese of Clifton until 15 February 1857 • resigned 2 July 1862 as coadjutor Archbishop of Westminster • appointed 1 September 1865 parish priest of St Mary's Church, Douglas, Isle of Man • nominated 27 January 1868 Apostolic Delegate in Scotland but declined the appointment 12 August 1868 • appointed Council Father at First Vatican Council 8 December 1869 to 20 October 1870 • retired 1 September 1874 to Prior Park, Bath • died 19 January 1886 at Prior Park, Bath aged 81 • buried at Prior Park College chapel, Bath. • *Prior Park College, Ralph Allan Drive, BATH BA2 5AH*

II.   † Rt Rev. Dr **WILLIAM VAUGHAN** DD: born 14 February 1814 at London • ordained priest (Western District) 10 March 1838 at Prior Park, Bath • ordained Bishop of Plymouth 16 September 1855 at Clifton, Bristol • appointed Council Father at First Vatican Council 8 December 1869 to 20 October 1870 • died 25 October 1902 at Newton Abbot aged 88 • buried at St Augustine's Convent, Newton Abbot • reinterred 13 December 1998 at the Cathedral Church of SS Mary and Boniface, Plymouth. • *St Augustine's Convent, 11 Devon Square, NEWTON ABBOT TQ12 2HN*

    a.   † Rt Rev. Dr **CHARLES MORICE GRAHAM** DD: see **III.** below.

III.   † Rt Rev. Dr **CHARLES MORICE GRAHAM** DD: born 5 April 1834 at Mhow (Madhya Pradesh), India • ordained priest (Plymouth) 19 December 1857 at Rome, Italy • ordained titular Bishop of *Cisamus* and appointed coadjutor Bishop of Plymouth 28 October 1891 at Plymouth • succeeded 25 October 1902 as Bishop of Plymouth • appointed 1 February 1911 titular Bishop of *Tiberias* and retired to Hayle • died 2 September 1912 at Hayle aged 78 • buried at Plymouth Cemetery • reinterred 13 December 1998 at the Cathedral Church of SS Mary and Boniface, Plymouth. • *The Downes, Foundry Hill, HAYLE TR27 4HW*

IV.   † Rt Rev. Dr **JOHN JOSEPH KEILY** DD: born 23 June 1854 at Limerick City (Limerick), Ireland • ordained priest (Plymouth) 18 May 1877 at Plymouth • ordained Bishop of Plymouth 13 June 1911 at Plymouth • died 23 September 1928 at Newton Abbot aged 74 • buried at St Augustine's Convent, Newton Abbot • reinterred 13 December 1998 at the Cathedral Church of SS Mary and Boniface, Plymouth. • *St Augustine's Convent, 11 Devon Square, NEWTON ABBOT TQ12 2HN*

V.   † Rt Rev. Dr **JOHN PATRICK BARRETT** BA DD PhD: born 31 October 1878 at Liverpool • ordained priest (Liverpool) 9 June 1906 at Upholland, Skelmersdale • ordained titular Bishop of *Assus* and appointed auxiliary Bishop of Birmingham 22 February 1927 at the Metropolitan Cathedral Church of St Chad, Birmingham • translated 7 June 1929 to Diocese of Plymouth • died 2 November 1946 at Torquay aged 68 • buried at the Abbey Church of St Mary, Buckfastleigh. • *Stoodley Knowle Convent, Ansteys Cove Road, TORQUAY TQ1 2JB*

VI. † Rt Rev. Dr **FRANCIS EDWARD JOSEPH GRIMSHAW**
DD: born 6 October 1901 at Bridgwater • ordained priest (Clifton) 27
February 1926 at Bristol • ordained Bishop of Plymouth 25 July 1947
at Plymouth • translated 11 May 1954 to Archdiocese of Birmingham •
appointed Council Father at Second Vatican Council 11 October 1962
to 21 November 1964 • died 22 March 1965 at Edgbaston, Birmingham aged 63 • buried at St Mary's College, Oscott, Sutton Coldfield.
• *Archbishop's House, 6 Norfolk Road, Edgbaston, BIRMINGHAM B15 3QD*

VII. † Rt Rev. **CYRIL EDWARD RESTIEAUX**: born 25 February 1910 at
Norwich • ordained priest (Nottingham) 1 November 1932 at Rome, Italy •
ordained Bishop of Plymouth 14 June 1955 at Plymouth • appointed Council
Father at Second Vatican Council 11 October 1962 to 8 December 1965 •
retired 15 January 1986 to Torquay • died 26 February 1996 at Torquay aged
86 • buried at the Cathedral Church of SS Mary and Boniface, Plymouth.
• *Stoodley Knowle Convent, Ansteys Cove Road, TORQUAY TQ1 2JB*

VIII. ® Rt Rev. Dr **HUGH CHRISTOPHER BUDD** PhL STL STD:
born 27 May 1937 at Romford • ordained priest (Brentwood) 8 July
1962 at Rome, Italy • ordained Bishop of Plymouth 15 January 1986
at Plymouth • retired 9 November 2013 to St Mary's, Isles of Scilly.
• *Star of the Sea, Strand, St Mary's, ISLES OF SCILLY TR21 0PT* (DEC-JUN)
• *The Presbytery, Silver Street, LYME REGIS DT7 3HS* (JUN-NOV)

IX. Rt Rev. **MARK O'TOOLE** BSc BD MPhil STL: born 22 June 1963 at
Southwark, London • ordained priest (Westminster) 9 June 1990 at the
Metropolitan Cathedral Church of the Most Precious Blood, Westminster,
London • ordained Bishop of Plymouth 28 January 2014 at Plymouth.
• *Bishop's House, 31 Wyndham Street West, PLYMOUTH PL1 5RZ*

DIOCESE OF PORTSMOUTH

(Dioecesis Portus Magni)

By Apostolic Brief of Pope Leo XIII, dated 19 May 1882, the Diocese of Portsmouth was formed by division of the Diocese of Southwark, with the episcopal see fixed at the Cathedral Church of St John the Evangelist, Portsmouth (1882–), consecrated on 29 March 1887.

From 19 May 1882, the Diocese of Portsmouth was a suffragan see within the Province of Westminster. At first, the Diocese of Portsmouth comprised the counties of Hampshire, Berkshire (south of the River Thames), Oxfordshire (south of the River Thames), with the islands of Wight, Jersey, Guernsey and others adjacent.

By Letters Apostolic (*Si qua est*) of Pope St Pius X, dated 28 October 1911, the Province of Westminster was divided into three new provinces of Birmingham, Liverpool and Westminster, with the Diocese of Portsmouth remaining part of the Province of Westminster. The episcopal see remained at the Cathedral Church of St John the Evangelist, Portsmouth (1882–).

By Letters Apostolic (*Romanorum pontificum*) of Pope Bl. Paul VI, dated 28 May 1965, the Province of Westminster was divided further into two new provinces of Southwark and Westminster, with the Diocese of Portsmouth being made part of the newly erected Province of Southwark. The episcopal see remained at the Cathedral Church of St John the Evangelist, Portsmouth (1882–).

The Diocese today comprises the counties of Hampshire, Oxfordshire (south of the River Thames), the Boroughs of Bournemouth and Christchurch in Dorset (except the parish of Kinson and Ensbury Park in Bournemouth), the unitary authorities of Bracknell Forest, Reading, West Berkshire, Windsor and Maidenhead and Wokingham, with the Isle of Wight and the Channel Islands.

I. † Rt Rev. Dr **JOHN VIRTUE (VERTUE)** DD: born 28 April 1826 at Holborn, London • ordained priest (Westminster) 20 December 1851 at Rome, Italy • entered diplomatic service to the Holy See 1853 at Rome, Italy • commissioned as military chaplain 1855 • released from military service 3 June 1882 • ordained Bishop of newly erected Diocese of Portsmouth 25 July 1882 at South Kensington, London • died 23 May 1900 at Portsmouth aged 74 • buried at Highland Road Cemetery, Southsea. • *Bishop's House, Edinburgh Road, PORTSMOUTH PO1 3HG*

    a. † Rt Rev. **JOHN BAPTIST CAHILL** BA: see **II.** below.

II. † Rt Rev. **JOHN BAPTIST CAHILL** BA: born 2 September 1841 at London • ordained priest (Southwark) 4 October 1864 at Bermondsey, London • ordained titular Bishop of *Thagora* and appointed auxiliary Bishop of Portsmouth 1 May 1900 at Portsmouth • translated 30 August 1900 to Diocese of Portsmouth • died 2 August 1910 at Portsmouth aged 68 • buried at Ryde Cemetery. • *Bishop's House, Edinburgh Road, PORTSMOUTH PO1 3HG*

    a. † Rt Rev. **WILLIAM TIMOTHY COTTER**: see **III.** below.

III. † Rt Rev. **WILLIAM TIMOTHY COTTER**: born 21 December 1866 at Cloyne (Cork), Ireland • ordained priest (Portsmouth) 19 June 1892 at Portsmouth • ordained titular Bishop of *Clazomenae* and appointed auxiliary Bishop of Portsmouth 19 March 1905 at Portsmouth • translated 24 November 1910 to Diocese of Portsmouth • died 24 October 1940 at Portsmouth aged 73 • buried at Waterlooville Convent Cemetery. • *Bishop's House, Edinburgh Road, PORTSMOUTH PO1 3HG*

    a. † Rt Rev. Dr **JOHN HENRY KING** PhD: see **IV.** below.

IV. † Most Rev. Dr **JOHN HENRY KING** PhD: born 16 September 1880 at Wardour, Salisbury • ordained priest (Portsmouth) 20 November 1904 at Jersey • ordained titular Bishop of *Opus* and appointed auxiliary Bishop of Portsmouth 15 July 1938 at Portsmouth • translated 4 June 1941 to Diocese of Portsmouth • appointed 6 June 1954 *Archbishop ad personam* at Vatican City • died 23 March 1965 at Winchester aged 84 • buried at Winchester Cemetery. • *Bishop's House, 29 Jewry Street, WINCHESTER SO23 8RY*

a. † Rt Rev. Dr **THOMAS HOLLAND** DSC DD PhD DLitt: born 11 June 1908 at Southport • ordained priest (Liverpool) 18 June 1933 at Southport • ordained titular Bishop of *Etenna* and appointed coadjutor Bishop of Portsmouth 21 December 1960 at Portsmouth • appointed Council Father at Second Vatican Council 11 October 1962 to 8 December 1965 • translated 3 September 1964 to Diocese of Salford • retired 21 June 1983 to Prestwich, Manchester • died 30 September 1999 at Prestwich, Manchester aged 91 • buried at the Cathedral Church of St John, Salford. • *Nazareth House, Scholes Lane, Prestwich, MANCHESTER M25 0NU*

V. † Rt Rev. **DEREK JOHN HARFORD WORLOCK** CH: born 4 February 1920 at St John's Wood, London • ordained priest (Westminster) 3 June 1944 at Old Hall Green, Ware • appointed Council Father at Second Vatican Council 14 September 1965 to 8 December 1965 • ordained Bishop of Portsmouth 21 December 1965 at Portsmouth • translated 7 February 1976 to Archdiocese of Liverpool • died 8 February 1996 at Mossley Hill, Liverpool aged 76 • buried at the Metropolitan Cathedral of Christ the King, Liverpool. • *Lowood, Carnatic Road, LIVERPOOL L18 8BY*

VI. † Rt Rev. **ANTHONY JOSEPH EMERY**: born 17 May 1918 at Burton-on-Trent • enlisted as military soldier 1940 • released from military service 1945 • ordained priest (Birmingham) 30 May 1953 at Oscott, Sutton Coldfield • ordained titular Bishop of *Tamallula* and appointed auxiliary Bishop of Birmingham 4 March 1968 at the Metropolitan Cathedral Church of St Chad, Birmingham • translated 5 November 1976 to Diocese of Portsmouth • died 5 April 1988 at Portsmouth aged 69 • buried at Milton Cemetery, Portsmouth. • *Bishop's House, Edinburgh Road, PORTSMOUTH PO1 3HG*

VII. ® Rt Rev. Dr **ROGER FRANCIS CRISPIAN HOLLIS** MA STL LLD: born 17 November 1936 at Bristol • ordained priest (Clifton)

11 July 1965 at Rome, Italy • ordained titular Bishop of *Cincari* and appointed auxiliary Bishop of Birmingham 5 May 1987 at the Metropolitan Cathedral Church of St Chad, Birmingham • translated 27 January 1989 to Diocese of Portsmouth • retired 11 July 2012 to Mells, Frome. • *Stable House, Fairview, Mells, FROME BA11 3PP*

VIII.   Rt Rev. Dr **PHILIP ANTHONY EGAN** BA STL PhD: born 14 November 1955 at Altrincham • ordained priest (Shrewsbury) 4 August 1984 at Altrincham • ordained Bishop of Portsmouth 24 September 2012 at Portsmouth. • *Bishop's House, Bishop Crispian Way, PORTSMOUTH PO1 3HG*

DIOCESE OF SALFORD

(Dioecesis Salfordensis)

By Letters Apostolic (*Universalis ecclesiae*) of Pope Bl. Pius IX, dated 29 September 1850, the Diocese of Salford was formed, with the episcopal see fixed at the Cathedral Church of St John the Evangelist, Salford (1850–), consecrated on 14 June 1890.

The Diocese of Salford was an original suffragan see within the Province of Westminster. At first, the Diocese of Salford comprised the Hundreds of Salford, Blackburn and Leyland in the County of Lancashire. By a re-script of the Letters Apostolic (*Universalis ecclesiae*) of Pope Bl. Pius IX, dated 27 June 1851, the Hundred of Leyland in the County of Lancashire was transferred from the Diocese of Salford to the Diocese of Liverpool, thus correcting a geographical error inherent in the original document.

By Letters Apostolic (*Si qua est*) of Pope St Pius X, dated 28 October 1911, the Province of Westminster was divided into three new Provinces of Birmingham, Liverpool and Westminster, with the Diocese of Salford being made part of the Province of Liverpool. The episcopal see remained at the Cathedral Church of St John the Evangelist, Salford (1850–).

The Diocese today comprises the Hundreds of Salford and Blackburn in the County of Lancashire.

a.   **APOSTOLIC ADMINISTRATOR:** † Rt Rev. Dr **GEORGE HILARY BROWN** DD: born 13 January 1786 at Clifton-in-the-Fylde, Preston • ordained priest (Northern District) 13 June 1810 at Ushaw, Durham • ordained titular Bishop of *Bugia* and appointed Vicar Apostolic for the Lancashire District 24 August 1840 at Vauxhall, Liverpool • appointed 22 April 1842 titular Bishop of *Tlos* • translated 29 September 1850 to restored Diocese of Liverpool • appointed 29 September 1850 Apostolic Administrator of the Diocese of Salford until 25 July 1851 • died 25 January 1856 at Litherland, Liverpool aged 70 • buried at St Oswald's Church, Old Swan, Liverpool.
• *17 Catharine Street, LIVERPOOL L8 7NH*

I.   † Rt Rev. Dr **WILLIAM TURNER** DD: born 25 September 1799 at Whittingham Hall, Preston • ordained priest (Northern District) 17 December 1825 at Rome, Italy • ordained Bishop of restored Diocese of Salford 25 July 1851 at Salford • appointed Council Father at First Vatican Council 8 December 1869 to 20 October 1870 • died 13 July 1872 at Salford aged 72 • buried at Salford Cemetery • reinterred 1 August 1875 at St Joseph's Cemetery, Moston, Manchester.
• *Bishop's House, Marlborough Road, SALFORD*

II.   † Rt Rev. Dr **HERBERT ALFRED HENRY VAUGHAN** DD: born 15 April 1832 at Gloucester • ordained priest (Westminster) 28 October 1854 at Lucca (Lucca), Italy • ordained Bishop of Salford 28 October 1872 at Salford • translated 29 March 1892 to Archdiocese of Westminster • elevated 16 January 1893 to Cardinal-Priest of Santi Andrea e Gregorio Magno al Monte Celio • died 19 June 1903 at Mill Hill, London aged 71 • buried at Mill Hill, London • reinterred 14 March 2005 at the Metropolitan Cathedral Church of the Most Precious Blood, Westminster, London.
• *Archbishop's House, 22 Carlisle Place, LONDON SW1P 1JA*

III.   † Rt Rev. Dr **JOHN BILSBORROW** DD: born 30 March 1836 at Singleton Lodge, Kirkham, Preston • ordained priest (Liverpool) 26 February 1865 at St Edward's College, Liverpool • ordained Bishop of Salford 24 August 1892 at Salford • died 5 March 1903 at Babbacombe, Torquay aged 66 • buried at St Joseph's Cemetery, Moston, Manchester.
• *7 Carlton Road, MANCHESTER*

IV.   † Rt Rev. Dr **LOUIS CHARLES CASARTELLI** DD DLitt MA: born 14 November 1852 at Cheetham Hill, Manchester • ordained priest (Salford) 10 September 1876 at Salford • ordained Bishop of Salford 21 September 1903 at Salford • died 18 January 1925 at Salford aged 72 • buried at St Joseph's Cemetery, Moston, Manchester. • *St Bede's College, Alexandra Road South, MANCHESTER M16 8HX*

a.   † Rt Rev. Dr **JOHN STEPHEN VAUGHAN** DD: born 24 January 1853 at Courtfield, Ross-on-Wye • ordained priest (Salford) 4 June 1876 at Salford • ordained titular Bishop of *Sebastopolis in Armenia* and appointed auxiliary Bishop of Salford 15 August 1909 at the Metropolitan Cathedral Church of the Most Precious Blood, Westminster, London • died 4 December 1925 at Great Harwood, Blackburn aged 72 • buried at St Hubert's Cemetery, Great Harwood, Blackburn. • *St Hubert's Presbytery, St Hubert's Street, Great Harwood, BLACKBURN BB6 7BE*

V.   † Rt Rev. Dr **THOMAS HENSHAW** DD: born 2 February 1873 at Miles Platting, Manchester • ordained priest (Salford) 18 October 1899 at Lisbon (Lisboa), Portugal • ordained Bishop of Salford 21 December 1925 at Salford • died 23 September 1938 at Worsley, Manchester aged 65 • buried at St Mary's Cemetery, Worsley, Manchester. • *Wardley Hall, Wardley Hall Road, Worsley, MANCHESTER M28 2ND*

VI.   † Rt Rev. **HENRY VINCENT MARSHALL**: born 19 July 1884 at Listowel (Kerry), Ireland • ordained priest (Salford) 24 June 1908 at Dublin City (Dublin), Ireland • ordained Bishop of Salford 21 September 1939 at Salford • died 14 April 1955 at Whalley Range, Manchester aged 70 • buried at St Joseph's Cemetery, Moston, Manchester. • *Wardley Hall, Wardley Hall Road, Worsley, MANCHESTER M28 2ND*

VII.   † Rt Rev. Dr **GEORGE ANDREW BECK** AA BA LLD: born 28 May 1904 at Streatham, London • ordained priest (Augustinians of the Assumption) 24 July 1927 at Louvain (Flemish Brabant), Belgium • ordained titular Bishop of *Tigias* and appointed coadjutor Bishop of Brentwood 21 September 1948 at the Metropolitan Cathedral Church of the Most Precious Blood, Westminster, London • succeeded 23 January 1951 as Bishop of Brentwood • translated 28 November 1955 to Diocese of Salford • appointed Council Father at Second Vatican Council 11 October

1962 to 8 December 1965 • translated 29 January 1964 to Archdiocese of Liverpool • retired 11 February 1976 to Upholland, Skelmersdale • died 13 September 1978 at Mossley Hill, Liverpool aged 74 • buried at the Metropolitan Cathedral Crypt of Christ the King, Liverpool. • *St Joseph's College, College Road, Upholland, SKELMERSDALE WN8 0PY*

VIII.   † Rt Rev. Dr **THOMAS HOLLAND** DSC DD PhD DLitt: born 11 June 1908 at Southport • ordained priest (Liverpool) 18 June 1933 at Southport • ordained titular Bishop of *Etenna* and appointed coadjutor Bishop of Portsmouth 21 December 1960 at Portsmouth • appointed Council Father at Second Vatican Council 11 October 1962 to 8 December 1965 • translated 3 September 1964 to Diocese of Salford • retired 21 June 1983 to Prestwich, Manchester • died 30 September 1999 at Prestwich, Manchester aged 91 • buried at the Cathedral Church of St John, Salford. • *Nazareth House, Scholes Lane, Prestwich, MANCHESTER M25 0NU*

a.   † Rt Rev. **GEOFFREY IGNATIUS BURKE** MA: born 31 July 1913 at Alexandra Park, Manchester • ordained priest (Salford) 29 June 1937 at Oscott, Sutton Coldfield • ordained titular Bishop of *Vagrauta* and appointed auxiliary Bishop of Salford 29 June 1967 at Salford • retired 31 July 1988 to Prestwich, Manchester thence to Longsight, Manchester • died 13 October 1999 at City of Manchester aged 86 • buried at St Mary's Cemetery, Worsley, Manchester. • *St Joseph's Home, 52 Plymouth Grove West, MANCHESTER M13 0AR*

IX.   ® Rt Rev. Dr **PATRICK ALTHAM KELLY** KC*HS DD LLD STL PhL: born 23 November 1938 at Morecambe • ordained priest (Lancaster) 18 February 1962 at Rome, Italy • ordained Bishop of Salford 3 April 1984 at Salford • translated 3 July 1996 to Archdiocese of Liverpool • resigned 27 February 2013 as Archbishop of Liverpool and retired to Southport. • *St Marie's House, 27 Seabank Road, SOUTHPORT PR9 0EJ*

X.   ® Rt Rev. **TERENCE JOHN BRAIN**: born 19 December 1938 at Coventry • ordained priest (Birmingham) 22 February 1964 at the Metropolitan Cathedral Church of St Chad, Birmingham • ordained titular Bishop of *Amudarsa* and appointed auxiliary Bishop of Birmingham 25 April 1991 at the Metropolitan Cathedral Church of St Chad, Birmingham • translated 7 October 1997

to Diocese of Salford • retired 30 September 2014 to Middleton, Manchester.
• *106 Crow Hill South, Middleton, MANCHESTER M24 1JU*

XI. Rt Rev. Dr **JOHN STANLEY KENNETH ARNOLD** LLB MA
JCD: born 12 June 1953 at Sheffield • professed (Institute of Charity) 19
March 1978 at Wonersh, Guildford • ordained priest (Westminster) 16
July 1983 at the Metropolitan Cathedral Church of the Most Precious
Blood, Westminster, London • ordained titular Bishop of *Lindisfarna*
and appointed auxiliary Bishop of Westminster 2 February 2006 at the
Metropolitan Cathedral Church of the Most Precious Blood, West-
minster, London • translated 30 September 2014 to Diocese of Salford.
• *Wardley Hall, Wardley Hall Road, Worsley, MANCHESTER M28 2ND*

DIOCESE OF SHREWSBURY

(Dioecesis Salopiensis)

By Letters Apostolic (*Universalis ecclesiae*) of Pope Bl. Pius IX, dated 29 September 1850, the Diocese of Shrewsbury was formed, with the episcopal see fixed at the Cathedral Church of Our Lady Help of Christians and St Peter of Alcantara, Shrewsbury (1856–), consecrated on 21 May 1891.

The Diocese of Shrewsbury was an original suffragan see within the Province of Westminster. At first, the Diocese of Shrewsbury comprised the counties of Anglesey, Caernarfon, Denbigh, Flint, Merioneth, Montgomery and Wrexham, with Cheshire and Shropshire.

By Apostolic Brief (*De animarum salute*) of Pope Leo XIII, dated 4 March 1895, the whole Principality of Wales except Glamorgan and Monmouthshire was made a separate Vicariate by division of the Diocese of Shrewsbury, taking the counties of Anglesey, Caernarfon, Denbigh, Flint, Merioneth, Montgomery and Wrexham from the Diocese of Shrewsbury.

By Letters Apostolic (*Si qua est*) of Pope St Pius X, dated 28 October 1911, the Province of Westminster was divided into three new Provinces of Birmingham, Liverpool and Westminster, with the Diocese of Shrewsbury being made part of the Province of Birmingham. The episcopal see remained at the Cathedral Church of Our Lady Help of Christians and St Peter of Alcantara, Shrewsbury (1856–).

The diocese today comprises the counties of Shropshire, Cheshire (south of the River Mersey) and the unitary authorities of Halton (south of the River Mersey), Stockport, Telford and the Wrekin and the Wirral.

a. **APOSTOLIC ADMINISTRATOR:** † Rt Rev. Dom. **THOMAS JOSEPH BROWN** OSB DD: born 2 May 1798 at Bath • professed (Order of Saint Benedict) 28 October 1814 at Downside, Radstock • ordained priest (Order of Saint Benedict) 7 April 1823 at London • ordained titular Bishop of *Apollonia* and appointed Vicar Apostolic for the Welsh District 28 October 1840 at Bath • translated 29 September 1850 to restored Diocese of Newport and Menevia • appointed 29 September 1850 Apostolic Administrator of the Diocese of Shrewsbury until 27 July 1851 • died 12 April 1880 at Lower Bullingham, Hereford aged 81 • buried at the Abbey Church of St Michael and All Angels, Belmont, Hereford. • *Manor House, Lower Bullingham, HEREFORD HR2 6EG*

I. † Rt Rev. Dr **JAMES BROWN** DD: born 11 January 1812 at Wolverhampton • ordained priest (Midland District) 18 February 1837 at Oscott, Sutton Coldfield • ordained Bishop of restored Diocese of Shrewsbury 27 July 1851 at the Cathedral Church of St George, Southwark, London • died 14 October 1881 at Grange Bank Farm, Shrewsbury aged 69 • buried at Pantasaph, Holywell. • *St Mary's Grange, Talcott Drive, SHREWSBURY SY3 9DQ*

a. † Rt Rev. **EDMUND KNIGHT**: see **II.** below.

II. † Rt Rev. **EDMUND KNIGHT**: born 27 August 1827 at Sheffield • ordained priest (Birmingham) 19 December 1857 at Rome, Italy • ordained titular Bishop of *Corycus* and appointed auxiliary Bishop of Shrewsbury 25 July 1879 at Birkenhead • translated 25 April 1882 to Diocese of Shrewsbury • Diocese of Shrewsbury restructured 4 March 1895 • appointed 11 May 1895 titular Bishop of *Flavias* and retired to Kensington, London • died 9 June 1905 at Kensington, London aged 77 • buried at Flaybrick Cemetery, Birkenhead. • *25 Kensington Court, LONDON W8 5DP*

a. † Rt Rev. **JOHN CARROLL**: see **III.** below.

III.   † Rt Rev. **JOHN CARROLL**: born 16 March 1838 at Castleblayney (Monaghan), Ireland • ordained priest (Shrewsbury) 22 December 1861 at Bruges (West Flanders), Belgium • ordained titular Bishop of *Acmonia* and appointed coadjutor Bishop of Shrewsbury 28 October 1893 at Birkenhead • succeeded 11 May 1895 as Bishop of Shrewsbury • died 14 January 1897 at Oxton, Birkenhead aged 58 • buried at Dukinfield Cemetery. • *Spring Villa, Roslin Road, Oxton, PRENTON CH43 5TE*

IV.   † Rt Rev. **SAMUEL WEBSTER ALLEN**: born 23 March 1844 at Stockport • ordained priest (Shrewsbury) 4 December 1870 at Liscard, Wallasey • ordained Bishop of Shrewsbury 16 June 1897 at Shrewsbury • died 13 May 1908 at Shrewsbury aged 64 • buried at Shrewsbury Cemetery. • *Cathedral House, 11 Belmont, SHREWSBURY SY1 1TE*

V.   † Rt Rev. **HUGH SINGLETON**: born 30 July 1851 at Birkenhead • ordained priest (Shrewsbury) 25 July 1880 at Birkenhead • ordained Bishop of Shrewsbury 21 September 1908 at Seacombe, Wallasey • died 17 December 1934 at Birkenhead aged 83 • buried at Landican Cemetery, Birkenhead. • *39 Beresford Road, PRENTON CH43 2JD*

    a.   † Rt Rev. Dr **AMBROSE JAMES MORIARTY** DD: see **VI.** below.

VI.   † Rt Rev. Dr **AMBROSE JAMES MORIARTY** DD: born 7 August 1870 at Stockport • ordained priest (Shrewsbury) 10 March 1894 at Shrewsbury • ordained titular Bishop of *Miletopolis* and appointed coadjutor Bishop of Shrewsbury 28 January 1932 at Shrewsbury • succeeded 17 December 1934 as Bishop of Shrewsbury • died 3 June 1949 at Shrewsbury aged 78 • buried at Shrewsbury Cemetery. • *The Council House, Castle Gates, SHREWSBURY SY1 2AQ*

    a.   † Rt Rev. Dr **JOHN ALOYSIUS MURPHY** DD: see **VII.** below.

VII.   † Rt Rev. Dr **JOHN ALOYSIUS MURPHY** DD: born 21 December 1905 at Birkenhead • ordained priest (Shrewsbury) 21 March 1931 at Lisbon (Lisboa), Portugal • ordained titular Bishop of *Appia* and appointed coadjutor Bishop of Shrewsbury 25 February 1948 at Chester • succeeded 3 June 1949 as Bishop of Shrewsbury • translated 26 August 1961 to Archdiocese of Cardiff • appointed Council Father at Second Vatican

Council 11 October 1962 to 8 December 1965 • retired 25 March 1983 to Malpas, Newport • died 18 November 1995 at Malpas, Newport aged 89 • buried at the Abbey Church of St Joseph, Llantarnam, Cwmbran.
• *St Joseph's Hospital, Harding Avenue, NEWPORT NP20 6ZE*

VIII.   † Rt Rev. Dr **WILLIAM ERIC GRASAR** JCD STL: born 18 May 1913 at Scunthorpe • ordained priest (Nottingham) 18 December 1937 at Nottingham • ordained Bishop of Shrewsbury 27 June 1962 at Shrewsbury • appointed Council Father at Second Vatican Council 11 October 1962 to 8 December 1965 • retired 30 August 1980 to Altrincham • died 28 December 1982 at Sefton Park, Liverpool aged 69 • buried at Our Lady's Church, Birkenhead.
• *St Vincent's Church, 2 Bentinck Road, ALTRINCHAM WA14 2BP*

a.   † Rt Rev. **JOHN (JACK) BREWER** STL JCL PhL: born 24 November 1929 at Burnage, Manchester • ordained priest (Shrewsbury) 8 July 1956 at Rome, Italy • ordained titular Bishop of *Britonia* and appointed auxiliary Bishop of Shrewsbury 28 July 1971 at Stockport • translated 15 November 1983 to coadjutor Bishop of Lancaster • succeeded 22 May 1985 as Bishop of Lancaster • died 10 June 2000 at Allithwaite, Grange-over-Sands aged 70 • buried at the Cathedral Churchyard of St Peter, Lancaster.
• *Bishop's House, Cannon Hill, LANCASTER LA1 5NG*

IX.   † Rt Rev. Dr **JOSEPH GRAY** JCD: born 20 October 1919 at Finternagh (Cavan), Ireland • ordained priest (Birmingham) 20 June 1943 at Cavan City (Cavan), Ireland • ordained titular Bishop of *Mercia* and appointed auxiliary Bishop of Liverpool 16 February 1969 at the Metropolitan Cathedral Church of Christ the King, Liverpool • translated 30 August 1980 to Diocese of Shrewsbury • retired 30 August 1995 to Birkenhead • died 7 May 1999 at Birkenhead aged 79 • buried at St Winefride's Church, Neston.
• *Bishop's House, 99 Eleanor Road, BIRKENHEAD CH43 7QW*

X.   ® Rt Rev. **BRIAN MICHAEL NOBLE**: born 11 April 1936 at Lancaster • ordained priest (Lancaster) 11 June 1960 at Lancaster • ordained Bishop of Shrewsbury 30 August 1995 at Wythenshawe, Manchester • retired 1 October 2010 to Heswall, Wirral.
• *Laburnum Cottage, 97 Barnston Road, Heswall, WIRRAL CH61 1BW*

a.   Rt Rev. **MARK DAVIES** BA: see **XI.** below.

XI.   Rt Rev. **MARK DAVIES** BA: born 12 May 1959 at Longsight, Manchester • ordained priest (Salford) 11 February 1984 at Reddish, Stockport • ordained coadjutor Bishop of Shrewsbury 22 February 2010 at Wythenshawe, Manchester • succeeded 1 October 2010 as Bishop of Shrewsbury. • *21 Churchwood View, LYMM WA13 0PU*

DIOCESE OF SOUTHWARK

(Dioecesis Southvarcensis)

By Letters Apostolic (*Universalis ecclesiae*) of Pope Bl. Pius IX, dated 29 September 1850, the Diocese of Southwark was formed, with the episcopal see fixed at the Cathedral Church of St George, Southwark, London (1850–1965), opened on 4 July 1848, consecrated on 7 November 1894, destroyed by fire bombs on 16 April 1941, rebuilt and consecrated again on 4 July 1958.

The Diocese of Southwark was an original suffragan see within the Province of Westminster. At first, the Diocese of Southwark comprised the counties of Berkshire (south of the River Thames), Hampshire, Surrey, Sussex and Kent, including the London boroughs south of the River Thames, with the islands of Wight, Jersey, Guernsey and others adjacent.

By Apostolic Brief of Pope Leo XIII, dated 19 May 1882, the Diocese of Portsmouth was formed by division of the Diocese of Southwark, taking the counties of Berkshire (south of the River Thames) and Hampshire, with the islands of Wight, Jersey, Guernsey and others adjacent from the Diocese of Southwark.

By Letters Apostolic (*Si qua est*) of Pope St Pius X, dated 28 October 1911, the Province of Westminster was divided into three new provinces of Birmingham, Liverpool and Westminster, with the Diocese of Southwark remaining part of the

Province of Westminster. The episcopal see remained at the Cathedral Church of St George, Southwark, London (1850–1965).

a.　**APOSTOLIC ADMINISTRATOR:** † + *His Eminence* **Cardinal** Dr **NICHOLAS PATRICK STEPHEN WISEMAN** DD: born 3 August 1802 at Seville (Sevilla), Spain • ordained priest (Northern District) 19 March 1825 at Rome, Italy • ordained titular Bishop of *Milopotamos* and appointed coadjutor Vicar Apostolic for the Midland District 8 June 1840 at Rome, Italy • translated 3 July 1840 to coadjutor Vicar Apostolic of the Central District • translated 29 August 1847 to coadjutor Vicar Apostolic of the London District • succeeded 18 February 1849 as Vicar Apostolic of the London District • translated 29 September 1850 to Archbishop and Metropolitan of newly raised and restored Archdiocese and Province of Westminster • appointed 29 September 1850 Apostolic Administrator of Diocese of Southwark until 4 July 1851 • elevated 30 September 1850 to Cardinal-Priest of Santa Pudenziana • died 15 February 1865 at Portman Square, London aged 62 • buried at St Mary's Cemetery, Kensal Green, London • reinterred 15 February 1907 at the Metropolitan Cathedral Church of the Most Precious Blood, Westminster, London. • *Archbishop's House, 8 York Place, LONDON W1H 6LA*

I.　† Rt Rev. Dr **THOMAS GRANT** DD: born 25 November 1816 at Ligny-lès-Aire (Pas-de-Calais), France • ordained priest 28 November 1841 at Rome, Italy • ordained Bishop of restored Diocese of Southwark 4 July 1851 at Rome, Italy • appointed Council Father at First Vatican Council 8 December 1869 • died 1 June 1870 at Rome, Italy aged 53 • buried at Upper Norwood, London. • *St George's Cathedral, Westminster Bridge Road, LONDON SE1 7HY*

II.　† Rt Rev. **JAMES DANELL**: born 14 July 1821 at Hampstead, London • ordained priest (London District) 6 June 1846 at Paris (Paris), France • ordained Bishop of Southwark 25 March 1871 at the Cathedral Church of St George, Southwark, London • died 14 June 1881 at Southwark, London aged 59 • buried at the Cathedral Church of St George, Southwark, London. • *St George's Cathedral, Westminster Bridge Road, LONDON SE1 7HY*

III.　† *CE* Rt Rev. Dr **ROBERT ASTON COFFIN** CSsR MA DD: born 19 July 1819 at Brighton • ordained Church of England deacon (Oxford) 18 December 1842 at Oxford • ordained Church of England priest (Oxford) 17

December 1843 at Oxford • received into Catholic Church 3 December 1845 at Prior Park, Bath • ordained priest (Confederation of Oratorians of St Philip Neri) 31 October 1847 at Rome, Italy • professed (Congregation of the Most Holy Redeemer) 2 February 1852 at Saint-Trond (Liège), Belgium • ordained Bishop of newly restructured Diocese of Southwark 11 June 1882 at Rome, Italy • died 6 April 1885 at Teignmouth aged 65 • buried at Teignmouth. • *St George's Cathedral, Westminster Bridge Road, LONDON SE1 7HY*

    a.   † Rt Rev. Dr **JOHN BAPTIST BUTT** DD: see **IV.** below.

IV.   † Rt Rev. Dr **JOHN BAPTIST BUTT** DD: born 20 April 1826 at Richmond • ordained priest (London District) 15 July 1849 at Hammersmith, London • commissioned as military chaplain 21 September 1854 • released from military service 1860 • ordained titular Bishop of *Milo* and appointed auxiliary Bishop of Southwark 29 January 1885 at Arundel • translated 26 June 1885 to Diocese of Southwark • appointed 9 April 1897 titular Bishop of *Sebastopolis in Thracia* and retired to Brighton thence to Arundel • died 1 November 1899 at Arundel aged 73 • buried at St John's College, Wonersh, Guildford. • *St Philip's, 2 Parsons Hill, ARUNDEL BN18 9AY*

    a.   † Rt Rev. FRANCIS ALPHONSUS BOURNE: see **V.** below.

V.   † Rt Rev. FRANCIS ALPHONSUS BOURNE: born 23 March 1861 at Clapham, London • ordained priest (Southwark) 11 June 1884 at Clapham, London • ordained titular Bishop of *Epiphania in Cilicia* and appointed coadjutor Bishop of Southwark 1 May 1896 at the Cathedral Church of St George, Southwark, London • succeeded 9 April 1897 as Bishop of Southwark • translated 11 September 1903 to Archdiocese of Westminster • elevated 27 November 1911 to Cardinal-Priest of Santa Pudenziana • Archdiocese of Westminster restructured 22 March 1917 • died 1 January 1935 at Westminster, London aged 73 • buried at St Edmund's College, Old Hall Green, Ware. • *Archbishop's House, Ambrosden Avenue, LONDON SW1P 1QJ*

VI.   † Most Rev. **PETER EMMANUEL AMIGO**: born 26 May 1864 at Gibraltar • ordained priest (Westminster) 25 February 1888 at South Kensington, London • ordained Bishop of Southwark 25 March 1904 at the Cathedral Church of St George, Southwark, London • appointed 25 February 1938 *Archbishop ad personam* at Vatican City • died 1 October 1949 at Southwark, London

aged 85 • buried at the Cathedral Church of St George, Southwark, London.
• *Bishop's House, 150 St George's Road, LONDON SE1 6HX*

a.   † Rt Rev. **WILLIAM FRANCIS BROWN**: born 3 May 1862
at Dundee • received into Catholic Church 1880 at Kensington,
London • ordained priest (Southwark) 20 March 1886 at the
Cathedral Church of St George, Southwark, London • appointed
1 June 1917 Apostolic Visitor to Scotland until 1 February 1920 •
ordained titular Bishop of *Pella* and appointed auxiliary Bishop
of Southwark 12 May 1924 at the Cathedral Church of St George,
Southwark, London • died 16 December 1951 at Vauxhall,
London aged 89 • buried at St Anne's Church, Vauxhall, London.
• *St Anne's Rectory, 363 Kennington Lane, LONDON SE11 5QY*

VII.   † Rt Rev. **CYRIL CONRAD COWDEROY**: born 5 May 1905
at Sidcup • ordained priest (Southwark) 30 May 1931 at the Cathedral
Church of St George, Southwark, London • ordained Bishop of Southwark
21 December 1949 at the Metropolitan Cathedral Church of the Most
Precious Blood, Westminster, London • appointed Council Father at
Second Vatican Council 11 October 1962 to 8 December 1965 • Archdiocese of Southwark restructured 28 May 1965 • appointed 28 May 1965
Archbishop and Metropolitan of newly raised Archdiocese and Province
of Southwark • died 10 October 1976 at West Malling aged 71 • buried
at the Metropolitan Cathedral Church of St George, Southwark, London.
• *Archbishop's House, 150 St George's Road, LONDON SE1 6HX*

ARCHDIOCESE OF SOUTHWARK

(Archidioecesis Southvarcensis)

By Letters Apostolic (*Romanorum pontificum*) of Pope Bl. Paul VI, dated 28 May 1965, the Province of Westminster was divided further into two new Provinces of Southwark and Westminster, with the Diocese of Southwark being raised to a metropolitan Archdiocese and province. The episcopal see remained at the Metropolitan Cathedral Church of St George, Southwark, London (1965–).

By the same Letters Apostolic (*Romanorum pontificum*) of Pope Bl. Paul VI, dated 28 May 1965, the Diocese of Arundel and Brighton was formed by division of the Diocese of Southwark, taking the County of Sussex and the part of Surrey (south of the River Thames) lying outside the Greater London boroughs from the newly restructured Archdiocese of Southwark.

The Province of Southwark comprises the Archdiocese of Southwark with the suffragan sees of Arundel and Brighton, Plymouth and Portsmouth. The Archdiocese today comprises those Greater London boroughs south of the River Thames, the County of Kent and the unitary authority of Medway.

VII.   † Most Rev. **CYRIL CONRAD COWDEROY**: born 5 May 1905 at Sidcup • ordained priest (Southwark) 30 May 1931 at the Cathedral Church of St George, Southwark, London • ordained Bishop of Southwark 21 December 1949 at the Metropolitan Cathedral Church of the Most Precious Blood, Westminster, London • appointed Council Father at Second Vatican Council 11 October 1962 to 8 December 1965 • Arch-diocese of Southwark restructured 28 May 1965 • appointed 28 May 1965 Archbishop and Metropolitan of newly raised Archdiocese and Province of Southwark • died 10 October 1976 at West Malling aged 71 • buried at the Metropolitan Cathedral Church of St George, Southwark, London.
• *Archbishop's House, 150 St George's Road, LONDON SE1 6eHX*

a.   † Rt Rev. **CHARLES JOSEPH HENDERSON** KCHS: born 14 April 1924 at Waterford City (Waterford), Ireland • ordained priest (Southwark) 6 June 1948 at Waterford City (Waterford), Ireland • ordained titular Bishop of *Trecalae* and appointed auxiliary Bishop of Southwark 8 December 1972 at the Metropolitan Cathedral Church of St George, Southwark, London • retired 26 January 2001 to Blackheath, London • died 10 April 2006 at Blackheath, London aged 81 • buried at the Metropolitan Cathedral Church of St George, Southwark, London.
• *Park House, 6a Cresswell Park, LONDON SE3 9RD*

VIII.   ® Most Rev. **MICHAEL GEORGE BOWEN** STL PhL: born 23 April 1930 at Gibraltar • ordained priest (Southwark) 6 July 1958 at Rome, Italy • incardinated 28 May 1965 into Diocese of Arundel and Brighton at Storrington, Pulborough • ordained titular Bishop of *Lamsorti* and appointed coadjutor Bishop of Arundel and Brighton 27 June 1970 at Arundel • succeeded 14 March 1971 as Bishop of Arundel and Brighton • translated 23 April 1977 to Archdiocese of Southwark • retired 6 November 2003 to Blackheath, London.
• *54 Parkside, Vanbrugh Fields, LONDON SE3 7QF*

a.   † Rt Rev. Dr Friar **JOHN PETER JUKES** OFM Conv. STL DUniv: born 7 August 1923 at Eltham, London • professed (Order of Friars Minor Conventual) 10 January 1947 at Mossley Hill, Liverpool • ordained priest (Order of Friars Minor Conventual) 20 July 1952 at Mossley Hill, Liverpool • ordained titular Bishop of *Strathernia* and appointed auxiliary Bishop of Southwark 30 January 1980 at the Metropolitan Cathedral Church of St George, Southwark, London • retired 11 December 1998 to West Malling • appointed 2002 parish

priest of St Margaret's Church, Huntly • retired 25 July 2008 to Huntly • died 21 November 2011 at Huntly aged 88 • buried at the Metropolitan Cathedral Church of St George, Southwark, London.
• *Willowbank, Gladstone Road, HUNTLY AB54 8BD*

b.   ℞ Rt Rev. **HOWARD GEORGE TRIPP**: born 3 July 1927 at Croydon • ordained priest (Southwark) 31 May 1953 at South Croydon • ordained titular Bishop of *Neoportus* and appointed auxiliary Bishop of Southwark 30 January 1980 at the Metropolitan Cathedral Church of St George, Southwark, London • retired 7 January 2004 to Wimbledon, London.
• *35 St Catherine's Close, LONDON SW20 9NL*

c.   **APOSTOLIC ADMINISTRATOR:** ℞ Rt Rev. **JOHN FRANK-LIN MELDON HINE** PhL STB: born 26 July 1938 at Tunbridge Wells • ordained priest (Southwark) 28 October 1962 at Rome, Italy • ordained titular Bishop of *Beverlacum* and appointed auxiliary Bishop of Southwark 27 February 2001 at the Metropolitan Cathedral Church of St George, Southwark, London • appointed 7 December 2009 Apostolic Administrator of the Archdiocese of Southwark until 10 June 2010 • retired 31 December 2013 to Tenterden.
• *St Andrew's Presbytery, 47 Ashford Road, TENTERDEN TN30 6LL*

IX.   ℞ Most Rev. Dr **KEVIN JOHN PATRICK McDONALD** BA STL STD: born 18 August 1947 at Stoke-on-Trent • ordained priest (Birmingham) 20 July 1974 at Rome, Italy • ordained Bishop of Northampton 2 May 2001 at Northampton • translated 8 December 2003 to Archdiocese of Southwark • resigned 4 December 2009 as Archbishop of Southwark and retired to Southwark, London.
• *c/o Archbishop's House, 150 St George's Road, LONDON SE1 6HX*

a.   Rt Rev. **PAUL HENDRICKS** BSc MA PhL: born 18 March 1956 at Beckenham • ordained priest (Southwark) 29 July 1984 at Orpington • ordained titular Bishop of *Rossmarkaeum* and appointed auxiliary Bishop of Southwark 14 February 2006 at the Metropolitan Cathedral Church of St George, Southwark, London.
• *95 Carshalton Road, SUTTON SM1 4LL*

b.   Rt Rev. **PATRICK KEVIN LYNCH** SS.CC MA MTh: born 27 April 1947 at Cork City (Cork), Ireland • professed (Congregation of the Sacred Hearts of Jesus and Mary) 23 August 1965 at Cootehill (Cavan), Ireland • ordained priest (Congregation of the Sacred Hearts of Jesus and Mary) 21 July 1972 at Cootehill (Cavan), Ireland • ordained titular Bishop of *Castrum* and appointed auxiliary Bishop of Southwark 14 February 2006 at the Metropolitan Cathedral Church of St George, Southwark, London.
• *Park House, 6a Cresswell Park, LONDON, SE3 9RD*

X.   Most Rev. Dr **PETER DAVID GREGORY SMITH** LLB JCD: born 21 October 1943 at Battersea, London • ordained priest (Southwark) 5 July 1972 at Wonersh, Guildford • ordained Bishop of East Anglia 27 May 1995 at Norwich • translated 26 October 2001 to Archdiocese of Cardiff • translated 30 April 2010 to Archdiocese of Southwark • appointed 4 October 2014 Apostolic Administrator of the Diocese of Arundel and Brighton until 28 May 2015.
• *Archbishop's House, 150 St George's Road, LONDON SE1 6HX*

DIOCESE OF WREXHAM

(Dioecesis Gurecsamiensis)

By Apostolic Decree (*Fiducia freti*) of Pope St John Paul II, dated 12 February 1987, the Diocese of Wrexham was formed by division of the Diocese of Menevia, with the episcopal see fixed at the Cathedral Church of Our Lady of Sorrows, Wrexham (1987–), consecrated on 7 November 1907.

By the same Apostolic Decree (*Fiducia freti*) of Pope St John Paul II, dated 12 February 1987, the episcopal see of the Diocese of Menevia was transferred from the Cathedral Church of Our Lady of Sorrows, Wrexham (1895–1987) to the Cathedral Church of St Joseph, Swansea (1987–) and the former County of West Glamorgan was transferred from the Archdiocese of Cardiff to the Diocese of Menevia.

Since 12 February 1987, the Diocese of Wrexham has been a suffragan see within the Province of Cardiff. At first, the Diocese of Wrexham comprised the counties of Anglesey, Caernarfon, Denbigh, Flint, Merioneth, Montgomery and Wrexham.

The Diocese today comprises the unitary authorities of Conwy, Denbighshire, Flintshire, Gwynedd and Wrexham, the District of Montgomery in Powys, and the Isle of Anglesey.

I. † Rt Rev. **JAMES HANNIGAN**: born 15 July 1928 at Glenfinn (Donegal), Ireland • ordained priest (Menevia) 27 June 1954 at Paris (Paris), France • ordained Bishop of Menevia 23 November 1983 at Wrexham • translated 12 February 1987 to newly erected Diocese of Wrexham • died 4 March 1994 at Chester aged 65 • buried at Wrexham.
• *Bishop's House, Sontley Road, WREXHAM LL13 7EW*

II. ® Rt Rev. **EDWIN REGAN**: born 31 December 1935 at Port Talbot • ordained priest (Cardiff) 5 July 1959 at Waterford City (Waterford), Ireland • ordained Bishop of Wrexham 13 December 1994 at Wrexham • retired 27 June 2012 to Wrexham thence to Blaenau Ffestiniog • appointed 1 November 2012 parish priest of St Mary Magdalene Church, Blaenau Ffestiniog.
• *Bethania, 6 Geufron Terrace, BLAENAU FFESTINIOG LL41 3BW*

III. Rt Rev. **PETER MALCOLM BRIGNALL**: born 5 July 1953 at Whetstone, London • ordained priest (Menevia) 18 February 1978 at New Southgate, London • incardinated 12 February 1987 into Diocese of Wrexham at Wrexham • ordained Bishop of Wrexham 12 September 2012 at Wrexham.
• *Bishop's House, Sontley Road, WREXHAM LL13 7EW*

SCOTLAND SINCE 1878

PROLOGUE

By Letters Apostolic (*Ex supremo apostolatus apice*) of POPE LEO XIII, dated 4 March 1878, the Scottish Hierarchy was restored and the metropolitan see fixed at Edinburgh. At first, the Hierarchy comprised the Archdiocese of St Andrews and Edinburgh with four suffragan sees: Aberdeen; Argyll and the Isles; Dunkeld; and Galloway. Furthermore, the Archdiocese of Glasgow was directly subject to the Holy See.

By Apostolic Constitution (*Dominici gregis*) of POPE VEN. PIUS XII, dated 25 May 1947, the Archdiocese of Glasgow was raised to a metropolitan Archdiocese and province, coming into effect on 5 April 1948. The Province of Glasgow then comprised the Archdiocese of Glasgow with the suffragan sees of Motherwell and Paisley.

By Apostolic Constitution (*Maxime interest*) of POPE VEN. PIUS XII, dated 25 May 1947, the Diocese of Motherwell was formed by division of the Archdiocese of Glasgow, comprising the County of Lanarkshire, with the episcopal see fixed at the Cathedral Church of Our Lady of Good Aid, Motherwell. The Diocese of Motherwell became a suffragan see within the Province of Glasgow, coming into effect on 5 April 1948.

By the same Apostolic Constitution (*Maxime interest*) of POPE VEN. PIUS XII, dated 25 May 1947, the Diocese of Paisley was formed by division of the Archdiocese of Glasgow and the Diocese of Galloway, comprising the County of Renfrewshire, with the episcopal see fixed at the Cathedral Church of St Mirin, Paisley. The Diocese of Paisley became a suffragan see within the Province of Glasgow, coming into effect on 5 April 1948.

By the same Apostolic Constitution (*Maxime interest*) of POPE PIUS VEN. XII, dated 25 May 1947, the Diocese of Galloway gained territory from the Archdiocese of Glasgow and was enlarged to include North Ayrshire (except the Isle of Arran) and the islands of Greater and Little Cumbrae, coming into effect on 5 April 1948.

By Apostolic Decree (*De sedis ac cathedrae episcopalis translatione*) of POPE ST JOHN XXIII, dated 12 March 1962, the episcopal see of the Diocese of Galloway was transferred from the Pro-Cathedral Church of St Andrew, Dumfries to the Cathedral Church of the Good Shepherd, Ayr.

By Apostolic Decree (*De episcopalis cathedrae translatione et ecclesiae cathedralis erectione*) of POPE BENEDICT XVI, dated 28 February 2007, the episcopal see of the Diocese of Galloway was transferred again from the Cathedral Church of the Good Shepherd, Ayr to the Cathedral Church of St Margaret, Ayr.

Today, the Hierarchy in Scotland now comprises two metropolitan Archdioceses and provinces with a further six suffragan sees. The Province of St Andrews and Edinburgh comprises the Archdiocese of St Andrews and Edinburgh with the suffragan sees of Aberdeen, Argyll and the Isles, Dunkeld and Galloway. The Province of Glasgow comprises the Archdiocese of Glasgow with the suffragan sees of Motherwell and Paisley.

Since the Restoration of the Hierarchy in Scotland, there have been fifty-six diocesan bishops, including three cardinals, who have carried out their ministry in this country, assisted by a further seven who remained as auxiliary Bishops. Of these sixty-three bishops, there have been five who were (or are) members of religious orders, another five auxiliary Bishops went on to become diocesan bishops and a further six were ordained as coadjutor Bishops, three of whom failed to succeed as the following diocesan bishop, including Mgr E. Hugh Cameron who declined his appointment as coadjutor Bishop of Argyll and the Isles.

In conclusion, eleven Popes have governed the Roman Catholic Church since the Restoration of the Hierarchy in Scotland. Great Britain has had nine Apostolic Nuncios appointed since 1938 and four Ukrainian Exarchs—with jurisdiction over Scotland—since 1968. Finally, the Bishopric of the Forces in Great Britain has been led by seven bishops since it was formed in 1918.

A variety of religious orders has been represented in the Catholic Hierarchy of Scotland. These have included two Benedictines (**OSB**), and one each from the Redemptorists (**CSsR**), Missionaries of Africa (White Fathers) (**MAfr**) and the Society of St Sulpice (**PSS**).

ARCHDIOCESE OF ST ANDREWS AND EDINBURGH

(Archidioecesis Sancti Andreae et Edimburgensis)

By Letters Apostolic (*Ex supremo apostolatus apice*) of Pope Leo XIII, dated 4 March 1878, the Archdiocese of St Andrews and Edinburgh was formed, with the episcopal see fixed at the Pro-Cathedral Church of St Mary, Edinburgh (1878–1886) then at the Metropolitan Cathedral Church of St Mary, Edinburgh (1886–), consecrated on 18 April 1978.

At first, the Metropolitan Archdiocese of St Andrews and Edinburgh comprised the counties of Berwickshire, part of Fife (south of the River Eden), East Lothian, Midlothian, Peeblesshire, Roxburghshire, Selkirkshire, Stirlingshire (except the districts of Baldernock and East Kilpatrick) and West Lothian.

The Province of St Andrews and Edinburgh comprises the Archdiocese of St Andrews and Edinburgh with the suffragan sees of Aberdeen, Argyll and the Isles, Dunkeld and Galloway. The Archdiocese today comprises the Metropolitan Cathedral City of Edinburgh, the counties of Berwickshire, part of Fife (south of the River Eden), East Lothian, Midlothian, Peeblesshire, Roxburghshire, Selkirkshire, Stirlingshire (except the districts of Baldernock and East Kilpatrick) and West Lothian.

a.   † Rt Rev. **JOHN MENZIES STRAIN**: see **I.** below.

I.   † Most Rev. **JOHN MENZIES STRAIN**: born 8 December 1810 at Edinburgh • ordained priest (Eastern District) 9 June 1833 at Rome, Italy • ordained titular Bishop of *Abila Lysaniae* and appointed Vicar Apostolic for the Eastern District 25 September 1864 at Rome, Italy • appointed Council Father at First Vatican Council 8 December 1869 to 20 October 1870 • translated 15 March 1878 to Archbishop and Metropolitan of newly raised and restored Archdiocese and Province of St Andrews and Edinburgh • died 2 July 1883 at St Mary's Cathedral, Edinburgh aged 72 • buried at the Metropolitan Cathedral Church of St Mary, Edinburgh. • *St Mary's Pro-Cathedral, Broughton Street (Chapel Lane), EDINBURGH EH1 3JR*

II.   † Most Rev. Dr **WILLIAM SMITH** DD: born 3 July 1819 at Edinburgh • ordained priest (Eastern District) 15 April 1843 at Rome, Italy • ordained Archbishop of St Andrews and Edinburgh 28 October 1885 at the Metropolitan Cathedral Church of St Mary, Edinburgh • appointed 6 September 1888 Apostolic Administrator of the Diocese of Dunkeld until 28 October 1890 • died 16 March 1892 at St Bennet's, Edinburgh aged 72 • buried at the Metropolitan Cathedral Church of St Mary, Edinburgh. • *St Bennet's, 42 Greenhill Gardens, EDINBURGH EH10 4BJ*

III.   † Most Rev. **ANGUS MacDONALD** BA: born 18 September 1844 at Borrodale, Arisaig • ordained priest (Western District) 7 July 1872 at Ushaw, Durham • ordained Bishop of restored Diocese of Argyll and the Isles 23 May 1878 at the Cathedral Church of St Andrew, Glasgow • translated 15 July 1892 to Archdiocese of St Andrews and Edinburgh • died 29 April 1900 at St Bennet's, Edinburgh aged 55 • buried at the Metropolitan Cathedral Church of St Mary, Edinburgh. • *St Bennet's, 42 Greenhill Gardens, EDINBURGH EH10 4B*

IV.   † Most Rev. **JAMES AUGUSTINE SMITH**: born 18 October 1841 at Edinburgh • ordained priest (Eastern District) 31 March 1866 at Rome, Italy • ordained Bishop of Dunkeld 28 October 1890 at Dundee • translated 30 August 1900 to Archdiocese of St Andrews and Edinburgh • died 25 November 1928 at St Bennet's, Edinburgh aged 87 • buried at the Metropolitan Cathedral Church of St Mary, Edinburgh. • *St Bennet's, 42 Greenhill Gardens, EDINBURGH EH10 4BJ*

a.　† Rt Rev. **HENRY GRAY (GREY) GRAHAM** MA BD: born 8 March 1874 at Maxton, Melrose • ordained Church of Scotland deacon (Presbytery of Selkirk) 9 March 1897 at Selkirk • ordained Church of Scotland priest (Presbytery of Hamilton) 14 November 1901 at Strathaven • received into Catholic Church 15 August 1903 at Fort Augustus • ordained priest (Glasgow) 22 December 1906 at Rome, Italy • ordained titular Bishop of *Tipasa in Numidia* and appointed auxiliary Bishop of St Andrews and Edinburgh 16 November 1917 at the Metropolitan Cathedral Church of St Mary, Edinburgh • resigned 31 March 1930 as auxiliary Bishop of St Andrews and Edinburgh and appointed parish priest of Holy Cross Church, Crosshill, Glasgow • died 5 December 1959 at Crosshill, Glasgow aged 85 • buried at St Peter's Cemetery, Dalbeth, Glasgow.
• *Holy Cross, 113 Dixon Avenue, GLASGOW G42 8ER*

V.　† Most Rev. Dom. **ANDREW THOMAS JOSEPH McDONALD** OSB: born 12 February 1871 at Invernevis, Fort William • professed (Order of Saint Benedict) 3 February 1890 at Fort Augustus • ordained priest (Order of Saint Benedict) 9 August 1896 at Fort Augustus • elected 27 August 1919 Abbot of the Abbey Church of St Benedict, Fort Augustus • ordained Archbishop of St Andrews and Edinburgh 24 September 1929 at the Metropolitan Cathedral Church of St Mary, Edinburgh • died 22 May 1950 at St Bennet's, Edinburgh aged 79 • buried at the Metropolitan Cathedral Church of St Mary, Edinburgh.
• *St Bennet's, 42 Greenhill Gardens, EDINBURGH EH10 4BJ*

VI.　† + *His Eminence* Cardinal Dr **GORDON JOSEPH GRAY** MA DD FEIS DUniv: born 10 August 1910 at Leith, Edinburgh • ordained priest (St Andrews and Edinburgh) 15 June 1935 at the Metropolitan Cathedral Church of St Mary, Edinburgh • ordained Archbishop of St Andrews and Edinburgh 21 September 1951 at the Metropolitan Cathedral Church of St Mary, Edinburgh • appointed Council Father at Second Vatican Council 11 October 1962 to 8 December 1965 • appointed 12 September 1963 Apostolic Administrator of the Diocese of Aberdeen until 25 March 1965 • elevated 28 April 1969 to Cardinal-Priest of Santa Chiara a Vigna Clara • retired 30 May 1985 to Edinburgh • died 19 July 1993 at Edinburgh aged 82 • buried at the Metropolitan Cathedral Church of St Mary, Edinburgh.
• *The Hermitage, 113–115 Whitehouse Loan, EDINBURGH EH9 1BB*

a. † Rt Rev. **JAMES MONAGHAN**: born 11 July 1914 at Bathgate
• ordained priest (St Andrews and Edinburgh) 11 June 1940 at the
Metropolitan Cathedral Church of St Mary, Edinburgh • ordained
titular Bishop of *Cell Ausaille* and appointed auxiliary Bishop of St
Andrews and Edinburgh 23 May 1970 at the Metropolitan Cathedral
Church of St Mary, Edinburgh • retired 13 July 1989 to Edinburgh
• died 3 June 1994 at Nazareth House, Lasswade aged 79 • buried
at the Metropolitan Cathedral Church of St Mary, Edinburgh.
• *252 Ferry Road, EDINBURGH EH5 3AN*

VII. ® + *His Eminence* Cardinal Dr **KEITH MICHAEL PATRICK
O'BRIEN** KM GCHS BSc DipEd DD LLD: born 17 March 1938 at Ballycastle (Antrim), Ireland • ordained priest (St Andrews and Edinburgh)
3 April 1965 at the Metropolitan Cathedral Church of St Mary, Edinburgh
• ordained Archbishop of St Andrews and Edinburgh 5 August 1985 at
the Metropolitan Cathedral Church of St Mary, Edinburgh • appointed
19 September 1996 Apostolic Administrator of the Diocese of Argyll and
the Isles until 7 December 1999 • elevated 21 October 2003 to Cardinal-
Priest of Santi Gioacchino ed Anna al Tuscolano • retired 25 February
2013 to Edinburgh • resigned 20 March 2015 the rights and privileges
of the Cardinal-Priest of Santi Gioacchino ed Anna al Tuscolano.
• *c/o Gillis Centre, 100 Strathearn Road, EDINBURGH EH9 1BB*

a. † Rt Rev. **KEVIN LAWRENCE RAFFERTY**: born 24 June
1933 at Garvagh, Coleraine (Derry), Ireland • ordained priest
(St Andrews and Edinburgh) 22 June 1957 at Kilkenny City
(Kilkenny), Ireland • ordained titular Bishop of *Ausuaga* and
appointed auxiliary Bishop of St Andrews and Edinburgh 15
August 1990 at the Metropolitan Cathedral Church of St Mary,
Edinburgh • died 19 April 1996 at Livingston aged 62 • buried
at Glenullin Cemetery, Garvagh, Coleraine (Derry), Ireland.
• *SS John Cantius and Nicholas, 34 West Main Street, BROXBURN
EH52 5RJ*

b. Rt Rev. Dr **STEPHEN ROBSON** BSc MTh STL JCL STD: born
1 April 1951 at Carlisle • received into Catholic Church 27 August
1972 at Carlisle • ordained priest (St Andrews and Edinburgh)
17 March 1979 at Carlisle • ordained titular Bishop of *Tunnuna*
and appointed auxiliary Bishop of St Andrews and Edinburgh

9 June 2012 at the Metropolitan Cathedral Church of St Mary, Edinburgh • translated 11 December 2013 to Diocese of Dunkeld.
• *Bishop's House, 29 Roseangle, DUNDEE DD1 4LS*

c.   **APOSTOLIC ADMINISTRATOR:** Most Rev. Dr **PHILIP TARTAGLIA** PhB STL STD: born 11 January 1951 at Govan, Glasgow • ordained priest (Glasgow) 30 June 1975 at Dennistoun, Glasgow • ordained Bishop of Paisley 20 November 2005 at Paisley • translated 24 July 2012 to Archdiocese of Glasgow • appointed 27 February 2013 Apostolic Administrator of the Archdiocese of St Andrews and Edinburgh until 21 September 2013.
• *Archbishop's House, 52 St Andrews Drive, GLASGOW G41 5HF*

VIII.   Most Rev. Dr **LEO WILLIAM CUSHLEY** PhB STB SLL JCD: born 18 June 1961 at Wester Moffat, Airdrie • ordained priest (Motherwell) 7 July 1985 at Uddingston, Glasgow • entered diplomatic service to the Holy See 1 July 1997 at Vatican City • ordained Archbishop of St Andrews and Edinburgh 21 September 2013 at the Metropolitan Cathedral Church of St Mary, Edinburgh.
• *St Bennet's, 42 Greenhill Gardens, EDINBURGH EH10 4BJ*

DIOCESE OF ABERDEEN

(Dioecesis Aberdonensis)

By Letters Apostolic (*Ex supremo apostolatus apice*) of Pope Leo XIII, dated 4 March 1878, the Diocese of Aberdeen was formed, with the episcopal see fixed at the Cathedral Church of St Mary of the Assumption, Aberdeen (1878–), consecrated on 5 October 1860.

Since 4 March 1878, the Diocese of Aberdeen has been a suffragan see within the Province of St Andrews and Edinburgh. At first, the Diocese of Aberdeen comprised the counties of Aberdeenshire, Banffshire, Caithness, Elgin or Moray, northern parts of Inverness-shire, Kincardineshire, Nairn, Ross and Cromarty (except Lewis in the Hebrides) and Sutherland, with the Orkney Islands and Shetland Islands.

The diocese today comprises the Cathedral City of Aberdeen, the counties of Aberdeenshire, Banffshire, Caithness, Moray, the northern part of Inverness-shire, Kincardineshire, Nairn, Ross and Cromarty and Sutherland, with the Orkney Islands and Shetland Islands.

a.   † Rt Rev. **JOHN MacDONALD**: see **I.** below.

I.   † Rt Rev. **JOHN MacDONALD**: born 2 July 1818 at Strath Glass, Beauly • ordained priest (Northern District) 4 November 1841 at Preshome, Buckie • ordained titular Bishop of *Nicopolis ad Iaterum* and appointed (coadjutor) Vicar Apostolic for the Northern District 24 February 1869 at Aberdeen (as his predecessor died the previous day) • appointed Council Father at First Vatican Council 8 December 1869 to 20 October 1870 • translated 15 March 1878 to restored Diocese of Aberdeen • died 4 February 1889 at Aberdeen aged 70 • buried at the Cathedral Church of St Mary of the Assumption, Aberdeen. • *Bishop's House, 20 Queen's Road, ABERDEEN AB15 4ZT*

II.   † Rt Rev. **COLIN CAMERON GRANT**: born 3 February 1832 at Glen Gairn, Ballater • ordained priest (Northern District) 22 December 1855 at Blairs, Aberdeen • ordained Bishop of Aberdeen 13 August 1889 at Aberdeen • died 26 September 1889 at Aberdeen aged 57 • buried at the Cathedral Church of St Mary of the Assumption, Aberdeen. • *Bishop's House, 20 Queen's Road, ABERDEEN AB15 4ZT*

III. † Rt Rev. **HUGH MacDONALD** CSsR: born 7 November 1841 at Borrodale, Arisaig • ordained priest (Western District) 21 September 1867 at Ushaw, Durham • professed (Congregation of the Most Holy Redeemer) 15 October 1871 at Bishop Eton, Liverpool • ordained Bishop of Aberdeen 23 October 1890 at Aberdeen • died 29 May 1898 at St Bennet's, Edinburgh aged 56 • buried at the Cathedral Church of St Mary of the Assumption, Aberdeen. • *Bishop's House, 20 Queen's Road, ABERDEEN AB15 4ZT*

IV.   † Rt Rev. Dr **AENEAS CHISHOLM** DD LLD: born 26 June 1836 at Inverness • ordained priest (Northern District) 15 May 1859 at Rome, Italy • ordained Bishop of Aberdeen 24 February 1899 at Aberdeen • died 13 January 1918 at St Patrick's, Edinburgh aged 81 • buried at St Mary's College Cemetery, Blairs, Aberdeen. • *Bishop's House, 19 Golden Square, ABERDEEN AB10 1RH*

V.   † Rt Rev. Dr **GEORGE HENRY BENNETT** PhD DD JCD LLD: born 24 June 1875 at St John's, Antigua • ordained priest (St Andrews and Edinburgh) 9 April 1898 at Rome, Italy • ordained Bishop of Aberdeen 1 August 1918 at Aberdeen • died 25 December

1946 at Aberdeen aged 71 • buried at Allenvale Cemetery, Aberdeen.
• *Bishop's House, 19 Golden Square, ABERDEEN AB10 1RH*

VI. † Rt Rev. Dr **JOHN ALEXANDER MATHESON** DD: born 28 April 1901 at Tomintoul, Ballindalloch • ordained priest (Aberdeen) 7 March 1925 at Rome, Italy • ordained Bishop of Aberdeen 24 September 1947 at Aberdeen • died 5 July 1950 at Aberdeen aged 49 • buried at the Catholic Cemetery, Tomintoul, Ballindalloch.
• *Bishop's House, 19 Golden Square, ABERDEEN AB10 1RH*

VII. † Rt Rev. Dr **FRANCIS PATRICK WALSH** MAfr PhD DD: born 15 September 1901 at Cirencester • ordained priest (Aberdeen) 7 March 1925 at Rome, Italy • professed (Missionaries of Africa (White Fathers)) 9 September 1931 at Sainte-Marie, Maison Carrée (Algiers), Algeria • ordained Bishop of Aberdeen 12 September 1951 at Aberdeen • appointed Council Father at Second Vatican Council 11 October 1962 to 8 December 1962 • resigned 12 September 1963 as Bishop of Aberdeen and appointed titular Bishop of *Birtha* • resigned 7 December 1970 as titular Bishop of *Birtha* and retired to Grantham • died 27 October 1974 at Grantham aged 73 • buried at Grantham Cemetery, Grantham.
• *The Rectory, 1 North Parade, GRANTHAM NG31 8AT*

a. **APOSTOLIC ADMINISTRATOR:** † Most Rev. Dr GORDON JOSEPH GRAY MA DD FEIS: born 10 August 1910 at Leith, Edinburgh • ordained priest (St Andrews and Edinburgh) 15 June 1935 at the Metropolitan Cathedral Church of St Mary, Edinburgh • ordained Archbishop of St Andrews and Edinburgh 21 September 1951 at the Metropolitan Cathedral Church of St Mary, Edinburgh • appointed Council Father at Second Vatican Council 11 October 1962 to 8 December 1965 • appointed 12 September 1963 Apostolic Administrator of the Diocese of Aberdeen until 25 March 1965 • elevated 28 April 1969 to Cardinal-Priest of Santa Chiara a Vigna Clara • retired 30 May 1985 to Edinburgh • died 19 July 1993 at Edinburgh aged 82 • buried at the Metropolitan Cathedral Church of St Mary, Edinburgh.
• *The Hermitage, Whitehouse Loan, EDINBURGH EH9 1BB*

VIII. † Rt Rev. **MICHAEL FOYLAN**: born 29 June 1907 at Shettleston, Glasgow • ordained priest (Dunkeld) 5 July 1931 at Kinnoull, Perth • ordained Bishop of Aberdeen 25 March 1965 at Aberdeen • appointed Council Father at Second

Vatican Council 14 September 1965 to 8 December 1965 • died 28 May 1976 at King's Gate, Aberdeen aged 68 • buried at St Ninian's Cemetery, Tynet, Buckie.
• *Bishop's House, 156 Kings Gate, ABERDEEN AB15 6BR*

IX. ® Rt Rev. Dr **MARIO JOSEPH CONTI** KC*HS PhL STL DD FRSE: born 20 March 1934 at Elgin • ordained priest (Aberdeen) 26 October 1958 at Rome, Italy • ordained Bishop of Aberdeen 3 May 1977 at Aberdeen • translated 22 February 2002 to Archdiocese of Glasgow • appointed 7 October 2004 Apostolic Administrator of the Diocese of Paisley until 20 November 2005 • retired 24 July 2012 to Glasgow.
• *40 Newlands Road, GLASGOW G43 2JD*

X. ® Rt Rev. **PETER ANTONY MORAN** PhL STL MA MEd LTCL: born 13 April 1935 at Hillhead, Glasgow • ordained priest (Glasgow) 19 March 1959 at Rome, Italy • incardinated 10 April 1992 into Diocese of Aberdeen at Aberdeen City • ordained Bishop of Aberdeen 1 December 2003 at Aberdeen • retired 4 June 2011 to Fortrose.
• *Regowan, 10 Cathedral Square, FORTROSE IV10 8TB*

XI. Rt Rev. Dom. **EDWARD HUGH GILBERT** OSB BA: born 15 March 1952 at Emsworth • received into Catholic Church 24 December 1970 at Polegate • professed (Order of Saint Benedict) 10 March 1979 at Pluscarden, Elgin • ordained priest (Order of Saint Benedict) 29 June 1982 at Pluscarden, Elgin • elected 29 October 1992 Abbot of the Abbey Church of Our Blessed Lady, St John the Baptist and St Andrew, Pluscarden, Elgin • ordained Bishop of Aberdeen 15 August 2011 at Aberdeen.
• *Bishop's House, 3 Queen's Cross, ABERDEEN AB15 4XU*

DIOCESE OF ARGYLL AND THE ISLES

(Dioecesis Ergadiensis et Insularum)

By Letters Apostolic (*Ex supremo apostolatus apice*) of Pope Leo XIII, dated 4 March 1878, the Diocese of Argyll and the Isles was formed, with the episcopal see fixed at the Cathedral Church of St Columba, Oban (1878–), which was rebuilt in 1932 and consecrated on 8 June 2004.

Since 4 March 1878, the Diocese of Argyll and the Isles has been a suffragan see within the Province of St Andrews and Edinburgh. At first, the Diocese of Argyll and the Isles comprised the counties of Argyll and parts of Inverness-shire, with the islands of Bute, Arran and the Hebrides.

The diocese today comprises the Cathedral City of Oban, the County of Argyll and the southern part of Inverness-shire, with the islands of Bute, Arran and the Hebrides.

I. † Rt Rev. **ANGUS MacDONALD** BA: born 18 September 1844 at Borrodale, Arisaig • ordained priest (Western District) 7 July 1872 at Ushaw, Durham • ordained Bishop of restored Diocese of Argyll and the Isles 23 May 1878 at the Cathedral Church of St Andrew, Glasgow • translated 15 July 1892 to Archdiocese of St Andrews and Edinburgh • died 29 April 1900 at St Bennet's, Edinburgh aged 55 • buried at Metropolitan Cathedral Church of St Mary, Edinburgh.
    • *St Bennet's, 42 Greenhill Gardens, EDINBURGH EH10 4BJ*

II. † Rt Rev. **GEORGE JOHN SMITH**: born 24 January 1840 at Cuttlebrae, Enzie, Buckie • ordained priest (Western District) 17 December 1864 at Paris (Paris), France • ordained Bishop of Argyll and the Isles 25 April 1893 at Oban • died 18 January 1918 at Oban aged 77 • buried at Pennyfuir Cemetery, Oban.
    • *Bishop's House, Corran Esplanade, OBAN PA34 5AB*

    a. †*M* Rev. Mgr **EWEN HUGH CAMERON**: born 20 April 1876 at Inveroy, Roy Bridge • ordained priest (Argyll and the Isles) 29 June 1900 at Oban • commissioned as military chaplain 3 December 1914 • nominated 13 November 1917 titular Bishop of *Usula* and appointed coadjutor Bishop of Argyll and the Isles but declined the appointment 20 November 1917 • released from military service 29 March 1919 • appointed 1928 parish priest at Kingussie • died 8 March 1931 at Rome, Italy aged 54 • buried at Scots College, Rome, Italy.
        • *Ardcolm, West Terrace, KINGUSSIE PH21 1HA*

III. † Rt Rev. **DONALD MARTIN**: born 6 October 1873 at Salen, Acharacle • ordained priest (Argyll and the Isles) 23 September 1905 at Oban • ordained Bishop of Argyll and the Isles 11 June 1919 at Oban • died 6 December 1938 at Oban aged 65 • buried at Pennyfuir Cemetery, Oban.
    • *Bishop's House, Corran Esplanade, OBAN PA34 5AB*

IV. † Rt Rev. Dr **DONALD ALPHONSUS CAMPBELL** DD: born 8 December 1894 at Bohuntin, Roy Bridge • ordained priest (Argyll and the Isles) 3 April 1920 at Rome, Italy • ordained Bishop of Argyll and the Isles 14 December 1939 at Oban • translated 6 January 1945 to Archdiocese of Glasgow • Archdiocese of Glasgow restructured 25 May 1947 • appointed 25 May 1947 Archbishop and Metropolitan of newly raised Archdiocese and Province of Glasgow • appointed 9 February 1954 Apostolic Administrator of the Diocese of Motherwell until 23 May 1955 •

appointed Council Father at Second Vatican Council 11 October 1962 to 8 December 1962 • died 22 July 1963 at Lourdes (Hautes-Pyrénées), France aged 68 • buried at St Peter's Cemetery, Dalbeth, Glasgow • reinterred 9 January 1980 at the Metropolitan Cathedral Church of St Andrew, Glasgow. • *Ardmory, 30 Langside Drive, GLASGOW G43 2QQ*

V. † Rt Rev. Dr **KENNETH GRANT** LLD: born 18 March 1900 at Fort William • enlisted as military soldier 18 July 1918 • released from military service 6 February 1919 • ordained priest (Glasgow) 24 April 1927 at the Cathedral Church of St Andrew, Glasgow • commissioned as military chaplain 3 November 1939 • released from military service 6 November 1945 • ordained Bishop of Argyll and the Isles 27 February 1946 at Oban • died 7 September 1959 at Glasgow aged 59 • buried at Cille Choireil Cemetery, Lochaber. • *Letterwalton House, Ledaig, OBAN PA37 1RY*

VI. † Rt Rev. **STEPHEN McGILL** PSS STL: born 4 January 1912 at Crosshill, Glasgow • ordained priest (Glasgow) 29 June 1936 at the Cathedral Church of St Andrew, Glasgow • joined Society of La Solitude de St Sulpice 1 July 1937 at Issy-les-Moulineaux (Hauts-de-Seine), France • ordained Bishop of Argyll and the Isles 22 June 1960 at Oban • appointed Council Father at Second Vatican Council 11 October 1962 to 8 December 1965 • translated 25 July 1968 to Diocese of Paisley • retired 30 March 1988 to Greenock • died 9 November 2005 at Cardonald, Glasgow aged 93 • buried at St Conval's Cemetery, Barrhead, Glasgow. • *Nazareth House, 1647 Paisley Road West, GLASGOW G52 3QT*

VII. † Rt Rev. Dr **COLIN ALOYSIUS MACPHERSON** STL LLD: born 5 August 1917 at Lochboisdale, Isle of South Uist • ordained priest (Argyll and the Isles) 23 March 1940 at Rome, Italy • ordained Bishop of Argyll and the Isles 6 February 1969 at Oban • died 24 March 1990 at Oban aged 72 • buried at Pennyfuir Cemetery, Oban. • *Bishop's House, Corran Esplanade, OBAN PA34 5AB*

VIII. † Rt Rev. **RODERICK WRIGHT**: born 28 June 1940 at Kinning Park, Glasgow • ordained priest (Glasgow) 29 June 1964 at the Metropolitan Cathedral Church of St Andrew, Glasgow • incardinated 12 August 1974 into Diocese of Argyll and the Isles at Dunoon • ordained Bishop of Argyll and the Isles 15 January 1991 at Oban • resigned 15 September 1996 as Bishop of Argyll and the Isles (renounced the dignity of bishop) and retired to Carnforth thence to

Napier (Hawke's Bay), New Zealand • died 23 May 2005 at Napier (Hawke's Bay), New Zealand aged 64 • buried at Napier (Hawke's Bay), New Zealand.
• *c/o Bishop's House, Corran Esplanade, OBAN PA34 5AB*

a. **APOSTOLIC ADMINISTRATOR:** ® Most Rev. KEITH MICHAEL PATRICK O'BRIEN KM GCHS BSc DipEd: born 17 March 1938 at Ballycastle (Antrim), Ireland • ordained priest (St Andrews and Edinburgh) 3 April 1965 at the Metropolitan Cathedral Church of St Mary, Edinburgh • ordained Archbishop of St Andrews and Edinburgh 5 August 1985 at the Metropolitan Cathedral Church of St Mary, Edinburgh • appointed 19 September 1996 Apostolic Administrator of the Diocese of Argyll and the Isles until 7 December 1999 • elevated 21 October 2003 to Cardinal-Priest of Santi Gioacchino ed Anna al Tuscolano • retired 25 February 2013 to Edinburgh • resigned 20 March 2015 the rights and privileges of the Cardinal-Priest of Santi Gioacchino ed Anna al Tuscolano.
• *c/o Gillis Centre, 100 Strathearn Road, EDINBURGH EH9 1BB*

IX. † Rt Rev. **IAN MURRAY** KC*HS BA: born 15 December 1932 at Lennoxtown, Glasgow • ordained priest (St Andrews and Edinburgh) 17 March 1956 at Valladolid (Valladolid), Spain • ordained Bishop of Argyll and the Isles 7 December 1999 at Oban • retired 16 October 2008 to Edinburgh. • died 22 January 2016 at Edinburgh aged 83 • buried at Pennyfuir Cemetery, Oban.
• *Cathedral House, 61 York Place, EDINBURGH EH1 3JD*

X. Rt Rev. **JOSEPH ANTHONY TOAL** KC*HS STB: born 13 October 1956 at Inverness • ordained priest (Argyll and the Isles) 10 July 1980 at Oban • ordained Bishop of Argyll and the Isles 8 December 2008 at Oban • appointed 31 May 2013 Apostolic Administrator of the Diocese of Motherwell until 29 April 2014 • translated 29 April 2014 to Diocese of Motherwell.
• *St Gerard's, Fleming Road, BELLSHILL ML4 1NF*

XI. Rt Rev. **BRIAN THOMAS McGEE** MA DipTh: born 8 October 1965 at Greenock • ordained priest (Paisley) 29 June 1989 at Greenock • ordained Bishop of Argyll and the Isles 18 February 2016 at Oban.
• *Bishop's House, Corran Esplanade, OBAN PA34 5AB*

DIOCESE OF DUNKELD

(Dioecesis Dunkeldensis)

By Letters Apostolic (*Ex supremo apostolatus apice*) of Pope Leo XIII, dated 4 March 1878, the Diocese of Dunkeld was formed, with the episcopal see fixed at the Pro-Cathedral Church of St Andrew, Dundee (1878–1923), then at the same Cathedral Church of St Andrew, Dundee (1923–), consecrated on 30 November 1987.

Since 4 March 1878, the Diocese of Dunkeld has been a suffragan see within the Province of St Andrews and Edinburgh. At first, the Diocese of Dunkeld comprised the counties of Angus, Clackmannanshire, part of Fife (north of the River Eden), Kinross and Perth.

The diocese today comprises the Cathedral City of Dundee, the counties of Angus, Clackmannanshire, part of Fife (north of the River Eden), and Perth and Kinross.

I.   † Rt Rev. **GEORGE RIGG**: born 19 July 1814 at Croghmore, Kirkpatrick Irongray, Kirkcudbright • ordained priest (Eastern District) 25 July 1838 at Valladolid (Valladolid), Spain • ordained Bishop of restored Diocese of Dunkeld 26 May 1878 at Rome, Italy • died 18 January 1887 at Perth aged 72 • buried at St John the Baptist Church, Perth. • *Bishop's House, 20 Melville Street, PERTH PH1 5PY*

a.   **APOSTOLIC ADMINISTRATOR:** † Most Rev. Dr **WILLIAM SMITH** DD: born 3 July 1819 at Edinburgh • ordained priest (Eastern District) 15 April 1843 at Rome, Italy • ordained Archbishop of St Andrews and Edinburgh 28 October 1885 at the Metropolitan Cathedral Church of St Mary, Edinburgh • appointed 6 September 1888 Apostolic Administrator of the Diocese of Dunkeld until 28 October 1890 • died 16 March 1892 at St Bennet's, Edinburgh aged 72 • buried at the Metropolitan Cathedral Church of St Mary, Edinburgh. • *St Bennet's, 42 Greenhill Gardens, EDINBURGH EH10 4BJ*

II.   † Rt Rev. **JAMES AUGUSTINE SMITH**: born 18 October 1841 at Edinburgh • ordained priest (Eastern District) 31 March 1866 at Rome, Italy • ordained Bishop of Dunkeld 28 October 1890 at Dundee • translated 30 August 1900 to Archdiocese of St Andrews and Edinburgh • died 25 November 1928 at Edinburgh aged 87 • buried at the Metropolitan Cathedral Church of St Mary, Edinburgh. • *St Bennet's, 42 Greenhill Gardens, EDINBURGH EH10 4BJ*

III. † Rt Rev. Dr **ANGUS MacFARLANE** DD: born 10 January 1843 at Spean Bridge • ordained priest (Western District) 26 April 1868 at Rome, Italy • ordained Bishop of Dunkeld 1 May 1901 at Dundee • died 24 September 1912 at Dundee aged 69 • buried at Balgay Cemetery, Dundee. • *Bishop's House, 29 Magdalen Yard Road, DUNDEE DD1 4LS*

IV.   † Rt Rev. Dr **ROBERT FRASER** DD LLD: born 10 August 1858 at Kennethmont, Huntly • ordained priest (Aberdeen) 13 August 1882 at Rome, Italy • ordained Bishop of Dunkeld 25 May 1913 at Rome, Italy • died 28 March 1914 at Dundee aged 55 • buried at Balgay Cemetery, Dundee. • *Bishop's House, 29 Magdalen Yard Road, DUNDEE DD1 4LS*

V.   † Rt Rev. **JOHN TONER**: born 14 March 1857 at Calton, Glasgow • ordained priest (Glasgow) 25 March 1882 at Palencia (Palencia), Spain • ordained

Bishop of Dunkeld 15 October 1914 at Dundee • appointed 12 June 1920 Apostolic Administrator of the Archdiocese of Glasgow until 21 May 1922 • died 31 May 1949 at Dundee aged 92 • buried at Balgay Cemetery, Dundee. • *Bishop's House, 29 Roseangle, DUNDEE DD1 4LS*

a.   † Rt Rev. **JAMES MAGUIRE**: born 29 August 1882 at Loanhead • ordained priest (St Andrews and Edinburgh) 22 July 1906 at the Metropolitan Cathedral Church of St Mary, Edinburgh • ordained titular Bishop of *Ilium* and appointed coadjutor Bishop of Dunkeld 30 November 1939 at Dundee • died 10 October 1944 at Dundee aged 62 • buried at Balgay Cemetery, Dundee. • *Cathedral House, 150 Nethergate, DUNDEE DD1 4EA*

b.   † Rt Rev. Dr **JAMES DONALD SCANLAN** LLB JCL JCD DD: see **VI.** below.

VI.   † Rt Rev. Dr **JAMES DONALD SCANLAN** LLB JCL JCD DD: born 24 January 1899 at Parkhead, Glasgow • enlisted as military soldier 12 September 1917 • released from military service 16 July 1919 • ordained priest (Westminster) 29 June 1929 at the Metropolitan Cathedral Church of the Most Precious Blood, Westminster, London • ordained titular Bishop of *Cyme* and appointed coadjutor Bishop of Dunkeld 20 June 1946 at Dundee • succeeded 31 May 1949 as Bishop of Dunkeld • translated 23 May 1955 to Diocese of Motherwell • appointed Council Father at Second Vatican Council 11 October 1962 to 8 December 1965 • translated 29 January 1964 to Archdiocese of Glasgow • retired 23 April 1974 to Kelvingrove, Glasgow thence to Marylebone, London • died 25 March 1976 at Marylebone, London aged 77 • buried at St Peter's Cemetery, Dalbeth, Glasgow • reinterred 9 January 1980 at the Metropolitan Cathedral Church of St Andrew, Glasgow. • *Tyburn Convent, 8–9 Hyde Park Place, LONDON W2 2LJ*

VII.   † Rt Rev. **WILLIAM ANDREW HART**: born 9 September 1904 at Dumbarton • ordained priest (Glasgow) 25 May 1929 at Valladolid (Valladolid), Spain • commissioned as military chaplain 28 October 1939 • released from military service 25 November 1945 • ordained Bishop of Dunkeld 21 September 1955 at Dundee • appointed Council Father at Second Vatican Council 11 October 1962 to 8 December 1965 • retired 26 January 1981 to Dundee • died 18 October 1992 at Dundee aged 88 • buried at Balgay Cemetery, Dundee. • *Little Sisters of the Poor, Wellburn Home, 118 Liff Road, DUNDEE DD2 2QT*

VIII.   ® Rt Rev. **VINCENT PAUL LOGAN** DipRE: born 30 June 1941 at Bathgate • ordained priest (St Andrews and Edinburgh) 14 March 1964 at the Metropolitan Cathedral Church of St Mary, Edinburgh • ordained Bishop of Dunkeld 26 February 1981 at Dundee • resigned 30 June 2012 as Bishop of Dunkeld and retired to Dundee. • *Croghmore, 10 Arnhall Drive, DUNDEE DD2 1LU*

IX.   Rt Rev. Dr **STEPHEN ROBSON** BSc MTh STL JCL STD: born 1 April 1951 at Carlisle • received into Catholic Church 27 August 1972 at Carlisle • ordained priest (St Andrews and Edinburgh) 17 March 1979 at Carlisle • ordained titular Bishop of *Tunnuna* and appointed auxiliary Bishop of St Andrews and Edinburgh 9 June 2012 at the Metropolitan Cathedral Church of St Mary, Edinburgh • translated 11 December 2013 to Diocese of Dunkeld. • *Bishop's House, 29 Roseangle, DUNDEE DD1 4LS*

DIOCESE OF GALLOWAY

(Dioecesis Candidae Casae o Gallovidianus)

By Letters Apostolic (*Ex supremo apostolatus apice*) of Pope Leo XIII, dated 4 March 1878, the Diocese of Galloway was formed, with the episcopal see fixed at the Pro-Cathedral Church of St Andrew, Dumfries (1878–1962), consecrated on 9 May 1813, re-ordered and re-opened on 13 November 1879 and destroyed by fire on 10 May 1961, then at the Cathedral Church of the Good Shepherd, Ayr (1962–2007), consecrated on 17 June 1962 and closed on 20 May 2007, then at the Cathedral Church of St Margaret, Ayr (2007–), consecrated on 10 June 1827.

Since 4 March 1878, the Diocese of Galloway has been a suffragan see within the Province of St Andrews and Edinburgh. At first, the Diocese of Galloway comprised the counties of Ayrshire (except North Ayrshire and the Isle of Arran), Dumfriesshire, Kirkcudbrightshire and Wigtownshire.

By Apostolic Constitution (*Maxime interest*) of Pope Ven. Pius XII, dated 25 May 1947, the Diocese of Galloway gained territory from the Archdiocese of Glasgow and was enlarged to include North Ayrshire (except the Isle of Arran) and the islands of Greater and Little Cumbrae.

The diocese today comprises the Cathedral City of Ayr, the counties of Ayrshire (except the Isle of Arran), Dumfriesshire, Kirkcudbrightshire, Wigtownshire, with the islands of Greater and Little Cumbrae.

I.   † Rt Rev. Dr **JOHN McLACHLAN** DD: born 7 September 1826 at Glasgow • ordained priest (Western District) 16 March 1850 at Rome, Italy • ordained Bishop of restored Diocese of Galloway 23 May 1878 at the Cathedral Church of St Andrew, Glasgow • died 16 January 1893 at Dumfries aged 66 • buried in the Pro-Cathedral Crypt of St Andrew, Dumfries.
      • *St Andrew's Pro-Cathedral, 27 Brooke Street, DUMFRIES DG1 2JL*

II.   † Rt Rev. **WILLIAM TURNER**: born 12 December 1844 at Aberdeen • ordained priest (Eastern District) 26 April 1868 at Rome, Italy • ordained Bishop of Galloway 25 July 1893 at Dumfries • died 19 January 1914 at Dumfries aged 69 • buried at Holy Cross Cemetery, Dumfries.
      • *St Benedict's, 17 Laurieknowe, DUMFRIES DG2 7AH*

III. † Rt Rev. **JAMES WILLIAM McCARTHY** KCHS: born 30 January 1853 at Newcastle upon Tyne • ordained priest (Glasgow) 4 May 1879 at the Cathedral Church of St Andrew, Glasgow • ordained Bishop of Galloway 9 June 1914 at Dumfries • died 24 December 1943 at Dumfries aged 90 • buried at St Andrew's Cemetery, Calside, Dumfries.
      • *Candida Casa, 17 Laurieknowe, DUMFRIES DG2 7AH*

a.   † Rt Rev. **WILLIAM HENRY MELLON**: see **IV.** below.

IV.   † Rt Rev. **WILLIAM HENRY MELLON**: born 6 January 1877 at Edinburgh • ordained priest (St Andrews and Edinburgh) 29 March 1902 at Rome, Italy • ordained titular Bishop of *Daulia* and appointed coadjutor Bishop of Galloway 28 October 1935 at the Metropolitan Cathedral Church of St Mary, Edinburgh • succeeded 24 December 1943 as Bishop of Galloway • died 2 February 1952 at Dumfries aged 75 • buried at St Andrew's Cemetery, Calside, Dumfries.
      • *Candida Casa, 17 Laurieknowe, DUMFRIES DG2 7AH*

V.   † Rt Rev. **JOSEPH MICHAEL McGEE**: born 13 December 1904 at Monzievaird and Strowan, Crieff • ordained priest (Dunkeld) 25 May 1929 at Valladolid (Valladolid), Spain • ordained Bishop of Galloway 11 November 1952 at Dumfries • appointed Council Father at Second Vatican

Council 11 October 1962 to 8 December 1965 • retired 4 April 1981 to Prestwick • died 5 March 1983 at Prestwick aged 78 • buried at Ayr Cemetery. • *32 Mansewell Road, PRESTWICK KA9 1BB*

VI.   ® Rt Rev. Dr **MAURICE TAYLOR** STL STD DD: born 5 May 1926 at Hamilton • enlisted as military soldier 17 August 1944 • released from military service 6 August 1947 • ordained priest (Motherwell) 2 July 1950 at Rome, Italy • ordained Bishop of Galloway 9 June 1981 at Coodham, Kilmarnock • retired 28 May 2004 to Ayr. • *41 Overmills Road, AYR KA7 3LH*

VII.   ® Rt Rev. Dr **JOHN CUNNINGHAM** JCD: born 22 February 1938 at Paisley • ordained priest (Paisley) 29 June 1961 at Paisley • ordained Bishop of Galloway 28 May 2004 at Ayr • retired 22 November 2014 to Greenock. • *24 Johnston Terrace, GREENOCK PA16 8BD*

VIII.   Rt Rev. **WILLIAM NOLAN** STL: born 26 January 1954 at Motherwell • ordained priest (Motherwell) 30 June 1977 at Motherwell • ordained Bishop of Galloway 14 February 2015 at Kilmarnock. • *Candida Casa, 8 Corsehill Road, AYR KA7 2ST*

ARCHDIOCESE OF GLASGOW

DA ROBUR FER AUXILIUM

(Archidioecesis Glasguensis)

By Letters Apostolic (*Ex supremo apostolatus apice*) of Pope Leo XIII, dated 4 March 1878, the Archdiocese of Glasgow was formed, with the episcopal see fixed at the Cathedral Church of St Andrew, Glasgow (1878–1947), consecrated on 28 April 1948.

The Archdiocese of Glasgow was directly subject to the Holy See. At first, the Archdiocese of Glasgow comprised the counties of Ayrshire (northern part), Dunbartonshire, Lanarkshire, Renfrewshire, the districts of Baldernock and East Kilpatrick in Stirlingshire, with the islands of Greater and Little Cumbrae.

By Apostolic Constitution (*Dominici gregis*) of Pope Ven. Pius XII, dated 25 May 1947, the Archdiocese of Glasgow was raised to a metropolitan Archdiocese and province, coming into effect on 5 April 1948 and the episcopal see remained at the Metropolitan Cathedral Church of St Andrew, Glasgow (1947–).

The Province of Glasgow comprises the Archdiocese of Glasgow with the suffragan sees of Motherwell and Paisley. The Archdiocese today comprises the Metropolitan Cathedral City of Glasgow (1947), the County of Dunbartonshire and the districts of Baldernock and East Kilpatrick in Stirlingshire.

a.   APOSTOLIC ADMINISTRATOR: † Rt Rev. Dr **CHARLES PETRE EYRE** LLD: see **I.** below.

I.   † Most Rev. Dr **CHARLES PETRE EYRE** LLD: born 7 November 1817 at Askham Bryan, York • ordained priest (Northern District (England & Wales)) 19 March 1842 at Rome, Italy • ordained titular Archbishop of *Anazarbus* and appointed Apostolic Delegate in Scotland 31 January 1869 at Rome, Italy • appointed 16 April 1869 Apostolic Administrator of the Western District until 15 March 1878 • translated 15 March 1878 to restored Archdiocese of Glasgow • died 27 March 1902 at Hillhead, Glasgow aged 84 • buried at St Peter's College chapel, Cardross, Dumbarton • reinterred 9 January 1980 at the Cathedral Church of St Andrew, Glasgow. • *Archbishop's House, 6 Bowmont Gardens, GLASGOW G12 9LR*

a.   † Rt Rev. **JOHN ALOYSIUS MAGUIRE**: see **II.** below.

II.   † Most Rev. **JOHN ALOYSIUS MAGUIRE**: born 8 September 1851 at Calton, Glasgow • ordained priest (Western District) 27 March 1875 at Rome, Italy • ordained titular Bishop of *Trocmades* and appointed auxiliary Bishop of Glasgow 11 June 1894 at the Cathedral Church of St Andrew, Glasgow • translated 4 August 1902 to Archdiocese of Glasgow • died 14 October 1920 at Charing Cross, Glasgow aged 69 • buried at St Peter's Cemetery, Dalbeth, Glasgow. • *Archbishop's House, 160 Renfrew Street, GLASGOW G3 6RF*

a.   † Rt Rev. **DONALD ALOYSIUS MACKINTOSH**: born 24 December 1844 at Bohuntin, Roy Bridge • ordained priest (Western District) 31 May 1871 at Blairs, Aberdeen • ordained titular Bishop of *Chersonesus in Zechia* and appointed coadjutor Archbishop of Glasgow 2 July 1912 at the Cathedral Church of St Andrew, Glasgow • died 8 October 1919 at Kinning Park, Glasgow aged 74 • buried at St Peter's Cemetery, Dalbeth, Glasgow. • *5 Westbourne Gardens, GLASGOW G12 9XD*

b.   APOSTOLIC ADMINISTRATOR: † Rt Rev. **JOHN TONER**: born 14 March 1857 at Calton, Glasgow • ordained priest (Glasgow) 25 March 1882 at Palencia (Palencia), Spain • ordained Bishop of Dunkeld 15 October 1914 at Dundee • appointed 12 June 1920 Apostolic Administrator of the Archdiocese of Glasgow until 21 May 1922 • died

31 May 1949 at Dundee aged 92 • buried at Balgay Cemetery, Dundee.
• *Bishop's House, 29 Roseangle, DUNDEE DD1 4LS*

III.   † Most Rev. Dr **DONALD MACKINTOSH** PhD DD: born 10 October 1877 at Glasnacardoch, Mallaig • ordained priest (Glasgow) 1 November 1900 at Rome, Italy • ordained Archbishop of Glasgow 21 May 1922 at Rome, Italy • died 8 December 1943 at Bearsden, Glasgow aged 66 • buried at St Peter's Cemetery, Dalbeth, Glasgow.
• *Archbishop's House, 2 Chesters Road, Bearsden, GLASGOW G61 4AG*

IV.   † Most Rev. Dr **DONALD ALPHONSUS CAMPBELL** DD: born 8 December 1894 at Bohuntin, Roy Bridge • ordained priest (Argyll and the Isles) 3 April 1920 at Rome, Italy • ordained Bishop of Argyll and the Isles 14 December 1939 at Oban • translated 6 January 1945 to Archdiocese of Glasgow • Archdiocese of Glasgow restructured 25 May 1947 • appointed 25 May 1947 Archbishop and Metropolitan of newly raised Archdiocese and Province of Glasgow • appointed 9 February 1954 Apostolic Administrator of the Diocese of Motherwell until 23 May 1955 • appointed Council Father at Second Vatican Council 11 October 1962 to 8 December 1962 • died 22 July 1963 at Lourdes (Hautes-Pyrénées, France aged 68 • buried at St Peter's College chapel, Cardross, Dumbarton • reinterred 9 January 1980 at the Metropolitan Cathedral Church of St Andrew, Glasgow.
• *Ardmory, 30 Langside Drive, GLASGOW G43 2QQ*

a.   † Rt Rev. **JAMES WARD**: born 4 September 1905 at Dumbarton • ordained priest (Glasgow) 29 June 1929 at the Cathedral Church of St Andrew, Glasgow • ordained titular Bishop of *Sita* and appointed auxiliary Bishop of Glasgow 21 September 1960 at the Metropolitan Cathedral Church of St Andrew, Glasgow • appointed Council Father at Second Vatican Council 11 October 1962 to 8 December 1965 • appointed 1 March 1965 parish priest of Holy Cross Church, Crosshill, Glasgow • died 21 October 1973 at Crosshill, Glasgow aged 68 • buried at St Peter's Cemetery, Dalbeth, Glasgow.
• *Holy Cross Parish, 113 Dixon Avenue, GLASGOW G42 8ER*

V.   † Most Rev. Dr **JAMES DONALD SCANLAN** LLB JCL JCD DD: born 24 January 1899 at Parkhead, Glasgow • enlisted as military soldier 12 September 1917 • released from military service 16 July 1919 • ordained priest (Westminster) 29 June 1929 at the Metropolitan Cathedral Church of the Most Precious Blood, Westminster, London • ordained titular Bishop of *Cyme* and appointed coadjutor Bishop of Dunkeld 20 June 1946 at Dundee • succeeded 31 May 1949 as Bishop of Dunkeld • translated 23 May 1955 to Diocese of Motherwell • appointed Council Father at Second Vatican Council 11 October 1962 to 8 December 1965 • translated 29 January 1964 to Archdiocese of Glasgow • retired 23 April 1974 to Kelvingrove Park, Glasgow thence to Marylebone, London • died 25 March 1976 at Marylebone, London aged 77 • buried at St Peter's Cemetery, Dalbeth, Glasgow • reinterred 9 January 1980 at the Metropolitan Cathedral Church of St Andrew, Glasgow. • *Tyburn Convent, 8–9 Hyde Park Place, LONDON W2 2LJ*

a.   † Rt Rev. Dr **THOMAS JOSEPH WINNING** STL JCD: see **VI.** below.

VI.   † + *His Eminence* Cardinal Dr **THOMAS JOSEPH WINNING** GCHS STL JCD DD DUniv LLD FEIS: born 3 June 1925 at Wishaw • ordained priest (Motherwell) 18 December 1948 at Rome, Italy • ordained titular Bishop of *Lugmad* and appointed auxiliary Bishop of Glasgow 30 November 1971 at the Metropolitan Cathedral Church of St Andrew, Glasgow • appointed 1 December 1971 parish priest of Our Holy Redeemer Church, Clydebank • translated 23 April 1974 to Archdiocese of Glasgow • elevated 26 November 1994 to Cardinal-Priest of Sant' Andrea delle Fratte • died 17 June 2001 at Newlands, Glasgow aged 76 • buried at the Metropolitan Cathedral Church of St Andrew, Glasgow. • *Archbishop's House, 40 Newlands Road, GLASGOW G43 2JD*

a.   ℞ Rt Rev. Dr **JOSEPH DEVINE** PhD: born 7 August 1937 at Kirkintilloch, Glasgow • ordained priest (Glasgow) 29 June 1960 at the Metropolitan Cathedral Church of St Andrew, Glasgow • ordained titular Bishop of *Voli* and appointed auxiliary Bishop of Glasgow 31 May 1977 at St Francis' Church, Gorbals, Glasgow • translated 13 May 1983 to Diocese of Motherwell • retired 31 May 2013 to Hamilton. • *27 Smithycroft, HAMILTON ML3 7UL*

b.   † Rt Rev. **CHARLES McDONALD RENFREW** PhL STL: born 21 June 1929 at Glasgow • ordained priest (Glasgow) 4 April 1953 at Rome, Italy • ordained titular Bishop of *Abula* and appointed auxiliary Bishop of Glasgow 31 May 1977 at St Francis' Church, Gorbals, Glasgow • died 27 February 1992 at Partick, Glasgow aged 62 •

buried at the Metropolitan Cathedral Church of St Andrew, Glasgow.
• *St Joseph's, 38–40 Mansionhouse Road, GLASGOW G41 3DW*

c. ® Rt Rev. **JOHN ALOYSIUS MONE**: born 22 June 1929 at
Crosshill, Glasgow • ordained priest (Glasgow) 12 June 1952 at the
Metropolitan Cathedral Church of St Andrew, Glasgow • ordained tit-
ular Bishop of *Abercornia* and appointed auxiliary Bishop of Glasgow
14 May 1984 at Holy Cross Church, Crosshill, Glasgow • translated 8
March 1988 to Diocese of Paisley • retired 7 October 2004 to Greenock.
• *Carnmore, 30 Esplanade, GREENOCK PA16 7RU*

VII. ® Most Rev. Dr **MARIO JOSEPH CONTI** KC*HS PhL STL DD
FRSE: born 20 March 1934 at Elgin • ordained priest (Aberdeen) 26
October 1958 at Rome, Italy • ordained Bishop of Aberdeen 3 May 1977
at Aberdeen • translated 22 February 2002 to Archdiocese of Glasgow
• appointed 7 October 2004 Apostolic Administrator of the Diocese
of Paisley until 20 November 2005 • retired 24 July 2012 to Glasgow.
• *40 Newlands Road, GLASGOW G43 2JD*

VIII. Most Rev. Dr **PHILIP TARTAGLIA** PhB STL STD: born 11 January 1951 at Govan, Glasgow • ordained priest (Glasgow) 30 June 1975
at Dennistoun, Glasgow • ordained Bishop of Paisley 20 November
2005 at Paisley • translated 24 July 2012 to Archdiocese of Glasgow •
appointed 27 February 2013 Apostolic Administrator of the Archdiocese of St Andrews and Edinburgh until 21 September 2013.
• *Archbishop's House, 52 St Andrews Drive, GLASGOW G41 5HF*

DIOCESE OF MOTHERWELL

(Dioecesis Matrisfontis)

By Apostolic Constitution (*Maxime interest*) of Pope Ven. Pius XII, dated 25 May 1947, the Diocese of Motherwell was formed by division of the Archdiocese of Glasgow, coming into effect on 5 April 1948, with the episcopal see fixed at the Cathedral Church of Our Lady of Good Aid, Motherwell (1947–), consecrated on 14 December 1900.

Since 25 May 1947, the Diocese of Motherwell has been a suffragan see within the Province of Glasgow. At first, the Diocese of Motherwell comprised the whole County of Lanarkshire.

The diocese today comprises the Cathedral City of Motherwell and the County of Lanarkshire (1947).

I.   † Rt Rev. **EDWARD WILSON DOUGLAS**: born 27 August 1901 at Crosshill, Glasgow • ordained priest (Glasgow) 1 May 1924 at the Cathedral Church of St Andrew, Glasgow • ordained Bishop of newly erected Diocese of Motherwell 21 April 1948 at Motherwell • appointed 9 February 1954 titular Bishop of *Botrys* and retired to Braemar thence to Fairlie, Largs • died 12 June 1967 at Glasgow aged 66 • buried at St Patrick's Cemetery, New Stevenston, Motherwell. • *58 Castlepark Drive, Fairlie, LARGS KA29 0DG*

a.   **APOSTOLIC ADMINISTRATOR:** † Most Rev. Dr **DONALD ALPHONSUS CAMPBELL** DD: born 8 December 1894 at Bohuntin, Roy Bridge • ordained priest (Argyll and the Isles) 3 April 1920 at Rome, Italy • ordained Bishop of Argyll and the Isles 14 December 1939 • translated 6 January 1945 to Archdiocese of Glasgow • Archdiocese of Glasgow restructured 25 May 1947 • appointed 25 May 1947 Archbishop and Metropolitan of newly raised Archdiocese and Province of Glasgow • appointed 9 February 1954 Apostolic Administrator of the Diocese of Motherwell until 23 May 1955 • appointed Council Father at Second Vatican Council 11 October 1962 to 8 December 1962 • died 22 July 1963 at Lourdes (Hautes-Pyrénées), France aged 68 • buried at St Peter's College chapel, Cardross, Dumbarton • reinterred 9 January 1980 at the Metropolitan Cathedral Church of St Andrew, Glasgow. • *Ardmory, 30 Langside Drive, GLASGOW G43 2QQ*

II. † Rt Rev. Dr **JAMES DONALD SCANLAN** LLB JCL JCD DD: born 24 January 1899 at Parkhead, Glasgow • enlisted as military soldier 12 September 1917 • released from military service 16 July 1919 • ordained priest (Westminster) 29 June 1929 at the Metropolitan Cathedral Church of the Most Precious Blood, Westminster, London • ordained titular Bishop of *Cyme* and appointed coadjutor Bishop of Dunkeld 20 June 1946 at Dundee • succeeded 31 May 1949 as Bishop of Dunkeld • translated 23 May 1955 to Diocese of Motherwell • appointed Council Father at Second Vatican Council 11 October 1962 to 8 December 1965 • translated 29 January 1964 to Archdiocese of Glasgow • retired 23 April 1974 to Kelvingrove, Glasgow thence to Marylebone, London • died 25 March 1976 at Marylebone, London aged 77 • buried at St Peter's Cemetery, Dalbeth, Glasgow • reinterred 9 January 1980 at the Metropolitan Cathedral Church of St Andrew, Glasgow. • *Tyburn Convent, 8–9 Hyde Park Place, LONDON W2 2LJ*

III.   † Rt Rev. **FRANCIS ALEXANDER SPALDING WARDEN THOMSON** BA MA STL: born 15 May 1917 at Edinburgh • ordained priest (St Andrews and Edinburgh) 15 June 1946 at the Metropolitan Cathedral Church of St Mary, Edinburgh • ordained Bishop of Motherwell 24 February 1965 at Motherwell • appointed Council Father at Second Vatican Council 14 September 1965 to 8 December 1965 • resigned 14 December 1982 as Bishop of Motherwell • appointed 14 December 1982 Apostolic Administrator of the Diocese of Motherwell until 13 May 1983 • appointed 12 September 1983 parish priest of St Isidore's Church, Biggar • died 6 December 1987 at Bon Secours Hospital, Glasgow aged 70 • buried at the Cathedral Church of Our Lady of Good Aid, Motherwell. • *St Isidore's, 6 Coulter Road, BIGGAR ML12 6EP*

a.   **APOSTOLIC ADMINISTRATOR:** Rt Rev. **FRANCIS ALEXANDER SPALDING WARDEN THOMSON** BA MA STL: see **III.** above.

IV.   ® Rt Rev. Dr **JOSEPH DEVINE** PhD: born 7 August 1937 at Kirkintilloch, Glasgow • ordained priest (Glasgow) 29 June 1960 at the Metropolitan Cathedral Church of St Andrew, Glasgow • ordained titular Bishop of *Voli* and appointed auxiliary Bishop of Glasgow 31 May 1977 at St Francis' Church, Gorbals, Glasgow • translated 13 May 1983 to Diocese of Motherwell • retired 31 May 2013 to Hamilton. • *27 Smithycroft, HAMILTON ML3 7UL*

a.   **APOSTOLIC ADMINISTRATOR:** Rt Rev. **JOSEPH ANTHONY TOAL** KC*HS STB: see **V.** below.

V.   Rt Rev. **JOSEPH ANTHONY TOAL** KC*HS STB: born 13 October 1956 at Inverness • ordained priest (Argyll and the Isles) 10 July 1980 at Oban • ordained Bishop of Argyll and the Isles 8 December 2008 at Oban • appointed 31 May 2013 Apostolic Administrator of the Diocese of Motherwell until 29 April 2014 • translated 29 April 2014 to Diocese of Motherwell. • *St Gerard's, Fleming Road, BELLSHILL ML4 1NF*

DIOCESE OF PAISLEY

(Dioecesis Pasletanus)

By Apostolic Constitution (*Maxime interest*) of Pope Ven. Pius XII, dated 25 May 1947, the Diocese of Paisley was formed by division of the Archdiocese of Glasgow, coming into effect on 5 April 1948, with the episcopal see fixed at the Cathedral Church of St Mirin, Paisley (1947–), consecrated on 27 November 1948.

Since 25 May 1947, the Diocese of Paisley has been a suffragan see within the Province of Glasgow. At first, the Diocese of Paisley comprised the whole County of Renfrewshire.

The diocese today comprises the Cathedral City of Paisley and the County of Renfrewshire (1947).

I. † Rt Rev. **JAMES BLACK**: born 25 June 1894 at Calton, Glasgow •
enlisted as military soldier 19 July 1917 • released from military service 18
December 1918 • ordained priest (Glasgow) 27 June 1920 at the Cathedral
Church of St Andrew, Glasgow • ordained Bishop of newly erected Diocese
of Paisley 14 April 1948 at Paisley • appointed Council Father at Second
Vatican Council 11 October 1962 to 8 December 1965 • died 29 March 1968
at Kilmacolm aged 73 • buried at St Conval's Cemetery, Barrhead, Glasgow.
• *Bishop's House, Porterfield Road, KILMACOLM PA13 4PD*

II. † Rt Rev. **STEPHEN McGILL** PSS STL: born 4 January 1912 at
Crosshill, Glasgow • ordained priest (Glasgow) 29 June 1936 at the
Cathedral Church of St Andrew, Glasgow • joined Society of La Soli-
tude de St Sulpice 1 July 1937 at Issy-les-Moulineaux (Hauts-de-Seine),
France • ordained Bishop of Argyll and the Isles 22 June 1960 at Oban
• appointed Council Father at Second Vatican Council 11 October 1962
to 8 December 1965 • translated 25 July 1968 to Diocese of Paisley •
retired 30 March 1988 to Greenock • died 9 November 2005 at Cardonald,
Glasgow aged 93 • buried at St Conval's Cemetery, Barrhead, Glasgow.
• *Nazareth House, 1647 Paisley Road West, GLASGOW G52 3QT*

III. ® Rt Rev. **JOHN ALOYSIUS MONE**: born 22 June 1929 at
Crosshill, Glasgow • ordained priest (Glasgow) 12 June 1952 at the
Metropolitan Cathedral Church of St Andrew, Glasgow • ordained
titular Bishop of *Abercornia* and appointed auxiliary Bishop of Glasgow
14 May 1984 at Holy Cross Church, Crosshill, Glasgow • translated 8
March 1988 to Diocese of Paisley • retired 7 October 2004 to Greenock.
• *Carnmore, 30 Esplanade, GREENOCK PA16 7RU*

a. **APOSTOLIC ADMINISTRATOR:** ® Most Rev. Dr **MARIO
JOSEPH CONTI** KC*HS PhL STL DD FRSE: born 20 March
1934 at Elgin • ordained priest (Aberdeen) 26 October 1958 at
Rome, Italy • ordained Bishop of Aberdeen 3 May 1977 at Aberdeen • translated 22 February 2002 to Archdiocese of Glasgow •
appointed 7 October 2004 Apostolic Administrator of the Diocese
of Paisley until 20 November 2005 • retired 24 July 2012 to Glasgow.
• *40 Newlands Road, GLASGOW G43 2JD*

IV. Rt Rev. Dr **PHILIP TARTAGLIA** PhB STL STD: born 11 January 1951 at Govan, Glasgow • ordained priest (Glasgow) 30 June 1975

at Dennistoun, Glasgow • ordained Bishop of Paisley 20 November 2005 at Paisley • translated 24 July 2012 to Archdiocese of Glasgow • appointed 27 February 2013 Apostolic Administrator of the Archdiocese of St Andrews and Edinburgh until 21 September 2013.
• *Archbishop's House, 52 St Andrews Drive, GLASGOW G41 5HF*

V.   Rt Rev. **JOHN KEENAN** LLB PhL STB: born 19 December 1964 at Cowcaddens, Glasgow • ordained priest (Glasgow) 9 July 1995 at Rome, Italy • ordained Bishop of Paisley 19 March 2014 at Paisley.
• *St Fergus, 35 Blackstoun Road, PAISLEY PA3 1LU*

CONTACT INFORMATION

NATIONAL JURISDICTIONS

(Dates are of consecration or translation)

APOSTOLIC NUNCIATURE TO GREAT BRITAIN

His Excellency Most Rev. Antonio Mennini (1974, 2010)

Apostolic Nunciature	T: 020 8944 7189
54 Parkside	E: nuntius@globalnet.co.uk
LONDON	W: www.vatican.va
SW19 5NE	

Retired Apostolic Nuncios: ® His Excellency Most Rev. Luigi Barbarito (1969, 1986) • ® His Excellency Most Rev. Pablo Puente Buces (1980, 1997)

BISHOPRIC OF THE FORCES IN GREAT BRITAIN

SEDE VACANTE

Bishop's Oak	T: 01252 373699
26 The Crescent	E: bishopricforces-rtrev@mod.uk
FARNBOROUGH	W: www.rcbishopricforces.org.uk
GU14 7AS	

Retired Bishop: ® Rt Rev. Francis Walmsley CBE (1979)

UKRAINIAN EPARCHY OF THE HOLY FAMILY OF LONDON

Most Rev. Hlib Lonchyna **MSU** (2002, 2004, 2009, 2013)

Ukrainian Catholic Cathedral   T: 020 7629 1073

22 Binney Street   E: hlib.lonchyna@gmail.com

LONDON   W: www.cerkva.org.uk

W1K 5BQ

Former Apostolic Exarch: Most Rev. Paul Chomnycky **OSBM** *(2002)*

PERSONAL ORDINARIATE OF OUR LADY OF WALSINGHAM

Rev. Mgr Keith Newton (2011)

24 Golden Square   T: 020 7440 5750

LONDON   E: keith.newton@ordinariate.org.uk

W1F 9JR   W: www.ordinariate.org.uk

DIOCESES IN ENGLAND AND WALES

(Dates are of consecration or translation)

WESTMINSTER

+ H.E. Vincent **Cardinal** Nichols (1992, 2000, 2009, 2014)

Archbishop's House	T: 020 7798 9033
Ambrosden Avenue	E: cardinalnichols@rcdow.org.uk
LONDON	W: www.rcdow.org.uk
SW1P 1QJ	

Auxiliary Bishops: Rt Rev. John Sherrington (2011) • Rt Rev. Nicholas Hudson (2014) • Rt Rev. Paul McAleenan (2016) • Rt Rev. John Wilson (2016)

*Retired Archbishop: ® + H.E. Cormac **Cardinal** Murphy-O'Connor (1977, 2000, 2001)*

ARUNDEL AND BRIGHTON

Rt Rev. Richard Moth (2009, 2015)

High Oaks	T: 01293 526428
Old Brighton Road	E: bishop@dabnet.org
Pease Pottage	W: www.dabnet.org
CRAWLEY	
RH11 9AJ	

Retired Bishop: ® Rt Rev. Kieran Conry (2001)

BIRMINGHAM

Most Rev. Bernard Longley (2003, 2009)

Archbishop's House
8 Shadwell Street
BIRMINGHAM
B4 6EY

T: 0121 236 9090
E: archbishop@rc-birmingham.org
W: www.birminghamdiocese.org.uk

*Auxiliary Bishops: Rt Rev. David McGough (2005) • Rt Rev. William Kenney CP
(1987, 2006) • Rt Rev. Robert Byrne CO (2014)*
Retired Auxiliary Bishop: ® Rt Rev. Philip Pargeter (1990)

BRENTWOOD

Rt Rev. Alan Williams **SM** (2014)

Cathedral House
Ingrave Road
BRENTWOOD
CM15 8AT

T: 01277 232266
E: bishopalan@dioceseofbrentwood.org
W: www.dioceseofbrentwood.net

Retired Bishop: ® Rt Rev. Thomas McMahon (1980)

CARDIFF

Most Rev. George Stack (2001, 2011)

Archbishop's House
43 Cathedral Road
CARDIFF
CF11 9HD

T: 029 2022 0411
E: arch@rcadc.org
W: www.rcadc.org

CLIFTON

Rt Rev. Declan Lang (2001)

St Ambrose   T: 0117 973 3072
North Road   E: declan.lang@cliftondiocese.com
Leigh Woods   W: www.cliftondiocese.com
BRISTOL
BS8 3PW

EAST ANGLIA

Rt Rev. Alan Hopes (2003, 2013)

The White House   T: 01508 492202
21 Upgate   E: office@east-angliadiocese.org.uk
Poringland   W: www.rcdea.org.uk
NORWICH
NR14 7SH

HALLAM

Rt Rev. Ralph Heskett **CSsR** (2010, 2014)

Bishop's House   T: 0114 278 7988
75 Norfolk Road   E: bishopofhallam@btinternet.com
SHEFFIELD   W: www.hallam-diocese.com
S2 2SZ

Retired Bishop: ® Rt Rev. John Rawsthorne (1981, 1997)

HEXHAM AND NEWCASTLE

Rt Rev. Séamus Cunningham (2009)

Bishop's House   T: 0191 228 0003
800 West Road   E: bishop@rcdhn.org.uk
NEWCASTLE UPON TYNE   W: www.rcdhn.org.uk
NE5 2BJ

LANCASTER

Rt Rev. Michael Campbell **OSA** (2008, 2009)

The Pastoral Centre	T: 01524 596050
Balmoral Road	E: bishop@lancasterrcdiocese.org.uk
LANCASTER	W: www.lancasterrcdiocese.org.uk
LA1 3BT	

Retired Bishop: ® Rt Rev. Patrick O'Donoghue (1993, 2001)

LEEDS

Rt Rev. Marcus Stock (2014)

Bishop's House	T: 0113 230 4533
13 North Grange Road	E: bishop@dioceseofleeds.org.uk
LEEDS	W: www.dioceseofleeds.org.uk
LS6 2BR	

Former Bishop: Most Rev. Arthur Roche (2001, 2002, 2004, 2012)
Retired Bishop: ® Rt Rev. David Konstant (1977, 1985)

LIVERPOOL

Most Rev. Malcolm McMahon **OP** (2000, 2014)

Archbishop's House	T: 0151 494 0686
19 Salisbury Road	E: archbishop.liverpool@rcaolp.co.uk
LIVERPOOL	W: www.liverpoolcatholic.org.uk
L19 0PH	

Auxiliary Bishop: Rt Rev. Thomas Williams (2003)
Retired Archbishop: ® Most Rev. Patrick Kelly (1984, 1996)
Retired Auxiliary Bishop: ® Rt Rev. Vincent Malone (1989)

MENEVIA

Rt Rev. Thomas Burns **SM** (2002, 2008)

Bryn Rhos
79 Walter Road
SWANSEA
SA1 4PS

T: 01792 650534
E: bishop@menevia.org
W: www.dioceseofmenevia.org

*Retired Bishops: ® Rt Rev. Daniel Mullins (1970, 1987) • ® Rt Rev. Dom. Mark
Jabalé **OSB** (2000, 2001)*

MIDDLESBROUGH

Rt Rev. Terence Drainey (2008)

Bishop's House
16 Cambridge Road
MIDDLESBROUGH
TS5 5NN

T: 01642 818253
E: bishop@dioceseofmiddlesbrough.co.uk
W: www.middlesbrough-diocese.org.uk

Retired Bishop: ® Rt Rev. John Crowley (1986, 1993)

NORTHAMPTON

Rt Rev. Peter Doyle (2005)

Bishop's House
Marriott Street
NORTHAMPTON
NN2 6AW

T: 01604 715635
E: bishopspa@northamptondiocese.com
W: www.northamptondiocese.org

Retired Bishop: ® Rt Rev. Leo McCartie (1977, 1990)

NOTTINGHAM
Rt Rev. Patrick McKinney (2015)

Bishop's House
27 Cavendish Road East
NOTTINGHAM
NG7 1BB

T: 0115 947 4786
E: bishop.secretary@nrcdt.org.uk
W: www.nottingham-diocese.org.uk

PLYMOUTH
Rt Rev. Mark O'Toole (2014)

Bishop's House
31 Wyndham Street West
PLYMOUTH
PL1 5RZ

T: 01752 224414
E: bishop@plymouth-diocese.org.uk
W: www.plymouth-diocese.org.uk

Retired Bishop: ® *Rt Rev. Christopher Budd (1986)*

PORTSMOUTH
Rt Rev. Philip Egan (2012)

Bishop's House
Bishop Crispian Way
PORTSMOUTH
PO1 3HG

T: 023 9282 0894
E: bishop@portsmouthdiocese.org.uk
W: www.portsmouthdiocese.org.uk

Retired Bishop: ® *Rt Rev. Crispian Hollis (1987, 1989)*

SALFORD

Rt Rev. John Arnold (2006, 2014)

Wardley Hall	T: 0161 794 2825
Wardley Hall Road	E: bishop@wardleyhall.org.uk
Worsley	W: www.salforddiocese.org.uk
MANCHESTER	
M28 2ND	

Retired Bishop: ® *Rt Rev. Terence Brain (1991, 1997)*

SHREWSBURY

Rt Rev. Mark Davies (2010)

21 Churchwood View	T: 0151 652 9855
LYMM	E: bishopmarkdavies@dioceseofshrewsbury.org
WA13 0PU	W: www.dioceseofshrewsbury.org

Retired Bishop: ® *Rt Rev. Brian Noble (1995)*

SOUTHWARK

Most Rev. Peter Smith (1995, 2001, 2010)

Archbishop's House	T: 020 7928 2495
150 St George's Road	E: aps@rcsouthwark.co.uk
LONDON	W: www.rcsouthwark.co.uk
SE1 6HX	

Auxiliary Bishops: Rt Rev. Paul Hendricks (2006) • *Rt Rev. Patrick Lynch* **SS.CC**
    (2006)

Retired Archbishops: ® *Most Rev. Michael Bowen (1970, 1977)* • ® *Most Rev.*
    Kevin McDonald (2001, 2003)

Retired Auxiliary Bishops: ® *Rt Rev. Howard Tripp (1980)* • ® *Rt Rev. John Hine*
    (2001)

WREXHAM

Rt Rev. Peter Brignall (2012)

Bishop's House
Sontley Road
WREXHAM
LL13 7EW

T: 01978 262726
E: curia@wrexhamdiocese.org.uk
W: www.wrexhamdiocese.org.uk

Retired Bishop: ® Rt Rev. Edwin Regan (1994)

DIOCESES IN SCOTLAND

(Dates are of consecration or translation)

ST ANDREWS AND EDINBURGH

Most Rev. Leo Cushley (2013)

St Bennet's T: 0131 623 8900
42 Greenhill Gardens E: chancellor@staned.org.uk
EDINBURGH W: www.archdiocese-edinburgh.com
EH10 4BJ

Retired Archbishop: ® + *H.E. Keith Patrick* **Cardinal** *O'Brien (1985, 2003)*

ABERDEEN

Rt Rev. Dom. Hugh Gilbert **OSB** (2011)

Bishop's House T: 01224 319154
3 Queen's Cross E: bishop@rcd-abdn.org
ABERDEEN W: www.dioceseofaberdeen.org
AB15 4XU

Retired Bishop: ® *Rt Rev. Peter Moran (2003)*

ARGYLL AND THE ISLES
Rt Rev. Brian McGee (2016)

Bishop's House	T: 01631 571395
Corran Esplanade	E: rcd.argyll@btconnect.com
OBAN	W: www.rcdai.org.uk
PA34 5AB	

DUNKELD
Rt Rev. Stephen Robson (2012, 2013)

Bishop's House	T: 01382 224327
29 Roseangle	E: bishop@dunkelddiocese.org.uk
DUNDEE	W: www.dunkelddiocese.org.uk
DD1 4LS	

Retired Bishop: ® Rt Rev. Vincent Logan (1981)

GALLOWAY
Rt Rev. William Nolan (2015)

Candida Casa	T: 01292 266750
8 Corsehill Road	E: bishop@gallowaydiocese.org.uk
AYR	W: www.gallowaydiocese.org.uk
KA7 2ST	

Retired Bishops: ® Rt Rev. Maurice Taylor (1981) • ® Rt Rev. John Cunningham (2004)

GLASGOW
Most Rev. Philip Tartaglia (2005, 2012)

52 St Andrews Drive	T: 0141 226 5898
GLASGOW	E: archbishop@rcag.org.uk
G41 5HF	W: www.rcag.org.uk

Retired Archbishop: ® Most Rev. Mario Conti (1977, 2002)

MOTHERWELL

Rt Rev. Joseph Toal (2008, 2014)

St Gerard's   T: 01698 841848

Fleming Road   E: bishop@rcdom.org.uk

BELLSHILL   W: www.rcdom.org.uk

ML4 1NF

Retired Bishop: ® *Rt Rev. Joseph Devine (1977, 1983)*

PAISLEY

Rt Rev. John Keenan (2014)

St Fergus   T: 0141 889 9277

35 Blackstoun Road   E: bishop@rcdop.org.uk

PAISLEY   W: www.rcdop.org.uk

PA3 1LU

Retired Bishop: ® *Rt Rev. John Mone (1984, 1988)*

BISHOPS IN ENGLAND AND WALES

ARNOLD, Rt Rev. John S. K., Bishop of Salford • Wardley Hall, Wardley Hall Road, Worsley, MANCHESTER M28 2ND • T: 0161 794 2825 • E: bishop@wardleyhall.org.uk

® **BOWEN**, Most Rev. Michael G., retired Archbishop of Southwark • 54 Parkside, Vanbrugh Fields, LONDON SE3 7QF • T: 020 7928 2495 • E: aps@rcsouthwark.co.uk

® **BRAIN**, Rt Rev. Terence J., retired Bishop of Salford • 106 Crow Hill South, Middleton, MANCHESTER M24 1JU • T: 0161 653 0820 • E: terence.brain@dioceseofsalford.org.uk

BRIGNALL, Rt Rev. Peter M., Bishop of Wrexham • Bishop's House, Sontley Road, WREXHAM LL13 7EW • T: 01978 262726 • E: curia@wrexhamdiocese.org.uk

® **BUDD**, Rt Rev. H. Christopher, retired Bishop of Plymouth • Star of the Sea, Strand, St Mary's, ISLES OF SCILLY TR21 0PT (DEC-JUN) • T: 01720 422356 • The Presbytery, Silver Street, LYME REGIS DT7 3HS (JUN-NOV) • T: 01297 599031 • E: hughchristopher@talktalk.net

BURNS SM, Rt Rev. Thomas M., Bishop of Menevia • Bryn Rhos, 79 Walter Road, SWANSEA SA1 4PS • T: 01792 650534 • E: bishop@menevia.org

BYRNE CO, Rt Rev. Robert, auxiliary Bishop of Birmingham • Oscott College, Chester Road, SUTTON COLDFIELD B73 5AA • T: 0121 321 5130 • E: bishop.robert@rc-birmingham.org

CAMPBELL OSA, Rt Rev. Michael G., Bishop of Lancaster • The Pastoral Centre, Balmoral Road, LANCASTER LA1 3BT • T: 01524 596050 • E: bishop@lancasterrcdiocese.org.uk

® **CONRY**, Rt Rev. Kieran T., retired Bishop of Arundel and Brighton • c/o High Oaks, Old Brighton Road, Pease Pottage, CRAWLEY RH11 9AJ • T: 01293 526428 • E: n/a

® **CROWLEY**, Rt Rev. John P., retired Bishop of Middlesbrough • 1 Kirkwick Avenue, HARPENDEN AL5 2QH • T: 01582 712245 • E: harpenden@rcdow.org.uk

CUNNINGHAM, Rt Rev. Séamus, Bishop of Hexham and Newcastle • Bishop's House, 800 West Road, NEWCASTLE UPON TYNE NE5 2BJ • T: 0191 228 0003 • E: bishop@rcdhn.org.uk

DAVIES, Rt Rev. Mark, Bishop of Shrewsbury • 21 Churchwood View, LYMM WA13 0PU • T: 01925 756271 • E: bishopmarkdavies@dioceseofshrewsbury.org

DOYLE, Rt Rev. Peter J. H., Bishop of Northampton • Bishop's House, Marriott Street, NORTHAMPTON NN2 6AW • T: 01604 715635 • E: admin@northamptondiocese.com

DRAINEY, Rt Rev. Terence P., Bishop of Middlesbrough • Bishop's House, 16 Cambridge Road, MIDDLESBROUGH TS5 5NN • T: 01642 818253 • E: bishop@dioceseofmiddlesbrough.co.uk

EGAN, Rt Rev. Philip A., Bishop of Portsmouth • Bishop's House, Bishop Crispian Way, PORTSMOUTH PO1 3HG • T: 023 9282 0894 • E: bishop@portsmouthdiocese.org.uk

HENDRICKS, Rt Rev. Paul, auxiliary Bishop of Southwark • 95 Carshalton Road, SUTTON SM1 4LL • T: 020 8643 8007 • E: bishop.hendricks@googlemail.com

HESKETT CSsR, Rt Rev. Ralph, Bishop of Hallam • Bishop's House, 75 Norfolk Road, SHEFFIELD S2 2SZ • T: 0114 278 7988 • E: bishopofhallam@btinternet.com

® **HINE**, Rt Rev. John F. M., retired auxiliary Bishop of Southwark • St Andrew's Presbytery, 47 Ashford Road, TENTERDEN TN30 6LL • T: 01580 762785 • E: jhine@absouthwark.org

® **HOLLIS**, Rt Rev. R. F. Crispian, retired Bishop of Portsmouth • Stable House, Fairview, Mells, FROME BA11 3PP • T: 01373 813284 • E: crispian.hollis@sky.com

CE **HOPES**, Rt Rev. Alan S., Bishop of East Anglia • The White House, 21 Upgate, Poringland, NORWICH NR14 7SH • T: 01508 492202 • E: office@east-angliadiocese.org.uk

HUDSON, Rt Rev. Nicholas G., auxiliary Bishop of Westminster • Flat 5, 8 Morpeth Terrace, LONDON SW1P 1EQ • T: 020 7931 6061 • E: nicholashudson@rcdow.org.uk

® **JABALÉ** OSB, Rt Rev. Dom. J. P. Mark, retired Bishop of Menevia • 14 Egerton Gardens, LONDON NW4 4BA • T: n/a • E: n/a

®   **KELLY**, Most Rev. Patrick A., retired Archbishop of Liverpool • St Marie's House, 27 Seabank Road, SOUTHPORT PR9 0EJ • T: 01704 542697 • E: pakelly@rcaolp.co.uk

KENNEY CP, Rt Rev. L. William, auxiliary Bishop of Birmingham • St Hugh's House, 27 Hensington Road, WOODSTOCK OX20 1JH • T: 01993 812234 • E: wk@sthughs.plus.com

®   **KONSTANT**, Rt Rev. David E., retired Bishop of Leeds • Ashlea, 62 Headingley Lane, LEEDS LS6 2BU • T: 0113 274 1670 • E: dekonstant@gmail.com

LANG, Rt Rev. Declan R., Bishop of Clifton • St Ambrose, North Road, Leigh Woods, BRISTOL BS8 3PW • T: 0117 973 3072 • E: declan.lang@cliftondiocese.com

LONCHYNA MSU, Most Rev. Hlib B. S., Bishop of Ukrainian Eparchy of the Holy Family of London • Ukrainian Catholic Cathedral, 22 Binney Street, LONDON W1K 5BQ • T: 020 7629 1073 • E: hlib.lonchyna@gmail.com

LONGLEY, Most Rev. Bernard, Archbishop of Birmingham • Archbishop's House, 8 Shadwell Street, BIRMINGHAM B4 6EY • T: 0121 236 9090 • E: archbishop@rc-birmingham.org

LYNCH SS.CC, Rt Rev. Patrick K., auxiliary Bishop of Southwark • 6a Cresswell Park, LONDON SE3 9RD • T: 020 8297 9219 • E: bishoplynch7@btinternet.com

®   **LYSYKANYCH**, Rev. Mgr B. Benjamin, retired Apostolic Administrator for the Ukrainian Exarchate in Great Britain • All Saints' Presbytery, Chadderton Way, OLDHAM OL9 6DH • T: 0161 633 5636 • E: n/a

McALEENAN, Rt Rev. Paul, auxiliary Bishop of Westminster • c/o Archbishop's House, Ambrosden Avenue, LONDON SW1P 1QJ • T: 020 7798 9033 • E: paulmcaleenan@rcdow.org.uk

®   **McCARTIE**, Rt Rev. P. Leo, retired Bishop of Northampton • Little Sisters of the Poor, 71 Queens Park Road, BIRMINGHAM B32 2LB • T: 0121 427 2486 • E: leo.mccartie@btinternet.com

®   **McDONALD**, Most Rev. Kevin J. P., retired Archbishop of Southwark • c/o Archbishop's House, 150 St George's Road, LONDON SE1 6HX • T: 020 7928 2495 • E: mail@kmcdonald.plus.com

McGOUGH, Rt Rev. David C., auxiliary Bishop of Birmingham • The Rocks, 106 Draycott Road, Tean, STOKE-ON-TRENT ST10 4JF • T: 01538 722433 • E: dmcgough@btinternet.com

McKINNEY, Rt Rev. Patrick J., Bishop of Nottingham • Bishop's House, 27 Cavendish Road East, NOTTINGHAM NG7 1BB • T: 0115 947 4786 • E: bishop.secretary@nrcdt.org.uk

McMAHON OP, Most Rev. Malcolm P., Archbishop of Liverpool • Archbishop's House, 19 Salisbury Road, LIVERPOOL L19 0PH • T: 0151 494 0686 • E: archbishop.liverpool@rcaolp.co.uk

® **McMAHON**, Rt Rev. Thomas, retired Bishop of Brentwood • Bishop's House, Stock Road, Stock, INGATESTONE CM4 9BU • T: 01277 840268 • E: stock@dioceseofbrentwood.org

® **MALONE**, Rt Rev. Vincent, retired auxiliary Bishop of Liverpool • 17 West Oakhill Park, LIVERPOOL L13 4BN • T: 0151 228 7637 • E: vmalone@rcaolp.co.uk

MENNINI, His Excellency Most Rev. Antonio, Apostolic Nuncio to Great Britain • The Apostolic Nunciature, 54 Parkside, LONDON SW19 5NE • T: 020 8944 7189 • E: nuntius@globalnet.co.uk

MOTH, Rt Rev. C. P. Richard, Bishop of Arundel and Brighton • High Oaks, Old Brighton Road, Pease Pottage, CRAWLEY RH11 9AJ • T: 01293 526428 • E: bishop@dabnet.org

® **MULLINS**, Rt Rev. Daniel J., retired Bishop of Menevia • 8 Rhodfa'r Gwendraeth, KIDWELLY SA17 4SR • T: 01554 890142 • E: n/a

® + **MURPHY-O'CONNOR**, *His Eminence Cormac*, retired Cardinal Archbishop of Westminster • St Edward's, 7 Dukes Avenue, LONDON W4 2AA • T: 020 8747 6922 • E: srdamian@rcdow.org.uk

CE **NEWTON**, Rev. Mgr Keith, Ordinary for Personal Ordinariate of Our Lady of Walsingham • 24 Golden Square, LONDON W1F 9JR • T: 020 7440 5750 • E: keith.newton@ordinariate.org.uk

+ **NICHOLS**, *His Eminence Vincent G.*, Cardinal Archbishop of Westminster • Archbishop's House, Ambrosden Avenue, LONDON SW1P 1QJ • T: 020 7798 9033 • E: cardinalnichols@rcdow.org.uk

® **NOBLE**, Rt Rev. Brian M., retired Bishop of Shrewsbury • Laburnam Cottage, 97 Barnston Road, Heswall, WIRRAL CH61 1BW • T: 0151 648 0623 • E: noblebrian@amisonline.co.uk

O'TOOLE, Rt Rev. Mark, Bishop of Plymouth • Bishop's House, 45 Cecil Street, PLYMOUTH PL1 5HW • T: 01752 224414 • E: bishopmark@prcdtr.org.uk

® **PARGETER**, Rt Rev. Philip, retired auxiliary Bishop of Birmingham • Grove House, 90 College Road, SUTTON COLDFIELD B73 5AH • T: 0121 354 4363 • E: bishoppargeter@yahoo.co.uk

® **RAWSTHORNE**, Rt Rev. John A., retired Bishop of Hallam • St Michael's Church, St Michael's Road, WIDNES WA8 8TF • T: 0151 424 4021 • E: jarawsthorne@live.co.uk

® **REGAN**, Rt Rev. Edwin, retired Bishop of Wrexham • Bethania, 6 Geufron Terrce, BLAENAU FFESTINIOG LL41 3BW • T: 01766 830409 • E: edwinregan@yahoo.co.uk

SHERRINGTON, Rt Rev. John F., auxiliary Bishop of Westminster • 81 Parkway, WELWYN GARDEN CITY AL8 6JF • T: 01707 322579 • E: johnsherrington@rcdow.org.uk

SMITH, Most Rev. Peter D. G., Archbishop of Southwark • Archbishop's House, 150 St George's Road, LONDON SE1 6HX • T: 020 7928 2495 • E: aps@rcsouthwark.co.uk

STACK, Most Rev. George, Archbishop of Cardiff • Archbishop's House, 43 Cathedral Road, CARDIFF CF11 9HD • T: 029 2022 0411 • E: arch@rcadc.org

CE **STOCK**, Rt Rev. Marcus N., Bishop of Leeds • Bishop's House, 13 North Grange Road, LEEDS LS6 2BR • T: 0113 230 4533 • E: bishop@dioceseofleeds.org.uk

® **TRIPP**, Rt Rev. Howard G., retired auxiliary Bishop of Southwark • 35 St Catherine's Close, LONDON SW20 9NL • T: 020 8542 4886 • E: howardtripp@outlook.com

® **WALMSLEY**, Rt Rev. Francis J., retired Bishop to HM Forces • St John's Convent, Linden Hill Lane, Kiln Green, READING RG10 9XP • T: 0118 940 2964 • E: n/a

WILLIAMS SM, Rt Rev. Alan, Bishop of Brentwood • Cathedral House, Ingrave Road, BRENTWOOD CM15 8AT • T: 01277 232266 • E: bishopalan@dioceseofbrentwood.org

WILLIAMS, Rt Rev. Thomas A., auxiliary Bishop of Liverpool • 14 Hope Place, LIVERPOOL L1 9BG • T: 0151 703 0109 • E: bpwilliams@rcaolp.co.uk

CE **WILSON**, Rt Rev. John, auxiliary Bishop of Westminster • c/o Archbishop's House, Ambrosden Avenue, LONDON SW1P 1QJ • T: 020 7798 9033 • E: johnwilson@rcdow.org.uk

<u>Bishops</u> . . . . .58 *of which:*

- Active 35

\+   • *Cardinals* 2

®   • Retired 23

CE   • Former C. of E. 4

Mgr   • Monsignor 2

     • Religious Orders 9

BISHOPS IN SCOTLAND

® **CONTI**, Most Rev. Mario J., retired Archbishop of Glasgow • 40 Newlands Road, GLASGOW G43 2JD • T: 0141 226 5898 • E: n/a

® **CUNNINGHAM**, Rt Rev. John, retired Bishop of Galloway • 24 Johnston Terrace, GREENOCK PA16 8BD • T: n/a • E: n/a

CUSHLEY, Most Rev. Leo W., Archbishop of St Andrews and Edinburgh • St Bennet's, 42 Greenhill Gardens, EDINBURGH EH10 4BJ • T: 0131 623 8900 • E: chancellor@staned.org.uk

® **DEVINE**, Rt Rev. Joseph, retired Bishop of Motherwell • 27 Smithycroft, HAMILTON ML3 7UL • T: 01698 459129 • E: bishop@rcdom.org.uk

CE **GILBERT** OSB, Rt Rev. Dom. E. Hugh, Bishop of Aberdeen • Bishop's House, 3 Queen's Cross, ABERDEEN AB15 4XU • T: 01224 319154 • E: bishop@rcd-abdn.org

KEENAN, Rt Rev. John, Bishop of Paisley • St Fergus, 35 Blackstoun Road, PAISLEY PA3 1LU • T: 0141 889 9277 • E: bishop@rcdop.org.uk

® **LOGAN**, Rt Rev. Vincent P., retired Bishop of Dunkeld • Croghmore, 10 Arnhall Drive, DUNDEE DD2 1LU • T: n/a • E: n/a

McGEE, Rt Rev. Brian T., Bishop of Argyll and the Isles • Bishop's House, Corran Esplanade, OBAN PA34 5AB • T: 01631 567436 • E: rcd.argyll@btconnect.com

® **MONE**, Rt Rev. John A., retired Bishop of Paisley • Carnmore, 30 Esplanade, GREENOCK PA16 7RU • T: 01475 802770 • E: bishopjohnmone@rcdop.org.uk

® **MORAN**, Rt Rev. Peter A., retired Bishop of Aberdeen • Regowan, 10 Cathedral Square, FORTROSE IV10 8TB • T: 01381 621088 • E: n/a

NOLAN, Rt Rev. William, Bishop of Galloway • Candida Casa, 8 Corsehill Road, AYR KA7 2ST • T: 01292 266750 • E: bishop@gallowaydiocese.org.uk

® + **O'BRIEN**, *His Eminence* Keith M. P., retired Cardinal Archbishop of St Andrews and Edinburgh • c/o Gillis Centre, 100 Strathearn Road, EDINBURGH EH9 1BB • T: 0131 623 8900 • E: chancellor@staned.org.uk

CE **ROBSON**, Rt Rev. Stephen, Bishop of Dunkeld • Bishop's House, 29 Roseangle, DUNDEE DD1 4LS • T: 01382 224327 • E: bishop@dunkelddiocese.org.uk

TARTAGLIA, Most Rev. Philip, Archbishop of Glasgow • 52 St Andrews Drive, GLASGOW G41 5HF • T: 0141 226 5898 • E: archbishop@rcag.org.uk

® **TAYLOR**, Rt Rev. Maurice, retired Bishop of Galloway • 41 Overmills Road, AYR KA7 3LH • T: 01292 285865 • E: mauricetaylor1926@sky.com

TOAL, Rt Rev. Joseph A., Bishop of Motherwell • St Gerard's, Fleming Road, BELLSHILL ML4 1NF • T: 01698 841848 • E: bishop@rcdom.org.uk

Bishops . . . . .16 *of which:*
- Active 8
+ • *Cardinals* 1
® • Retired 8
CE • Former C. of E. 2
- Religious Orders 1

BISHOPS AROUND THE WORLD

®   **BARBARITO**, His Excellency Most Rev. Luigi, retired Apostolic Nuncio to Great Britain • Suore Francescane, via Grottone 28, 83030 PIETRADEFUSI (Avellino), Italy • T: +39 08 2596 2636 • E: barbarito1@alice.it

BURNETTE, Rt Rev. Kurt R., Bishop of Passaic (Ruthenian) • 445 Lackawanna Avenue, WOODLAND PARK NJ 07424, USA • T: +1 973 890 7777 • E: bishop@dioceseofpassaic.org

CHOMNYCKY OSBM, Most Rev. Paul P., former Apostolic Exarch for Ukrainians in Great Britain • Chancery Office, 14 Peveril Road, STAMFORD CT 06902, USA • T: +1 203 324 7698 • E: paulosbm@catholic.org

DUNN, Rt Rev. Patrick J., Bishop of Auckland • Pompallier Diocesan Centre, 30 New Street, Ponsonby, AUCKLAND 1011, New Zealand • T: n/a • E: n/a

CE   **ENTWISTLE**, Rev. Mgr Harry, ordinary for Personal Ordinariate of Our Lady of the Southern Cross • Our Lady of the Southern Cross, 40a Mary Street, HIGHGATE WA 6003, Australia • T: +61 8 9422 7988 • E: ordinariate@iinet.net.au

®   **FITZGERALD MAfr**, His Excellency Most Rev. Michael L., retired Apostolic Nuncio to Egypt • c/o Padri Bianchi, via Aurelia 269, 00165 ROME, Italy • T: +39 06 3936 341 • E: m.afr@mafroma.org

GALLAGHER, His Excellency Most Rev. Paul R., Secretariat of State (Relations with States) • Palazzo Apostolico Vaticano, 00120 VATICAN CITY • T: +39 06 6988 3913 • E: gallagherpaulus@gmail.com

McPARTLAND SMA, Rev. Mgr Michael B., Apostolic Prefect of Falkland Islands • St Mary's Church, 12 Ross Road, STANLEY, Falkland Islands, FIQQ 1ZZ • T: +500 21204 • E: stmarys@horizon.co.fk

®   **O'DONOGHUE**, Rt Rev. Patrick, retired Bishop of Lancaster • Nazareth House, Drommahane, MALLOW (Cork), Ireland • T: +353 22 21561 • E: nazarethmallow@eircom.net

®   **PUENTE BUCES**, His Excellency Most Rev. Pablo, retired Apostolic Nuncio to Great Britain • La Parroquia de San Juan Bautista, 39750 COLINDRES, Spain • T: +34 942 650293 • E: n/a

ROCHE, Most Rev. Arthur, secretary of the Congregation for Divine Worship and Discipline of the Sacraments • Palazzo delle Congregazioni, Piazza Pio XII 10, 00193 ROME, Italy • T: +39 06 69 88 40 05 • E: n/a

       Bishops . . . . .11 *of which:*

        • Active 7

®   • Retired 4

CE   • Former C. of E. 1

Mgr   • Monsignor 2

        • Religious Orders 4

ALMANAC

INDEX OF DATES

PRE-1800

☌ CHIARAMONTI **OSB**, B. N. M. L. Gregorio (POPE PIUS VII): born 14 August 1742 at Cesena (Forli-Cesena), Italy.

CHIARAMONTI **OSB**, B. N. M. L. Gregorio (POPE PIUS VII): professed (Order of Saint Benedict) 20 August 1758 at Cesena (Forli-Cesena), Italy.

☌ della GENGA, Annibale (POPE LEO XII): born 22 August 1760 at Castello della Genga (Ancona), Italy.

☌ CASTIGLIONI, Francesco S. M. F. (POPE PIUS VIII): born 20 November 1761 at Cingoli (Macerata), Italy.

☌ CAPPELLARI **OSB**, B. A. Mauro (POPE GREGORY XVI): born 18 September 1765 at Belluno (Belluno), Italy.

CHIARAMONTI **OSB**, B. N. M. L. Gregorio (POPE PIUS VII): ordained priest (Order of Saint Benedict) 21 September 1765 at Cesena (Forli-Cesena), Italy.

CHIARAMONTI **OSB**, B. N. M. L. Gregorio (POPE PIUS VII): ordained Bishop of Tivoli 21 December 1782 at Tivoli (Roma), Italy.

della GENGA, Annibale (POPE LEO XII): ordained priest (Rome) 4 June 1783 at Rome, Italy.

CHIARAMONTI **OSB**, B. N. M. L. Gregorio (POPE PIUS VII): translated 14 February 1785 to Diocese of Imola.

+ CHIARAMONTI **OSB**, B. N. M. L. Gregorio (POPE PIUS VII): elevated 14 February 1785 to Cardinal-Priest of San Callisto.

CASTIGLIONI, Francesco S. M. F. (POPE PIUS VIII): ordained priest (Cingoli) 17 December 1785 at Cingoli (Macerata), Italy.

CAPPELLARI **OSB**, B. A. Mauro (POPE GREGORY XVI): professed (Order of Saint Benedict) 1786 at Murano (Venezia), Italy.

ơ   BROWN, George H.: born 13 January 1786 at Clifton-in-the-Fylde, Preston.

ơ   HOGARTH, William: born 25 March 1786 at Dodding Green, Kendal.

CAPPELLARI **OSB**, B. A. Mauro (**POPE GREGORY XVI**): ordained priest (Order of Saint Benedict) 1787 at Murano (Venezia), Italy.

ơ   BRIGGS, John: born 20 May 1788 at Barton-upon-Irwell, Manchester.

ơ   WAREING, William: born 14 February 1791 at Lincoln's Inn Fields, London.

ơ   BURGESS **OSB**, T. Lawrence: born 1 October 1791 at Clayton Green, Chorley.

ơ   HENDREN **OSF**, Joseph W. F.: born 19 October 1791 at Birmingham.

ơ   MASTAI-FERRETTI, Giovanni M. (**POPE BL. PIUS IX**): born 13 May 1792 at Senigallia (Ancona), Italy.

della GENGA, Annibale (**POPE LEO XII**): entered diplomatic service to the Holy See 1794 at Rome, Italy.

della GENGA, Annibale (**POPE LEO XII**): ordained titular Archbishop of *Tyrus* and appointed Apostolic Nuncio to Germany 24 February 1794 at Rome, Italy.

ơ   BROWN **OSB**, T. Joseph: born 2 May 1798 at Bath.

ơ   TURNER, William: born 25 September 1799 at Whittingham Hall, Preston.

1800

x   CHIARAMONTI **OSB**, B. N. M. L. Gregorio (**POPE PIUS VII**): elected Pope 14 March 1800 at Rome, Italy.

CHIARAMONTI **OSB**, B. N. M. L. Gregorio (**POPE PIUS VII**): installed 21 March 1800 at Rome, Italy.

CASTIGLIONI, Francesco S. M. F. (**POPE PIUS VIII**): ordained Bishop of Montalto (delle Marche) 17 August 1800 at Rome, Italy.

1802

♂ WISEMAN, Nicholas P. S.: born 3 August 1802 at Seville (Sevilla), Spain.

1804

♂ ERRINGTON, George: born 14 September 1804 at Clints Hall, Marske, Richmond.

1806

♂ ULLATHORNE OSB, W. Bernard: born 7 May 1806 at Pocklington, York.
HENDREN OSF, Joseph W. F.: professed (Order of Saint Francis) 2 August 1806 at Abergavenny.

1807

BURGESS OSB, T. Lawrence: professed (Order of Saint Benedict) 13 October 1807 at Ampleforth, York.

1808

♂ MANNING, Henry E.: born 15 July 1808 at Totteridge, London.

1809

HOGARTH, William: ordained priest (Northern District) 20 December 1809 at Ushaw, Durham.

1810

♂ PECCI, Vincenzo G. R. L. (**POPE LEO XIII**): born 2 March 1810 at Carpineto Romano (Roma), Italy.

BROWN, George H.: ordained priest (Northern District) 13 June 1810 at Ushaw, Durham.

♂ STRAIN, John M.: born 8 December 1810 at Edinburgh.

1812

♂ BROWN, James: born 11 January 1812 at Wolverhampton.

1813

♂ CHADWICK, James: born 24 April 1813 at Drogheda (Louth), Ireland.

1814

BURGESS OSB, T. Lawrence: ordained priest (Order of Saint Benedict) 1814 at Ushaw, Durham.

♂ VAUGHAN, William: born 14 February 1814 at London.

♂ GOSS, Alexander: born 5 July 1814 at Ormskirk.

BRIGGS, John: ordained priest (Northern District) 19 July 1814 at Ushaw, Durham.

♂ RIGG, George: born 19 July 1814 at Croghmore, Kirkpatrick Irongray, Kirkcudbright.

BROWN OSB, T. Joseph: professed (Order of Saint Benedict) 28 October 1814 at Downside, Radstock.

♂ WEATHERS, William: born 12 November 1814 at London.

1815

HENDREN **OSF**, Joseph W. F.: ordained priest (Order of Saint Francis) 28 September 1815 at Wolverhampton.

WAREING, William: ordained priest (Midland District) 28 September 1815 at Wolverhampton.

1816

CASTIGLIONI, Francesco S. M. F. (**POPE PIUS VIII**): translated 8 March 1816 to Diocese of Cesena.

+ CASTIGLIONI, Francesco S. M. F. (**POPE PIUS VIII**): elevated 8 March 1816 to **Cardinal-Priest of Santa Maria in Traspontina**.

CHIARAMONTI **OSB**, B. N. M. L. Gregorio (**POPE PIUS VII**): resigned 8 March 1816 as Bishop of Imola.

della GENGA, Annibale (**POPE LEO XII**): translated 8 March 1816 to Diocese of Senigallia.

della GENGA, Annibale (**POPE LEO XII**): appointed *Archbishop ad personam* 8 March 1816 at Rome, Italy.

+ della GENGA, Annibale (**POPE LEO XII**): elevated 8 March 1816 to **Cardinal-Priest of Santa Maria in Trastevere**.

della GENGA, Annibale (**POPE LEO XII**): resigned 10 September 1816 as Bishop of Senigallia.

♂ GRANT, Thomas: born 25 November 1816 at Ligny-lès-Aire (Pas-de-Calais), France.

1817

♂ ROSKELL, Richard B.: born 15 August 1817 at Gateacre, Liverpool.

♂ EYRE, Charles P.: born 7 November 1817 at Askham Bryan, York.

1818

♂ CORNTHWAITE, Robert: born 9 May 1818 at Preston.

σ   MacDONALD, John: born 2 July 1818 at Strath Glass, Beauly.

1819

σ   AMHERST, Francis K.: born 21 March 1819 at Marylebone, London.
    MASTAI-FERRETTI, Giovanni M. (POPE BL. PIUS IX): ordained priest (Senigallia) 10 April 1819 at Senigallia (Ancona), Italy.

σ   SMITH, William: born 3 July 1819 at Edinburgh.

σ   COFFIN CSsR, Robert A.: born 19 July 1819 at Brighton.

1820

    della GENGA, Annibale (POPE LEO XII): appointed 9 May 1820 Prefect of the Roman Curia.

1821

    della GENGA, Annibale (POPE LEO XII): appointed 10 February 1821 Archpriest of the Basilica of St Mary Major.

σ   DANELL, James: born 14 July 1821 at Hampstead, London.

+   CASTIGLIONI, Francesco S. M. F. (POPE PIUS VIII): elevated 13 August 1821 to Cardinal-Bishop of Frascati and appointed Prefect of the Roman Curia.

1822

σ   PATTERSON, James L.: born 16 November 1822 at Marylebone, London.

1823

BROWN OSB, T. Joseph: ordained priest (Order of Saint Benedict) 7 April 1823 at London.

† CHIARAMONTI OSB, B. N. M. L. Gregorio (POPE PIUS VII): died 20 August 1823 at the Apostolic Palace, Rome, Italy aged 81 • buried at St Peter's Basilica, Vatican City.

x della GENGA, Annibale (POPE LEO XII): elected Pope 28 September 1823 at Rome, Italy.

della GENGA, Annibale (POPE LEO XII): installed 5 October 1823 at Rome, Italy.

σ CLIFFORD, William H. J.: born 24 December 1823 at Irnham, Grantham.

1824

σ O'REILLY, Bernard: born 10 January 1824 at Ballybeg (Meath), Ireland.

σ BEWICK, John W.: born 20 April 1824 at Minsteracres, Consett.

1825

+ CAPPELLARI OSB, B. A. Mauro (POPE GREGORY XVI): elevated 21 March 1825 to Cardinal-Priest *in pectore*.

WISEMAN, Nicholas P. S.: ordained priest (Northern District) 19 March 1825 at Rome, Italy.

ULLATHORNE OSB, W. Bernard: professed (Order of Saint Benedict) 5 April 1825 at Downside, Radstock.

σ WILKINSON, Thomas W.: born 5 April 1825 at Harperley, Stanley.

TURNER, William: ordained priest (Northern District) 17 December 1825 at Rome, Italy.

1826

+   CAPPELLARI **OSB**, B. A. Mauro (**POPE GREGORY XVI**): elevated 13 March 1826 to **Cardinal-Priest of San Callisto.**

ơ   BUTT, John B.: born 20 April 1826 at Richmond.

ơ   VIRTUE (VERTUE), John: born 28 April 1826 at Holborn, London.

ơ   McLACHLAN, John: born 7 September 1826 at Glasgow.

    CAPPELLARI **OSB**, B. A. Mauro (**POPE GREGORY XVI**): appointed 1 October 1826 Prefect of the Congregation for the Doctrine of the Faith at Rome, Italy.

1827

ơ   O'CALLAGHAN, Henry: born 29 March 1827 at London.

    MASTAI-FERRETTI, Giovanni M. (**POPE BL. PIUS IX**): ordained Archbishop of Spoleto 3 June 1827 at Spoleto (Perugia), Italy.

ơ   KNIGHT, Edmund: born 27 August 1827 at Sheffield.

    ERRINGTON, George: ordained priest (Northern District) 22 December 1827 at Rome, Italy.

1829

ơ   BAGSHAWE **CO**, Edward G.: born 12 January 1829 at Holborn, London.

†   della GENGA, Annibale (**POPE LEO XII**): died 10 February 1829 at the Apostolic Palace, Rome, Italy aged 68 • buried at St Peter's Basilica, Vatican City.

x   CASTIGLIONI, Francesco S. M. F. (**POPE PIUS VIII**): elected Pope 31 March 1829 at Rome, Italy.

    CASTIGLIONI, Francesco S. M. F. (**POPE PIUS VIII**): installed 5 April 1829 at Rome, Italy.

1830

σ   BROWNLOW, William R. B.: born 4 July 1830 at Wilmslow.

†   CASTIGLIONI, Francesco S. M. F. (**POPE PIUS VIII**): died 30 November 1830 at the Apostolic Palace, Rome, Italy aged 69 • buried at St Peter's Basilica, Vatican City.

1831

x   CAPPELLARI **OSB**, B. A. Mauro (**POPE GREGORY XVI**): elected Pope 2 February 1831 at Rome, Italy.
     CAPPELLARI **OSB**, B. A. Mauro (**POPE GREGORY XVI**): ordained Bishop of Rome and installed 6 February 1831 at Rome, Italy.

σ   GORDON, William: born 24 September 1831 at Thirsk.
     ULLATHORNE **OSB**, W. Bernard: ordained priest (Order of Saint Benedict) 24 September 1831 at Ushaw, Durham.

1832

σ   GRANT, Colin C.: born 3 February 1832 at Glen Gairn, Ballater.

σ   VAUGHAN, Herbert A. H.: born 15 April 1832 at Gloucester.

σ   JOHNSON, William A.: born 20 August 1832 at Somers Town, London.
     MASTAI-FERRETTI, Giovanni M. (**POPE BL. PIUS IX**): translated 17 December 1832 to Archdiocese of Imola.
     MASTAI-FERRETTI, Giovanni M. (**POPE BL. PIUS IX**): appointed 17 December 1832 *Archbishop ad personam* at Rome, Italy.
     MANNING, Henry E.: ordained Church of England deacon (Oxford) 23 December 1832 at Oxford.

1833

CE   MANNING, Henry E.: ordained Church of England priest (Chichester) 9 June 1833 at Lincoln's Inn, London.

STRAIN, John M.: ordained priest (Eastern District) 9 June 1833 at Rome, Italy.

BRIGGS, John: ordained titular Bishop of *Trachis* and appointed coadjutor Vicar Apostolic for the Northern District 29 June 1833 at Ushaw, Durham.

1834

♂ GRAHAM, Charles M.: born 5 April 1834 at Mhow (Madhya Pradesh), India.

1835

♂ SARTO, Giuseppe M. (**POPE ST PIUS X**): born 2 June 1835 at Riese Pio X (Treviso), Italy.

1836

BRIGGS, John: succeeded 28 January 1836 as Vicar Apostolic for the Northern District.

♂ BILSBORROW, John: born 30 March 1836 at Singleton Lodge, Kirkham, Preston.

♂ CHISHOLM, Aeneas: born 26 June 1836 at Inverness.

♂ RIDDELL, Arthur G.: born 15 September 1836 at York.

1837

BROWN, James: ordained priest (Midland District) 18 February 1837 at Oscott, Sutton Coldfield.

♂ HEDLEY OSB, J. E. Cuthbert: born 15 April 1837 at Carlisle House, Morpeth.

♂ FENTON, Patrick: born 19 August 1837 at Soho, London.

♂ BRINDLE, Robert: born 4 November 1837 at Everton, Liverpool.

CHADWICK, James: ordained priest (Northern District) 17 December 1837 at Ushaw, Durham.

PECCI, Vincenzo G. R. L. (POPE LEO XIII): ordained priest (Anagni) 31 December 1837 at Rome, Italy.

1838

WEATHERS, William: ordained priest (London District) 1838 at Old Hall Green, Ware.

VAUGHAN, William: ordained priest (Western District) 10 March 1838 at Prior Park, Bath.

♂ CARROLL, John: born 16 March 1838 at Castleblayney (Monaghan), Ireland.

♂ ILSLEY, Edward: born 11 May 1838 at Appleyard Court, Stafford.

RIGG, George: ordained priest (Eastern District) 25 July 1838 at Valladolid (Valladolid), Spain.

1839

+ MASTAI-FERRETTI, Giovanni M. (POPE BL. PIUS IX): elevated 23 December 1839 to Cardinal-Priest *in pectore*.

1840

♂ SMITH, George J.: born 24 January 1840 at Cuttlebrae, Enzie.

WISEMAN, Nicholas P. S.: ordained titular Bishop of *Milopotamos* and appointed coadjutor Vicar Apostolic for the Midland District 8 June 1840 at Rome, Italy.

ROSKELL, Richard B.: ordained priest (Lancashire District) 9 June 1840 at Rome, Italy.

BRIGGS, John: translated 3 July 1840 to Vicar Apostolic for the Yorkshire District.

WISEMAN, Nicholas P. S.: translated 3 July 1840 to coadjutor Vicar Apostolic of the Midland District.

BROWN, George H.: ordained titular Bishop of *Bugia* and appointed Vicar Apostolic for the Lancashire District 24 August 1840 at Vauxhall, Liverpool.

WAREING, William: ordained titular Bishop of *Areopolis* and appointed Vicar Apostolic for the Eastern District 21 September 1840 at Oscott, Sutton Coldfield.

BROWN OSB, T. Joseph: ordained titular Bishop of *Apollonia* and appointed Vicar Apostolic for the Welsh District 28 October 1840 at Bath.

+ MASTAI-FERRETTI, Giovanni M. (POPE BL. PIUS IX): elevated 14 December 1840 to Cardinal-Priest of Santi Marcellino e Pietro.

1841

♂ LACY, Richard: born 16 January 1841 at Navan (Meath), Ireland.

GOSS, Alexander: ordained priest (Lancashire District) 4 July 1841 at Rome, Italy.

♂ CAHILL, John B.: born 2 September 1841 at London.

♂ SMITH, James A.: born 18 October 1841 at Edinburgh.

MacDONALD, John: ordained priest (Northern District) 4 November 1841 at Preshome, Buckie.

♂ MacDONALD CSsR, Hugh: born 7 November 1841 at Borrodale, Arisaig.

GRANT, Thomas: ordained priest 28 November 1841 at Rome, Italy.

1842

EYRE, Charles P.: ordained priest (Northern District (England & Wales)) 19 March 1842 at Rome, Italy.

BROWN, George H.: appointed 22 April 1842 titular Bishop of *Tlos*.

COFFIN CSsR, Robert A.: ordained Church of England deacon (Oxford) 18 December 1842 at Oxford.

1843

PECCI, Vincenzo G. R. L. (POPE LEO XIII): entered diplomatic service to the Holy See 1843 at Rome, Italy.

♂ MacFARLANE, Angus: born 10 January 1843 at Spean Bridge.

PECCI, Vincenzo G. R. L. (POPE LEO XIII): ordained titular Archbishop of *Tamiathis* and appointed Apostolic Nuncio to Belgium 19 February 1843 at Rome, Italy.

SMITH, William: ordained priest (Eastern District) 15 April 1843 at Rome, Italy.

♂ STANLEY, A. Charles: born 16 September 1843 at Winnington, Northwich.

CE COFFIN CSsR, Robert A.: ordained Church of England priest (Oxford) 17 December 1843 at Oxford.

1844

♂ ALLEN, Samuel W.: born 23 March 1844 at Stockport

♂ MacDONALD, Angus: born 18 September 1844 at Borrodale, Arisaig.

♂ TURNER, William: born 12 December 1844 at Aberdeen.

PATTERSON, James L.: ordained Church of England deacon (Oxford) 21 December 1844 at Oxford.

♂ MACKINTOSH, Donald A.: born 24 December 1844 at Bohuntin, Roy Bridge.

1845

CORNTHWAITE, Robert: ordained priest (Northern District) 9 November 1845 at Rome, Italy.

COFFIN CSsR, Robert A.: received into Catholic Church 3 December 1845 at Prior Park, Bath.

CE PATTERSON, James L.: ordained Church of England priest (Oxford) 21 December 1845 at Oxford.

1846

PECCI, Vincenzo G. R. L. (POPE LEO XIII): translated 18 January 1846 to Archdiocese of Perugia.

PECCI, Vincenzo G. R. L. (POPE LEO XIII): appointed 18 January 1846 *Archbishop ad personam* at Rome, Italy.

† CAPPELLARI OSB, B. A. Mauro (POPE GREGORY XVI): died 1 June 1846 at the Apostolic Palace, Rome, Italy aged 80 • buried at St Peter's Basilica, Vatican City.

AMHERST, Francis A.: ordained priest (Central District) 6 June 1846 at Oscott, Sutton Coldfield.

DANELL, James: ordained priest (London District) 6 June 1846 at Paris (Paris), France.

x MASTAI-FERRETTI, Giovanni M. (POPE BL. PIUS IX): elected Pope 16 June 1846 at Rome, Italy.

MASTAI-FERRETTI, Giovanni M. (POPE BL. PIUS IX): installed 21 June 1846 at Rome, Italy.

ULLATHORNE OSB, W. Bernard: ordained titular Bishop of *Hetalonia* and appointed Vicar Apostolic for the Western District 21 June 1846 at Coventry.

WILKINSON, Thomas W.: received into Catholic Church 29 December 1846 at Leeds.

1847

O'REILLY, Bernard: ordained priest (Lancashire District) 9 May 1847 at Ushaw, Durham.

WISEMAN, Nicholas P. S.: translated 29 August 1847 to coadjutor Vicar Apostolic of the London District.

COFFIN **CSsR**, Robert A.: ordained priest (Confederation of Oratorians of St Philip Neri) 31 October 1847 at Rome, Italy.

1848

ULLATHORNE **OSB**, W. Bernard: translated 28 July 1848 to Vicar Apostolic for the Central District.

HOGARTH, William: ordained titular Bishop of *Samosata* and appointed Vicar Apostolic for the Northern District 24 August 1848 at Ushaw, Durham.

HENDREN **OSF**, Joseph W. F.: ordained titular Bishop of *Verinopolis* and appointed Vicar Apostolic for the Western District 10 September 1848 at Bristol.

WILKINSON, Thomas W.: ordained priest (Northern District) 23 December 1848 at Ushaw, Durham.

1849

WISEMAN, Nicholas P. S.: succeeded 18 February 1849 as Vicar Apostolic of the London District.

BUTT, John B.: ordained priest (London District) 15 July 1849 at Hammersmith, London.

BAGSHAWE **CO**, Edward G.: professed (Confederation of Oratorians of St Philip Neri) 2 November 1849 at Strand, London.

1850

McLACHLAN, John: ordained priest (Western District) 16 March 1850 at Rome, Italy.

PATTERSON, James L.: received into Catholic Church 30 March 1850 at Jerusalem, Israel.

BEWICK, John W.: ordained priest (Northern District) 27 May 1850 at Ushaw, Durham.

CLIFFORD, William H. J.: ordained priest (Western District) 25 August 1850 at Clifton, Bristol.

ENGLAND AND WALES: Hierarchy restored 29 September 1850.

BRIGGS, John: translated 29 September 1850 to restored Diocese of Beverley.

BROWN, George H.: translated 29 September 1850 to restored Diocese of Liverpool.

* BROWN, George H.: appointed 29 September 1850 Apostolic Administrator of the Diocese of Salford until 25 July 1851.

BROWN OSB, T. Joseph: translated 29 September 1850 to restored Diocese of Newport and Menevia.

* BROWN OSB, T. Joseph: appointed 29 September 1850 Apostolic Administrator of the Diocese of Shrewsbury until 27 July 1851.

HENDREN OSF, Joseph W. F.: translated 29 September 1850 to restored Diocese of Clifton.

* HENDREN OSF, Joseph W. F.: appointed 29 September 1850 Apostolic Administrator of Diocese of Plymouth until 22 June 1851.

HOGARTH, William: translated 29 September 1850 to restored Diocese of Hexham.

ULLATHORNE OSB, W. Bernard: translated 29 September 1850 to restored Diocese of Birmingham.

* ULLATHORNE OSB, W. Bernard: appointed 29 September 1850 Apostolic Administrator of the Diocese of Nottingham until 22 June 1851.

WAREING, William: translated 29 September 1850 to restored Diocese of Northampton.

WISEMAN, Nicholas P. S.: translated 29 September 1850 to Archbishop and Metropolitan of newly raised and restored Archdiocese and Province of Westminster.

* WISEMAN, Nicholas P. S.: appointed 29 September 1850 Apostolic Administrator of Diocese of Southwark until 4 July 1851.

+ WISEMAN, Nicholas P. S.: elevated 30 September 1850 to Cardinal-Priest of Santa Pudenziana.

1851

O'CALLAGHAN, Henry: ordained priest (Westminster) 15 March 1851 at Old Hall Green, Ware.

MANNING, Henry E.: received into Catholic Church 6 April 1851 at Mayfair, London.

MANNING, Henry E.: ordained priest (Westminster) 14 June 1851 at Mayfair, London.

HENDREN OSF, Joseph W. F.: translated 22 June 1851 to restored Diocese of Nottingham.

DIOCESE OF LIVERPOOL: restructured 27 June 1851.

DIOCESE OF SALFORD: restructured 27 June 1851.

GRANT, Thomas: ordained Bishop of restored Diocese of Southwark 4 July 1851 at Rome, Italy.

ERRINGTON, George: ordained Bishop of restored Diocese of Plymouth 25 July 1851 at Salford.

TURNER, William: ordained Bishop of restored Diocese of Salford 25 July 1851 at Salford.

BROWN, James: ordained Bishop of restored Diocese of Shrewsbury 27 July 1851 at the Cathedral Church of St George, Southwark, London.

BURGESS OSB, T. Lawrence: ordained Bishop of Clifton 27 July 1851 at the Cathedral Church of St George, Southwark, London.

♂ SINGLETON, Hugh: born 30 July 1851 at Birkenhead.

♂ MAGUIRE, John A.: born 8 September 1851 at Calton, Glasgow.

VIRTUE (VERTUE), John: ordained priest (Westminster) 20 December 1851 at Rome, Italy.

1852

COFFIN CSsR, Robert A.: professed (Congregation of the Most Holy Redeemer) 2 February 1852 at Saint-Trond (Liège), Belgium.

BAGSHAWE CO, Edward G.: ordained priest (Confederation of Oratorians of St Philip Neri) 6 March 1852 at Strand, London.

♂ BURTON, George C. A.: born 7 June 1852 at Hull.

♂ CASARTELLI, Louis C.: born 14 November 1852 at Cheetham Hill, Manchester.

1853

VIRTUE (VERTUE), John: entered diplomatic service to the Holy See 1853 at Rome, Italy.

♂ VAUGHAN, John S.: born 24 January 1853 at Courtfield, Ross-on-Wye.

♂ McCARTHY, James W.: born 30 January 1853 at Newcastle upon Tyne.

® HENDREN OSF, Joseph W. F.: appointed 23 February 1853 titular Bishop of *Martyropolis* and retired to Birmingham thence to Taunton.

ROSKELL, Richard B.: ordained Bishop of Nottingham 21 September 1853 at Nottingham.

GOSS, Alexander: ordained titular Bishop of *Gerrha* and appointed coadjutor Bishop of Liverpool 25 September 1853 at the Pro-Cathedral Church of St Nicholas, Liverpool.

BROWNLOW, William R. B.: ordained Church of England deacon (Lichfield) 18 December 1853 at Lichfield.

+ PECCI, Vincenzo G. R. L. (**POPE LEO XIII**): elevated 19 December 1853 to **Cardinal-Priest of San Crisogono**.

1854

♂ KEILY, John J.: born 23 June 1854 at Limerick City (Limerick), Ireland.

BUTT, John B.: commissioned as military chaplain 21 September 1854.

♂ GLANCEY, Michael F.: born 25 October 1854 at Wolverhampton.

VAUGHAN, Herbert A. H.: ordained priest (Westminster) 28 October 1854 at Lucca (Lucca), Italy.

♂ *DELLA* CHIESA, Giacomo P. G.-B. (**POPE BENEDICT XV**): born 21 November 1854 at Pegli (Genova), Italy.

† BURGESS OSB, T. Lawrence: died 27 November 1854 at Westbury-on-Trym, Bristol aged 63 • buried at the Pro-Cathedral Church of the Twelve Apostles, Clifton, Bristol.

1855

PATTERSON, James L.: ordained priest (Westminster) 1855 at Moorfields, City of London.

VIRTUE (VERTUE), John: commissioned as military chaplain 1855.

HEDLEY OSB, J. E. Cuthbert: professed (Order of Saint Benedict) 1 January 1855 at Ampleforth, York.

♂ McINTYRE, John: born 1 January 1855 at Snow Hill, Birmingham.

ERRINGTON, George: translated 30 March 1855 to titular Archbishop of *Trapezus* and appointed coadjutor Archbishop of Westminster.

VAUGHAN, William: ordained Bishop of Plymouth 16 September 1855 at Clifton, Bristol.

* ERRINGTON, George: appointed 22 October 1855 Apostolic Administrator of the Diocese of Clifton until 15 February 1857.

GRANT, Colin C.: ordained priest (Northern District) 22 December 1855 at Blairs, Aberdeen.

1856

† BROWN, George H.: died 25 January 1856 at Litherland, Liverpool aged 70 • buried at St Oswald's Church, Old Swan, Liverpool.

GOSS, Alexander: succeeded 25 January 1856 as Bishop of Liverpool.

CE BROWNLOW, William R. B.: ordained Church of England priest (Lichfield) 18 May 1856 at St Paul's Cathedral, City of London.

♂ PRESTON, Richard: born 12 December 1856 at St Leonards Gate, Lancaster.

1857

♂ WARD, Bernard F. N.: born 4 February 1857 at Old Hall Green, Ware.

CLIFFORD, William H. J.: ordained Bishop of Clifton 15 February 1857 at Rome, Italy.

♂ TONER, John: born 14 March 1857 at Calton, Glasgow.

♂   COLLINS, Richard: born 5 April 1857 at Newbury.

♂   WHITESIDE, Thomas: born 17 April 1857 at Lancaster.

♂   RATTI, Ambrogio D. A. (POPE PIUS XI): born 31 May 1857 at
Desio (Monza e Brianza), Italy.

GRAHAM, Charles M.: ordained priest (Plymouth) 19 December
1857 at Rome, Italy.

JOHNSON, William A.: ordained priest (Westminster) 19
December 1857 at Rome, Italy.

KNIGHT, Edmund: ordained priest (Birmingham) 19 December
1857 at Rome, Italy.

1858

®   WAREING, William: appointed 11 February 1858 titular Bishop of
Rhithymna and retired to Old Hall Convent, East Bergholt, Colchester.

DIOCESE OF PLYMOUTH: cathedral transferred 25 March
1858.

AMHERST, Francis K.: ordained Bishop of Northampton 4 July
1858 at Northampton.

♂   FRASER, Robert: born 10 August 1858 at Kennethmont, Huntly.

SARTO, Giuseppe M. (POPE ST PIUS X): ordained priest (Treviso)
18 September 1858 at Treviso (Treviso), Italy.

1859

GORDON, William: ordained priest (Beverley) 10 February 1859 at
York.

CHISHOLM, Aeneas: ordained priest (Northern District) 15 May
1859 at Rome, Italy.

♂   KEATING, Frederick W.: born 13 June 1859 at City of Birmingham.

RIDDELL, Arthur G.: ordained priest (Beverley) 24 September 1859
at Ushaw, Durham.

1860

BUTT, John B.: released from military service 1860.

♂ COWGILL, Joseph R.: born 23 February 1860 at Broughton in Craven, Skipton.

♂ MOSTYN, Francis E. J.: born 6 August 1860 at Talacre, Holywell.

® BRIGGS, John: retired 7 November 1860 to Fulford, York.

1861

† BRIGGS, John: died 4 January 1861 at Fulford, York aged 72 • buried at St Leonard's chapel, Hazlewood, Tadcaster.

♂ BOURNE, Francis A.: born 23 March 1861 at Clapham, London.

DIOCESE OF HEXHAM AND NEWCASTLE: renamed 23 May 1861.

HOGARTH, William: translated 23 May 1861 to renamed Diocese of Hexham and Newcastle.

ILSLEY, Edward: ordained priest (Birmingham) 29 June 1861 at the Cathedral Church of St Chad, Birmingham.

CORNTHWAITE, Robert: ordained Bishop of Beverley 10 November 1861 at Moorfields, City of London.

CARROLL, John: ordained priest (Shrewsbury) 22 December 1861 at Bruges (West Flanders), Belgium.

1862

♂ BROWN, William F.: born 3 May 1862 at Dundee.

® ERRINGTON, George: resigned 2 July 1862 as coadjutor Archbishop of Westminster.

♂ BILSBORROW OSB, J. Romanus: born 27 August 1862 at Walton-le-Dale, Preston.

HEDLEY OSB, J. E. Cuthbert: ordained priest (Order of Saint Benedict) 19 October 1862 at Ampleforth, York.

BRINDLE, Robert: ordained priest (Plymouth) 27 December 1862 at Lisbon (Lisboa), Portugal.

1863

BROWNLOW, William R. B.: received into Catholic Church 1 November 1863 at Edgbaston, Birmingham.

1864

♂ AMIGO, Peter E.: born 26 May 1864 at Gibraltar.
DIOCESE OF BEVERLEY: pro-cathedral transferred 1 June 1864.
STRAIN, John M.: ordained titular Bishop of *Abila Lysaniae* and appointed Vicar Apostolic for the Eastern District 25 September 1864 at Rome, Italy.
CAHILL, John B.: ordained priest (Southwark) 4 October 1864 at Bermondsey, London.
SMITH, George J.: ordained priest (Western District) 17 December 1864 at Paris (Paris), France.

1865

† WISEMAN, Nicholas P. S.: died 15 February 1865 at Portman Square, London aged 62 • buried at St Mary's Cemetery, Kensal Green, London.
BILSBORROW, John: ordained priest (Liverpool) 26 February 1865 at St Edward's College, Liverpool.
MANNING, Henry E.: ordained Archbishop of Westminster 8 June 1865 at Moorfields, City of London.
♂ HINSLEY, Arthur: born 25 August 1865 at Carlton, Selby.
ERRINGTON, George: appointed 1 September 1865 parish priest of St Mary's Church, Douglas, Isle of Man.
♂ DOUBLEDAY, Arthur H.: born 16 October 1865 at Pietermaritzburg (Natal), South Africa.
† WAREING, William: died 26 December 1865 at Old Hall Convent, East Bergholt, Colchester aged 74 • buried at Old Hall Convent, East Bergholt, Colchester.

1866

†   HOGARTH, William: died 29 January 1866 at Darlington aged 79 • buried at St Cuthbert's College, Ushaw, Durham.

SMITH, James A.: ordained priest (Eastern District) 31 March 1866 at Rome, Italy.

FENTON, Patrick: ordained priest (Westminster) 22 September 1866 at Old Hall Green, Ware.

CHADWICK, James: ordained Bishop of Hexham and Newcastle 28 October 1866 at Ushaw, Durham.

†   HENDREN OSF, Joseph W. F.: died 14 November 1866 at Taunton aged 75 • buried at the Franciscan Convent, Taunton.

♂   COTTER, William T.: born 21 December 1866 at Cloyne (Cork), Ireland.

STANLEY, A. Charles: ordained Church of England deacon (Worcester) 21 December 1866 at Worcester.

BROWNLOW, William R. B.: ordained priest (Plymouth) 22 December 1866 at Rome, Italy.

1867

♂   DOBSON, Robert: born 21 January 1867 at New Orleans (LA), USA.

MacDONALD CSsR, Hugh: ordained priest (Western District) 21 September 1867 at Ushaw, Durham.

MANNING, Henry E.: appointed 1 October 1867 Apostolic Visitor to Scotland.

LACY, Richard: ordained priest (Beverley) 21 December 1867 at Rome, Italy.

1868

ERRINGTON, George: nominated 27 January 1868 Apostolic Delegate in Scotland but declined the appointment 12 August 1868.

♂   CARY-ELWES, Dudley C.: born 5 February 1868 at Nice (Alpes-Maritimes), France.

MacFARLANE, Angus: ordained priest (Western District) 26 April 1868 at Rome, Italy.

TURNER, William: ordained priest (Eastern District) 26 April 1868 at Rome, Italy.

CE STANLEY, A. Charles: ordained Church of England priest (Worcester) 7 June 1868 at Coventry.

1869

EYRE, Charles P.: ordained titular Archbishop of *Anazarbus* and appointed Apostolic Delegate in Scotland 31 January 1869 at Rome, Italy.

MacDONALD, John: ordained titular Bishop of *Nicopolis ad Iaterum* and appointed (coadjutor) Vicar Apostolic for the Northern District 24 February 1869 at Aberdeen (as his predecessor died the previous day).

ơ BUTT, Joseph: born 27 March 1869 at Richmond.

* EYRE, Charles P.: appointed 16 April 1869 Apostolic Administrator of the Western District until 15 March 1878

ARCHDIOCESE OF WESTMINSTER: pro-cathedral transferred 2 July 1869.

ơ KEATINGE, William L.: born 1 August 1869 at London.

ơ DEY, James: born 14 October 1869 at Walsall.

FIRST VATICAN COUNCIL: 8 December 1869 to 20 October 1870.

1870

ơ PEARSON OSB, T. Wulstan: born 4 January 1870 at Preston.

† GRANT, Thomas: died 1 June 1870 at Rome, Italy aged 53 • buried at Upper Norwood, London.

ơ DUNN, Thomas: born 28 July 1870 at Marylebone, London.

ơ MORIARTY, Ambrose J.: born 7 August 1870 at Stockport.

ALLEN, Samuel W.: ordained priest (Shrewsbury) 4 December 1870 at Liscard, Wallasey.

1871

ơ   McDONALD **OSB**, A. T. Joseph: born 12 February 1871 at Invernevis, Fort William.

DANELL, James: ordained Bishop of Southwark 25 March 1871 at the Cathedral Church of St George, Southwark, London.

MACKINTOSH, Donald A.: ordained priest (Western District) 31 May 1871 at Blairs, Aberdeen.

ơ   THORMAN, Joseph: born 6 August 1871 at Gateshead.

MacDONALD **CSsR**, Hugh: professed (Congregation of the Most Holy Redeemer) 15 October 1871 at Bishop Eton, Liverpool.

1872

ơ   SHINE, Thomas: born 11 February 1872 at Knocknaveigh (Tipperary), Ireland.

ơ   BIDWELL, Manuel J.: born 29 June 1872 at Palma de Mallorca (Islas Baleares), Spain.

MacDONALD, Angus: ordained priest (Western District) 7 July 1872 at Ushaw, Durham.

†   TURNER, William: died 13 July 1872 at Salford aged 72 • buried at Salford Cemetery.

†   GOSS, Alexander: died 3 October 1872 at St Edward's college, Everton, Liverpool aged 58 • buried at Ford Cemetery, Litherland, Liverpool.

VAUGHAN, Herbert A. H.: ordained Bishop of Salford 28 October 1872 at Salford.

WEATHERS, William: ordained titular Bishop of *Amycla* and appointed auxiliary Bishop of Westminster 28 October 1872 at Salford.

ơ   YOUENS **SMA**, Laurence W.: born 14 December 1872 at High Wycombe.

1873

ơ   HENSHAW, Thomas: born 2 February 1873 at Miles Platting, Manchester.

O'REILLY, Bernard: ordained Bishop of Liverpool 19 March 1873 at St Vincent de Paul Church, Liverpool.

HEDLEY OSB, J. E. Cuthbert: ordained titular Bishop of *Caesaropolis* and appointed auxiliary Bishop of Newport and Menevia 29 September 1873 at Belmont, Hereford.

ơ MARTIN, Donald: born 6 October 1873 at Salen, Acharacle.

1874

BRINDLE, Robert: commissioned as military chaplain 12 January 1874.

ơ GRAHAM, Henry G.: born 8 March 1874 at Maxton, Melrose.

® ERRINGTON, George: retired 1 September 1874 to Prior Park, Bath.

BAGSHAWE CO, Edward G.: ordained Bishop of Nottingham 12 November 1874 at Brompton Oratory, London.

® ROSKELL, Richard B.: appointed 12 November 1874 titular Bishop of *Abdera* and retired to Glascoed, Wrexham thence to Whitewell, Clitheroe.

1875

MAGUIRE, John A.: ordained priest (Western District) 27 March 1875 at Rome, Italy.

+ MANNING, Henry E.: elevated 31 March 1875 to Cardinal-Priest of Santi Andrea e Gregorio Magno al Monte Celio.

ơ BENNETT, George H.: born 24 June 1875 at St John's, Antigua.

† TURNER, William: reinterred 1 August 1875 at St Joseph's Cemetery, Moston, Manchester.

ơ MYERS, Edward: born 8 September 1875 at Walmgate, York.

ơ LEE, William: born 27 September 1875 at Mitchelstown (Cork), Ireland.

1876

♂ PACELLI, Eugenio M. G. G. (**POPE VEN. PIUS XII**): born 2
March 1876 at Rome, Italy.

♂ CAMERON, E. Hugh: born 20 April 1876 at Inveroy, Roy Bridge.

VAUGHAN, John S.: ordained priest (Salford) 4 June 1876 at
Salford.

CASARTELLI, Louis C.: ordained priest (Salford) 10 September
1876 at Salford.

1877

♂ MELLON, William H.: born 6 January 1877 at Edinburgh.

♂ WILLIAMS, Thomas L.: born 20 March 1877 at Handsworth,
Birmingham.

♂ VAUGHAN, Francis J.: born 5 May 1877 at Courtfield,
Ross-on-Wye.

KEILY, John J.: ordained priest (Plymouth) 18 May 1877 at Plymouth.

♂ MACKINTOSH, Donald: born 10 October 1877 at Glasnacardoch,
Mallaig.

GLANCEY, Michael F.: ordained priest (Birmingham) 22 December
1877 at Olton, Solihull.

1878

† MASTAI-FERRETTI, Giovanni M. (**POPE BL. PIUS IX**): died 7
February 1878 at the Apostolic Palace, Rome, Italy aged 85 • buried at St
Peter's Basilica, Vatican City.

x PECCI, Vincenzo G. R. L. (**POPE LEO XIII**): elected Pope 20
February 1878 at Rome, Italy.

PECCI, Vincenzo G. R. L. (**POPE LEO XIII**): installed 3 March
1878 at Rome, Italy.

SCOTLAND: Hierarchy restored 4 March 1878.

EYRE, Charles P.: translated 15 March 1878 to restored Archdiocese
of Glasgow.

MacDONALD, John: translated 15 March 1878 to restored Diocese of Aberdeen.

STRAIN, John M.: translated 15 March 1878 to Archbishop and Metropolitan of newly raised and restored Archdiocese and Province of St Andrews and Edinburgh.

MacDONALD, Angus: ordained Bishop of restored Diocese of Argyll and the Isles 23 May 1878 at the Cathedral Church of St Andrew, Glasgow.

McLACHLAN, John: ordained Bishop of restored Diocese of Galloway 23 May 1878 at the Cathedral Church of St Andrew, Glasgow.

RIGG, George: ordained Bishop of restored Diocese of Dunkeld 26 May 1878 at Rome, Italy.

♂ BARRETT, John P.: born 31 October 1878 at Liverpool.

DIOCESE OF LEEDS: erected 20 December 1878.

DIOCESE OF MIDDLESBROUGH: erected 20 December 1878.

CORNTHWAITE, Robert: translated 20 December 1878 to newly erected Diocese of Leeds.

* CORNTHWAITE, Robert: appointed 20 December 1878 Apostolic Administrator of Diocese of Middlesbrough until 18 December 1879.

DELLA CHIESA, Giacomo P. G.-B. (POPE BENEDICT XV): ordained priest (Rome) 21 December 1878 at Rome, Italy.

1879

STANLEY, A. Charles: received into Catholic Church 1879 at London.

® AMHERST, Francis K.: resigned 2 April 1879 as Bishop of Northampton.

* AMHERST, Francis K.: appointed 2 April 1879 Apostolic Administrator of the Diocese of Northampton until 9 June 1880.

McCARTHY, James W.: ordained priest (Glasgow) 4 May 1879 at the Cathedral Church of St Andrew, Glasgow.

KNIGHT, Edmund: ordained titular Bishop of *Corycus* and appointed auxiliary Bishop of Shrewsbury 25 July 1879 at Birkenhead.

♂ McNULTY, John F.: born 11 August 1879 at Collyhurst, Manchester.

ILSLEY, Edward: ordained titular Bishop of *Fesseë* and appointed auxiliary Bishop of Birmingham 4 December 1879 at the Cathedral Church of St Chad, Birmingham.

LACY, Richard: ordained Bishop of newly erected Diocese of Middlesbrough 18 December 1879 at Middlesbrough.

RATTI, Ambrogio D. A. (**POPE PIUS XI**): ordained priest (Milano) 27 December 1879 at Rome, Italy.

1880

BROWN, William F.: received into Catholic Church 1880 at Kensington, London.

ơ FLYNN, Thomas E.: born 6 January 1880 at Portsmouth.

† BROWN OSB, T Joseph: died 12 April 1880 at Lower Bullingham, Hereford aged 81 • buried at the Abbey Church of St Michael and All Angels, Belmont, Hereford.

PATTERSON, James L: ordained titular Bishop of *Emmaüs* and appointed auxiliary Bishop of Westminster 10 May 1880 at Rome, Italy.

McINTYRE, John: ordained priest (Birmingham) 22 May 1880 at Rome, Italy.

RIDDELL, Arthur G.: ordained Bishop of Northampton 9 June 1880 at Northampton.

SINGLETON, Hugh: ordained priest (Shrewsbury) 25 July 1880 at Birkenhead.

® AMHERST, Francis K.: appointed 27 July 1880 titular Bishop of *Sozusa in Palaestina* and retired to Fieldgate House, Kenilworth.

ơ KING, John H.: born 16 September 1880 at Wardour, Salisbury.

STANLEY, A. Charles: ordained priest (Westminster) 18 December 1880 at Rome, Italy.

1881

HEDLEY OSB, J. E. Cuthbert: translated 18 February 1881 to Diocese of Newport and Menevia.

♂ DOWNEY, Richard J.: born 5 May 1881 at Kilkenny City (Kilkenny), Ireland.

† DANELL, James: died 14 June 1881 at Southwark, London aged 59 • buried at the Cathedral Church of St George, Southwark, London.

† MASTAI-FERRETTI, Giovanni M. (POPE BL. PIUS IX): reinterred 13 July 1881 at St Lawrence's Basilica (outside the walls), Rome, Italy.

† BROWN, James: died 14 October 1881 at Grange Bank Farm, Shrewsbury aged 69 • buried at Pantasaph, Holywell.

♂ RONCALLI, Angelo G. (POPE ST JOHN XXIII): born 25 November 1881 at Sotto il Monte Giovanni XXIII (Bergamo), Italy.

1882

♂ McGRATH, Michael J.: born 24 March 1882 at Kilkenny City (Kilkenny), Ireland.

TONER, John: ordained priest (Glasgow) 25 March 1882 at Palencia (Palencia), Spain.

KNIGHT, Edmund: translated 25 April 1882 to Diocese of Shrewsbury.

† CHADWICK, James: died 14 May 1882 at Newcastle upon Tyne aged 69 • buried at St Cuthbert's College, Ushaw, Durham.

DIOCESE OF PORTSMOUTH: erected 19 May 1882.

DIOCESE OF SOUTHWARK: restructured 19 May 1882.

VIRTUE (VERTUE), John: released from military service 3 June 1882.

COFFIN CSsR, Robert A.: ordained Bishop of newly restructured Diocese of Southwark 11 June 1882 at Rome, Italy.

VIRTUE (VERTUE), John: ordained Bishop of newly erected Diocese of Portsmouth 25 July 1882 at South Kensington, London.

FRASER, Robert: ordained priest (Aberdeen) 13 August 1882 at Rome, Italy.

† AMHERST, Francis K.: died 21 August 1882 at Fieldgate House, Kenilworth aged 63 • buried at the Cathedral Church of Our Lady and St Thomas, Northampton.

♂ MAGUIRE, James: born 29 August 1882 at Loanhead.

WARD, Bernard F. N.: ordained priest (Westminster) 8 October 1882 at Old Hall Green, Ware.

BEWICK, John W.: ordained Bishop of Hexham and Newcastle 18 October 1882 at Newcastle upon Tyne.

KEATING, Frederick W.: ordained priest (Birmingham) 20 October 1882 at Olton, Solihull.

1883

† ROSKELL, Richard B.: died 27 January 1883 at Whitewell, Clitheroe aged 65 • buried at St Hubert's Church, Dunsop Bridge, Clitheroe.

COWGILL, Joseph R.: ordained priest (Leeds) 19 May 1883 at Rome, Italy.

† STRAIN, John M.: died 2 July 1883 at St Mary's Cathedral, Edinburgh aged 72 • buried at the Metropolitan Cathedral Church of St Mary, Edinburgh.

1884

BILSBORROW OSB, J. Romanus: professed (Order of Saint Benedict) 25 January 1884 at Belmont, Hereford.

♂ CRAVEN, George L.: born 1 February 1884 at Wednesbury.

PRESTON, Richard: ordained priest (Liverpool) 7 June 1884 at Rome, Italy.

BOURNE, Francis A.: ordained priest (Southwark) 11 June 1884 at Clapham, London.

♂ HANNON, Daniel J.: born 12 June 1884 at Rotherham.

♂ MARSHALL, Henry V.: born 19 July 1884 at Listowel (Kerry), Ireland.

MOSTYN, Francis E. J.: ordained priest (Shrewsbury) 14 September 1884 at Ushaw, Durham.

SARTO, Giuseppe M. (POPE ST PIUS X): ordained Bishop of Mantova 20 November 1884 at Mantua (Mantua), Italy.

1885

BUTT, John B.: ordained titular Bishop of *Milo* and appointed auxiliary Bishop of Southwark 29 January 1885 at Arundel.

† COFFIN CSsR, Robert A.: died 6 April 1885 at Teignmouth aged 65 • buried at Teignmouth.

COLLINS, Richard: ordained priest (Hexham and Newcastle) 30 May 1885 at Ushaw, Durham.

WHITESIDE, Thomas: ordained priest (Liverpool) 30 May 1885 at Rome, Italy.

BUTT, John B.: translated 26 June 1885 to Diocese of Southwark.

SMITH, William: ordained Archbishop of St Andrews and Edinburgh 28 October 1885 at the Metropolitan Cathedral Church of St Mary, Edinburgh.

1886

† ERRINGTON, George: died 19 January 1886 at Prior Park, Bath aged 81 • buried at Prior Park College chapel, Bath.

BROWN, William F.: ordained priest (Southwark) 20 March 1886 at the Cathedral Church of St George, Southwark, London.

† BEWICK, John W.: died 29 October 1886 at Tynemouth, North Shields aged 62 • buried at Ashburton Cemetery, Gosforth, Newcastle upon Tyne.

1887

† RIGG, George: died 18 January 1887 at Perth aged 72 • buried at St John the Baptist Church, Perth.

♂ McCORMACK, Joseph: born 17 May 1887 at Broadway.

♂ PARKER, Thomas L.: born 21 December 1887 at Sutton Coldfield.

1888

O'CALLAGHAN, Henry: ordained Bishop of Hexham and Newcastle 18 January 1888 at Rome, Italy (*never took up residence in the diocese*).

ILSLEY, Edward: translated 17 February 1888 to Diocese of Birmingham.

®   ULLATHORNE OSB, W. Bernard: appointed 17 February 1888 titular Archbishop of *Cabasa* and retired to Oscott, Sutton Coldfield.

AMIGO, Peter E.: ordained priest (Westminster) 25 February 1888 at South Kensington, London.

WILKINSON, Thomas W.: ordained titular Bishop of *Cisamus* and appointed auxiliary Bishop of Hexham and Newcastle 25 July 1888 at Ushaw, Durham.

♂   POSKITT, Henry J.: born 6 September 1888 at Birkin, Selby.

＊   SMITH, William: appointed 6 September 1888 Apostolic Administrator of the Diocese of Dunkeld until 28 October 1890.

DOUBLEDAY, Arthur H.: ordained priest (Southwark) 22 December 1888 at the Cathedral Church of St George, Southwark, London.

1889

†   MacDONALD, John: died 4 February 1889 at Aberdeen aged 70 • buried at the Cathedral Church of St Mary of the Assumption, Aberdeen.

†   ULLATHORNE OSB, W. Bernard: died 21 March 1889 at Oscott, Sutton Coldfield aged 82 • buried at Aston Hall, Stone.

BILSBORROW OSB, J. Romanus: ordained priest (Order of Saint Benedict) 23 June 1889 at Douai (Nord), France.

GRANT, Colin C.: ordained Bishop of Aberdeen 13 August 1889 at Aberdeen.

♂   BRUNNER, George: born 21 August 1889 at Hull.

♂   GODFREY, William: born 25 September 1889 at Kirkdale, Liverpool.

†   GRANT, Colin C.: died 26 September 1889 at Aberdeen aged 57 • buried at the Cathedral Church of St Mary of the Assumption, Aberdeen.

® O'CALLAGHAN, Henry: resigned 27 September 1889 as Bishop of Hexham and Newcastle and appointed titular Archbishop of *Nicosia* and retired to Rome, Italy.

WILKINSON, Thomas W.: translated 28 December 1889 to Diocese of Hexham and Newcastle.

1890

YOUENS SMA, Laurence W.: received into Catholic Church 1890 at High Wycombe.

McDONALD OSB, A. T. Joseph: professed (Order of Saint Benedict) 3 February 1890 at Fort Augustus.

GORDON, William: ordained titular Bishop of *Arcadiopolis in Asia* and appointed coadjutor Bishop of Leeds 24 February 1890 at Leeds.

BURTON, George C. A.: ordained priest (Hexham and Newcastle) 31 May 1890 at Rome, Italy.

† CORNTHWAITE, Robert: died 16 June 1890 at Leeds aged 72 • buried at the Church of Mary Immaculate, Sicklinghall, Wetherby.

GORDON, William: succeeded 16 June 1890 as Bishop of Leeds.

MacDONALD CSsR, Hugh: ordained Bishop of Aberdeen 23 October 1890 at Aberdeen.

SMITH, James A.: ordained Bishop of Dunkeld 28 October 1890 at Dundee.

PEARSON OSB, T. Wulstan: professed (Order of Saint Benedict) 12 December 1890 at Belmont, Hereford.

1891

DOBSON, Robert: ordained priest (Liverpool) 23 May 1891 at Upholland, Skelmersdale.

GRAHAM, Charles M.: ordained titular Bishop of *Cisamus* and appointed coadjutor Bishop of Plymouth 28 October 1891 at Plymouth.

1892

† MANNING, Henry E.: died 14 January 1892 at Westminster, London aged 83 • buried at St Mary's Cemetery, Kensal Green, London.

† SMITH, William: died 16 March 1892 at St Bennet's, Edinburgh aged 72 • buried at the Metropolitan Cathedral Church of St Mary, Edinburgh.

VAUGHAN, Herbert A. H.: translated 29 March 1892 to Archdiocese of Westminster.

COTTER, William T.: ordained priest (Portsmouth) 19 June 1892 at Portsmouth.

MacDONALD, Angus: translated 15 July 1892 to Archdiocese of St Andrews and Edinburgh.

BILSBORROW, John: ordained Bishop of Salford 24 August 1892 at Salford.

1893

+ VAUGHAN, Herbert A. H.: elevated 16 January 1893 to Cardinal-Priest of Santi Andrea e Gregorio Magno al Monte Celio.

† McLACHLAN, John: died 16 January 1893 at Dumfries aged 66 • buried in the Pro-Cathedral Crypt of St Andrew, Dumfries.

DUNN, Thomas: ordained priest (Westminster) 2 February 1893 at South Kensington, London.

SMITH, George J.: ordained Bishop of Argyll and the Isles 25 April 1893 at Oban.

+ SARTO, Giuseppe M. (POPE ST PIUS X): elevated 12 June 1893 to Cardinal-Priest of San Bernardo alle Terme.

SARTO, Giuseppe M. (POPE ST PIUS X): translated 15 June 1893 to Patriarch Archdiocese of Venice.

TURNER, William: ordained Bishop of Galloway 25 July 1893 at Dumfries.

† CLIFFORD, William H. J.: died 14 August 1893 at Prior Park, Bath aged 69 • buried at Prior Park College chapel, Bath.

KEATINGE, William L.: ordained priest (Southwark) 27 August 1893 at Rome, Italy.

CARROLL, John: ordained titular Bishop of *Acmonia* and appointed coadjutor Bishop of Shrewsbury 28 October 1893 at Birkenhead.

♂   CLARKE, John M.: born 20 December 1893 at Bootle, Liverpool.
HINSLEY, Arthur: ordained priest (Leeds) 23 December 1893 at Rome, Italy.

1894

DEY, James: ordained priest (Birmingham) 17 February 1894 at Oscott, Sutton Coldfield.

MORIARTY, Ambrose J.: ordained priest (Shrewsbury) 10 March 1894 at Shrewsbury.

♂   WALL, Bernard P.: born 15 March 1894 at Tonbridge.

†   O'REILLY, Bernard: died 9 April 1894 at St Edward's college, Everton, Liverpool aged 70 • buried at Upholland, Skelmersdale.

BROWNLOW, William R. B.: ordained Bishop of Clifton 1 May 1894 at Clifton, Bristol.

MAGUIRE, John A.: ordained titular Bishop of *Trocmades* and appointed auxiliary Bishop of Glasgow 11 June 1894 at the Cathedral Church of St Andrew, Glasgow.

♂   BLACK, James: born 25 June 1894 at Calton, Glasgow.

SHINE, Thomas: ordained priest (Leeds) 29 June 1894 at Leeds.

WHITESIDE, Thomas: ordained Bishop of Liverpool 15 August 1894 at the Pro-Cathedral Church of St Nicholas, Liverpool.

♂   CAMPBELL, Donald A.: born 8 December 1894 at Bohuntin, Roy Bridge.

1895

DIOCESE OF SHREWSBURY: restructured 4 March 1895.

DIOCESE OF NEWPORT: restructured and renamed 4 March 1895.

VICARIATE OF WALES: erected 4 March 1895.

HEDLEY OSB, J. E. Cuthbert: translated 4 March 1895 to renamed Diocese of Newport.

†   WEATHERS, William: died 4 March 1895 at Isleworth aged 80 • buried at St Edmund's College, Old Hall Green, Ware.

♂   O'HARA, Gerald P. A.: born 4 May 1895 at Scranton (PA), USA.

CARROLL, John: succeeded 11 May 1895 as Bishop of Shrewsbury.

®   KNIGHT, Edmund: appointed 11 May 1895 titular Bishop of *Flavias* and retired to Kensington, London.

♂   PETIT, John E.: born 22 June 1895 at Highgate, London.

MOSTYN, Francis E. J.: ordained titular Bishop of *Ascalon* and appointed Vicar Apostolic for the Welsh District 14 September 1895 at Birkenhead.

1896

BOURNE, Francis A.: ordained titular Bishop of *Epiphania in Cilicia* and appointed coadjutor Bishop of Southwark 1 May 1896 at the Cathedral Church of St George, Southwark, London.

CARY-ELWES, Dudley C.: ordained priest (Northampton) 30 May 1896 at Rome, Italy.

McDONALD OSB, A. T. Joseph: ordained priest (Order of Saint Benedict) 9 August 1896 at Fort Augustus.

THORMAN, Joseph: ordained priest (Hexham and Newcastle) 27 September 1896 at Ushaw, Durham.

1897

†   CARROLL, John: died 14 January 1897 at Oxton, Birkenhead aged 58 • buried at Dukinfield Cemetery.

GRAHAM, Henry G.: ordained Church of Scotland deacon (presbytery of Selkirk) 9 March 1897 at Selkirk.

BOURNE, Francis A.: succeeded 9 April 1897 as Bishop of Southwark.

®   BUTT, John B.: appointed 9 April 1897 titular Bishop of *Sebastopolis in Thracia* and retired to Brighton thence to Arundel.

KEATINGE, William L.: commissioned as military chaplain 1 May 1897.

ALLEN, Samuel W.: ordained Bishop of Shrewsbury 16 June 1897 at Shrewsbury.

BUTT, Joseph: ordained priest (Southwark) 18 July 1897 at Wonersh, Guildford.

♂ MONTINI, Giovanni-Battista E. A. M. (POPE BL. PAUL VI): born 26 September 1897 at Concesio (Brescia), Italy.

PEARSON OSB, T. Wulstan: ordained priest (Order of Saint Benedict) 26 September 1897 at Downside, Radstock.

1898

BENNETT, George H.: ordained priest (St Andrews and Edinburgh) 9 April 1898 at Rome, Italy.

BIDWELL, Manuel J.: ordained priest (Westminster) 8 May 1898 at Rome, Italy.

DIOCESE OF MENEVIA: erected 12 May 1898.

MOSTYN, Francis E. J.: translated 12 May 1898 to newly erected Diocese of Menevia.

† MacDONALD CSsR, Hugh: died 29 May 1898 at St Bennet's, Edinburgh aged 56 • buried at the Cathedral Church of St Mary of the Assumption, Aberdeen.

1899

♂ SCANLAN, James D.: born 24 January 1899 at Parkhead, Glasgow.

♂ MASTERSON, Joseph: born 29 January 1899 at Manchester.

♂ GRIFFIN, Bernard W.: born 21 February 1899 at Cannon Hill, Birmingham.

CHISHOLM, Aeneas: ordained Bishop of Aberdeen 24 February 1899 at Aberdeen.

BRINDLE, Robert: ordained titular Bishop of *Hermopolis Maior* and appointed auxiliary Bishop of Westminster 12 March 1899 at Rome, Italy.

PACELLI, Eugenio M. G. G. (POPE VEN. PIUS XII): ordained priest (Rome) 2 April 1899 at Rome, Italy.

♂ RUDDERHAM, Joseph E.: born 17 June 1899 at Norwich.

♂ ELLIS, Edward: born 30 June 1899 at Radford, Nottingham.

BRINDLE, Robert: released from military service 5 July 1899.

HENSHAW, Thomas: ordained priest (Salford) 18 October 1899 at Lisbon (Lisboa), Portugal.

† BUTT, John B.: died 1 November 1899 at Arundel aged 73 • buried at St John's College, Wonersh, Guildford.

1900

♂ GRANT, Kenneth: born 18 March 1900 at Fort William.

† MacDONALD, Angus: died 29 April 1900 at St Bennet's, Edinburgh aged 55 • buried at the Metropolitan Cathedral Church of St Mary, Edinburgh.

CAHILL, John B.: ordained titular Bishop of *Thagora* and appointed auxiliary Bishop of Portsmouth 1 May 1900 at Portsmouth.

† VIRTUE (VERTUE), John: died 23 May 1900 at Portsmouth aged 74 • buried at Highland Road Cemetery, Southsea.

CAMERON, E. Hugh: ordained priest (Argyll and the Isles) 29 June 1900 at Oban.

PRESTON, Richard: ordained titular Bishop of *Phocaea* and appointed auxiliary Bishop of Hexham and Newcastle 25 July 1900 at Ushaw, Durham.

WILLIAMS, Thomas L.: ordained priest (Birmingham) 24 August 1900 at Oscott, Sutton Coldfield.

CAHILL, John B.: translated 30 August 1900 to Diocese of Portsmouth.

SMITH, James A.: translated 30 August 1900 to Archdiocese of St Andrews and Edinburgh.

MACKINTOSH, Donald: ordained priest (Glasgow) 1 November 1900 at Rome, Italy.

1901

LEE, William: ordained priest (Clifton) 2 March 1901 at Oscott, Sutton Coldfield.

♂ MATHESON, John A.: born 28 April 1901 at Tomintoul, Ballindalloch.

MacFARLANE, Angus: ordained Bishop of Dunkeld 1 May 1901 at Dundee.

YOUENS SMA, Laurence W.: ordained priest (Society of African Missionaries) 30 June 1901 at Choubrah (Cairo), Egypt.

♂ DOUGLAS, Edward W.: born 27 August 1901 at Crosshill, Glasgow.

♂ WALSH MAfr, Francis P.: born 15 September 1901 at Cirencester.

♂ GRIMSHAW, Francis E. J.: born 6 October 1901 at Bridgwater.

† BROWNLOW, William R. B.: died 9 November 1901 at Clifton, Bristol aged 71 • buried at Holy Souls Chapel Crypt, Arnos Vale, Bristol.

GRAHAM, Henry G.: ordained Church of Scotland priest (presbytery of Hamilton) 14 November 1901 at Strathaven.

® BAGSHAWE CO, Edward G.: resigned 25 November 1901 as Bishop of Nottingham.

BRINDLE, Robert: translated 6 December 1901 to Diocese of Nottingham.

1902

♂ MATHEW, David J.: born 16 January 1902 at Lyme Regis.

BAGSHAWE CO, Edward G.: appointed 27 January 1902 titular Bishop of *Hypaepa*.

♂ HALSALL, Joseph F.: born 15 February 1902 at Ainsdale, Southport.

† EYRE, Charles P.: died 27 March 1902 at Hillhead, Glasgow aged 84 • buried at St Peter's College chapel, Cardross, Dumbarton.

MELLON, William H.: ordained priest (St Andrews and Edinburgh) 29 March 1902 at Rome, Italy.

BURTON, George C. A.: ordained Bishop of Clifton 1 May 1902 at Clifton, Bristol.

♂ BUTLER OSB, B. E. Christopher: born 7 May 1902 at Reading.

MAGUIRE, John A.: translated 4 August 1902 to Archdiocese of Glasgow.

GRAHAM, Charles M.: succeeded 25 October 1902 as Bishop of Plymouth.

† VAUGHAN, William: died 25 October 1902 at Newton Abbot aged 88 • buried at St Augustine's convent, Newton Abbot.

† PATTERSON, James L.: died 2 December 1902 at Chelsea, London aged 80 • buried at St Edmund's College, Old Hall Green, Ware.

MYERS, Edward: ordained priest (Westminster) 7 December 1902 at Oscott, Sutton Coldfield.

1903

♂ BRIGHT, Humphrey P.: born 27 January 1903 at Brentwood.

† BILSBORROW, John: died 5 March 1903 at Babbacombe, Torquay aged 66 • buried at St Joseph's Cemetery, Moston, Manchester.

STANLEY, A. Charles: ordained titular Bishop of *Emmaüs* and appointed auxiliary Bishop of Westminster 15 March 1903 at Rome, Italy (*never took up residence in the diocese*).

† VAUGHAN, Herbert A. H.: died 19 June 1903 at Mill Hill, London aged 71 • buried at Mill Hill, London.

VAUGHAN, Francis J.: ordained priest (Newport) 5 July 1903 at Ushaw, Durham.

† PECCI, Vincenzo G. R. L. (**POPE LEO XIII**): died 20 July 1903 at the Apostolic Palace, Rome, Italy aged 93 • buried at the Basilica of St John Lateran, Rome, Italy.

x SARTO, Giuseppe M. (**POPE ST PIUS X**): elected Pope 4 August 1903 at Rome, Italy.

DEY, James: commissioned as military chaplain 7 August 1903.

SARTO, Giuseppe M. (**POPE ST PIUS X**): installed 9 August 1903 at Rome, Italy.

GRAHAM, Henry G.: received into Catholic Church 15 August 1903 at Fort Augustus.

BOURNE, Francis A.: translated 11 September 1903 to Archdiocese of Westminster.

CASARTELLI, Louis C.: ordained Bishop of Salford 21 September 1903 at Salford.

ARCHDIOCESE OF WESTMINSTER: Cathedral transferred 24 December 1903.

1904

HINSLEY, Arthur: incardinated 1904 into Diocese of Southwark at Southwark, London.

® BAGSHAWE CO, Edward G.: appointed 17 January 1904 titular Archbishop of *Selucia in Isauria* and retired to Gunnersbury, London.

AMIGO, Peter E.: ordained Bishop of Southwark 25 March 1904 at the Cathedral Church of St George, Southwark, London.

RONCALLI, Angelo G. (**POPE ST JOHN XXIII**): ordained priest (Bergamo) 10 August 1904 at Bergamo (Bergamo), Italy.

FENTON, Patrick: ordained titular Bishop of *Amycla* and appointed auxiliary Bishop of Westminster 1 May 1904 at the Metropolitan Cathedral Church of the Most Precious Blood, Westminster, London.

♂ BECK **AA**, George A.: born 28 May 1904 at Streatham, London.

DIOCESE OF LEEDS: cathedral transferred 16 June 1904.

♂ HART, William A.: born 9 September 1904 at Dumbarton.

YOUENS **SMA**, Laurence W.: incardinated 23 September 1904 into Diocese of Northampton at High Wycombe.

† O'CALLAGHAN, Henry: died 11 October 1904 at Florence (Firenze), Italy aged 79 • buried at San Miniato al Monte, Florence (Firenze), Italy.

KING, John H.: ordained priest (Portsmouth) 20 November 1904 at Jersey.

♂ McGEE, Joseph M.: born 13 December 1904 at Monzievaird and Strowan, Crieff.

® PRESTON, Richard: resigned 22 December 1904 as auxiliary Bishop of Hexham and Newcastle and retired to Southfield, Lancaster.

1905

♂ HEENAN, John C.: born 26 January 1905 at Ilford.

† PRESTON, Richard: died 9 February 1905 at Southfield, Lancaster aged 48 • buried at St Cuthbert's College, Ushaw, Durham.

COTTER, William T.: ordained titular Bishop of *Clazomenae* and appointed auxiliary Bishop of Portsmouth 19 March 1905 at Portsmouth.

♂ COWDEROY, Cyril C.: born 5 May 1905 at Sidcup.

†   KNIGHT, Edmund: died 9 June 1905 at Kensington, London aged 77 • buried at Flaybrick Cemetery, Birkenhead.

COLLINS, Richard: ordained titular Bishop of *Selinus* and appointed auxiliary Bishop of Hexham and Newcastle 29 June 1905 at Newcastle upon Tyne.

♂   WARD, James: born 4 September 1905 at Dumbarton.

MARTIN, Donald: ordained priest (Argyll and the Isles) 23 September 1905 at Oban.

COWGILL, Joseph R.: ordained titular Bishop of *Olena* and appointed coadjutor Bishop of Leeds 30 November 1905 at Leeds.

♂   MURPHY, John A.: born 21 December 1905 at Birkenhead.

1906

JOHNSON, William A.: ordained titular Bishop of *Arindela* and appointed auxiliary Bishop of Westminster 1 May 1906 at the Metropolitan Cathedral Church of the Most Precious Blood, Westminster, London.

BARRETT, John P.: ordained priest (Liverpool) 9 June 1906 at Upholland, Skelmersdale.

MAGUIRE, James: ordained priest (St Andrews and Edinburgh) 22 July 1906 at the Metropolitan Cathedral Church of St Mary, Edinburgh.

♂   GRANT, Charles A.: born 25 October 1906 at Cambridge.

GRAHAM, Henry G.: ordained priest (Glasgow) 22 December 1906 at Rome, Italy.

1907

♂   PEARSON, Thomas B.: born 18 January 1907 at Preston.

†   MANNING, Henry E.: reinterred 15 February 1907 at the Metropolitan Cathedral Church of the Most Precious Blood, Westminster, London.

†   WISEMAN, Nicholas P. S.: reinterred 15 February 1907 at the Metropolitan Cathedral Church of the Most Precious Blood, Westminster, London.

DOWNEY, Richard J.: ordained priest (Liverpool) 25 May 1907 at Upholland, Skelmersdale.

♂ FOYLAN, Michael: born 29 June 1907 at Shettleston, Glasgow.

† RIDDELL, Arthur G.: died 15 September 1907 at Northampton aged 71 • buried at Kingsthorpe Cemetery, Northampton.

HANNON, Daniel J.: ordained priest (Newport) 22 September 1907 at Oscott, Sutton Coldfield.

DELLA CHIESA, Giacomo P. G.-B. (**POPE BENEDICT XV**): ordained Archbishop of Bologna 22 December 1907 at Rome, Italy.

1908

KEATING, Frederick W.: ordained Bishop of Northampton 25 February 1908 at the Cathedral Church of St Chad, Birmingham.

† ALLEN, Samuel W.: died 13 May 1908 at Shrewsbury aged 64 • buried at Shrewsbury Cemetery.

♂ HOLLAND, Thomas: born 11 June 1908 at Southport.

FLYNN, Thomas E.: ordained priest (Liverpool) 13 June 1908 at Upholland, Skelmersdale.

MARSHALL, Henry V.: ordained priest (Salford) 24 June 1908 at Dublin City (Dublin), Ireland.

McGRATH, Michael J.: ordained priest (Clifton) 12 July 1908 at Clifton, Bristol.

SINGLETON, Hugh: ordained Bishop of Shrewsbury 21 September 1908 at Seacombe, Wallasey.

♂ DWYER, George P.: born 25 September 1908 at Miles Platting, Manchester.

1909

† JOHNSON, William A.: died 27 March 1909 at Westminster, London aged 76 • buried at St Edmund's College, Old Hall Green, Ware.

♂ ENRICI, Domenico: born 9 April 1909 at Cervasca (Cuneo), Italy.

† WILKINSON, Thomas W.: died 17 April 1909 at Ushaw, Durham aged 84 • buried at St Cuthbert's College, Ushaw, Durham.

COLLINS, Richard: translated 21 June 1909 to Diocese of Hexham and Newcastle.

VAUGHAN, John S.: ordained titular Bishop of *Sebastopolis in Armenia* and appointed auxiliary Bishop of Salford 15 August 1909 at the Metropolitan Cathedral Church of the Most Precious Blood, Westminster, London.

♂ TICKLE, Gerard W.: born 2 November 1909 at Birkenhead.

1910

♂ RESTIEAUX, Cyril E.: born 25 February 1910 at Norwich.

♂ WHEELER, William G.: born 5 May 1910 at Dobcross, Oldham.

♂ FOLEY, Brian C.: born 25 May 1910 at Ilford.

† CAHILL, John B.: died 2 August 1910 at Portsmouth aged 68 • buried at Ryde Cemetery.

♂ GRAY, Gordon J.: born 10 August 1910 at Leith, Edinburgh.

♂ CUNNINGHAM, James: born 15 August 1910 at Rusholme, Manchester.

COTTER, William T.: translated 24 November 1910 to Diocese of Portsmouth.

1911

POSKITT, Henry J.: ordained Church of England deacon (Ripon) 1911 at Ripon.

® GRAHAM, Charles M.: appointed 1 February 1911 titular Bishop of *Tiberias* and retired to Hayle.

BILSBORROW OSB, J. Romanus: ordained Bishop of Port-Louis, Mauritius 24 February 1911 at Upper Woolhampton, Reading.

BUTT, Joseph: ordained titular Bishop of *Cambysopolis* and appointed auxiliary Bishop of Westminster 24 February 1911 at the Metropolitan Cathedral Church of the Most Precious Blood, Westminster, London.

♂ HEIM, Bruno B.: born 5 March 1911 at Neuendorf (Solothurn), Switzerland.

McNULTY, John F.: ordained priest (Salford) 16 April 1911 at Salford.

COWGILL, Joseph R.: succeeded 7 June 1911 as Bishop of Leeds.

† GORDON, William: died 7 June 1911 at Leeds aged 79 • buried at Killingbeck Cemetery, Leeds.

KEILY, John J.: ordained Bishop of Plymouth 13 June 1911 at Plymouth.

ENGLAND AND WALES: restructured 28 October 1911.

ILSLEY, Edward: appointed 28 October 1911 Archbishop and Metropolitan of newly raised Archdiocese and Province of Birmingham.

WHITESIDE, Thomas: appointed 28 October 1911 Archbishop and Metropolitan of newly raised Archdiocese and Province of Liverpool.

+ BOURNE, Francis A.: elevated 27 November 1911 to Cardinal-Priest of Santa Pudenziana.

1912

CE POSKITT, Henry J.: ordained Church of England priest (Ripon) 1912 at Ripon.

RATTI, Ambrogio D. A. (POPE PIUS XI): entered diplomatic service to the Holy See 1912 at Rome, Italy.

♂ McGILL PSS, Stephen: born 4 January 1912 at Crosshill, Glasgow.

CRAVEN, George L.: ordained priest (Westminster) 29 June 1912 at the Metropolitan Cathedral Church of the Most Precious Blood, Westminster, London.

MACKINTOSH, Donald A.: ordained titular Bishop of *Chersonesus in Zechia* and appointed coadjutor Archbishop of Glasgow 2 July 1912 at the Cathedral Church of St Andrew, Glasgow.

McINTYRE, John: ordained titular Bishop of *Lamus* and appointed auxiliary Bishop of Birmingham 30 July 1912 at the Metropolitan Cathedral Church of St Chad, Birmingham.

McCORMACK, Joseph: ordained priest (Hexham and Newcastle) 11 August 1912 at Ushaw, Durham.

† GRAHAM, Charles M.: died 2 September 1912 at Hayle aged 78 • buried at Plymouth Cemetery.

♂ CLEARY, Joseph F.: born 4 September 1912 at Dublin City (Dublin), Ireland.

† MacFARLANE, Angus: died 24 September 1912 at Dundee aged 69
• buried at Balgay Cemetery, Dundee.

♂ LUCIANI, Albino (**POPE JOHN PAUL I**): born 17 October 1912 at
Forno di Canale (Belluno), Italy.

♂ CASHMAN, David J.: born 27 December 1912 at Bristol.

1913

♂ GRASAR, William E.: born 18 May 1913 at Scunthorpe.
FRASER, Robert: ordained Bishop of Dunkeld 25 May 1913 at Rome,
Italy.

♂ BURKE, Geoffrey I.: born 31 July 1913 at Alexandra Park,
Manchester.

♂ CASEY, Patrick J.: born 20 November 1913 at Stoke Newington,
London.

1914

† TURNER, William: died 19 January 1914 at Dumfries aged 69 •
buried at Holy Cross Cemetery, Dumfries.

† FRASER, Robert: died 28 March 1914 at Dundee aged 55 • buried at
Balgay Cemetery, Dundee.

+ *DELLA* CHIESA, Giacomo P. G.-B. (**POPE BENEDICT XV**):
elevated 25 May 1914 to **Cardinal-Priest of Santi Quattro Coronati**.
McCARTHY, James W.: ordained Bishop of Galloway 9 June 1914 at
Dumfries.

♂ MONAGHAN, James: born 11 July 1914 at Bathgate.

† SARTO, Giuseppe M. (**POPE ST PIUS X**): died 20 August 1914 at
the Apostolic Palace, Rome, Italy aged 79 • buried at St Peter's Basilica,
Vatican City.

x *DELLA* CHIESA, Giacomo P. G.-B. (**POPE BENEDICT XV**):
elected Pope 3 September 1914 at Rome, Italy.
DELLA CHIESA, Giacomo P. G.-B. (**POPE BENEDICT XV**):
installed 6 September 1914 at Rome, Italy.

♂ McCLEAN, John G.: born 24 September 1914 at Redcar.

TONER, John: ordained Bishop of Dunkeld 15 October 1914 at Dundee.

CAMERON, E. Hugh: commissioned as military chaplain 3 December 1914.

1915

† BAGSHAWE CO, Edward G.: died 6 February 1915 at Gunnersbury, London aged 86 • buried at Isleworth Cemetery.

♂ HARVEY, Philip J. B.: born 6 March 1915 at Richmond.

PARKER, Thomas L.: ordained priest (Salford) 29 May 1915 at Ushaw, Durham.

® BRINDLE, Robert: appointed 1 June 1915 titular Bishop of *Tacapae* and retired to Spinkhill, Sheffield.

POSKITT, Henry J.: received into Catholic Church 25 September 1915 at Ampleforth, York.

† HEDLEY OSB, J. E. Cuthbert: died 11 November 1915 at Llanishen, Cardiff aged 78 • buried at Cathays Cemetery, Cardiff.

1916

ENGLAND AND WALES: restructured 7 February 1916.

BILSBORROW OSB, J. Romanus: translated 7 February 1916 to Archbishop and Metropolitan of newly raised Archdiocese and Province of Cardiff.

DUNN, Thomas: ordained Bishop of Nottingham 25 February 1916 at Nottingham.

† BRINDLE, Robert: died 27 June 1916 at Spinkhill, Sheffield aged 78 • buried at the Cathedral Church of St Barnabas, Nottingham.

♂ CARDINALE, Igino E.: born 14 October 1916 at Fondi (Latina), Italy.

GODFREY, William: ordained priest (Liverpool) 28 October 1916 at Rome, Italy.

1917

PACELLI, Eugenio M. G. G. (POPE VEN. PIUS XII): entered diplomatic service to the Holy See 1917 at Rome, Italy.

♂ FOX, Langton D.: born 21 February 1917 at Golders Green, London.

DIOCESE OF ESSEX: erected 22 March 1917.

ARCHDIOCESE OF WESTMINSTER: restructured 22 March 1917.

* WARD, Bernard F. N.: appointed 22 March 1917 Apostolic Administrator of the newly erected Diocese of Essex until 20 July 1917.

BRUNNER, George: ordained priest (Middlesbrough) 9 April 1917 at Ushaw, Durham.

® FENTON, Patrick: retired 10 April 1917 to Bexhill-on-Sea.

WARD, Bernard F. N.: ordained titular Bishop of *Lydda* 10 April 1917 at the Metropolitan Cathedral Church of the Most Precious Blood, Westminster, London.

PACELLI, Eugenio M. G. G. (POPE VEN. PIUS XII): ordained titular Archbishop of *Sardes* and appointed Apostolic Nuncio to Germany 13 May 1917 at Rome, Italy.

♂ THOMSON, Francis A. S. W.: born 15 May 1917 at Edinburgh.

BROWN, William F.: appointed 1 June 1917 Apostolic Visitor to Scotland until 1 February 1920.

POSKITT, Henry J.: ordained priest (Middlesbrough) 15 July 1917 at Rome, Italy.

BLACK, James: enlisted as military soldier 19 July 1917.

DIOCESE OF BRENTWOOD: renamed 20 July 1917.

WARD, Bernard F. N.: translated 20 July 1917 to renamed Diocese of Brentwood.

♂ MACPHERSON, Colin A.: born 5 August 1917 at Lochboisdale, Isle of South Uist.

McINTYRE, John: appointed 24 August 1917 titular Archbishop of *Oxyrynchus* and appointed auxiliary Bishop of Birmingham.

SCANLAN, James D.: enlisted as military soldier 12 September 1917.

♂ HARRIS, Augustine: born 27 October 1917 at West Derby, Liverpool.

CAMERON, E. Hugh: nominated 13 November 1917 titular Bishop of *Usula* and appointed coadjutor Bishop of Argyll and the Isles but declined the appointment 20 November 1917.

GRAHAM, Henry G.: ordained titular Bishop of *Tipasa in Numidia* and appointed auxiliary Bishop of St Andrews and Edinburgh 16 November 1917 at the Metropolitan Cathedral Church of St Mary, Edinburgh.

CLARKE, John M.: ordained priest (Saint Joseph's Missionary Society of Mill Hill) 2 December 1917 at Bootle, Liverpool.

BIDWELL, Manuel J.: ordained titular Bishop of *Miletopolis* and appointed auxiliary Bishop of Westminster 8 December 1917 at the Metropolitan Cathedral Church of the Most Precious Blood, Westminster, London.

1918

† CHISHOLM, Aeneas: died 13 January 1918 at St Patrick's, Edinburgh aged 81 • buried at St Mary's College Cemetery, Blairs, Aberdeen.

† SMITH, George J.: died 18 January 1918 at Oban aged 77 • buried at Pennyfuir Cemetery, Oban.

KEATINGE, William L.: ordained titular Bishop of *Metellopolis* and appointed Vicar Delegate to the Army and Royal Air Force 25 February 1918 at Rome, Italy.

PETIT, John E.: ordained priest (Brentwood) 9 May 1918 at Old Hall Green, Ware.

ơ EMERY, Anthony J.: born 17 May 1918 at Burton-on-Trent.

WALL, Bernard P.: ordained priest (Southwark) 14 July 1918 at Wonersh, Guildford.

GRANT, Kenneth: enlisted as military soldier 18 July 1918.

BENNETT, George H.: ordained Bishop of Aberdeen 1 August 1918 at Aberdeen.

† FENTON, Patrick: died 22 August 1918 at Bexhill-on-Sea aged 81 • buried at St Edmund's College, Old Hall Green, Ware.

BLACK, James: released from military service 18 December 1918.

1919

GRANT, Kenneth: released from military service 6 February 1919.

CAMERON, E. Hugh: released from military service 29 March 1919.

MARTIN, Donald: ordained Bishop of Argyll and the Isles 11 June 1919 at Oban.

SCANLAN, James D.: released from military service 16 July 1919.

ơ CLARK, Alan C.: born 9 August 1919 at Bickley, Bromley.

McDONALD OSB, A. T. Joseph: elected 27 August 1919 Abbot of the Abbey Church of St Benedict, Fort Augustus.

ơ HORNYAK OSBM, Augustine E.: born 7 October 1919 at Kucura (Backa), Serbia.

† MACKINTOSH, Donald A.: died 8 October 1919 at Kinning Park, Glasgow aged 74 • buried at St Peter's Cemetery, Dalbeth, Glasgow.

ơ GRAY, Joseph: born 20 October 1919 at Finternagh (Cavan), Ireland.

RATTI, Ambrogio D. A. (POPE PIUS XI): ordained titular Archbishop of *Naupactus* and appointed Apostolic Nuncio to Poland 28 October 1919 at Rome, Italy.

1920

† WARD, Bernard F. N.: died 21 January 1920 at Brentwood aged 62 • buried at St Edmund's College, Old Hall Green, Ware.

ơ WORLOCK, Derek J. H.: born 4 February 1920 at St John's Wood, London.

ARCHDIOCESE OF CARDIFF: cathedral transferred 12 March 1920.

ơ GUAZZELLI, Victor: born 19 March 1920 at Stepney, London.

CAMPBELL, Donald A.: ordained priest (Argyll and the Isles) 3 April 1920 at Rome, Italy.

O'HARA, Gerald P. A.: ordained priest (Philadelphia) 3 April 1920 at Philadelphia (PA), USA.

ơ WOJTYŁA, Karol J. (POPE ST JOHN PAUL II): born 18 May 1920 at Wadowice (Wadowice), Poland.

MONTINI, Giovanni-Battista E. A. M. (POPE BL. PAUL VI): ordained priest (Brescia) 29 May 1920 at Brescia (Brescia), Italy.

* TONER, John: appointed 12 June 1920 Apostolic Administrator of the Archdiocese of Glasgow until 21 May 1922.

DOUBLEDAY, Arthur H.: ordained Bishop of Brentwood 23 June 1920 at the Cathedral Church of St George, Southwark, London.

BLACK, James: ordained priest (Glasgow) 27 June 1920 at the Cathedral Church of St Andrew, Glasgow.

® BILSBORROW OSB, J. Romanus: resigned 1 September 1920 as Archbishop of Cardiff.

† MAGUIRE, John A.: died 14 October 1920 at Charing Cross, Glasgow aged 69 • buried at St Peter's Cemetery, Dalbeth, Glasgow.

CLARKE, John M.: released from St Joseph's Missionary Society of Mill Hill 1 November 1920.

® BILSBORROW OSB, J. Romanus: appointed 16 December 1920 titular Archbishop of *Cius* and retired to Upper Woolhampton, Reading thence to St Pierre de Moka, Mauritius.

1921

GRANT, Charles A.: received into Catholic Church 1921 at Cambridge.

® ILSLEY, Edward: appointed 15 January 1921 titular Archbishop of *Macra* and retired to Harvington Hall, Kidderminster thence to Oscott, Sutton Coldfield.

† WHITESIDE, Thomas: died 28 January 1921 at Princes Park, Liverpool aged 63 • buried at Ford Cemetery, Litherland, Liverpool.

MOSTYN, Francis E. J.: translated 7 March 1921 to Archdiocese of Cardiff.

* MOSTYN, Francis E. J.: appointed 7 March 1921 Apostolic Administrator of the Diocese of Menevia until 8 September 1926.

RATTI, Ambrogio D. A. (POPE PIUS XI): translated 29 April 1921 to titular Archbishop of *Adana*.

KEATING, Frederick W.: translated 13 June 1921 to Archdiocese of Liverpool.

RATTI, Ambrogio D. A. (POPE PIUS XI): translated 13 June 1921 to Archdiocese of Milan.

+ RATTI, Ambrogio D. A. (POPE PIUS XI): elevated 13 June 1921 to Cardinal-Priest of Santi Silvestro e Martino ai Monti.

McINTYRE, John: translated 16 June 1921 to Archdiocese of Birmingham.

SHINE, Thomas: ordained titular Bishop of *Lamus* and appointed coadjutor Bishop of Middlesbrough 29 June 1921 at Middlesbrough.

CARY-ELWES, Dudley C.: ordained Bishop of Northampton 15 December 1921 at Northampton.

† BAGSHAWE CO, Edward G.: reinterred 16 December 1921 at the Cathedral Church of St Barnabas, Nottingham.

1922

† *DELLA* CHIESA, Giacomo P. G.-B. (POPE BENEDICT XV): died 22 January 1922 at the Apostolic Palace, Rome, Italy aged 67 • buried at St Peter's Basilica, Vatican City.

x RATTI, Ambrogio D. A. (POPE PIUS XI): elected Pope 6 February 1922 at Rome, Italy.

RATTI, Ambrogio D. A. (POPE PIUS XI): installed 12 February 1922 at Rome, Italy.

♂ BARBARITO, Luigi: born 19 April 1922 at Atripalda (Avellino), Italy.

♂ MOVERLEY, Gerald: born 19 April 1922 at Bradford.

♂ MAHON MHM, Gerald T.: born 4 May 1922 at Fulham, London.

MACKINTOSH, Donald: ordained Archbishop of Glasgow 21 May 1922 at Rome, Italy.

ELLIS, Edward: ordained priest (Nottingham) 15 October 1922 at Nottingham.

DOBSON, Robert: ordained titular Bishop of *Cynopolis in Arcadia* and appointed auxiliary Bishop of Liverpool 30 November 1922 at the Pro-Cathedral Church of St Nicholas, Liverpool.

1923

♂ KUCHMIAK CSsR, Michael: born 5 February 1923 at Obertyn (pov. Horodenka), Ukraine.

♂ O'BRIEN, T. Kevin: born 18 February 1923 at Cork City (Cork), Ireland.

♂ HUME OSB, G. Basil: born 2 March 1923 at Newcastle upon Tyne.

♂ JUKES OFM Conv., John P.: born 7 August 1923 at Eltham, London.

1924

† COLLINS, Richard: died 9 February 1924 at Newcastle upon Tyne aged 66 • buried at St Cuthbert's College, Ushaw, Durham.

♂ HENDERSON, Charles J.: born 14 April 1924 at Waterford City (Waterford), Ireland.

DOUGLAS, Edward W.: ordained priest (Glasgow) 1 May 1924 at the Cathedral Church of St Andrew, Glasgow.

BROWN, William F.: ordained titular Bishop of *Pella* and appointed auxiliary Bishop of Southwark 12 May 1924 at the Cathedral Church of St George, Southwark, London.

MASTERSON, Joseph: ordained priest (Salford) 27 July 1924 at Rome, Italy.

GLANCEY, Michael F.: ordained titular Bishop of *Flaviopolis* and appointed auxiliary Bishop of Birmingham 29 September 1924 at the Metropolitan Cathedral Church of St Chad, Birmingham.

GRIFFIN, Bernard W.: ordained priest (Birmingham) 1 November 1924 at Rome, Italy.

DIOCESE OF HEXHAM AND NEWCASTLE: restructured 22 November 1924.

DIOCESE OF LANCASTER: erected 22 November 1924.

ARCHDIOCESE OF LIVERPOOL: restructured 22 November 1924.

KEATINGE, William L.: released from military service 31 December 1924.

1925

RONCALLI, Angelo G. (POPE ST JOHN XXIII): entered diplomatic service to the Holy See 1925 at Rome, Italy.

† CASARTELLI, Louis C.: died 18 January 1925 at Salford aged 72 •
buried at St Joseph's Cemetery, Moston, Manchester.

THORMAN, Joseph: ordained Bishop of newly restructured
Diocese of Hexham and Newcastle 27 January 1925 at Newcastle upon
Tyne.

PEARSON OSB, T. Wulstan: ordained Bishop of newly erected
Diocese of Lancaster 24 February 1925 at Lancaster.

MATHESON, John A.: ordained priest (Aberdeen) 7 March 1925 at
Rome, Italy.

WALSH MAfr, Francis P.: ordained priest (Aberdeen) 7 March 1925
at Rome, Italy.

RONCALLI, Angelo G (POPE ST JOHN XXIII): ordained titular
Archbishop of *Areopolis* and appointed Apostolic Official to Bulgaria 19
March 1925 at Rome, Italy.

♂ WINNING, Thomas J.: born 3 June 1925 at Wishaw.

♂ ALEXANDER, Mervyn A. N.: born 29 June 1925 at Highbury,
London.

♂ McCARTIE, P. Leo: born 5 September 1925 at West Hartlepool.

♂ McGUINNESS, James J.: born 2 October 1925 at Londonderry
(Derry), Ireland.

† GLANCEY, Michael F.: died 16 October 1925 at Edgbaston,
Birmingham aged 70 • buried at St Mary's College, Oscott, Sutton
Coldfield.

† VAUGHAN, John S.: died 4 December 1925 at Great Harwood,
Blackburn aged 72 • buried at St Hubert's Cemetery, Great Harwood,
Blackburn.

HENSHAW, Thomas: ordained Bishop of Salford 21 December 1925
at Salford.

1926

GRIMSHAW, Francis E. J.: ordained priest (Clifton) 27 February
1926 at Bristol.

♂ TAYLOR, Maurice: born 5 May 1926 at Hamilton.

VAUGHAN, Francis J.: ordained Bishop of Menevia 8 September
1926 at the Metropolitan Cathedral Church of St David, Cardiff.

BUTLER OSB, B. E. Christopher: ordained Church of England deacon (Oxford) 19 September 1926 at Christ Church, Oxford.

RUDDERHAM, Joseph: ordained priest (Northampton) 31 October 1926 at Rome, Italy.

♂ WALMSLEY, Francis J.: born 9 November 1926 at Woolwich, London.

HINSLEY, Arthur: ordained titular Bishop of *Sebastopolis in Armenia* 30 November 1926 at Rome, Italy.

† ILSLEY, Edward: died 1 December 1926 at Oscott, Sutton Coldfield aged 88 • buried at the Metropolitan Cathedral Church of St Chad, Birmingham.

1927

BARRETT, John P.: ordained titular Bishop of *Assus* and appointed auxiliary Bishop of Birmingham 22 February 1927 at the Metropolitan Cathedral Church of St Chad, Birmingham.

♂ RATZINGER, Joseph A. (POPE BENEDICT XVI): born 16 April 1927 at Marktl am Inn (Bavaria), Germany.

GRANT, Kenneth: ordained priest (Glasgow) 24 April 1927 at the Cathedral Church of St Andrew, Glasgow.

♂ LINDSAY, Hugh: born 20 June 1927 at Jesmond, Newcastle upon Tyne.

♂ TRIPP, Howard G.: born 3 July 1927 at Croydon.

BECK AA, George A.: ordained priest (Augustinians of the Assumption) 24 July 1927 at Louvain (Flemish Brabant), Belgium.

1928

BUTLER OSB, B. E. Christopher: received into Catholic Church 1928 at Downside, Radstock.

CAMERON, E. Hugh: appointed 1928 parish priest at Kingussie.

† KEATING, Frederick W.: died 7 February 1928 at Princes Park, Liverpool aged 68 • buried at Upholland, Skelmersdale.

† STANLEY, A. Charles: died 23 April 1928 at Rome, Italy aged 84 • buried at Rome, Italy.

♂ SWINDLEHURST, Owen F.: born 10 May 1928 at Newburn, Newcastle upon Tyne.

BRIGHT, Humphrey P.: ordained priest (Birmingham) 2 June 1928 at Oscott, Sutton Coldfield.

♂ HANNIGAN, James: born 15 July 1928 at Glenfinn (Donegal), Ireland.

DOWNEY, Richard J.: ordained Archbishop of Liverpool 21 September 1928 at the Pro-Cathedral Church of St Nicholas, Liverpool.

† KEILY, John J: died 23 September 1928 at Newton Abbot aged 74 • buried at St Augustine's convent, Newton Abbot.

® McINTYRE, John: appointed 16 November 1928 titular Archbishop of *Odessus* and retired to Edgbaston, Birmingham.

† SMITH, James A.: died 25 November 1928 at St Bennet's, Edinburgh aged 87 • buried at the Metropolitan Cathedral Church of St Mary, Edinburgh.

♂ GRIFFITHS OSB, M. Ambrose: born 4 December 1928 at Twickenham.

1929

BUTLER OSB, B. E. Christopher: professed (Order of Saint Benedict) 1929 at Downside, Radstock.

♂ WARD OFM Cap., John A.: born 24 January 1929 at Leeds.

♂ HRYNCHYSHYN CSsR, Michel: born 18 February 1929 at Buchanan (SK), Canada.

† LACY, Richard: died 11 April 1929 at Middlesbrough aged 88 • buried at St Joseph's Cemetery, North Ormesby, Middlesbrough.

SHINE, Thomas: succeeded 11 April 1929 as Bishop of Middlesbrough.

♂ O'CONNOR, Kevin: born 20 May 1929 at Kirkdale, Liverpool.

O'HARA, Gerald P. A.: ordained titular Bishop of *Heliopolis in Phoenicia* and appointed auxiliary Bishop of Philadelphia (PA), USA 21 May 1929 at Philadelphia (PA), USA.

HART, William A.: ordained priest (Glasgow) 25 May 1929 at Valladolid (Valladolid), Spain.

McGEE, Joseph M.: ordained priest (Dunkeld) 25 May 1929 at Valladolid (Valladolid), Spain.

MATHEW, David J.: ordained priest (Cardiff) 25 May 1929 at Rome, Italy.

BARRETT, John P.: translated 7 June 1929 to Diocese of Plymouth.

♂ RENFREW, Charles M.: born 21 June 1929 at Glasgow.

♂ MONE, John A.: born 22 June 1929 at Crosshill, Glasgow.

♂ COUVE DE MURVILLE, Maurice N. L.: born 27 June 1929 at Saint Germain en Laye (Yvelines), France.

SCANLAN, James D.: ordained priest (Westminster) 29 June 1929 at the Metropolitan Cathedral Church of the Most Precious Blood, Westminster, London.

WARD, James: ordained priest (Glasgow) 29 June 1929 at the Cathedral Church of St Andrew, Glasgow.

♂ MULLINS, Daniel J.: born 10 July 1929 at Kilfinane (Limerick), Ireland.

WILLIAMS, Thomas L.: ordained Archbishop of Birmingham 25 July 1929 at the Metropolitan Cathedral Church of St Chad, Birmingham.

McDONALD OSB, A. T. Joseph: ordained Archbishop of St Andrews and Edinburgh 24 September 1929 at the Metropolitan Cathedral Church of St Mary, Edinburgh.

DEY, James: released from military service 17 October 1929.

♂ BREWER, John (Jack): born 24 November 1929 at Burnage, Manchester.

+ PACELLI, Eugenio M. G. G. (POPE VEN. PIUS XII): elevated 16 December 1929 to Cardinal-Priest of Santi Giovanni e Paolo.

1930

HINSLEY, Arthur: appointed 9 January 1930 titular Archbishop of *Sardes* and appointed Apostolic Delegate to West Africa.

PACELLI, Eugenio M. G. G. (POPE VEN. PIUS XII): appointed 9 February 1930 Secretary of the Secretariat of State, Vatican City.

® GRAHAM, Henry G.: resigned 31 March 1930 as auxiliary Bishop of St Andrews and Edinburgh and appointed parish priest of Holy Cross Church, Crosshill, Glasgow.

HALSALL, Joseph F.: ordained priest (Liverpool) 19 April 1930 at Rome, Italy.

♂ BOWEN, Michael G.: born 23 April 1930 at Gibraltar.

♂ HITCHEN, Anthony: born 23 May 1930 at Chorley.

♂ THOMAS, Francis G.: born 29 May 1930 at Stone.

♂ KONSTANT, David E.: born 16 June 1930 at Blackheath, London.

HEENAN, John C.: ordained priest (Brentwood) 6 July 1930 at Ilford.

† BIDWELL, Manuel J.: died 11 July 1930 at Chelsea, London aged 58 • buried at St Vincent's Hospital, Pinner.

♂ O'BRIEN, James J.: born 5 August 1930 at Wood Green, London.

CLARKE, John M.: commissioned as military chaplain 10 December 1930.

1931

† BURTON, George C. A.: died 8 February 1931 at Leigh Woods, Bristol aged 78 • buried at Holy Souls Chapel Crypt, Arnos Vale, Bristol.

† CAMERON, E. Hugh: died 8 March 1931 at Rome, Italy aged 54 • buried at Scots College, Rome, Italy.

MURPHY, John A.: ordained priest (Shrewsbury) 21 March 1931 at Lisbon (Lisboa), Portugal.

COWDEROY, Cyril C.: ordained priest (Southwark) 30 May 1931 at the Cathedral Church of St George, Southwark, London.

♂ PUENTE BUCES, Pablo: born 16 June 1931 at Colindres (Cantabria), Spain.

† BILSBORROW OSB, J. Romanus: died 19 June 1931 at Belle Rose, Mauritius aged 68 • buried at the Cathedral Church of St Louis, Port-Louis, Mauritius.

FOYLAN, Michael: ordained priest (Dunkeld) 5 July 1931 at Kinnoull, Perth.

WALSH MAfr, Francis P.: professed (Missionaries of Africa (White Fathers)) 9 September 1931 at Sainte-Marie, Maison Carrée (Algiers), Algeria.

♂ MALONE, Vincent: born 11 September 1931 at Old Swan, Liverpool.

†   DUNN, Thomas: died 21 September 1931 at Nottingham aged 61 • buried at the Cathedral Church of St Barnabas, Nottingham.
RONCALLI, Angelo G. (POPE ST JOHN XXIII): appointed 16 October 1931 Apostolic Delegate to Bulgaria.

1932

LEE, William: ordained Bishop of Clifton 26 January 1932 at Clifton, Bristol.
MORIARTY, Ambrose J.: ordained titular Bishop of *Miletopolis* and appointed coadjutor Bishop of Shrewsbury 28 January 1932 at Shrewsbury.

†   CARY-ELWES, Dudley C.: died 1 May 1932 at Hampstead, London aged 64 • buried at Great Billing, Northampton.
McNULTY, John F.: ordained Bishop of Nottingham 11 June 1932 at Nottingham.
MYERS, Edward: ordained titular Bishop of *Lamus* and appointed auxiliary Bishop of Westminster 25 July 1932 at the Metropolitan Cathedral Church of the Most Precious Blood, Westminster, London.

♂   MURPHY-O'CONNOR, Cormac: born 24 August 1932 at Reading.
DWYER, George P.: ordained priest (Salford) 1 November 1932 at Rome, Italy.
RESTIEAUX, Cyril E.: ordained priest (Nottingham) 1 November 1932 at Rome, Italy.

♂   MURRAY, Ian: born 15 December 1932 at Lennoxtown, Glasgow.

1933

BUTLER OSB, B. E. Christopher: ordained priest (Order of Saint Benedict) 10 June 1933 at Downside, Radstock.

♂   PARGETER, Philip: born 13 June 1933 at Wolverhampton.
HOLLAND, Thomas: ordained priest (Liverpool) 18 June 1933 at Southport.

♂ RAFFERTY, Kevin L.: born 24 June 1933 at Garvagh, Coleraine (Derry), Ireland.

ENRICI, Domenico: ordained priest (Cuneo) 29 June 1933 at Cuneo (Cuneo), Italy.

YOUENS SMA, Laurence W.: ordained Bishop of Northampton 25 July 1933 at Northampton.

♂ JABALÉ OSB, J. P. Mark: born 16 October 1933 at Alexandria (Alexandria), Egypt.

PEARSON, Thomas B.: ordained priest (Lancaster) 1 November 1933 at Rome, Italy.

WHEELER, William G.: ordained Church of England deacon (Chichester) 21 December 1933 at Chichester.

1934

† KEATINGE, William L.: died 21 February 1934 at Westminster, London aged 64 • buried at St Mary's Cemetery, Kensal Green, London.

♂ CONTI, Mario J.: born 20 March 1934 at Elgin.

♂ O'DONOGHUE, Patrick: born 4 May 1934 at Mourne Abbey (Cork), Ireland.

TICKLE, Gerard W.: ordained priest (Shrewsbury) 28 October 1934 at Rome, Italy.

† McINTYRE, John: died 21 November 1934 at Edgbaston, Birmingham aged 79 • buried at the Metropolitan Cathedral Church of St Chad, Birmingham.

RONCALLI, Angelo G. (POPE ST JOHN XXIII): translated 30 November 1934 to titular Archbishop of *Mesembria*.

MORIARTY, Ambrose J.: succeeded 17 December 1934 as Bishop of Shrewsbury.

† SINGLETON, Hugh: died 17 December 1934 at Birkenhead aged 83 • buried at Landican Cemetery, Birkenhead.

CE WHEELER, William G.: ordained Church of England priest (Derby) 23 December 1934 at Derby.

1935

†   BOURNE, Francis A.: died 1 January 1935 at Westminster, London aged 73 • buried at St Edmund's College, Old Hall Green, Ware.
RONCALLI, Angelo G. (**POPE ST JOHN XXIII**): appointed 12 January 1935 Apostolic Delegate to Greece and Turkey.

†   VAUGHAN, Francis J.: died 13 March 1935 at Wrexham aged 57 • buried at Wrexham.
PACELLI, Eugenio M. G. G. (**POPE VEN. PIUS XII**): appointed 1 April 1935 Camerlengo of the Apostolic Chamber.

ơ   MORAN, Peter A.: born 13 April 1935 at Hillhead, Glasgow.
HINSLEY, Arthur: translated 29 April 1935 to Archdiocese of Westminster.
DEY, James: ordained titular Bishop of *Sebastopolis in Armenia* and appointed Vicar Delegate to the Army and Royal Air Force 2 June 1935 at Oscott, Sutton Coldfield.
GRAY, Gordon J.: ordained priest (St Andrews and Edinburgh) 15 June 1935 at the Metropolitan Cathedral Church of St Mary, Edinburgh.
GRANT, Charles A.: ordained priest (Northampton) 16 June 1935 at Oscott, Sutton Coldfield.
LUCIANI, Albino (**POPE JOHN PAUL I**): ordained priest (Belluno e Feltre) 7 July 1935 at Belluno (Belluno), Italy.
McGRATH, Michael J.: ordained Bishop of Menevia 24 September 1935 at Wrexham.
MELLON, William H.: ordained titular Bishop of *Daulia* and appointed coadjutor Bishop of Galloway 28 October 1935 at the Metropolitan Cathedral Church of St Mary, Edinburgh.
O'HARA, Gerald P. A.: translated 16 November 1935 to Diocese of Savannah (GA), USA.

ơ   REGAN, Edwin: born 31 December 1935 at Port Talbot.

1936

ơ   NOBLE, Brian M.: born 11 April 1936 at Lancaster.
†   COWGILL, Joseph R.: died 12 May 1936 at Leeds aged 76 • buried at Killingbeck Cemetery, Leeds.
ơ   McMAHON, Thomas: born 17 June 1936 at Dorking.

McGILL **PSS**, Stephen: ordained priest (Glasgow) 29 June 1936 at the Cathedral Church of St Andrew, Glasgow.

† WHITESIDE, Thomas: reinterred 8 September 1936 at the Metropolitan Cathedral Crypt of Christ the King, Liverpool.

WHEELER, William G.: received into Catholic Church 18 September 1936 at Downside, Radstock.

POSKITT, Henry J.: ordained Bishop of Leeds 21 September 1936 at Leeds.

† THORMAN, Joseph: died 7 October 1936 at Newcastle upon Tyne aged 65 • buried at St Cuthbert's College, Ushaw, Durham.

ơ RAWSTHORNE, John A.: born 12 November 1936 at Crosby, Liverpool.

ơ HOLLIS, R. F. Crispian: born 17 November 1936 at Bristol.

ơ BERGOGLIO **SJ**, Jorge M. (**POPE FRANCIS**): born 17 December 1936 at Buenos Aires (Buenos Aires), Argentina.

1937

O'HARA, Gerald P. A.: translated 5 January 1937 to renamed Diocese of Savannah-Atlanta (GA), USA.

McCORMACK, Joseph: ordained Bishop of Hexham and Newcastle 4 February 1937 at Newcastle upon Tyne.

CUNNINGHAM, James: ordained priest (Salford) 22 May 1937 at Upholland, Skelmersdale.

ơ BUDD, H. Christopher: born 27 May 1937 at Romford.

ơ SAINZ MUÑOZ, Faustino: born 5 June 1937 at Almadén (Ciudad Real), Spain.

BURKE, Geoffrey I.: ordained priest (Salford) 29 June 1937 at Oscott, Sutton Coldfield.

McGILL **PSS**, Stephen: joined Society of La Solitude de St Sulpice 1 July 1937 at Issy-les-Moulineaux (Hauts-de-Seine), France.

FOLEY, Brian C.: ordained priest (Brentwood) 25 July 1937 at Rome, Italy.

ơ DEVINE, Joseph: born 7 August 1937 at Kirkintilloch, Glasgow.

ơ FITZGERALD **MAfr**, Michael L.: born 17 August 1937 at Walsall.

+ HINSLEY, Arthur: elevated 16 December 1937 to Cardinal-Priest of Santa Susanna.

GRASAR, William E.: ordained priest (Nottingham) 18 December 1937 at Nottingham.

1938

ENRICI, Domenico: entered diplomatic service to the Holy See 1938 at Vatican City.

GODFREY, William: entered diplomatic service to the Holy See 1938 at Vatican City.

σ   CUNNINGHAM, John: born 22 February 1938 at Paisley.

AMIGO, Peter E.: appointed 25 February 1938 *Archbishop ad personam* at Vatican City.

σ   O'BRIEN, Keith M. P.: born 17 March 1938 at Ballycastle (Antrim), Ireland.

®   BUTT, Joseph: appointed 23 April 1938 titular Archbishop of *Nicopsis* and retired to Downside, Radstock.

HEIM, Bruno B.: ordained priest (Basel) 29 June 1938 at Solothurn (Solothurn), Switzerland.

GRIFFIN, Bernard W.: ordained titular Bishop of *Appia* and appointed auxiliary Bishop of Birmingham 30 June 1938 at the Metropolitan Cathedral Church of St Chad, Birmingham.

KING, John H.: ordained titular Bishop of *Opus* and appointed auxiliary Bishop of Portsmouth 15 July 1938 at Portsmouth.

σ   HINE, John F. M.: born 26 July 1938 at Tunbridge Wells.

†   HENSHAW, Thomas: died 23 September 1938 at Worsley, Manchester aged 65 • buried at St Mary's Cemetery, Worsley, Manchester.

APOSTOLIC DELEGATION: formed 21 November 1938, with jurisdiction over Great Britain, Malta and Gibraltar (with Bermuda added later).

σ   KELLY, Patrick A: born 23 November 1938 at Morecambe.

†   PEARSON OSB, T Wulstan: died 1 December 1938 at Preston aged 68 • buried at the Cathedral Church of St Peter, Lancaster.

†   MARTIN, Donald: died 6 December 1938 at Oban aged 65 • buried at Pennyfuir Cemetery, Oban.

σ   BRAIN, Terence J.: born 19 December 1938 at Coventry.

GODFREY, William: ordained titular Archbishop of *Cius* and appointed Apostolic Delegate to Great Britain, Malta and Gibraltar 21 December 1938 at Rome, Italy.

MATHEW, David J.: ordained titular Bishop of *Aeliae* and appointed auxiliary Bishop of Westminster 21 December 1938 at the Metropolitan Cathedral Church of the Most Precious Blood, Westminster, London.

CASHMAN, David J.: ordained priest (Birmingham) 24 December 1938 at Rome, Italy.

1939

BRIGHT, Humphrey P.: commissioned as military chaplain 26 January 1939.

† RATTI, Ambrogio D. A. (**POPE PIUS XI**): died 10 February 1939 at the Apostolic Palace, Vatican City aged 81 • buried at St Peter's Basilica, Vatican City.

x PACELLI, Eugenio M. G. G. (**POPE VEN. PIUS XII**): elected Pope 2 March 1939 at Vatican City.

PACELLI, Eugenio M. G. G. (**POPE VEN. PIUS XII**): installed 12 March 1939 at Vatican City.

HARVEY, Philip J. B.: ordained priest (Westminster) 3 June 1939 at the Metropolitan Cathedral Church of the Most Precious Blood, Westminster, London.

CLEARY, Joseph F.: ordained priest (Birmingham) 29 June 1939 at Oscott, Sutton Coldfield.

FLYNN, Thomas E.: ordained Bishop of Lancaster 24 July 1939 at Lancaster.

CASEY, Patrick J.: ordained priest (Westminster) 3 September 1939 at the Metropolitan Cathedral Church of the Most Precious Blood, Westminster, London.

MARSHALL, Henry V.: ordained Bishop of Salford 21 September 1939 at Salford.

σ McPARTLAND **SMA**, Michael B.: born 29 September 1939 at Middlesbrough.

† MOSTYN, Francis E. J.: died 25 October 1939 at Cardiff aged 79 • buried at Cathays Cemetery, Cardiff.

HART, William A.: commissioned as military chaplain 28 October 1939.

GRANT, Kenneth: commissioned as military chaplain 3 November 1939.

† YOUENS SMA, Laurence W.: died 14 November 1939 at Northampton aged 66 • buried at the Abbey Church of St Michael and All Angels, Belmont, Hereford.

MAGUIRE, James: ordained titular Bishop of *Ilium* and appointed coadjutor Bishop of Dunkeld 30 November 1939 at Dundee.

CAMPBELL, Donald A.: ordained Bishop of Argyll and the Isles 14 December 1939 at Oban.

1940

EMERY, Anthony J.: enlisted as military soldier 1940.

MACPHERSON, Colin A.: ordained priest (Argyll and the Isles) 23 March 1940 at Rome, Italy.

WHEELER, William G.: ordained priest (Westminster) 31 March 1940 at the Metropolitan Cathedral Church of the Most Precious Blood, Westminster, London.

♂ ENTWISTLE, Harry: born 31 May 1940 at Chorley.

MONAGHAN, James: ordained priest (St Andrews and Edinburgh) 11 June 1940 at the Metropolitan Cathedral Church of St Mary, Edinburgh.

McGRATH, Michael J.: translated 20 June 1940 to Archdiocese of Cardiff.

♂ WRIGHT, Roderick: born 28 June 1940 at Kinning Park, Glasgow.

† COTTER, William T.: died 24 October 1940 at Portsmouth aged 73 • buried at Waterlooville convent Cemetery.

1941

PARKER, Thomas L.: ordained Bishop of Northampton 11 February 1941 at Northampton.

HANNON, Daniel J.: ordained Bishop of Menevia 1 May 1941 at
Wrexham.

KING, John H.: translated 4 June 1941 to Diocese of Portsmouth.

♂ CROWLEY, John P.: born 23 June 1941 at Newbury.

♂ LOGAN, Vincent P.: born 30 June 1941 at Bathgate.

CARDINALE, Igino E.: ordained priest (Naples) 13 July 1941 at
Naples (Napoli), Italy.

♂ CAMPBELL OSA, Michael G.: born 2 October 1941 at Larne
(Antrim), Ireland.

TICKLE, Gerard W.: commissioned as military chaplain 15
December 1941.

1942

† DOBSON, Robert: died 6 January 1942 at Sefton Park, Liverpool
aged 74 • buried at Upholland, Skelmersdale.

McCLEAN, John G.: ordained priest (Middlesbrough) 22 March
1942 at Ushaw, Durham.

FOX, Langton D.: ordained priest (Southwark) 30 May 1942 at
Wonersh, Guildford.

HARRIS, Augustine: ordained priest (Liverpool) 30 May 1942 at
Upholland, Skelmersdale.

♂ CUNNINGHAM, Séamus: born 7 July 1942 at Castlebar (Mayo),
Ireland.

HUME OSB, G. Basil: professed (Order of Saint Benedict) 23
September 1942 at Ampleforth, York.

1943

♂ LYSYKANYCH, B. Benjamin: born 2 January 1943 at Bielefield
(Nord Rhein-Westfalia), Germany.

† HINSLEY, Arthur: died 17 March 1943 at Hare Street, Buntingford
aged 77 • buried at the Metropolitan Cathedral Church of the Most
Precious Blood, Westminster, London.

†   McNULTY, John F.: died 8 June 1943 at Dollis Hill, London aged 63 • buried at the Cathedral Church of St Barnabas, Nottingham.

GRAY, Joseph: ordained priest (Birmingham) 20 June 1943 at Cavan City (Cavan), Ireland.

ơ   SMITH, Peter D. G.: born 21 October 1943 at Battersea, London.

†   MACKINTOSH, Donald: died 8 December 1943 at Bearsden, Glasgow aged 66 • buried at St Peter's Cemetery, Dalbeth, Glasgow.

GRIFFIN, Bernard W.: translated 18 December 1943 to Archdiocese of Westminster.

†   McCARTHY, James W.: died 24 December 1943 at Dumfries aged 90 • buried at St Andrew's Cemetery, Calside, Dumfries.

MELLON, William H.: succeeded 24 December 1943 as Bishop of Galloway.

1944

CLARKE, John M.: incardinated 1944 into Archdiocese of Westminster at Westminster, London.

ơ   HOPES, Alan S.: born 14 March 1944 at Oxford.

ELLIS, Edward: ordained Bishop of Nottingham 1 May 1944 at Nottingham.

ơ   DOYLE, Peter J. H.: born 3 May 1944 at Wilpshire, Blackburn.

ơ   BURNS SM, Thomas M.: born 3 June 1944 at Belfast (Antrim), Ireland.

WORLOCK, Derek J. H.: ordained priest (Westminster) 3 June 1944 at Old Hall Green, Ware.

TAYLOR, Maurice: enlisted as military soldier 17 August 1944.

BARBARITO, Luigi: ordained priest (Avellino) 20 August 1944 at Avellino (Avellino), Italy.

†   BUTT, Joseph: died 23 August 1944 at Downside, Radstock aged 75 • buried at the Abbey Church of St Gregory, Downside, Radstock.

BRIGHT, Humphrey P.: released from military service 31 August 1944.

†   MAGUIRE, James: died 10 October 1944 at Dundee aged 62 • buried at Balgay Cemetery, Dundee.

BRIGHT, Humphrey P.: ordained titular Bishop of *Soli* and appointed auxiliary Bishop of Birmingham 28 October 1944 at the Metropolitan Cathedral Church of St Chad, Birmingham.

♂ McGOUGH, David C.: born 20 November 1944 at Tunstall, Stoke-on-Trent.

RONCALLI, Angelo G. (POPE ST JOHN XXIII): appointed 23 December 1944 Apostolic Nuncio to France.

1945

EMERY, Anthony J.: released from military service 1945.

CAMPBELL, Donald A.: translated 6 January 1945 to Archdiocese of Glasgow.

CLARK, Alan C.: ordained priest (Southwark) 11 February 1945 at Bromley.

GUAZZELLI, Victor: ordained priest (Westminster) 17 March 1945 at Lisbon (Lisboa), Portugal.

HORNYAK OSBM, Augustine E.: ordained priest (Philadelphia-Ukrainian) 25 March 1945 at Rome, Italy.

HALSALL, Joseph F.: ordained titular Bishop of *Zabi* and appointed auxiliary Bishop of Liverpool 21 September 1945 at the Pro-Cathedral Church of St Nicholas, Liverpool.

GRANT, Kenneth: released from military service 6 November 1945.

♂ NICHOLS, Vincent G.: born 8 November 1945 at Crosby, Liverpool.

HART, William A.: released from military service 25 November 1945.

1946

CARDINALE, Igino E.: entered diplomatic service to the Holy See 1946 at Vatican City.

+ GRIFFIN, Bernard W.: elevated 18 February 1946 to Cardinal-Priest of Santi Andrea e Gregorio Magno al Monte Celio.

GRANT, Kenneth: ordained Bishop of Argyll and the Isles 27 February 1946 at Oban.

† WILLIAMS, Thomas L.: died 1 April 1946 at Edgbaston, Birmingham aged 69 • buried at St Mary's College, Oscott, Sutton Coldfield.

† HANNON, Daniel J.: died 26 April 1946 at Wrexham aged 61 • buried at Wrexham.

MOVERLEY, Gerald: ordained priest (Leeds) 28 April 1946 at Leeds.

♂ KENNEY CP, L. William: born 7 May 1946 at Newcastle upon Tyne.

♂ STACK, George: born 9 May 1946 at Cork City (Cork), Ireland.

MATHEW, David J.: translated 10 May 1946 to titular Archbishop of *Apamea in Bithynia* and appointed Apostolic Delegate to British East and West Africa.

* CLARKE, John M.: appointed 8 June 1946 Apostolic Administrator of the Bishopric of the Forces in Great Britain until 23 April 1954.

† DEY, James: died 8 June 1946 at Barton on Sea, New Milton aged 76 • buried at St Mary's College, Oscott, Sutton Coldfield.

THOMSON, Francis A. S. W.: ordained priest (St Andrews and Edinburgh) 15 June 1946 at the Metropolitan Cathedral Church of St Mary, Edinburgh.

SCANLAN, James D.: ordained titular Bishop of *Cyme* and appointed coadjutor Bishop of Dunkeld 20 June 1946 at Dundee.

MAHON MHM, Gerald T.: ordained priest (Saint Joseph's Missionary Society of Mill Hill) 14 July 1946 at Mill Hill, London.

BRUNNER, George: ordained titular Bishop of *Elis* and appointed auxiliary Bishop of Middlesbrough 25 July 1946 at Middlesbrough.

HRYNCHYSHYN CSsR, Michel: professed (Congregation of the Most Holy Redeemer) 28 July 1946 at Yorkton (SK), Canada.

TICKLE, Gerard W.: released from military service 24 August 1946.

BUTLER OSB, B. E. Christopher: elected 12 September 1946 Abbot of the Abbey Church of St Gregory, Downside, Radstock.

WOJTYŁA, Karol J. (POPE ST JOHN PAUL II): ordained priest (Kraków) 1 November 1946 at Kraków (Kraków), Poland.

† BARRETT, John P.: died 2 November 1946 at Torquay aged 68 • buried at the Abbey Church of St Mary, Buckfastleigh.

† BENNETT, George H.: died 25 December 1946 at Aberdeen aged 71 • buried at Allenvale Cemetery, Aberdeen.

1947

HEIM, Bruno B.: entered diplomatic service to the Holy See 1947 at Vatican City.

O'HARA, Gerald P. A.: entered diplomatic service to the Holy See 1947 at Vatican City.

JUKES OFM Conv., John P.: professed (Order of Friars Minor Conventual) 10 January 1947 at Mossley Hill, Liverpool.

O'HARA, Gerald P. A.: appointed 19 February 1947 Apostolic Nuncio to Romania.

MASTERSON, Joseph: ordained Archbishop of Birmingham 19 March 1947 at the Metropolitan Cathedral Church of St Chad, Birmingham.

PETIT, John E.: ordained Bishop of Menevia 25 March 1947 at Llandudno.

♂ LYNCH SS.CC, Patrick K.: born 27 April 1947 at Cork City (Cork), Ireland.

DIOCESE OF GALLOWAY: restructured 25 May 1947.

ARCHDIOCESE OF GLASGOW: restructured 25 May 1947.

DIOCESE OF MOTHERWELL: erected 25 May 1947.

DIOCESE OF PAISLEY: erected 25 May 1947.

CAMPBELL, Donald A.: appointed 25 May 1947 Archbishop and Metropolitan of newly raised Archdiocese and Province of Glasgow.

CRAVEN, George L.: ordained titular Bishop of *Sebastopolis in Armenia* and appointed auxiliary Bishop of Westminster 25 July 1947 at the Metropolitan Cathedral Church of the Most Precious Blood, Westminster, London.

GRIMSHAW, Francis E. J.: ordained Bishop of Plymouth 25 July 1947 at Plymouth.

TAYLOR, Maurice: released from military service 6 August 1947.

♂ McDONALD, Kevin J. P.: born 18 August 1947 at Stoke-on-Trent.

♂ MENNINI, Antonio: born 2 September 1947 at Rome, Italy.

MATHESON, John A.: ordained Bishop of Aberdeen 24 September 1947 at Aberdeen.

1948

♂   WILLIAMS, Thomas A.: born 10 February 1948 at Vauxhall, Liverpool.

MURPHY, John A.: ordained titular Bishop of *Appia* and appointed coadjutor Bishop of Shrewsbury 25 February 1948 at Chester.

BLACK, James: ordained Bishop of newly erected Diocese of Paisley 14 April 1948 at Paisley.

DOUGLAS, Edward W.: ordained Bishop of newly erected Diocese of Motherwell 21 April 1948 at Motherwell.

HENDERSON, Charles J.: ordained priest (Southwark) 6 June 1948 at Waterford City (Waterford), Ireland.

O'BRIEN, T. Kevin: ordained priest (Leeds) 20 June 1948 at Dublin City (Dublin), Ireland.

ALEXANDER, Mervyn A. N.: ordained priest (Clifton) 18 July 1948 at Rome, Italy.

BECK AA, George A.: ordained titular Bishop of *Tigias* and appointed coadjutor Bishop of Brentwood 21 September 1948 at the Metropolitan Cathedral Church of the Most Precious Blood, Westminster, London.

†   LEE, William: died 21 September 1948 at Leigh Woods, Bristol aged 72 • buried at Holy Souls Cemetery, Arnos Vale, Bristol.

KUCHMIAK CSsR, Michael: professed (Congregation of the Most Holy Redeemer) 3 October 1948 at Mercato San Severino (Salerno), Italy.

WINNING, Thomas J.: ordained priest (Motherwell) 18 December 1948 at Rome, Italy.

1949

SCANLAN, James D.: succeeded 31 May 1949 as Bishop of Dunkeld.

†   TONER, John: died 31 May 1949 at Dundee aged 92 • buried at Balgay Cemetery, Dundee.

†   MORIARTY, Ambrose J.: died 3 June 1949 at Shrewsbury aged 78 • buried at Shrewsbury Cemetery.

MURPHY, John A.: succeeded 3 June 1949 as Bishop of Shrewsbury.

♂ McMAHON **OP**, Malcolm P.: born 14 June 1949 at Brixton, London.

McCARTIE, P. Leo: ordained priest (Birmingham) 17 July 1949 at Trent Vale, Stoke-on-Trent.

PEARSON, Thomas B.: ordained titular Bishop of *Sinda* and appointed auxiliary Bishop of Lancaster 25 July 1949 at Lancaster.

RUDDERHAM, Joseph E.: ordained Bishop of Clifton 25 July 1949 at Clifton, Bristol.

♂ DRAINEY, Terence P.: born 1 August 1949 at Droylesden, Manchester.

† AMIGO, Peter E.: died 1 October 1949 at Southwark, London aged 85 • buried at the Cathedral Church of St George, Southwark, London.

COWDEROY, Cyril C.: ordained Bishop of Southwark 21 December 1949 at the Metropolitan Cathedral Church of the Most Precious Blood, Westminster, London.

1950

WARD **OFM Cap.**, John A.: professed (Order of Friars Minor Capuchin) 25 January 1950 at Peckham, London.

♂ DUNN, Patrick J.: born 5 February 1950 at London.

† POSKITT, Henry J.: died 19 February 1950 at Leeds aged 61 • buried at St Edward's Church, Clifford, Wetherby.

♂ ROCHE, Arthur: born 6 March 1950 at Batley Carr, Dewsbury.

♂ LANG, Declan R.: born 15 April 1950 at Cowes.

† McDONALD **OSB**, A. T. Joseph: died 22 May 1950 at St Bennet's, Edinburgh aged 79 • buried at the Metropolitan Cathedral Church of St Mary, Edinburgh.

McGUINNESS, James J.: ordained priest (Nottingham) 3 June 1950 at Nottingham.

TAYLOR, Maurice: ordained priest (Motherwell) 2 July 1950 at Rome, Italy.

† MATHESON, John A.: died 5 July 1950 at Aberdeen aged 49 • buried at the Catholic Cemetery, Tomintoul, Ballindalloch.

♂ DUNN, Kevin J.: born 9 July 1950 at Clayton, Newcastle.

O'HARA, Gerald P. A.: appointed 12 July 1950 *Archbishop ad personam* at Vatican City.

HUME OSB, G. Basil: ordained priest (Order of Saint Benedict) 23 July 1950 at Ampleforth, York.

1951

σ TARTAGLIA, Philip: born 11 January 1951 at Govan, Glasgow.

BECK AA, George A.: succeeded 23 January 1951 as Bishop of Brentwood.

† DOUBLEDAY, Arthur H.: died 23 January 1951 at Brentwood aged 85 • buried at the Cathedral Church Cemetery of the Sacred Heart and St Helen, Brentwood.

σ CONRY, Kieran T.: born 1 February 1951 at Coventry.

HEENAN, John C.: ordained Bishop of Leeds 12 March 1951 at Leeds.

σ WILLIAMS SM, Alan: born 15 March 1951 at Oldham.

σ ROBSON, Stephen: born 1 April 1951 at Carlisle.

MYERS, Edward: appointed 20 May 1951 titular Archbishop of *Beroea* and appointed coadjutor Archbishop of Westminster *sedi datus sine jure successionis.*

BL. SARTO, Giuseppe M. (POPE ST PIUS X): beatified 3 June 1951 at Vatican City.

RATZINGER, Joseph A. (POPE BENEDICT XVI): ordained priest (München und Freising) 29 June 1951 at Freising (Bavaria), Germany.

σ McALEENAN, Paul: born 15 July 1951 at Belfast (Antrim), Ireland.

σ EVANS, Michael C.: born 10 August 1951 at Camberwell, London.

WALSH MAfr, Francis P.: ordained Bishop of Aberdeen 12 September 1951 at Aberdeen.

GRAY, Gordon J.: ordained Archbishop of St Andrews and Edinburgh 21 September 1951 at the Metropolitan Cathedral Church of St Mary, Edinburgh.

GRIFFITHS OSB, M. Ambrose: professed (Order of Saint Benedict) 25 September 1951 at Ampleforth, York.

O'HARA, Gerald P. A.: appointed 27 November 1951 Apostolic Nuncio to Ireland.

† BROWN, William F.: died 16 December 1951 at Vauxhall, London aged 89 • buried at St Anne's Church, Vauxhall, London.

1952

†   MELLON, William H.: died 2 February 1952 at Dumfries aged 75 • buried at St Andrew's Cemetery, Calside, Dumfries.

♂   GILBERT OSB, E. Hugh: born 15 March 1952 at Emsworth.

♂   NEWTON, Keith: born 10 April 1952 at Liverpool.

HRYNCHYSHYN CSsR, Michel: ordained priest (Congregation of the Most Holy Redeemer) 25 May 1952 at Toronto (ON), Canada.

MONE, John A.: ordained priest (Glasgow) 12 June 1952 at the Metropolitan Cathedral Church of St Andrew, Glasgow.

JUKES OFM Conv., John P.: ordained priest (Order of Friars Minor Conventual) 20 July 1952 at Mossley Hill, Liverpool.

McGEE, Joseph M.: ordained Bishop of Galloway 11 November 1952 at Dumfries.

1953

BARBARITO, Luigi: entered diplomatic service to the Holy See 1953 at Vatican City.

+   RONCALLI, Angelo G. (POPE ST JOHN XXIII): elevated 12 January 1953 to Cardinal-Priest of Santa Prisca.

RONCALLI, Angelo G. (POPE ST JOHN XXIII): translated 15 January 1953 to Patriarch Archdiocese of Venice.

♂   HESKETT CSsR, Ralph: born 3 March 1953 at Sunderland.

RENFREW, Charles M.: ordained priest (Glasgow) 4 April 1953 at Rome, Italy.

MULLINS, Daniel J.: ordained priest (Cardiff) 12 April 1953 at Oscott, Sutton Coldfield.

EMERY, Anthony J.: ordained priest (Birmingham) 30 May 1953 at Oscott, Sutton Coldfield.

WALMSLEY, Francis J.: ordained priest (Southwark) 30 May 1953 at Wonersh, Guildford.

TRIPP, Howard G.: ordained priest (Southwark) 31 May 1953 at South Croydon.

WARD OFM Cap., John A.: ordained priest (Order of Friars Minor Capuchin) 7 June 1953 at Peckham, London.

♂   ARNOLD, John S. K.: born 12 June 1953 at Sheffield.

†   DOWNEY, Richard J.: died 16 June 1953 at Gateacre Grange, Liverpool aged 72 • buried at the Metropolitan Cathedral Crypt of Christ the King, Liverpool.

♂   BRIGNALL, Peter M.: born 5 July 1953 at Whetstone, London.

LINDSAY, Hugh: ordained priest (Hexham and Newcastle) 19 July 1953 at Newcastle upon Tyne.

JABALÉ OSB, J. P. Mark: professed (Order of Saint Benedict) 29 September 1953 at Belmont, Hereford.

GODFREY, William: translated 14 November 1953 to Archdiocese of Liverpool.

BISHOPRIC OF THE FORCES: established 21 November 1953, which came into effect on 23 April 1954.

†   MASTERSON, Joseph: died 30 November 1953 at Edgbaston, Birmingham aged 54 • buried at St Mary's College, Oscott, Sutton Coldfield.

1954

♂   GALLAGHER, Paul R.: born 23 January 1954 at Liverpool.

♂   NOLAN, William: born 26 January 1954 at Motherwell.

*   CAMPBELL, Donald A: appointed 9 February 1954 Apostolic Administrator of the Diocese of Motherwell until 23 May 1955.

®   DOUGLAS, Edward W.: appointed 9 February 1954 titular Bishop of *Botrys* and retired to Braemar thence to Fairlie, Largs.

♂   LONCHYNA MSU, Hlib B. S.: born 23 February 1954 at Steubenville (OH), USA.

CLARKE, John M.: released from military service 23 April 1954 and appointed chaplain to St Margaret's Chapel, Tichborne House, Alresford.

MATHEW, David J.: commissioned as military chaplain and translated 23 April 1954 to Military Vicar to HM Forces.

♂   McKINNEY, Patrick J.: born 30 April 1954 at Balsall Heath, Birmingham.

GRIMSHAW, Francis E. J.: translated 11 May 1954 to Archdiocese of Birmingham.

♂   CHOMNYCKY OSBM, Paul P.: born 19 May 1954 at Vancouver (BC), Canada.

ST SARTO, Giuseppe M. (POPE ST PIUS X): canonised 29 May 1954 at Vatican City.

KING, John H.: appointed 6 June 1954 *Archbishop ad personam* at Vatican City.

O'HARA, Gerald P. A.: appointed 8 June 1954 Apostolic Delegate to Great Britain, Malta, Gibraltar and Bermuda.

KONSTANT, David E.: ordained priest (Westminster) 12 June 1954 at the Metropolitan Cathedral Church of the Most Precious Blood, Westminster, London.

O'BRIEN, James J.: ordained priest (Westminster) 12 June 1954 at the Metropolitan Cathedral Church of the Most Precious Blood, Westminster, London.

O'CONNOR, Kevin: ordained priest (Liverpool) 12 June 1954 at Upholland, Skelmersdale.

HANNIGAN, James: ordained priest (Menevia) 27 June 1954 at Paris (Paris), France.

SWINDLEHURST, Owen F.: ordained priest (Hexham and Newcastle) 11 July 1954 at Rome, Italy.

MONTINI, Giovanni-Battista E. A. M. (POPE BL. PAUL VI): ordained Archbishop of Milan 12 December 1954 at Milan (Milano), Italy.

1955

SHINE, Thomas: appointed 19 January 1955 *Archbishop ad personam* at Vatican City.

σ LONGLEY, Bernard: born 5 April 1955 at City of Manchester.

† MARSHALL, Henry V.: died 14 April 1955 at Whalley Range, Manchester aged 70 • buried at St Joseph's Cemetery, Moston, Manchester.

SCANLAN, James D.: translated 23 May 1955 to Diocese of Motherwell.

THOMAS, Francis G.: ordained priest (Birmingham) 5 June 1955 at Oscott, Sutton Coldfield.

RESTIEAUX, Cyril E.: ordained Bishop of Plymouth 14 June 1955 at Plymouth.

HITCHEN, Anthony: ordained priest (Liverpool) 17 July 1955 at Chorley.

MALONE, Vincent: ordained priest (Liverpool) 18 September 1955 at Old Swan, Liverpool.

HART, William A.: ordained Bishop of Dunkeld 21 September 1955 at Dundee.

ENRICI, Domenico: ordained titular Archbishop of *Ancusa* and appointed Apostolic Inter-nuncio to Indonesia 1 November 1955 at Vatican City.

♂ BURNETTE, Kurt R.: born 7 November 1955 at Fakenham.

♂ EGAN, Philip A.: born 14 November 1955 at Altrincham.

† SHINE, Thomas: died 22 November 1955 at Middlesbrough aged 83 • buried at St Joseph's Cemetery, North Ormesby, Middlesbrough.

BECK AA, George A.: translated 28 November 1955 to Diocese of Salford.

1956

WALL, Bernard P.: ordained Bishop of Brentwood 18 January 1956 at Brompton Oratory, Kensington, London.

MURRAY, Ian: ordained priest (St Andrews and Edinburgh) 17 March 1956 at Valladolid (Valladolid), Spain.

♂ HENDRICKS, Paul: born 18 March 1956 at Beckenham.

PUENTE BUCES, Pablo: ordained priest (Santander) 2 April 1956 at Santander (Cantabria), Spain.

KUCHMIAK CSsR, Michael: ordained priest (Congregation of the Most Holy Redeemer) 13 May 1956 at Meadowvale (ON), Canada.

BRUNNER, George: translated 7 June 1956 to Diocese of Middlesbrough.

O'HARA, Gerald P. A.: translated 2 July 1956 to newly restructured Diocese of Savannah (GA), USA.

BREWER, John (Jack): ordained priest (Shrewsbury) 8 July 1956 at Rome, Italy.

† GRIFFIN, Bernard W.: died 20 August 1956 at Polzeath, Wadebridge aged 57 • buried at the Metropolitan Cathedral Church of the Most Precious Blood, Westminster, London.

FITZGERALD **MAfr**, Michael L.: professed (Missionaries of Africa (White Fathers)) 7 September 1956 at s'Heerenberg (Gelderland), Netherlands.

† MYERS, Edward: died 13 September 1956 at Chelsea, London aged 81 • buried at St Edmund's College, Old Hall Green, Ware.

ơ BYRNE **CO**, Robert: born 22 September 1956 at Urmston, Manchester.

ơ TOAL, Joseph A.: born 13 October 1956 at Inverness.

MURPHY-O'CONNOR, Cormac: ordained priest (Portsmouth) 28 October 1956 at Rome, Italy.

GODFREY, William: translated 3 December 1956 to Archdiocese of Westminster.

1957

HEENAN, John C.: translated 7 May 1957 to Archdiocese of Liverpool.

UKRAINIAN EXARCHATE: erected 10 June 1957 for the faithful of the Byzantine-Ukrainian Rite resident in England and Wales.

GODFREY, William: appointed 10 June 1957 to the Apostolic Exarchate for Ukrainians in England and Wales.

RAFFERTY, Kevin L.: ordained priest (St Andrews and Edinburgh) 22 June 1957 at Kilkenny City (Kilkenny), Ireland.

COUVE DE MURVILLE, Maurice N. L.: ordained priest (Southwark) 29 June 1957 at Leatherhead.

GRIFFITHS **OSB**, M. Ambrose: ordained priest (Order of Saint Benedict) 21 July 1957 at Ampleforth, York.

DWYER, George P.: ordained Bishop of Leeds 24 September 1957 at Leeds.

CUNNINGHAM, James: ordained titular Bishop of *Ios* and appointed auxiliary Bishop of Hexham and Newcastle 12 November 1957 at Newcastle upon Tyne.

1958

CLARKE, John M.: appointed administrator of St Bede's Church, Croxley Green, Rickmansworth.

♂ SHERRINGTON, John F.: born 5 January 1958 at Leicester.

ENRICI, Domenico: appointed 30 January 1958 Apostolic Nuncio to Haiti.

† McCORMACK, Joseph: died 2 March 1958 at Newcastle upon Tyne aged 70 • buried at St Cuthbert's College, Ushaw, Durham.

† HALSALL, Joseph F.: died 13 March 1958 at Allithwaite, Grange-over-Sands aged 56 • buried at SS Peter and Paul Church, Great Crosby, Liverpool.

CASHMAN, David J.: ordained titular Bishop of *Cantanus* and appointed auxiliary Bishop of Westminster 27 May 1958 at the Metropolitan Cathedral Church of the Most Precious Blood, Westminster, London.

CUNNINGHAM, James: translated 1 July 1958 to Diocese of Hexham and Newcastle.

BOWEN, Michael G.: ordained priest (Southwark) 6 July 1958 at Rome, Italy.

♂ MOTH, C. P. Richard: born 8 July 1958 at Chingola (Copperbelt), Zambia.

JABALÉ OSB, J. P. Mark: ordained priest (Order of Saint Benedict) 13 July 1958 at Belmont, Hereford.

WOJTYŁA, Karol J. (POPE ST JOHN PAUL II): ordained titular Bishop of *Ombi* and appointed auxiliary Bishop of Kraków 28 September 1958 at Kraków (Kraków), Poland.

† PACELLI, Eugenio M. G. G. (POPE VEN. PIUS XII): died 9 October 1958 at Castel Gandolfo (Roma), Italy aged 82 • buried at St Peter's Basilica, Vatican City.

ARCHDIOCESE OF LIVERPOOL: pro-cathedral transferred 26 October 1958.

CONTI, Mario J: ordained priest (Aberdeen) 26 October 1958 at Rome, Italy.

x RONCALLI, Angelo G. (POPE ST JOHN XXIII): elected Pope 28 October 1958 at Vatican City.

RONCALLI, Angelo G. (POPE ST JOHN XXIII): installed 4 November 1958 at Vatican City.

+ GODFREY, William: elevated 15 December 1958 to Cardinal-Priest of Santi Nereo ed Achilleo.

+   MONTINI, Giovanni-Battista E. A. M. (**POPE BL. PAUL VI**): elevated 15 December 1958 to Cardinal-Priest of Santi Silvestro e Martino ai Monti.
LUCIANI, Albino (**POPE JOHN PAUL I**): ordained Bishop of Vittorio Veneto 27 December 1958 at Vittorio Veneto (Treviso), Italy.

1959

♂   HUDSON, Nicholas G. E.: born 14 February 1959 at Hammersmith, London.
PARGETER, Philip: ordained priest (Birmingham) 21 February 1959 at Oscott, Sutton Coldfield.
MORAN, Peter A.: ordained priest (Glasgow) 19 March 1959 at Rome, Italy.

♂   DAVIES, Mark: born 12 May 1959 at Longsight, Manchester.
REGAN, Edwin: ordained priest (Cardiff) 5 July 1959 at Waterford City (Waterford), Ireland.

†   GRANT, Kenneth: died 7 September 1959 at Glasgow aged 59 • buried at Cille Choireil Cemetery, Lochaber.

®   O'HARA, Gerald P. A.: resigned 12 November 1959 as Bishop of Savannah (GA), USA and appointed titular Archbishop of *Pessinus*.
McMAHON, Thomas: ordained priest (Brentwood) 28 November 1959 at Wonersh, Guildford.

†   GRAHAM, Henry G.: died 5 December 1959 at Crosshill, Glasgow aged 85 • buried at St Peter's Cemetery, Dalbeth, Glasgow.

1960

®   CLARKE, John M.: retired 1960 to Dublin City (Dublin), Ireland.
ENRICI, Domenico: appointed 5 January 1960 Apostolic Internuncio to Japan.
BERGOGLIO SJ, Jorge M. (**POPE FRANCIS**): professed (Society of Jesus) 12 March 1960 at San Miguel (Corrientes), Argentina.
NOBLE, Brian M.: ordained priest (Lancaster) 11 June 1960 at Lancaster.

HORNYAK **OSBM**, Augustine E.: professed (Basilian Order of St Josaphat) 19 June 1960 at Mundare (AB), Canada.

McGILL **PSS**, Stephen: ordained Bishop of Argyll and the Isles 22 June 1960 at Oban.

DEVINE, Joseph: ordained priest (Glasgow) 29 June 1960 at the Metropolitan Cathedral Church of St Andrew, Glasgow.

WARD, James: ordained titular Bishop of *Sita* and appointed auxiliary Bishop of Glasgow 21 September 1960 at the Metropolitan Cathedral Church of St Andrew, Glasgow.

WALMSLEY, Francis J.: commissioned as military chaplain 3 October 1960.

HOLLAND, Thomas: ordained titular Bishop of *Etenna* and appointed coadjutor Bishop of Portsmouth 21 December 1960 at Portsmouth.

1961

FITZGERALD **MAfr**, Michael L.: ordained priest (Missionaries of Africa (White Fathers)) 3 February 1961 at Whetstone, London.

† McGRATH, Michael J.: died 28 February 1961 at Cardiff aged 78 • buried at the Abbey Church of St Joseph, Llantarnam, Cwmbran.

GRANT, Charles A.: ordained titular Bishop of *Alinda* and appointed auxiliary Bishop of Northampton 25 April 1961 at Northampton.

ơ CUSHLEY, Leo W.: born 18 June 1961 at Wester Moffat, Airdrie.

CUNNINGHAM, John: ordained priest (Paisley) 29 June 1961 at Paisley.

MURPHY, John A.: translated 26 August 1961 to Archdiocese of Cardiff.

ơ STOCK, Marcus N.: born 27 August 1961 at London.

HORNYAK **OSBM**, Augustine E.: ordained titular Bishop of *Hermonthis* and appointed auxiliary Bishop of the Apostolic Exarchate for Ukrainians in England and Wales 26 October 1961 at Philadelphia (PA), USA.

† FLYNN, Thomas E.: died 4 November 1961 at Lancaster aged 81 • buried at the Cathedral Church of St Peter, Lancaster.

HEIM, Bruno B.: ordained titular Archbishop of *Xanthus* and appointed Apostolic Delegate to Scandinavia 10 December 1961 at Solothurn (Solothurn), Switzerland.

1962

PUENTE BUCES, Pablo: entered diplomatic service to the Holy See 1962 at Vatican City.

KELLY, Patrick A.: ordained priest (Lancaster) 18 February 1962 at Rome, Italy.

DIOCESE OF GALLOWAY: cathedral transferred 12 March 1962.

FOLEY, Brian C.: ordained Bishop of Lancaster 13 June 1962 at Lancaster.

RAWSTHORNE, John A.: ordained priest (Liverpool) 16 June 1962 at Upholland, Skelmersdale.

GRASAR, William E.: ordained Bishop of Shrewsbury 27 June 1962 at Shrewsbury.

BUDD, H. Christopher: ordained priest (Brentwood) 8 July 1962 at Rome, Italy.

SECOND VATICAN COUNCIL (I): 11 October 1962 to 8 December 1962.

ENRICI, Domenico: appointed 12 October 1962 Apostolic Delegate to Australia, New Zealand and Oceania.

HINE, John F. M.: ordained priest (Southwark) 28 October 1962 at Rome, Italy.

1963

† GODFREY, William: died 22 January 1963 at Westminster, London aged 73 • buried at the Metropolitan Cathedral Church of the Most Precious Blood, Westminster, London.

® MATHEW, David J.: released from military service and retired 29 March 1963 to Stonor Park, Henley-on-Thames.

HUME OSB, G. Basil: elected 17 April 1963 abbot of the Abbey Church of St Laurence, Ampleforth, York.

HORNYAK OSBM, Augustine E.: translated 18 April 1963 to the Apostolic Exarchate for Ukrainians in England and Wales.

† CLARKE, John M.: died 5 May 1963 at Dublin City (Dublin), Ireland aged 69 • buried at Deans Grange Cemetery, Dun Laoghaire (Dublin), Ireland.

† RONCALLI, Angelo G. (POPE ST JOHN XXIII): died 3 June 1963 at the Apostolic Palace, Vatican City aged 81 • buried at St Peter's Basilica, Vatican City.

x MONTINI, Giovanni-Battista E. A. M. (POPE BL. PAUL VI): elected Pope 21 June 1963 at Vatican City.

♂ O'TOOLE, Mark: born 22 June 1963 at Southwark, London.

MONTINI, Giovanni-Battista E. A. M. (POPE BL. PAUL VI): installed 30 June 1963 at Vatican City.

† O'HARA, Gerald P. A.: died 16 July 1963 at Wimbledon, London aged 68 • buried at the Cathedral Church of SS Peter and Paul, Philadelphia (PA), USA.

† CAMPBELL, Donald A.: died 22 July 1963 at Lourdes (Hautes-Pyrénées), France aged 68 • buried at St Peter's College chapel, Cardross, Dumbarton.

KENNEY CP, L. William: professed (Congregation of the Passion of Jesus Christ) 1 September 1963 at Broadway.

HEENAN, John C.: translated 2 September 1963 to Archdiocese of Westminster.

* GRAY, Gordon J.: appointed 12 September 1963 Apostolic Administrator of the Diocese of Aberdeen until 25 March 1965.

® WALSH MAfr, Francis P.: resigned 12 September 1963 as Bishop of Aberdeen and appointed titular Bishop of *Birtha*.

ENTWISTLE, Harry: ordained Church of England deacon (Blackburn) 22 September 1963 at Blackburn.

SECOND VATICAN COUNCIL (II): 29 September 1963 to 4 December 1963.

CARDINALE, Igino E.: ordained titular Archbishop of *Nepte* and appointed Apostolic Delegate to Great Britain, Malta, Gibraltar and Bermuda 20 October 1963 at Vatican City.

TICKLE, Gerard W.: ordained titular Bishop of *Bela* and appointed Military Vicar to HM Forces 30 November 1963 at Rome, Italy.

1964

†   RIDDELL, Arthur G.: reinterred 1964 at the Cathedral Church of Our Lady and St Thomas, Northampton.

WOJTYŁA, Karol J. (POPE ST JOHN PAUL II): translated 13 January 1964 to Archdiocese of Kraków.

BECK AA, George A.: translated 29 January 1964 to Archdiocese of Liverpool.

SCANLAN, James D.: translated 29 January 1964 to Archdiocese of Glasgow.

BRAIN, Terence J.: ordained priest (Birmingham) 22 February 1964 at the Metropolitan Cathedral Church of St Chad, Birmingham.

LOGAN, Vincent P.: ordained priest (St Andrews and Edinburgh) 14 March 1964 at the Metropolitan Cathedral Church of St Mary, Edinburgh.

WHEELER, William G.: ordained titular Bishop of *Theudalis* and appointed coadjutor Bishop of Middlesbrough 19 March 1964 at Middlesbrough.

†   BRIGHT, Humphrey P.: died 26 March 1964 at Tunstall, Stoke-on-Trent aged 61 • buried at St Mary's College, Oscott, Sutton Coldfield.

WRIGHT, Roderick: ordained priest (Glasgow) 29 June 1964 at the Metropolitan Cathedral Church of St Andrew, Glasgow.

HOLLAND, Thomas: translated 3 September 1964 to Diocese of Salford.

SECOND VATICAN COUNCIL (III): 14 September 1964 to 21 November 1964.

CE   ENTWISTLE, Harry: ordained Church of England priest (Blackburn) 20 September 1964 at Blackburn.

♂   KEENAN, John: born 19 December 1964 at Cowcaddens, Glasgow..

SAINZ MUÑOZ, Faustino: ordained priest (Madrid) 19 December 1964 at Madrid (Madrid), Spain.

1965

CLEARY, Joseph F.: ordained titular Bishop of *Cresima* and appointed auxiliary Bishop of Birmingham 25 January 1965 at the Metropolitan Cathedral Church of St Chad, Birmingham.

+   HEENAN, John C.: elevated 22 February 1965 to Cardinal-Priest of San Silvestro in Capite.

THOMSON, Francis A. S. W.: ordained Bishop of Motherwell 24 February 1965 at Motherwell.

WARD, James: appointed 1 March 1965 parish priest of Holy Cross Church, Crosshill, Glasgow.

†   GRIMSHAW, Francis E. J.: died 22 March 1965 at Edgbaston, Birmingham aged 63 • buried at St Mary's College, Oscott, Sutton Coldfield.

†   KING, John H.: died 23 March 1965 at Winchester aged 84 • buried at Winchester Cemetery.

FOYLAN, Michael: ordained Bishop of Aberdeen 25 March 1965 at Aberdeen.

O'BRIEN, Keith M. P.: ordained priest (St Andrews and Edinburgh) 3 April 1965 at the Metropolitan Cathedral Church of St Mary, Edinburgh.

ENGLAND AND WALES: restructured 28 May 1965.

ARCHDIOCESE OF SOUTHWARK: restructured 28 May 1965.

DIOCESE OF ARUNDEL AND BRIGHTON: erected 28 May 1965.

BOWEN, Michael G.: incardinated 28 May 1965 into Diocese of Arundel and Brighton at Storrington, Pulborough.

CASHMAN, David J.: translated 28 May 1965 to newly erected Diocese of Arundel and Brighton.

COUVE DE MURVILLE, Maurice N. L.: incardinated 28 May 1965 into Diocese of Arundel and Brighton at Storrington, Pulborough.

COWDEROY, Cyril C.: appointed 28 May 1965 Archbishop and Metropolitan of newly raised Archdiocese and Province of Southwark.

CROWLEY, John P.: ordained priest (Westminster) 12 June 1965 at the Metropolitan Cathedral Church of the Most Precious Blood, Westminster, London.

HOLLIS, R. F. Crispian: ordained priest (Clifton) 11 July 1965 at Rome, Italy.

LYNCH SS.CC, Patrick K.: professed (Congregation of the Sacred Hearts of Jesus and Mary) 23 August 1965 at Cootehill (Cavan), Ireland.

BURNS SM, Thomas M.: professed (Society of Mary) 12 September 1965 at Paignton.

SECOND VATICAN COUNCIL (IV): 14 September 1965 to 8 December 1965.

♂   McGEE, Brian T.: born 8 October 1965 at Greenock.

FOX, Langton D.: ordained titular Bishop of *Maura* and appointed coadjutor Bishop of Menevia 16 December 1965 at Wrexham.

DWYER, George P.: translated 21 December 1965 to Archdiocese of Birmingham.

WORLOCK, Derek J. H.: ordained Bishop of Portsmouth 21 December 1965 at Portsmouth.

1966

CASEY, Patrick J.: ordained titular Bishop of *Sufar* and appointed auxiliary Bishop of Westminster 2 February 1966 at the Metropolitan Cathedral Church of the Most Precious Blood, Westminster, London.

HARRIS, Augustine: ordained titular Bishop of *Socia* and appointed auxiliary Bishop of Liverpool 11 February 1966 at the Pro-Cathedral Pontifical Crypt of Christ the King, Liverpool.

HEIM, Bruno B.: appointed 16 February 1966 Apostolic Pro-Nuncio to Finland.

WHEELER, William G.: translated 3 May 1966 to Diocese of Leeds.

CUNNINGHAM, Séamus: ordained priest (Hexham and Newcastle) 12 June 1966 at Waterford City (Waterford), Ireland.

CAMPBELL OSA, Michael G.: professed (Order of St Augustine) 17 September 1966 at Clare, Sudbury.

BUTLER OSB, B. E. Christopher: ordained titular Bishop of *Nova Barbara* and appointed auxiliary Bishop of Westminster 21 December 1966 at the Metropolitan Cathedral Church of the Most Precious Blood, Westminster, London.

1967

®   PARKER, Thomas L.: appointed 17 January 1967 titular Bishop of *Magarmel* and retired to Poringland, Norwich thence to Burnham, Slough.

McCLEAN, John G.: ordained titular Bishop of *Maxita* and appointed coadjutor Bishop of Middlesbrough 24 February 1967 at Middlesbrough.

† CRAVEN, George L.: died 15 March 1967 at Marylebone, London aged 83 • buried at St Edmund's College, Old Hall Green, Ware.

GRANT, Charles A.: translated 25 March 1967 to Diocese of Northampton.

ARCHDIOCESE OF LIVERPOOL: cathedral transferred 14 May 1967.

HOPES, Alan S.: ordained Church of England deacon (London) 21 May 1967 at St Paul's Cathedral, City of London.

O'DONOGHUE, Patrick: ordained priest (Westminster) 25 May 1967 at Analeentha, Mourne Abbey (Cork), Ireland.

® BRUNNER, George: appointed 12 June 1967 titular Bishop of *Murustaga* and retired to Middlesbrough.

† DOUGLAS, Edward W.: died 12 June 1967 at Glasgow aged 66 • buried at St Patrick's Cemetery, New Stevenston, Motherwell.

McCLEAN, John G.: succeeded 12 June 1967 as Bishop of Middlesbrough.

+ WOJTYŁA, Karol J. (POPE ST JOHN PAUL II): elevated 26 June 1967 to Cardinal-Priest of San Cesario in Palatio.

BURKE, Geoffrey I.: ordained titular Bishop of *Vagrauta* and appointed auxiliary Bishop of Salford 29 June 1967 at Salford.

1968

MOVERLEY, Gerald: ordained titular Bishop of *Tinis in Proconsulari* and appointed auxiliary Bishop of Leeds 25 January 1968 at Sheffield.

EMERY, Anthony J.: ordained titular Bishop of *Tamallula* and appointed auxiliary Bishop of Birmingham 4 March 1968 at the Metropolitan Cathedral Church of St Chad, Birmingham.

† BLACK, James: died 29 March 1968 at Kilmacolm aged 73 • buried at St Conval's Cemetery, Barrhead, Glasgow.

UKRAINIAN EXARCHATE: extended 12 May 1968 to Scotland and Great Britain.

UKRAINIAN EXARCHATE: cathedral transferred 12 May 1968.

HORNYAK **OSBM**, Augustine E: translated 12 May 1968 to the Apostolic Exarchate for Ukrainians in Great Britain.

DOYLE, Peter J. H.: ordained priest (Portsmouth) 8 June 1968 at Portsmouth.

CE HOPES, Alan S.: ordained Church of England priest (London) 9 June 1968 at St Paul's Cathedral, City of London.

ơ WILSON, John: born 4 July 1968 at Sheffield.

McGILL **PSS**, Stephen: translated 25 July 1968 to Diocese of Paisley.

1969

MACPHERSON, Colin A.: ordained Bishop of Argyll and the Isles 6 February 1969 at Oban.

GRAY, Joseph: ordained titular Bishop of *Mercia* and appointed auxiliary Bishop of Liverpool 16 February 1969 at the Metropolitan Cathedral Church of Christ the King, Liverpool.

† BRUNNER, George: died 21 March 1969 at Middlesbrough aged 79 • buried at St Joseph's Cemetery, North Ormesby, Middlesbrough.

® WALL, Bernard P.: appointed 15 April 1969 titular Bishop of *Othona* and retired to South Woodford, London.

CARDINALE, Igino E.: appointed 19 April 1969 Apostolic Nuncio to Belgium and Luxembourg.

ENRICI, Domenico: appointed 26 April 1969 Apostolic Delegate to Great Britain, Malta, Gibraltar and Bermuda.

+ GRAY, Gordon J.: elevated 28 April 1969 to Cardinal-Priest of Santa Chiara a Vigna Clara.

HEIM, Bruno B.: appointed 7 May 1969 Apostolic Pro-Nuncio to Egypt.

CLARK, Alan C.: ordained titular Bishop of *Elmhama* and appointed auxiliary Bishop of Northampton 13 May 1969 at Northampton.

KENNEY **CP**, L. William: ordained priest (Congregation of the Passion of Jesus Christ) 29 June 1969 at the Metropolitan Cathedral Church of St Chad, Birmingham.

BARBARITO, Luigi: ordained titular Archbishop of *Fiorentino* and appointed Apostolic Nuncio to Haiti 10 August 1969 at Vatican City.

CASEY, Patrick J.: translated 28 November 1969 to Diocese of Brentwood.

LINDSAY, Hugh.: ordained titular Bishop of *Cuncacestre* and appointed auxiliary Bishop of Hexham and Newcastle 11 December 1969 at Newcastle upon Tyne.

BERGOGLIO **SJ**, Jorge M. (**POPE FRANCIS**): ordained priest (Society of Jesus) 13 December 1969 at San Miguel (Corrientes), Argentina.

LUCIANI, Albino (**POPE JOHN PAUL I**): translated 15 December 1969 to Patriarch Archdiocese of Venice.

NICHOLS, Vincent G.: ordained priest (Liverpool) 21 December 1969 at Rome, Italy.

1970

SAINZ MUÑOZ, Faustino: entered diplomatic service to the Holy See 1970 at Vatican City.

McGOUGH, David C.: ordained priest (Birmingham) 14 March 1970 at Tunstall, Stoke-on-Trent.

MULLINS, Daniel J.: ordained titular Bishop of *Sidnacestre* and appointed auxiliary Bishop of Cardiff 1 April 1970 at the Metropolitan Cathedral Church of St David, Cardiff.

GUAZZELLI, Victor: ordained titular Bishop of *Lindisfarna* and appointed auxiliary Bishop of Westminster 23 May 1970 at the Metropolitan Cathedral Church of the Most Precious Blood, Westminster, London.

MAHON MHM, Gerald T.: ordained titular Bishop of *Eanach Dúin* and appointed auxiliary Bishop of Westminster 23 May 1970 at the Metropolitan Cathedral Church of the Most Precious Blood, Westminster, London.

MONAGHAN, James: ordained titular Bishop of *Cell Ausaille* and appointed auxiliary Bishop of St Andrews and Edinburgh 23 May 1970 at the Metropolitan Cathedral Church of St Mary, Edinburgh.

BOWEN, Michael G.: ordained titular Bishop of *Lamsorti* and appointed coadjutor Bishop of Arundel and Brighton 27 June 1970 at Arundel.

CARDINALE, Igino E.: appointed 10 November 1970 Apostolic Nuncio to the European Community.

®   WALSH MAfr, Francis P.: resigned 7 December 1970 as titular Bishop of *Birtha* and retired to Grantham.

GILBERT OSB, E. Hugh: received into Catholic Church 24 December 1970 at Polegate.

1971

BOWEN, Michael G.: succeeded 14 March 1971 as Bishop of Arundel and Brighton.

†   CASHMAN, David J.: died 14 March 1971 at Arundel aged 58 • buried at the Cathedral Churchyard of Our Lady and St Philip Howard, Arundel.

BREWER, John (Jack): ordained titular Bishop of *Britonia* and appointed auxiliary Bishop of Shrewsbury 28 July 1971 at Stockport.

HESKETT CSsR, Ralph: professed (Congregation of the Most Holy Redeemer) 28 August 1971 at Kinnoul, Perth.

CAMPBELL OSA, Michael G.: ordained priest (Order of St Augustine) 16 September 1971 at Carlisle.

WINNING, Thomas J.: ordained titular Bishop of *Lugmad* and appointed auxiliary Bishop of Glasgow 30 November 1971 at the Metropolitan Cathedral Church of St Andrew, Glasgow.

WINNING, Thomas J.: appointed 1 December 1971 parish priest of Our Holy Redeemer Church, Clydebank.

BURNS SM, Thomas M.: ordained priest (Society of Mary) 16 December 1971 at Paignton.

1972

McGUINNESS, James J.: ordained titular Bishop of *Sanctus Germanus* and appointed coadjutor Bishop of Nottingham 23 March 1972 at Nottingham.

ALEXANDER, Mervyn A. N.: ordained titular Bishop of *Pinhel* and appointed auxiliary Bishop of Clifton 25 April 1972 at Clifton, Bristol.

STACK, George: ordained priest (Westminster) 21 May 1972 at Poplar, London.

WILLIAMS, Thomas A.: ordained priest (Liverpool) 27 May 1972 at the Metropolitan Cathedral Church of Christ the King, Liverpool.

FOX, Langton D.: translated 16 June 1972 to Diocese of Menevia.

® PETIT, John E.: retired 16 June 1972 to Wrexham.

SMITH, Peter D. G.: ordained priest (Southwark) 5 July 1972 at Wonersh, Guildford.

LYNCH SS.CC, Patrick K.: ordained priest (Congregation of the Sacred Hearts of Jesus and Mary) 21 July 1972 at Cootehill (Cavan), Ireland.

ROBSON, Stephen: received into Catholic Church 27 August 1972 at Carlisle.

HENDERSON, Charles J.: ordained titular Bishop of *Trecalae* and appointed auxiliary Bishop of Southwark 8 December 1972 at the Metropolitan Cathedral Church of St George, Southwark, London.

1973

† BURGESS OSB, T. Lawrence: reinterred 4 March 1973 at Holy Souls Chapel Crypt, Arnos Vale, Bristol.

+ LUCIANI, Albino (POPE JOHN PAUL I): elevated 5 March 1973 to Cardinal-Priest of San Marco.

† PETIT, John E.: died 3 June 1973 at Wrexham aged 77 • buried at Pantasaph, Holywell.

DIOCESE OF CLIFTON: cathedral transferred 29 June 1973.

ENRICI, Domenico: appointed 16 July 1973 official of State at the Roman Curia.

HEIM, Bruno B.: appointed 16 July 1973 Apostolic Delegate to Great Britain, Malta, Gibraltar and Bermuda.

† WARD, James: died 21 October 1973 at Crosshill, Glasgow aged 68 • buried at St Peter's Cemetery, Dalbeth, Glasgow.

1974

®   SCANLAN, James D.: retired 23 April 1974 to Kelvingrove, Glasgow thence to Marylebone, London.

WINNING, Thomas J.: translated 23 April 1974 to Archdiocese of Glasgow.

®   CUNNINGHAM, James: resigned 16 May 1974 as Bishop of Hexham and Newcastle and retired to Newcastle upon Tyne.

†   CUNNINGHAM, James: died 10 July 1974 at Newcastle upon Tyne aged 63 • buried at St Cuthbert's College, Ushaw, Durham.

McDONALD, Kevin J. P.: ordained priest (Birmingham) 20 July 1974 at Rome, Italy.

WRIGHT, Roderick: incardinated 12 August 1974 into Diocese of Argyll and the Isles at Dunoon.

®   RUDDERHAM, Joseph E.: retired 31 August 1974 to Charlton Kings, Cheltenham.

McPARTLAND SMA, Michael B.: professed (Society of African Missions) 27 September 1974 at New Barnet, Barnet.

†   WALSH MAfr, Francis P.: died 27 October 1974 at Grantham aged 73 • buried at Grantham Cemetery, Grantham.

®   ELLIS, Edward: retired 31 October 1974 to Nottingham.

McGUINNESS, James J.: succeeded 31 October 1974 as Bishop of Nottingham.

LINDSAY, Hugh: translated 12 December 1974 to Diocese of Hexham and Newcastle.

MENNINI, Antonio: ordained priest (Rome) 14 December 1974 at Rome, Italy.

ALEXANDER, Mervyn A. N.: translated 20 December 1974 to Diocese of Clifton.

1975

†   PARKER, Thomas L.: died 25 March 1975 at Kiln Green, Reading aged 87 • buried at the Cathedral Church of Our Lady and St Thomas, Northampton.

BARBARITO, Luigi: appointed 5 April 1975 Apostolic Pro-Nuncio to Senegal, Niger, Upper Volta, Mali, Mauritania, Guinea Bissau and Cape Verde Islands.

LANG, Declan R.: ordained priest (Portsmouth) 7 June 1975 at Portsmouth.

EVANS, Michael C.: ordained priest (Southwark) 22 June 1975 at Wonersh, Guildford.

NEWTON, Keith: ordained Church of England deacon (Chelmsford) 29 June 1975 at Chelmsford.

TARTAGLIA, Philip: ordained priest (Glasgow) 30 June 1975 at Dennistoun, Glasgow.

DRAINEY, Terence P.: ordained priest (Salford) 12 July 1975 at Fairfield, Manchester.

CONRY, Kieran T.: ordained priest (Birmingham) 19 July 1975 at Coventry.

ROCHE, Arthur: ordained priest (Leeds) 19 July 1975 at Batley Carr, Dewsbury.

† HEENAN, John C.: died 7 November 1975 at Westminster, London aged 70 • buried at the Metropolitan Cathedral Church of the Most Precious Blood, Westminster, London.

† MATHEW, David J.: died 12 December 1975 at St John's Wood, London aged 73 • buried at the Abbey Church of St Gregory, Downside, Radstock.

1976

DUNN, Kevin J.: ordained priest (Birmingham) 17 January 1976 at Clayton, Newcastle.

WORLOCK, Derek J. H.: translated 7 February 1976 to Archdiocese of Liverpool.

® BECK AA, George A.: retired 11 February 1976 to Upholland, Skelmersdale.

DIOCESE OF EAST ANGLIA: erected 13 March 1976.

DIOCESE OF NORTHAMPTON: restructured 13 March 1976.

HUME OSB, G. Basil: ordained Archbishop of Westminster 25 March 1976 at the Metropolitan Cathedral Church of the Most Precious Blood, Westminster, London.

† SCANLAN, James D.: died 25 March 1976 at Marylebone, London aged 77 • buried at St Peter's Cemetery, Dalbeth, Glasgow.

GRIFFITHS **OSB**, M. Ambrose: elected 7 April 1976 Abbot of the Abbey Church of St Laurence, Ampleforth, York.

DUNN, Patrick J.: ordained priest (Auckland) 24 April 1976 at Remuera (Auckland), New Zealand.

+ HUME OSB, G. Basil: elevated 24 May 1976 to Cardinal-Priest of San Silvestro in Capite.

† FOYLAN, Michael: died 28 May 1976 at Kings Gate, Aberdeen aged 68 • buried at St Ninian's Cemetery, Tynet, Buckie.

CLARK, Alan C.: translated 2 June 1976 to newly erected Diocese of East Anglia.

† WALL, Bernard P.: died 18 June 1976 at South Woodford, London aged 82 • buried at St John's College, Wonersh, Guildford.

CE NEWTON, Keith: ordained Church of England priest (Chelmsford) 27 June 1976 at Chelmsford.

HESKETT **CSsR**, Ralph: ordained priest (Congregation of the Most Holy Redeemer) 10 July 1976 at Sunderland.

WILLIAMS **SM**, Alan: professed (Society of Mary) 8 September 1976 at Whitechapel, London.

† COWDEROY, Cyril C.: died 10 October 1976 at West Malling aged 71 • buried at the Metropolitan Cathedral Church of St George, Southwark, London.

EMERY, Anthony J.: translated 5 November 1976 to Diocese of Portsmouth.

LONCHYNA **MSU**, Hlib B. S.: professed (Order of Ukrainian Studite Monks) 19 December 1976 at Grottaferrata (Roma), Italy.

1977

BOWEN, Michael G.: translated 23 April 1977 to Archdiocese of Southwark.

HARVEY, Philip J. B.: ordained titular Bishop of *Bahanna* and appointed auxiliary Bishop of Westminster 25 April 1977 at the Metropolitan Cathedral Church of the Most Precious Blood, Westminster, London.

KONSTANT, David E.: ordained titular Bishop of *Betagbarar* and appointed auxiliary Bishop of Westminster 25 April 1977 at the Metropolitan Cathedral Church of the Most Precious Blood, Westminster, London.

CONTI, Mario J.: ordained Bishop of Aberdeen 3 May 1977 at Aberdeen.

McCARTIE, P. Leo: ordained titular Bishop of *Elmhama* and appointed auxiliary Bishop of Birmingham 20 May 1977 at the Metropolitan Cathedral Church of St Chad, Birmingham.

RATZINGER, Joseph A. (POPE BENEDICT XVI): ordained Archbishop of München und Freising 28 May 1977 at Munich (Bavaria), Germany.

DEVINE, Joseph: ordained titular Bishop of *Voli* and appointed auxiliary Bishop of Glasgow 31 May 1977 at St Francis' Church, Gorbals, Glasgow.

RENFREW, Charles M.: ordained titular Bishop of *Abula* and appointed auxiliary Bishop of Glasgow 31 May 1977 at St Francis' Church, Gorbals, Glasgow.

+ RATZINGER, Joseph A. (POPE BENEDICT XVI): elevated 27 June 1977 to Cardinal-Priest of Santa Maria Consolatrice al Tiburtino.

NOLAN, William: ordained priest (Motherwell) 30 June 1977 at Motherwell.

LONCHYNA MSU, Hlib B. S.: ordained priest (Order of Ukrainian Studite Monks) 3 July 1977 at Grottaferrata (Roma), Italy.

SWINDLEHURST, Owen F.: ordained titular Bishop of *Cuncacestre* and appointed auxiliary Bishop of Hexham and Newcastle 25 July 1977 at Newcastle upon Tyne.

GALLAGHER, Paul R.: ordained priest (Liverpool) 31 July 1977 at the Metropolitan Cathedral Church of Christ the King, Liverpool.

® BUTLER OSB, B. E. Christopher: retired 21 September 1977 to Old Hall Green, Ware.

O'BRIEN, James J.: ordained titular Bishop of *Manaccenser* and appointed auxiliary Bishop of Westminster 21 September 1977 at the Metropolitan Cathedral Church of the Most Precious Blood, Westminster, London.

McMAHON OP, Malcolm P.: professed (Order of Preachers) 16 December 1977 at Haverstock Hill, London.

MURPHY-O'CONNOR, Cormac: ordained Bishop of Arundel and Brighton 21 December 1977 at Arundel.

1978

BRIGNALL, Peter M.: ordained priest (Menevia) 18 February 1978 at New Southgate, London.

ARNOLD, John S. K.: professed (Institute of Charity) 19 March 1978 at Wonersh, Guildford.

McPARTLAND SMA, Michael B.: ordained priest (Society of African Missions) 14 May 1978 at Grove Hill, Middlesbrough.

BARBARITO, Luigi: appointed 10 June 1978 Apostolic Pro-Nuncio to Australia.

McKINNEY, Patrick J.: ordained priest (Birmingham) 29 July 1978 at Buncrana (Donegal), Ireland.

† MONTINI, Giovanni-Battista E. A. M. (POPE BL. PAUL VI): died 6 August 1978 at Castel Gandolfo (Roma), Italy aged 80 • buried at St Peter's Basilica, Vatican City.

x LUCIANI, Albino (POPE JOHN PAUL I): elected Pope 26 August 1978 at Vatican City.

† McCLEAN, John G.: died 27 August 1978 at Blackley, Manchester aged 63 • buried at St Joseph's Cemetery, North Ormesby, Middlesbrough.

LUCIANI, Albino (POPE JOHN PAUL I): installed 3 September 1978 at Vatican City.

† BECK AA, George A.: died 13 September 1978 at Mossley Hill, Liverpool aged 74 • buried at the Metropolitan Cathedral Crypt of Christ the King, Liverpool.

† LUCIANI, Albino (POPE JOHN PAUL I): died 28 September 1978 at the Apostolic Palace, Vatican City aged 65 • buried at St Peter's Basilica, Vatican City.

x WOJTYŁA, Karol J. (POPE ST JOHN PAUL II): elected Pope 16 October 1978 at Vatican City.

WOJTYŁA, Karol J. (POPE ST JOHN PAUL II): installed 22 October 1978 at Vatican City.

HARRIS, Augustine: translated 20 November 1978 to Diocese of Middlesbrough.

1979

®   TICKLE, Gerard W.: released from military service and retired 8 January 1979 to Neston thence to Ruthin.

WALMSLEY, Francis J.: released from military service 8 January 1979.

WALMSLEY, Francis J.: ordained titular Bishop of *Tamalluma* and appointed Military Vicar to HM Forces 22 February 1979 at Aldershot.

†   RUDDERHAM, Joseph E.: died 24 February 1979 at Charlton Kings, Cheltenham aged 79 • buried at Holy Souls Cemetery, Arnos Vale, Bristol.

GILBERT OSB, E. Hugh: professed (Order of Saint Benedict) 10 March 1979 at Pluscarden, Elgin.

ROBSON, Stephen: ordained priest (St Andrews and Edinburgh) 17 March 1979 at Carlisle.

HITCHEN, Anthony: ordained titular Bishop of *Othona* and appointed auxiliary Bishop of Liverpool 3 July 1979 at the Metropolitan Cathedral Church of Christ the King, Liverpool.

O'CONNOR, Kevin: ordained titular Bishop of *Glastonia* and appointed auxiliary Bishop of Liverpool 3 July 1979 at the Metropolitan Cathedral Church of Christ the King, Liverpool.

†   ELLIS, Edward: died 6 July 1979 at Nottingham aged 80 • buried at the Cathedral Church of St Barnabas, Nottingham.

®   ENRICI, Domenico: retired 1 December 1979 to Cervasca (Cuneo), Italy.

®   CASEY, Patrick J.: resigned 11 December 1979 as Bishop of Brentwood and appointed parish priest of Holy Redeemer and St Thomas More Church, Chelsea, London.

1980

†   CAMPBELL, Donald A.: reinterred 9 January 1980 at the Cathedral Church of St Andrew, Glasgow.

†   EYRE, Charles P.: reinterred 9 January 1980 at the Cathedral Church of St Andrew, Glasgow.

†   SCANLAN, James D.: reinterred 9 January 1980 at the Cathedral Church of St Andrew, Glasgow.

JUKES **OFM Conv.**, John P.: ordained titular Bishop of *Strathernia* and appointed auxiliary Bishop of Southwark 30 January 1980 at the Metropolitan Cathedral Church of St George, Southwark, London.

TRIPP, Howard G.: ordained titular Bishop of *Neoportus* and appointed auxiliary Bishop of Southwark 30 January 1980 at the Metropolitan Cathedral Church of St George, Southwark, London.

PUENTE BUCES, Pablo: ordained titular Archbishop of *Macri* and appointed appointed 25 May 1980 Apostolic Pro-Nuncio to Indonesia at Vatican City.

DIOCESE OF HALLAM: erected 30 May 1980.

DIOCESE OF LEEDS: restructured 30 May 1980.

DIOCESE OF NOTTINGHAM: restructured 30 May 1980.

MOVERLEY, Gerald: translated 30 May 1980 to newly erected Diocese of Hallam.

TOAL, Joseph A.: ordained priest (Argyll and the Isles) 10 July 1980 at Oban.

McMAHON, Thomas: ordained Bishop of Brentwood 17 July 1980 at Brentwood.

® GRASAR, William E.: retired 30 August 1980 to Altrincham.

GRAY, Joseph: translated 30 August 1980 to Diocese of Shrewsbury.

WARD **OFM Cap.**, John A.: ordained coadjutor Bishop of Menevia 1 October 1980 at Wrexham.

1981

MENNINI, Antonio: entered diplomatic service to the Holy See 1981 at Vatican City.

® HART, William A.: retired 26 January 1981 to Dundee.

® FOX, Langton D.: retired 5 February 1981 to Wrexham.

WARD **OFM Cap.**, John A.: succeeded 5 February 1981 as Bishop of Menevia.

LOGAN, Vincent P.: ordained Bishop of Dunkeld 26 February 1981 at Dundee.

® McGEE, Joseph M.: retired 4 April 1981 to Prestwick.

TAYLOR, Maurice: ordained Bishop of Galloway 9 June 1981 at Coodham, Kilmarnock.

® DWYER, George P.: retired 1 September 1981 to Selly Park, Birmingham.

RATZINGER, Joseph A. (POPE BENEDICT XVI): appointed 25 November 1981 Prefect of the Congregation for the Doctrine of the Faith at Vatican City.

O'BRIEN, T. Kevin: ordained titular Bishop of *Árd Carna* and appointed auxiliary Bishop of Middlesbrough 8 December 1981 at Middlesbrough.

LONGLEY, Bernard: ordained priest (Arundel and Brighton) 12 December 1981 at Wonersh, Guildford.

RAWSTHORNE, John A.: ordained titular Bishop of *Rotdon* and appointed auxiliary Bishop of Liverpool 16 December 1981 at the Metropolitan Cathedral Church of Christ the King, Liverpool.

1982

APOSTOLIC NUNCIATURE: raised 16 January 1982 to Nunciature (without overseas territories).

HEIM, Bruno B.: appointed 16 January 1982 Apostolic Pro-Nuncio to Great Britain (without overseas territories).

® RATZINGER, Joseph A. (POPE BENEDICT XVI): resigned 15 February 1982 as Archbishop of München und Freising.

COUVE DE MURVILLE, Maurice N. L.: ordained Archbishop of Birmingham 25 March 1982 at the Metropolitan Cathedral Church of St Chad, Birmingham.

LYSYKANYCH, B. Benjamin: ordained priest (Salford) 4 April 1982 at Rochdale.

DIOCESE OF LEEDS: restructured 2 May 1982.

DIOCESE OF MIDDLESBROUGH: restructured 2 May 1982.

McMAHON OP, Malcolm P.: ordained priest (Order of Preachers) 26 June 1982 at Haverstock Hill, London.

GILBERT OSB, E. Hugh: ordained priest (Order of Saint Benedict) 29 June 1982 at Pluscarden, Elgin.

MOTH, C. P. Richard: ordained priest (Southwark) 3 July 1982 at Wonersh, Guildford.

® GRANT, Charles A.: retired 29 September 1982 to Kiln Green, Reading.

THOMAS, Francis G.: ordained Bishop of Northampton 29 September 1982 at Northampton.

BYRNE CO, Robert: professed (Congregation of the Oratory) 30 September 1982 at Edgbaston, Birmingham.

CHOMNYCKY OSBM, Paul P.: professed (Basilian Order of St Josaphat) 1 November 1982 at Glen Cove (NY), USA.

® THOMSON, Francis A. S. W.: resigned 14 December 1982 as Bishop of Motherwell.

* THOMSON, Francis A. S. W.: appointed 14 December 1982 Apostolic Administrator of the Diocese of Motherwell until 13 May 1983.

† GRASAR, William E.: died 28 December 1982 at Sefton Park, Liverpool aged 69 • buried at Our Lady's Church, Birkenhead.

1983

HRYNCHYSHYN CSsR, Michel: ordained titular Bishop of *Zygris* and appointed Bishop of the Apostolic Exarchate for Ukrainians in France, Benelux and Switzerland 30 January 1983 at Rome, Italy.

† McGEE, Joseph M.: died 5 March 1983 at Prestwick aged 78 • buried at Ayr Cemetery.

† CARDINALE, Igino E.: died 24 March 1983 at Brussels (Capitale), Belgium aged 66 • buried at Castel di Guido (Roma), Italy.

® MURPHY, John A.: retired 25 March 1983 to Malpas, Newport.

WARD OFM Cap., John A.: translated 25 March 1983 to Archdiocese of Cardiff.

WILLIAMS SM, Alan: ordained priest (Society of Mary) 30 April 1983 at Whitechapel, London.

DEVINE, Joseph: translated 13 May 1983 to Diocese of Motherwell.

® HOLLAND, Thomas: retired 21 June 1983 to Prestwich, Manchester.

ARNOLD, John S. K.: ordained priest (Westminster) 16 July 1983 at the Metropolitan Cathedral Church of the Most Precious Blood, Westminster, London.

THOMSON, Francis A. S. W.: appointed 12 September 1983 parish priest of St Isidore's Church, Biggar.

® PEARSON, Thomas B.: retired 31 October 1983 to Carlisle.

BREWER, John (Jack): translated 15 November 1983 to coadjutor Bishop of Lancaster.

HANNIGAN, James: ordained Bishop of Menevia 23 November 1983 at Wrexham.

1984

DAVIES, Mark: ordained priest (Salford) 11 February 1984 at Reddish, Stockport.

KELLY, Patrick A.: ordained Bishop of Salford 3 April 1984 at Salford.

® GRIFFITHS OSB, M. Ambrose: resigned 5 April 1984 as Abbot of the Abbey Church of St Laurence, Ampleforth, York and appointed titular Abbot of *Westminster* and parish priest of St Mary's Church, Leyland.

GALLAGHER: Paul R.: entered diplomatic service to the Holy See 1 May 1984 at Vatican City.

MONE, John A.: ordained titular Bishop of *Abercornia* and appointed auxiliary Bishop of Glasgow 14 May 1984 at Holy Cross Church, Crosshill, Glasgow.

HENDRICKS, Paul: ordained priest (Southwark) 29 July 1984 at Orpington.

EGAN, Philip A.: ordained priest (Shrewsbury) 4 August 1984 at Altrincham.

1985

BYRNE CO, Robert: ordained priest (Congregarion of the Oratory) 5 January 1985 at Edgbaston, Birmingham.

WILSON, John: received into Catholic Church 23 February 1985 at Sheffield.

BREWER, John (Jack): succeeded 22 May 1985 as Bishop of Lancaster.

® FOLEY, Brian C.: retired 22 May 1985 to Lancaster.

® GRAY, Gordon J.: retired 30 May 1985 to Edinburgh.

McALEENAN, Paul: ordained priest (Westminster) 8 June 1985 at the Metropolitan Cathedral Church of the Most Precious Blood, Westminster, London.

CUSHLEY, Leo W.: ordained priest (Motherwell) 7 July 1985 at Uddingston, Glasgow.

® HEIM, Bruno B.: resigned 31 July 1985 as Apostolic Pro-Nuncio to Great Britain and retired to Olten (Solothurn), Switzerland.

O'BRIEN, Keith M. P.: ordained Archbishop of St Andrews and Edinburgh 5 August 1985 at the Metropolitan Cathedral Church of St Mary, Edinburgh.

® WHEELER, William G.: retired 10 September 1985 to Headingley, Leeds.

KONSTANT, David E.: translated 25 September 1985 to Diocese of Leeds.

1986

BUDD, H. Christopher: ordained Bishop of Plymouth 15 January 1986 at Plymouth.

® RESTIEAUX, Cyril E.: retired 15 January 1986 to Torquay.

BARBARITO, Luigi: appointed 21 January 1986 Apostolic Pro-Nuncio to Great Britain.

PUENTE BUCES, Pablo: appointed 15 March 1986 Apostolic Pro-Nuncio to Cape Verde, Mali and Senegal and Apostolic Delegate to Guinea-Bissau and Mauritania.

HUDSON, Nicholas G. E.: ordained priest (Southwark) at Wimbledon, London.

WALMSLEY, Francis J.: appointed 21 July 1986 Bishop in Ordinary to HM Forces.

BURNS SM, Thomas M.: commissioned as military chaplain 8 September 1986.

† BUTLER OSB, B. E. Christopher: died 20 September 1986 at St John's Wood, London aged 84 • buried at the Abbey Church of St Gregory, Downside, Radstock.

CROWLEY, John P.: ordained titular Bishop of *Thala* and appointed auxiliary Bishop of Westminster 8 December 1986 at the Metropolitan Cathedral Church of the Most Precious Blood, Westminster, London.

DIOCESE OF MIDDLESBROUGH: cathedral transferred 20
December 1986.

1987

FITZGERALD MAfr, Michael L.: appointed 22 January 1987
Secretary of the Pontifical Council for Inter-religious Dialogue at
Vatican City.

DIOCESE OF MENEVIA: cathedral transferred and restructured
12 February 1987.

DIOCESE OF WREXHAM: erected 12 February 1987.

BRIGNALL, Peter M.: incardinated 12 February 1987 into Diocese
of Wrexham at Wrexham.

HANNIGAN, James: translated 12 February 1987 to newly erected
Diocese of Wrexham.

MULLINS, Daniel J.: translated 12 February 1987 to newly
restructured Diocese of Menevia.

HOLLIS, R. F. Crispian: ordained titular Bishop of *Cincari*
and appointed auxiliary Bishop of Birmingham 5 May 1987 at the
Metropolitan Cathedral Church of St Chad, Birmingham.

SHERRINGTON, John F.: ordained priest (Nottingham) 13 June
1987 at Leicester.

KENNEY CP, L. William: ordained titular Bishop of *Midica* and
appointed auxiliary Bishop of Stockholm 24 August 1987 at Stockholm
(Stockholm), Sweden.

® CLEARY, Joseph F.: retired 4 September 1987 to Wolverhampton.

† DWYER, George P.: died 17 September 1987 at Selly Park,
Birmingham aged 78 • buried at St Mary's College, Oscott, Sutton
Coldfield.

® HORNYAK OSBM, Augustine E.: resigned 29 September 1987 as
Apostolic Exarch for Ukrainians in Great Britain and retired to Acton,
London.

* HRYNCHYSHYN CSsR, Michel: appointed 29 September 1987
Apostolic Administrator of the Apostolic Exarchate for Ukrainians in
Great Britain until 24 June 1989.

† PEARSON, Thomas B.: died 17 November 1987 at Carlisle aged 80 •
buried at the Cathedral Church of St Peter, Lancaster.

† THOMSON, Francis A. S. W.: died 6 December 1987 at Bon Secours Hospital, Glasgow aged 70 • buried at the Cathedral Church of Our Lady of Good Aid, Motherwell.

1988

MONE, John A.: translated 8 March 1988 to Diocese of Paisley.

® McGILL PSS, Stephen: retired 30 March 1988 to Greenock.

MOTH, C. P. Richard: commissioned as military chaplain 1 April 1988.

† EMERY, Anthony J.: died 5 April 1988 at Portsmouth aged 69 • buried at Milton Cemetery, Portsmouth.

† HITCHEN, Anthony: died 10 April 1988 at Freshfield, Liverpool aged 57 • buried at St Gregory's Church, Chorley.

KUCHMIAK CSsR, Michael: ordained titular Bishop of *Agathopolis* and appointed auxiliary Bishop of the Apostolic Exarchate for Ukrainians in Philadelphia (PA), USA 27 April 1988 at Philadelphia (PA), USA.

® BURKE, Geoffrey I.: retired 31 July 1988 to Prestwich, Manchester thence to Longsight, Manchester.

STOCK, Marcus N.: ordained priest (Birmingham) 13 August 1988 at Caversham, Reading.

CHOMNYCKY OSBM, Paul P.: ordained priest (Basilian Order of St Josaphat) 1 October 1988 at Vancouver (BC), Canada.

SAINZ MUÑOZ, Faustino: ordained titular Archbishop of *Novaliciana* and appointed Apostolic Pro-Nuncio to Cuba 18 December 1988 at Vatican City.

† THOMAS, Francis G.: died 25 December 1988 at Beaconsfield aged 58 • buried at the Cathedral Church of Our Lady and St Thomas, Northampton.

1989

HOLLIS, R. F. Crispian: translated 27 January 1989 to Diocese of Portsmouth.

†   GRANT, Charles A.: died 24 April 1989 at Kiln Green, Reading aged 82 • buried at Woburn Sands, Milton Keynes.

BURNETTE, Kurt R.: ordained priest (Van Nuys (Ruthenian)) 26 April 1989 at Sherman Oaks (CA), USA.

KUCHMIAK CSsR, Michael: translated 24 June 1989 to the Apostolic Exarchate for Ukrainians in Great Britain.

McGEE, Brian T.: ordained priest (Paisley) 29 June 1989 at Greenock.

MALONE, Vincent: ordained titular Bishop of *Abora* and appointed auxiliary Bishop of Liverpool 3 July 1989 at the Metropolitan Cathedral Church of Christ the King, Liverpool.

®   MONAGHAN, James: retired 13 July 1989 to Edinburgh.

PUENTE BUCES, Pablo: appointed 31 July 1989 Apostolic Nuncio to Lebanon.

®   CASEY, Patrick J.: retired 25 September 1989 to Leigh-on-Sea.

1990

PARGETER, Philip: ordained titular Bishop of *Valentiniana* and appointed auxiliary Bishop of Birmingham 21 February 1990 at the Metropolitan Cathedral Church of St Chad, Birmingham.

McCARTIE, P. Leo: translated 19 March 1990 to Diocese of Northampton.

†   MACPHERSON, Colin A.: died 24 March 1990 at Oban aged 72 • buried at Pennyfuir Cemetery, Oban.

O'TOOLE, Mark: ordained priest (Westminster) 9 June 1990 at the Metropolitan Cathedral Church of the Most Precious Blood, Westminster, London.

®   HARVEY, Philip J. B.: retired 3 July 1990 to Whitton, Twickenham.

RAFFERTY, Kevin L.: ordained titular Bishop of *Ausuaga* and appointed auxiliary Bishop of St Andrews and Edinburgh 15 August 1990 at the Metropolitan Cathedral Church of St Mary, Edinburgh.

1991

WRIGHT, Roderick: ordained Bishop of Argyll and the Isles 15 January 1991 at Oban.

† CLEARY, Joseph F.: died 25 February 1991 at Wolverhampton aged 78 • buried at Banbury.

BRAIN, Terence J.: ordained titular Bishop of *Amudarsa* and appointed auxiliary Bishop of Birmingham 25 April 1991 at the Metropolitan Cathedral Church of St Chad, Birmingham.

1992

® MOTH, C. P. Richard: resigned from active military service 1992.

FITZGERALD MAfr, Michael L.: ordained titular Bishop of *Nepte* 6 January 1992 at Vatican City.

® LINDSAY, Hugh: resigned 11 January 1992 as Bishop of Hexham and Newcastle and retired to Allithwaite, Grange-over-Sands.

NICHOLS, Vincent G.: ordained titular Bishop of *Othona* and appointed auxiliary Bishop of Westminster 24 January 1992 at the Metropolitan Cathedral Church of the Most Precious Blood, Westminster, London.

† MAHON MHM, Gerald T.: died 29 January 1992 at Littlehampton aged 69 • buried at Mill Hill, London.

† RENFREW, Charles M.: died 27 February 1992 at Partick, Glasgow aged 62 • buried at the Metropolitan Cathedral Church of St Andrew, Glasgow.

GRIFFITHS OSB, M. Ambrose: ordained Bishop of Hexham and Newcastle 20 March 1992 at Newcastle upon Tyne.

MORAN, Peter A.: incardinated 10 April 1992 into Diocese of Aberdeen at Aberdeen City.

BERGOGLIO SJ, Jorge M. (POPE FRANCIS): ordained titular Bishop of *Auca* and appointed auxiliary Bishop of Buenos Aires 27 June 1992 at Buenos Aires (Buenos Aires), Argentina.

SAINZ MUÑOZ, Faustino: appointed 7 October 1992 Apostolic Nuncio to Democratic Republic of Congo.

† HART, William A.: died 18 October 1992 at Dundee aged 88 • buried at Balgay Cemetery, Dundee.

GILBERT OSB, E. Hugh: elected 29 October 1992 Abbot of the Abbey Church of Our Blessed Lady, St John the Baptist and St Andrew, Pluscarden, Elgin.

® HARRIS, Augustine: retired 3 November 1992 to Ince Blundell, Liverpool.

1993

CROWLEY, John P.: translated 18 January 1993 to Diocese of Middlesbrough.

+ RATZINGER, Joseph A (POPE BENEDICT XVI): elevated 5 April 1993 to Cardinal-Bishop of Velletri Segni.

† O'CONNOR, Kevin: died 5 May 1993 at Fleetwood aged 63 • buried at SS Peter and Paul Church, Great Crosby, Liverpool.

PUENTE BUCES, Pablo: appointed 25 May 1993 Apostolic Nuncio to Kuwait.

O'DONOGHUE, Patrick: ordained titular Bishop of *Tulana* and appointed auxiliary Bishop of Westminster 29 June 1993 at the Metropolitan Cathedral Church of the Most Precious Blood, Westminster, London.

† GRAY, Gordon J.: died 19 July 1993 at Edinburgh aged 82 • buried at the Metropolitan Cathedral Church of St Mary, Edinburgh.

JABALÉ OSB, J. P. Mark: elected 1 September 1993 Abbot of the Abbey Church of St Michael and All Angels, Belmont, Hereford.

1994

BARBARITO, Luigi: appointed 1 January 1994 Apostolic Nuncio to Great Britain.

† HANNIGAN, James: died 4 March 1994 at Chester aged 65 • buried at Wrexham.

† MONAGHAN, James: died 3 June 1994 at Nazareth House, Lasswade aged 79 • buried at the Metropolitan Cathedral Church of St Mary, Edinburgh.

DUNN, Patrick J.: ordained titular Bishop of *Fesseë* and appointed auxiliary Bishop of Auckland 25 July 1994 at Auckland (Auckland), New Zealand.

† TICKLE, Gerard W.: died 14 September 1994 at Colwyn Bay aged 84 • buried at St Winefride's Church, Neston.

+ WINNING, Thomas J.: elevated 26 November 1994 to Cardinal-Priest of Sant' Andrea delle Fratte.

HOPES, Alan S.: received into Catholic Church 8 December 1994 at Kensington, London.

REGAN, Edwin: ordained Bishop of Wrexham 13 December 1994 at Wrexham.

DUNN, Patrick J.: translated 19 December 1994 to Diocese of Auckland.

1995

® CLARK, Alan C.: retired 27 May 1995 to Poringland, Norwich thence to Norwich.

SMITH, Peter D. G.: ordained Bishop of East Anglia 27 May 1995 at Norwich.

KEENAN, John: ordained priest (Glasgow) 9 July 1995 at Rome, Italy.

WILSON, John: ordained priest (Leeds) 29 July 1995 at Halifax.

† SWINDLEHURST, Owen F.: died 28 August 1995 at Sunderland aged 67 • buried at Our Lady Immaculate Church, Washington.

® GRAY, Joseph: retired 30 August 1995 to Birkenhead.

NOBLE, Brian M.: ordained Bishop of Shrewsbury 30 August 1995 at Wythenshawe, Manchester.

† MURPHY, John A.: died 18 November 1995 at Malpas, Newport aged 89 • buried at the Abbey Church of St Joseph, Llantarnam, Cwmbran.

HOPES, Alan S.: ordained priest (Westminster) 4 December 1995 at the Metropolitan Cathedral Church of the Most Precious Blood, Westminster, London.

1996

† WORLOCK, Derek J. H.: died 8 February 1996 at Mossley Hill, Liverpool aged 76 • buried at the Metropolitan Cathedral of Christ the King, Liverpool.

† RESTIEAUX, Cyril E.: died 26 February 1996 at Torquay aged 86 • buried at the Cathedral Church of SS Mary and Boniface, Plymouth.

† RAFFERTY, Kevin L.: died 19 April 1996 at Livingston aged 62 • buried at Glenullin Cemetery, Garvagh, Coleraine (Derry), Ireland.

KELLY, Patrick A.: translated 3 July 1996 to Archdiocese of Liverpool.

® MOVERLEY, Gerald: retired 8 July 1996 to Sheffield.

® WRIGHT, Roderick: resigned 15 September 1996 as Bishop of Argyll and the Isles (renounced the dignity of bishop) and retired to Carnforth thence to Napier (Hawke's Bay), New Zealand.

* O'BRIEN, Keith M. P.: appointed 19 September 1996 Apostolic Administrator of the Diocese of Argyll and the Isles until 7 December 1999.

† MOVERLEY, Gerald: died 14 December 1996 at Sheffield aged 74 • buried at the Cathedral Church of St Marie, Sheffield.

* HRYNCHYSHYN CSsR, Michel: appointed 16 December 1996 Apostolic Administrator of the Apostolic Exarchate for Ukrainians in Germany and Scandinavia until 20 November 2000.

® GUAZZELLI, Victor: retired 21 December 1996 to Westminster, London.

1997

BERGOGLIO SJ, Jorge M. (POPE FRANCIS): translated 3 June 1997 to coadjutor Archbishop of Buenos Aires.

CUSHLEY, Leo W.: entered diplomatic service to the Holy See 1 July 1997 at Vatican City.

RAWSTHORNE, John A.: translated 3 July 1997 to Diocese of Hallam.

† FOX, Langton D.: died 26 July 1997 at Wrexham aged 80 • buried at Wrexham.

® BARBARITO, Luigi: retired 31 July 1997 to Rome, Italy thence to Pietradefusi (Avellino), Italy.

PUENTE BUCES, Pablo: appointed 31 July 1997 Apostolic Nuncio to Great Britain.

† HENDREN OSF, Joseph W. F.: reinterred 4 October 1997 at St George's Church, Taunton.

BRAIN, Terence J.: translated 7 October 1997 to Diocese of Salford.

† ENRICI, Domenico: died 3 December 1997 at Cervasca (Cuneo), Italy aged 88 • buried at Cervasca (Cuneo), Italy.

1998

† WHEELER, William G.: died 20 February 1998 at Headingley, Leeds aged 87 • buried at St Edward's Church, Clifford, Wetherby.

BERGOGLIO SJ, Jorge M. (POPE FRANCIS): succeeded 28 February 1998 as Archbishop of Buenos Aires.

WALMSLEY, Francis J.: resigned 7 March 1998 as titular Bishop of *Tamalluma*.

® O'BRIEN, T. Kevin: retired 25 June 1998 to Hull thence to Headingley, Leeds.

® JUKES OFM Conv., John P.: retired 11 December 1998 to West Malling.

† GRAHAM, Charles M.: reinterred 13 December 1998 at the Cathedral Church of SS Mary and Boniface, Plymouth.

† KEILY, John J.: reinterred 13 December 1998 at the Cathedral Church of SS Mary and Boniface, Plymouth.

† VAUGHAN, William: reinterred 13 December 1998 at the Cathedral Church of SS Mary and Boniface, Plymouth.

1999

SAINZ MUÑOZ, Faustino: appointed 21 January 1999 Apostolic Nuncio to European Community.

† CASEY, Patrick J.: died 26 January 1999 at Leigh-on-Sea aged 85 • buried at the Cathedral Church Cemetery of SS Mary and Helen, Brentwood.

† GRAY, Joseph: died 7 May 1999 at Birkenhead aged 79 • buried at St Winefride's Church, Neston.

® COUVE DE MURVILLE, Maurice N. L.: retired 12 June 1999 to Seaford thence to Horsham.

† HUME OSB, G. Basil: died 17 June 1999 at St John's Wood, London aged 76 • buried at the Metropolitan Cathedral Church of the Most Precious Blood, Westminster, London.

† HOLLAND, Thomas: died 30 September 1999 at Prestwich, Manchester aged 91 • buried at the Cathedral Church of St John, Salford.

† BURKE, Geoffrey I.: died 13 October 1999 at City of Manchester aged 86 • buried at St Mary's Cemetery, Worsley, Manchester.

MURRAY, Ian: ordained Bishop of Argyll and the Isles 7 December 1999 at Oban.

† FOLEY, Brian C.: died 23 December 1999 at Lancaster aged 89 • buried at the Cathedral Church of St Peter, Lancaster.

2000

MURPHY-O'CONNOR, Cormac: translated 22 March 2000 to Archdiocese of Westminster.

NICHOLS, Vincent G.: translated 29 March 2000 to Archdiocese of Birmingham.

† BREWER, John (Jack): died 10 June 2000 at Allithwaite, Grange-over-Sands aged 70 • buried at the Cathedral Churchyard of St Peter, Lancaster.

BL. MASTAI-FERRETTI, Giovanni M. (POPE BL. PIUS IX): beatified 3 September 2000 at Vatican City.

BL. RONCALLI, Angelo G. (POPE ST JOHN XXIII): beatified 3 September 2000 at Vatican City.

MENNINI, Antonio: ordained titular Archbishop of *Ferentium* and appointed Apostolic Nuncio to Bulgaria 12 September 2000 at Vatican City.

JABALÉ OSB, J. P. Mark: ordained coadjutor Bishop of Menevia 7 December 2000 at Swansea.

® McGUINNESS, James J.: retired 8 December 2000 to Nottingham thence to Ednaston, Ashbourne.

McMAHON OP, Malcolm P.: ordained Bishop of Nottingham 8 December 2000 at Nottingham.

2001

® HENDERSON, Charles J.: retired 26 January 2001 to Blackheath, London.

+ BERGOGLIO SJ, Jorge M. (POPE FRANCIS): elevated 21 February 2001 to Cardinal-Priest of San Roberto Bellarmino.

+ MURPHY-O'CONNOR, Cormac: elevated 21 February 2001 to Cardinal-Priest of Santa Maria sopra Minerva.

HINE, John F. M.: ordained titular Bishop of *Beverlacum* and appointed auxiliary Bishop of Southwark 27 February 2001 at the Metropolitan Cathedral Church of St George, Southwark, London.

® ALEXANDER, Mervyn A. N.: retired 28 March 2001 and appointed parish priest of St Joseph's Church, Weston-super-Mare.

LANG, Declan R.: ordained Bishop of Clifton 28 March 2001 at Clifton, Bristol.

® McCARTIE, P. Leo: retired 29 March 2001 to Aston, Stone thence to Harborne, Birmingham.

McDONALD, Kevin J. P.: ordained Bishop of Northampton 2 May 2001 at Northampton.

ROCHE, Arthur: ordained titular Bishop of *Rusticiana* and appointed auxiliary Bishop of Westminster 10 May 2001 at the Metropolitan Cathedral Church of the Most Precious Blood, Westminster, London.

STACK, George: ordained titular Bishop of *Gemellae in Numidia* and appointed auxiliary Bishop of Westminster 10 May 2001 at the Metropolitan Cathedral Church of the Most Precious Blood, Westminster, London.

CONRY, Kieran T.: ordained Bishop of Arundel and Brighton 9 June 2001 at Arundel.

JABALÉ OSB, J. P. Mark: succeeded 12 June 2001 as Bishop of Menevia.

® MULLINS, Daniel J.: retired 12 June 2001 to Kidwelly.

†   WINNING, Thomas J.: died 17 June 2001 at Newlands, Glasgow aged 76 • buried at the Metropolitan Cathedral Church of St Andrew, Glasgow.

O'DONOGHUE, Patrick: translated 4 July 2001 to Diocese of Lancaster.

SMITH, Peter D. G.: translated 26 October 2001 to Archdiocese of Cardiff.

®   WARD OFM Cap., John A.: retired 26 October 2001 to Ystradowen, Cowbridge.

2002

JUKES OFM Conv., John P.: appointed 2002 parish priest of St Margaret's Church, Huntly.

CONTI, Mario J.: translated 22 February 2002 to Archdiocese of Glasgow.

LONCHYNA MSU, Hlib B. S.: ordained titular Bishop of *Bareta* and appointed auxiliary Bishop of the Ukrainian Archeparchy of Lviv 27 February 2002 at Lviv (Lviv), Ukraine.

NEWTON, Keith: ordained bishop suffragan of Richborough (Provincial Episcopal Visitor) 9 March 2002 at Chelmsford.

®   WALMSLEY, Francis J.: released from military service and retired 24 May 2002 to Kiln Green, Reading.

CHOMNYCKY OSBM, Paul P.: ordained titular Bishop of *Buffada* and appointed Bishop of the Apostolic Exarchate for Ukrainians in Great Britain 11 June 2002 at Edmonton (AB), Canada.

®   KUCHMIAK CSsR, Michael: retired 11 June 2002 to Newark (NJ), USA thence to Yorkton (SK), Canada.

BURNS SM, Thomas M.: ordained Bishop in Ordinary to HM Forces 18 June 2002 at Aldershot.

†   CLARK, Alan C.: died 16 July 2002 at Norwich aged 82 • buried at the Catholic National Shrine of Our Lady of Walsingham, Houghton St Giles, Walsingham.

ROCHE, Arthur: translated 16 July 2002 to coadjutor Bishop of Leeds.

McPARTLAND SMA, Michael B.: appointed 31 July 2002
Apostolic Prefect of Falkland Islands and Superior *missio sui iuris* of
Saint Helena, Ascension and Tristan da Cunha.

FITZGERALD MAfr, Michael L.: appointed titular Archbishop
of *Nepte* and President of the Pontifical Council for Inter-religious
Dialogue 1 October 2002 at Vatican City.

MENNINI, Antonio: appointed 6 November 2002 Apostolic Nuncio
to Russian Federation.

+ RATZINGER, Joseph A. (POPE BENEDICT XVI): elevated 30
November 2002 to Cardinal-Bishop of Ostia and appointed Dean of the
College of Cardinals.

2003

HOPES, Alan S.: ordained titular Bishop of *Cuncacestre* and
appointed auxiliary Bishop of Westminster 24 January 2003 at
the Metropolitan Cathedral Church of the Most Precious Blood,
Westminster, London.

LONGLEY, Bernard: ordained titular Bishop of *Zarna* and
appointed auxiliary Bishop of Westminster 24 January 2003 at
the Metropolitan Cathedral Church of the Most Precious Blood,
Westminster, London.

† HARVEY, Philip J. B.: died 2 February 2003 at Whitton,
Twickenham aged 87 • buried at St Mary's Cemetery, Kensal Green,
London.

† HEIM, Bruno B.: died 18 March 2003 at Olten (Solothurn),
Switzerland aged 92 • buried at Neuendorf (Solothurn), Switzerland.

EVANS, Michael C.: ordained Bishop of East Anglia 19 March 2003
at Norwich.

WILLIAMS, Thomas A.: ordained titular Bishop of *Mageó*
and appointed auxiliary Bishop of Liverpool 27 May 2003 at the
Metropolitan Cathedral Church of Christ the King, Liverpool.

+ O'BRIEN, Keith M. P.: elevated 21 October 2003 to Cardinal-Priest
of Santi Gioacchino ed Anna al Tuscolano.

® BOWEN, Michael G.: retired 6 November 2003 to Blackheath,
London.

†   HORNYAK OSBM, Augustine E.: died 16 November 2003 at Acton, London aged 84 • buried at Kucura (Backa), Serbia.

MORAN, Peter A.: ordained Bishop of Aberdeen 1 December 2003 at Aberdeen.

McDONALD, Kevin J. P.: translated 8 December 2003 to Archdiocese of Southwark.

2004

®   TRIPP, Howard G.: retired 7 January 2004 to Wimbledon, London.

GALLAGHER, Paul R.: ordained titular Archbishop of *Hodelm* and appointed 13 March 2004 Apostolic Nuncio to Burundi at Rome, Italy.

®   GRIFFITHS OSB, M. Ambrose: retired 26 March 2004 to Leyland.

®   KONSTANT, David E.: retired 7 April 2004 to Headingley, Leeds.

ROCHE, Arthur: succeeded 7 April 2004 as Bishop of Leeds.

DUNN, Kevin J.: ordained Bishop of Hexham and Newcastle 25 May 2004 at Newcastle upon Tyne.

CUNNINGHAM, John: ordained Bishop of Galloway 28 May 2004 at Ayr.

®   TAYLOR, Maurice: retired 28 May 2004 to Ayr.

†   GUAZZELLI, Victor: died 1 June 2004 at Vauxhall, London aged 84 • buried at St Mary's Cemetery, Kensal Green, London.

*   CONTI, Mario J.: appointed 7 October 2004 Apostolic Administrator of the Diocese of Paisley until 20 November 2005.

®   MONE, John A.: retired 7 October 2004 to Greenock.

®   PUENTE BUCES, Pablo: resigned 23 October 2004 as Apostolic Nuncio to Great Britain and retired to Colindres (Cantabria), Spain.

LONCHYNA MSU, Hlib B. S.: translated 6 December 2004 to auxiliary Bishop of the Ukrainian Archeparchy of Kyiv-Halyč (Kiev), Ukraine.

SAINZ MUÑOZ, Faustino: appointed 11 December 2004 Apostolic Nuncio to Great Britain.

†   O'BRIEN, T. Kevin: died 27 December 2004 at Headingley, Leeds aged 81 • buried at the Cathedral Church of St Mary, Coulby Newham, Middlesbrough.

2005

† VAUGHAN, Herbert A. H.: reinterred 14 March 2005 at the Metropolitan Cathedral Church of the Most Precious Blood, Westminster, London.

† WOJTYŁA, Karol J. (POPE ST JOHN PAUL II): died 2 April 2005 at the Apostolic Palace, Vatican City aged 84 • buried at St Peter's Basilica, Vatican City.

x RATZINGER, Joseph A. (POPE BENEDICT XVI): elected Pope 19 April 2005 at Vatican City.

RATZINGER, Joseph A. (POPE BENEDICT XVI): installed 24 April 2005 at Vatican City.

† WRIGHT, Roderick: died 23 May 2005 at Napier (Hawke's Bay), New Zealand aged 64 • buried at Napier (Hawke's Bay), New Zealand.

DOYLE, Peter J. H.: ordained Bishop of Northampton 28 June 2005 at Northampton.

† BRUNNER, George: reinterred 7 June 2005 at the Cathedral Church of St Mary, Coulby Newham, Middlesbrough.

† LACY, Richard: reinterred 7 June 2005 at the Cathedral Church of St Mary, Coulby Newham, Middlesbrough.

† McCLEAN, John G.: reinterred 7 June 2005 at the Cathedral Church of St Mary, Coulby Newham, Middlesbrough.

† SHINE, Thomas: reinterred 7 June 2005 at the Cathedral Church of St Mary, Coulby Newham, Middlesbrough.

® O'BRIEN, James J.: retired 30 June 2005 to London Colney, St Albans.

† McGILL PSS, Stephen: died 9 November 2005 at Cardonald, Glasgow aged 93 • buried at St Conval's Cemetery, Barrhead, Glasgow.

TARTAGLIA, Philip: ordained Bishop of Paisley 20 November 2005 at Paisley.

McGOUGH, David C.: ordained titular Bishop of *Chunavia* and appointed auxiliary Bishop of Birmingham 8 December 2005 at the Metropolitan Cathedral Church of St Chad, Birmingham.

2006

ARNOLD, John S. K.: ordained titular Bishop of *Lindisfarna* and appointed auxiliary Bishop of Westminster 2 February 2006 at the Metropolitan Cathedral Church of the Most Precious Blood, Westminster, London.

HENDRICKS, Paul: ordained titular Bishop of *Rossmarkaeum* and appointed auxiliary Bishop of Southwark 14 February 2006 at the Metropolitan Cathedral Church of St George, Southwark, London.

LYNCH ss.cc, Patrick K.: ordained titular Bishop of *Castrum* and appointed auxiliary Bishop of Southwark 14 February 2006 at the Metropolitan Cathedral Church of St George, Southwark, London.

FITZGERALD MAfr, Michael L.: appointed 15 February 2006 Apostolic Nuncio to Egypt.

CHOMNYCKY OSBM, Paul P.: translated 20 February 2006 to the Apostolic Exarchate for Ukrainians in Stamford (CT), USA.

* LYSYKANYCH, B. Benjamin: appointed 21 February 2006 Apostolic Administrator of the Apostolic Exarchate for Ukrainians in Great Britain until 2 June 2009.

† HENDERSON, Charles J.: died 10 April 2006 at Blackheath, London aged 81 • buried at the Metropolitan Cathedral Church of St George, Southwark, London.

KENNEY CP, L. William: translated 17 October 2006 to auxiliary Bishop of Birmingham.

® MALONE, Vincent: retired 26 October 2006 to Old Swan, Liverpool.

2007

DIOCESE OF GALLOWAY: cathedral transferred 28 February 2007.

† WARD OFM Cap., John A.: died 27 March 2007 at Ystradowen, Cowbridge aged 78 • buried at the Abbey Church of St Joseph, Llantarnam, Cwmbran.

† McGUINNESS, James J.: died 6 April 2007 at Ednaston, Ashbourne aged 81 • buried at the Cathedral Church of St Barnabas, Nottingham.

†   O'BRIEN, James J.: died 11 April 2007 at London Colney, St Albans aged 76 • cremated and interred at Our Lady of Lourdes Church, New Southgate, London.

®   CROWLEY, John P.: retired 3 May 2007 to Wanstead, London thence to Harpenden.

†   HARRIS, Augustine: died 30 August 2007 at Ince Blundell, Liverpool aged 89 • buried at the Cathedral Church of St Mary, Coulby Newham, Middlesbrough.

†   COUVE DE MURVILLE, Maurice N. L.: died 3 November 2007 at Storrington, Pulborough aged 78 • buried at St Mary's College, Oscott, Sutton Coldfield.

2008

DRAINEY, Terence P.: ordained Bishop of Middlesbrough 25 January 2008 at Coulby Newham, Middlesbrough.

®   ALEXANDER, Mervyn A. N.: retired 20 February 2008 to Clifton Down, Bristol.

†   DUNN, Kevin J.: died 1 March 2008 at Newcastle upon Tyne aged 57 • buried at the Cathedral Crypt of St Mary, Newcastle upon Tyne.

CAMPBELL OSA, Michael G.: ordained coadjutor Bishop of Lancaster 31 March 2008 at Lancaster.

®   JUKES OFM Conv., John P.: retired 25 July 2008 to Huntly.

MENNINI, Antonio: appointed 26 July 2008 Apostolic Nuncio to Uzbekistan.

†   KUCHMIAK CSsR, Michael: died 26 August 2008 at Saskatoon (SK), Canada aged 85 • buried at Holy Family Cemetery, Winnipeg (MB), Canada.

BURNS SM, Thomas M.: released from military service 16 October 2008.

®   JABALÉ OSB, J. P. Mark: retired 16 October 2008 and appointed parish priest of Holy Trinity Church, Chipping Norton.

®   MURRAY, Ian: retired 16 October 2008 to Edinburgh.

BURNS SM, Thomas M.: translated 1 December 2008 to Diocese of Menevia.

TOAL, Joseph A.: ordained Bishop of Argyll and the Isles 8 December 2008 at Oban.

2009

†   LINDSAY, Hugh: died 19 January 2009 at Allithwaite, Grange-over-Sands aged 81 • buried at the Cathedral Crypt of St Mary, Newcastle upon Tyne.

GALLAGHER, Paul R.: appointed 19 February 2009 Apostolic Nuncio to Guatemala.

CUNNINGHAM, Séamus: ordained Bishop of Hexham and Newcastle 20 March 2009 at Newcastle upon Tyne.

®   MURPHY-O'CONNOR, Cormac: retired 3 April 2009 to Chiswick, London.

CAMPBELL OSA, Michael G.: succeeded 1 May 2009 as Bishop of Lancaster.

®   O'DONOGHUE, Patrick: retired 1 May 2009 to Bantry (Cork), Ireland.

NICHOLS, Vincent G.: translated 21 May 2009 to Archdiocese of Westminster.

*   KENNEY, L. William: appointed 22 May 2009 Apostolic Administrator of the Archdiocese of Birmingham until 8 December 2009.

*   LONCHYNA MSU, Hlib B. S.: appointed 2 June 2009 Apostolic Administrator of the Apostolic Exarchate for Ukrainians in Great Britain until 14 June 2011.

®   LYSYKANYCH, B. Benjamin: retired 2 June 2009 and appointed parish priest of All Saints' Ukrainian Church, Oldham.

O'DONOGHUE, Patrick: appointed 3 July 2009 assistant priest of St Finbarr's parish, Bantry (Cork), Ireland.

MOTH, C. P. Richard: released from military service 25 July 2009.

®   PARGETER, Philip: retired 31 July 2009 to Sutton Coldfield.

MOTH, C. P. Richard: ordained Bishop in Ordinary to HM Forces 29 September 2009 at the Metropolitan Cathedral Church of the Most Precious Blood, Westminster, London.

LONGLEY, Bernard: translated 1 October 2009 to Archdiocese of Birmingham.

®   McDONALD, Kevin J. P.: resigned 4 December 2009 as Archbishop of Southwark and retired to Southwark, London.

*   HINE, John F. M.: appointed 7 December 2009 Apostolic Administrator of the Archdiocese of Southwark until 10 June 2010.

BURNETTE, Kurt R.: incardinated 18 December 2009 into Eparchy of Holy Protection of Mary of Phoenix (Ruthenian) at Sherman Oaks (CA), USA.

V. PACELLI, Eugenio M. G. G. (**POPE VEN. PIUS XII**): proclaimed *Venerable* 19 December 2009 at Vatican City.

2010

DAVIES, Mark: ordained coadjutor Bishop of Shrewsbury 22 February 2010 at Wythenshawe, Manchester.

SMITH, Peter D. G.: translated 30 April 2010 to Archdiocese of Southwark.

HESKETT **CSsR**, Ralph: ordained Bishop of Gibraltar 10 July 2010 at Gibraltar.

† ALEXANDER, Mervyn A. N.: died 14 August 2010 at Clifton Down, Bristol aged 85 • buried at the Cathedral Churchyard of SS Peter and Paul, Clifton, Bristol.

DAVIES, Mark: succeeded 1 October 2010 as Bishop of Shrewsbury.

® NOBLE, Brian M.: retired 1 October 2010 to Heswall, Wirral.

® SAINZ MUÑOZ, Faustino: resigned 5 December 2010 as Apostolic Nuncio to Great Britain and retired to Madrid (Madrid), Spain.

MENNINI, Antonio: appointed 18 December 2010 Apostolic Nuncio to Great Britain.

® NEWTON, Keith: resigned 31 December 2010 as bishop suffragan of Richborough and Church of England priest.

2011

NEWTON, Keith: received into Catholic Church 1 January 2011 at the Metropolitan Cathedral Church of the Most Precious Blood, Westminster, London.

OUR LADY OF WALSINGHAM: erected 15 January 2011.

NEWTON, Keith: ordained priest (Our Lady of Walsingham) 15 January 2011 at the Metropolitan Cathedral Church of the Most Precious Blood, Westminster, London.

NEWTON, Keith: appointed 15 January 2011 as ordinary for Personal Ordinariate of Our Lady of Walsingham.

STACK, George: translated 19 April 2011 to Archdiocese of Cardiff.

BL. WOJTYŁA, Karol J. (POPE ST JOHN PAUL II): beatified 1 May 2011 at Vatican City.

®   MORAN, Peter A.: retired 4 June 2011 to Fortrose.

†   GRIFFITHS OSB, M. Ambrose: died 14 June 2011 at Leyland aged 82 • buried at the Abbey Church of St Laurence, Ampleforth, York.

LONCHYNA MSU, Hlib B. S.: translated 14 June 2011 to the Apostolic Exarchate for Ukrainians in Great Britain.

†   EVANS, Michael C.: died 11 July 2011 at Norwich aged 59 • cremated and interred at the Cathedral Church of St John the Baptist, Norwich.

GILBERT OSB, E. Hugh: ordained Bishop of Aberdeen 15 August 2011 at Aberdeen.

SHERRINGTON, John F.: ordained titular Bishop of *Hilta* and appointed auxiliary Bishop of Westminster 14 September 2011 at the Metropolitan Cathedral Church of the Most Precious Blood, Westminster, London.

†   JUKES OFM Conv., John P.: died 21 November 2011 at Huntly aged 88 • buried at the Metropolitan Cathedral Church of St George, Southwark, London.

2012

ROBSON, Stephen: ordained titular Bishop of *Tunnuna* and appointed auxiliary Bishop of St Andrews and Edinburgh 9 June 2012 at the Metropolitan Cathedral Church of St Mary, Edinburgh.

ENTWISTLE, Harry: received into Catholic Church 10 June 2012 at Guildford (WA), Australia.

ENTWISTLE, Harry: ordained priest (Our Lady of the Southern Cross) 15 June 2012 at Perth (WA), Australia.

ENTWISTLE, Harry: appointed 15 June 2012 as ordinary for Personal Ordinariate of Our Lady of the Southern Cross, Australia.

ROCHE, Arthur: appointed 26 June 2012 secretary of the Congregation for Divine Worship and Discipline of the Sacraments.

ROCHE, Arthur: appointed 26 June 2012 *Archbishop ad personam* at Vatican City.

® REGAN, Edwin: retired 27 June 2012 to Wrexham thence to Blaenau Ffestiniog.

® LOGAN, Vincent P.: resigned 30 June 2012 as Bishop of Dunkeld and retired to Dundee.

® HOLLIS, R. F. Crispian: retired 11 July 2012 to Mells, Frome.

® HRYNCHYSHYN CSsR, Michel: retired 21 July 2012 to Vincennes (Val-de-Marne), France.

® CONTI, Mario J.: retired 24 July 2012 to Glasgow.

TARTAGLIA, Philip: translated 24 July 2012 to Archdiocese of Glasgow.

BRIGNALL, Peter M.: ordained Bishop of Wrexham 12 September 2012 at Wrexham.

EGAN, Philip A.: ordained Bishop of Portsmouth 24 September 2012 at Portsmouth.

® FITZGERALD MAfr, Michael L.: retired 23 October 2012 to Rome, Italy.

† SAINZ MUÑOZ, Faustino: died 31 October 2012 at Madrid (Madrid), Spain aged 75 • buried at Madrid (Madrid), Spain.

REGAN, Edwin: appointed 1 November 2012 parish priest of St Mary Magdalene Church, Blaenau Ffestiniog.

† HRYNCHYSHYN CSsR, Michel: died 12 November 2012 at Vincennes (Val-de-Marne), France aged 83 • buried at Winnipeg (MB), Canada.

GALLAGHER, Paul R.: appointed 11 December 2012 Apostolic Nuncio to Australia.

2013

EPARCHY OF THE HOLY FAMILY OF LONDON: erected 18 January 2013.

LONCHYNA MSU, Hlib B. S.: appointed 18 January 2013 Bishop of the Ukrainian Eparchy of the Holy Family of London.

® O'BRIEN, Keith M. P.: retired 25 February 2013 to Edinburgh.

® KELLY, Patrick A.: resigned 27 February 2013 as Archbishop of Liverpool and retired to Southport.

*   TARTAGLIA, Philip: appointed 27 February 2013 Apostolic Administrator of the Archdiocese of St Andrews and Edinburgh until 21 September 2013.

*   WILLIAMS, Thomas A.: appointed 27 February 2013 Apostolic Administrator of the Archdiocese of Liverpool until 1 May 2014.

®   RATZINGER, Joseph A. (POPE BENEDICT XVI): resigned 28 February 2013 as Pope and retired to Vatican City.

x   BERGOGLIO SJ, Jorge M. (POPE FRANCIS): elected Pope 13 March 2013 at Vatican City.

      BERGOGLIO SJ, Jorge M. (POPE FRANCIS): installed 19 March 2013 at Vatican City.

®   O'DONOGHUE, Patrick: retired 2 April 2013 to Mallow (Cork), Ireland.

®   DEVINE, Joseph: retired 31 May 2013 to Hamilton.

*   TOAL, Joseph A.: appointed 31 May 2013 Apostolic Administrator of the Diocese of Motherwell until 29 April 2014.

      HOPES, Alan S.: translated 11 June 2013 to Diocese of East Anglia.

      CUSHLEY, Leo W.: ordained Archbishop of St Andrews and Edinburgh 21 September 2013 at the Metropolitan Cathedral Church of St Mary, Edinburgh.

®   BUDD, H. Christopher: retired 9 November 2013 to St Mary's, Isles of Scilly.

      BURNETTE, Kurt R.: ordained Bishop of Passaic (Ruthenian) 4 December 2013 at Passaic (NJ), USA.

      ROBSON, Stephen: translated 11 December 2013 to Diocese of Dunkeld.

®   HINE, John F. M.: retired 31 December 2013 to Tenterden.

2014

      O'TOOLE, Mark: ordained Bishop of Plymouth 28 January 2014 at Plymouth.

+   NICHOLS, Vincent G.: elevated 22 February 2014 to Cardinal-Priest of Santissimo Redentore e Sant'Alfonso in Via Merulana.

      KEENAN, John: ordained Bishop of Paisley 19 March 2014 at Paisley.

      McMAHON OP, Malcolm P.: translated 21 March 2014 to Archdiocese of Liverpool.

® McMAHON, Thomas: retired 14 April 2014 to Stock, Ingatestone.

ST RONCALLI, Angelo G. (POPE ST JOHN XXIII): canonised 27 April 2014 at Vatican City.

ST WOJTYŁA, Karol J. (POPE ST JOHN PAUL II): canonised 27 April 2014 at Vatican City.

TOAL, Joseph A.: translated 29 April 2014 to Diocese of Motherwell.

BYRNE CO, Robert: ordained titular Bishop of *Cuncacestre* and appointed auxiliary Bishop of Birmingham 13 May 2014 at the Metropolitan Cathedral Church of St Chad, Birmingham.

HESKETT CSsR, Ralph: translated 20 May 2014 to Diocese of Hallam.

® RAWSTHORNE, John A.: retired 20 May 2014 to Widnes.

HUDSON, Nicholas G. E.: ordained titular Bishop of *Sanctus Germanus* and appointed auxiliary Bishop of Westminster 4 June 2014 at the Metropolitan Cathedral Church of the Most Precious Blood, Westminster, London.

WILLIAMS SM, Alan: ordained Bishop of Brentwood 1 July 2014 at Brentwood.

ARNOLD, John S. K.: translated 30 September 2014 to Diocese of Salford.

® BRAIN, Terence J.: retired 30 September 2014 to Middleton, Manchester.

® CONRY, Kieran T.: resigned 4 October 2014 as Bishop of Arundel and Brighton and retired to Pease Pottage, Crawley.

★ SMITH, Peter D. G.: appointed 4 October 2014 Apostolic Administrator of the Diocese of Arundel and Brighton until 28 May 2015.

BL. MONTINI, Giovanni-Battista E. A. M. (POPE BL. PAUL VI): beatified 19 October 2014 at Vatican City.

GALLAGHER, Paul R.: appointed Secretary of the Secretariat of State 8 November 2014 at Vatican City.

STOCK, Marcus N.: ordained Bishop of Leeds 13 November 2014 at Leeds.

® CUNNINGHAM, John: retired 22 November 2014 to Greenock.

2015

NOLAN, William: ordained Bishop of Galloway 14 February 2015 at Kilmarnock.

+ O'BRIEN, Keith M. P.: resigned 20 March 2015 the rights and privileges of the Cardinal-Priest of Santi Gioacchino ed Anna al Tuscolano.

MOTH, C. P. Richard: translated 21 March 2015 to Diocese of Arundel and Brighton.

McKINNEY, Patrick J.: ordained Bishop of Nottingham 3 July 2015 at Nottingham.

2016

† MURRAY, Ian: died 22 January 2016 at Edinburgh • buried at Pennyfuir Cemetery, Oban.

McALEENAN, Paul: ordained titular Bishop of *Mercia* and appointed auxiliary Bishop of Westminster 25 January 2016 at the Metropolitan Cathedral Church of the Most Precious Blood, Westminster, London.

WILSON, John: ordained titular Bishop of *Lindisfarna* and appointed auxiliary Bishop of Westminster 25 January 2016 at the Metropolitan Cathedral Church of the Most Precious Blood, Westminster, London.

McGEE, Brian T.: ordained Bishop of Argyll and the Isles 18 February 2016 at Oban.

INDEXES

INDEX OF TITULAR SEES

Archbishop ad personam	† AMIGO, P. E.
	† KING, J. H.
† x MASTAI-FERRETTI, G. M. (POPE BL. PIUS IX)	
	† O'HARA, G. P. A.
† x PECCI, V. G. R. L. (POPE LEO XIII)	
	ROCHE, A.
	† SHINE, T.
Abdera (Abderitanus)	† ROSKELL, R. B.
Abercornia (Abercorniensis)	® MONE, J. A.
Abila Lysaniae (Abilenus Lysaniae)	† STRAIN, J. M.
Abora (Aborensis)	® MALONE, V.
Abula (Ablensis)	† RENFREW, C. M.
Acmonia (Acmoniensis)	† CARROLL, J.
Aeliae (Aeliensis)	† MATHEW, D. J.
Agathopolis (Agathopolitanus)	† KUCHMIAK CSsR, M.
Alinda (Alindensis)	† GRANT, C. A.
Amudarsa (Amudarsensis)	BRAIN, T. J.
Amycla (Amyclaeensis)	† FENTON, P.
	† WEATHERS, W.
Anazarbus (Anazarbensis)	† EYRE, C. P.
Ancusa (Ancusensis)	† ENRICI, D.
Apamea in Bithynia (Apamenus in Bithynia)	† MATHEW, D. J.
Apollonia (Apolloniensis)	† BROWN OSB, T. J.
Appia (Appianus)	† + GRIFFIN, B. W.
	† MURPHY, J. A.
Arcadiopolis in Asia (Arcadiopolitanus in Asia)	† GORDON, W.
Árd Carna (Ardcarnensis)	† O'BRIEN, T. K.
Areopolis (Areopolitanus) † x RONCALLI, A. G. (POPE ST JOHN XXIII)	
	† WAREING, W.

Arindela (Arindelensis)	† JOHNSON, W. A.
Ascalon (Ascalonitanus)	† MOSTYN, F. E. J.
Assus (Assiensis)	† BARRETT, J. P.
Auca (Aucensis)	x BERGOGLIO SJ, J. M. (POPE FRANCIS)
Ausuaga (Ausuagensis)	† RAFFERTY, K. L.
Bahanna (Bahannensis)	† HARVEY, P. J. H.
Bareta (Baretensis)	LONCHYNA MSU, H. B. S.
Bela (Belensis)	† TICKLE, G. W.
Beroea (Beroeensis)	† MYERS, E.
Betagbarar (Betagbarensis)	® KONSTANT, D. E.
Beverlacum (Beverlacensis)	® HINE, J. F. M.
Birtha (Birthensis)	† WALSH MAfr, F. P.
Botrys (Botryensis)	† DOUGLAS, E. W.
Britonia (Britoniensis)	† BREWER, J.
Buffada (Buffadensis)	CHOMNYCKY OSBM, P. P.
Bugia (Bugiensis)	† BROWN, G. H.
Cabasa (Cabasitanus)	† ULLATHORNE OSB, W. B.
Caesaropolis (Caesaropolitanus)	† HEDLEY OSB, J. E. C.
Cambysopolis (Cambysopolitanus)	† BUTT, J.
Cantanus (Cantanensis)	† CASHMAN, D. J.
Castrum (Castrensis)	LYNCH SS.CC, P. K.
Cell Ausaille (Cellae Sancti Auxilii)	† MONAGHAN, J.
Chersonesus in Zechia (Chersonensis in Zechia)	† MACKINTOSH, D. A.
Chunavia (Chunaviensis)	McGOUGH, D. C.
Cincari (Cincaritanus)	HOLLIS, R. F. C.
Cisamus (Cisamensis)	† GRAHAM, C. M.
	† WILKINSON, T. W.
Cius (Cianensis)	† BILSBORROW OSB, J. R.
	† + GODFREY, W.
Clazomenae (Clazomeniensis)	† COTTER, W. T.
Corycus (Coryciensis)	† KNIGHT, E.
Cresima (Cresimensis)	† CLEARY, J. F.
Cuncacestre (Cuncacestrensis)	BYRNE CO, R.
	HOPES, A. S.
	† LINDSAY, H.
	† SWINDLEHURST, O. F.
Cyme (Cymaeus)	† SCANLAN, J. D.
Cynopolis in Arcadia (Cynopolitanus in Arcadia)	† DOBSON, R.
Daulia (Dauliensis o Davaliensis)	† MELLON, W. H.

Eanach Dúin (Enachdunensis)	† MAHON MHM, G. T.
Elis (Elidensis)	† BRUNNER, G.
Elmhama (Helmamensis)	† CLARK, A. C.
	® McCARTIE, P. L.
Emmaüs (Emmausensis)	† PATTERSON, J. L.
	† STANLEY, A. C.
Epiphania in Cilicia (Epiphanensis in Cilicia)	† + BOURNE, F. A.
Etenna (Etennensis)	† HOLLAND, T.
Ferentium (Ferentiensis)	MENNINI, A.
Fesseë (Fesseitanus)	DUNN, P. J.
	† ILSLEY, E.
Fiorentino (Florentinensis)	® BARBARITO, L.
Flavias (Flaviensis)	† KNIGHT, E.
Flaviopolis (Flaviopolitanus)	† GLANCEY, M. F.
Gemellae in Numidia (Gemellensis in Numidia)	STACK, G.
Gerrha (Gerrhensis)	† GOSS, A.
Glastonia (Glastoniensis)	† O'CONNOR, K.
Heliopolis in Phoenicia (Heliopolitanus in Phoenicia)	† O'HARA, G. P. A.
Hermonthis (Hermonthitanus)	† HORNYAK OSBM, A. E.
Hermopolis Maior (Hermopolitanus)	† BRINDLE, R.
Hetalonia (Hetaloniensis)	† ULLATHORNE OSB, W. B.
Hilta (Hiltensis)	SHERRINGTON, J. F.
Hodelm (Hodelmensis)	GALLAGHER, P. R.
Hypaepa (Hypaepenus)	† BAGSHAWE CO, E. P.
Ilium (Iliensis)	† MAGUIRE, J.
Ios (Iotanus)	† CUNNINGHAM, J.
Lamsorti (Lamsortensis)	® BOWEN, M. G.
Lamus (Lamenus)	† McINTYRE, J.
	† MYERS, E.
	† SHINE, T.
Lindisfarna (Lindisfarnensis)	ARNOLD, J. S. K.
	† GUAZZELLI, V.
	WILSON, J.
Lugmad (Lugmadensis)	† + WINNING, T. J.
Lydda (Lyddensis)	† WARD, B. F. N.
Macra (Macrensis in Rhodope)	† ILSLEY, E.
Macri (Macrensis in Mauretania)	® PUENTE BUCES, P.
Magarmel (Magarmelitanus)	† PARKER, T. L.
Mageó (Mugensis)	WILLIAMS, T. A.

Manaccenser (Manaccenseritanus)	† O'BRIEN, J. J.
Martyropolis (Martyropolitanus)	† HENDREN OSF, J. W. F.
Maura (Maurensis)	† FOX, L. D.
Maxita (Maxitensis)	† McCLEAN, J. G.
Mercia (Merciorum)	† GRAY, J.
	McALEENAN, P.
Mesembria (Mesembrianus)	
† x RONCALLI, A. G. (POPE ST JOHN XXIII)	
Metellopolis (Metellopolitanus)	† KEATINGE, W. L.
Midica (Midicensis)	KENNEY CP, L. W.
Miletopolis (Miletopolitanus)	† BIDWELL, M. J.
	† MORIARTY, A. J.
Milo (Milensis)	† BUTT, J. B.
Milopotamos (Milopotamensis)	† + WISEMAN, N. P. S.
Murustaga (Murustagensis)	† BRUNNER, G.
Naupactus (Naupactensis)	† x RATTI, A. D. A. (POPE PIUS XI)
Neoportus (Neoportensis)	® TRIPP, H. G.
Nepte (Neptensis)	† CARDINALE, I. E.
	® FITZGERALD MAfr, M. L.
Nicopolis ad Iaterum (Nicopolitanus ad Iaterum)	† MacDONALD, J.
Nicopsis (Nicopsitanus)	† BUTT, J.
Nicosia (Nicosiensis)	† O'CALLAGHAN, H.
Nova Barbara (Novabarbarensis)	† BUTLER OSB, B. E. C.
Novaliciana (Novalicianensis)	† SAINZ MUÑOZ, F.
Odessus (Odessitanus)	† McINTYRE, J.
Olena (Olenensis)	† COWGILL, J. R.
Ombi (Obitanus)	† x WOJTYŁA, K. J. (POPE ST JOHN PAUL II)
Opus (Opuntius)	† KING, J. H.
Othona (Othonensis)	† HITCHEN, A.
	+ NICHOLS, V. G.
	† WALL, B. P.
Oxyrynchus (Oxyrynchitanus)	† McINTYRE, J.
Pella (Pellensis)	† BROWN, W. F.
Pessinus (Pessinuntinus)	† O'HARA, G. P. A.
Phocaea (Phocaeensis)	† PRESTON, R.
Pinhel (Pinhelensis)	† ALEXANDER, M. A. N.
Rhithymna (Rhithymnensis)	† WAREING, W.
Rossmarkaeum (Rossmarkensis)	HENDRICKS, P.
Rotdon (Rotdonensis)	® RAWSTHORNE, J. A.

Rusticiana (Rusticianensis)	ROCHE, A.
Samosata (Samosatensis)	† HOGARTH, W.
Sanctus Germanus (Cornubiensis)	HUDSON, N. G. E.
	† McGUINNESS, J. J.
Sardes (Sardianus)	† + HINSLEY, A.
† x PACELLI, E. M. G. G. (POPE VEN. PIUS XII)	
Sebastopolis in Armenia (Sebastopolitanus in Armenia)	† DEY, J.
	† CRAVEN, G. L.
	† + HINSLEY, A.
	† VAUGHAN, J. S.
Sebastopolis in Thracia (Sebastopolitanus in Thracia)	† BUTT, J. B.
Selinus (Selinusiensis)	† COLLINS, R.
Selucia in Isauria (Seleuciensis in Isauria)	† BAGSHAWE CO, E. G.
Sidnacestre (Syddensis)	® MULLINS, D. J.
Sinda (Sindensis)	† PEARSON, T. B.
Sita (Sitensis)	† WARD, J.
Socia (Sociensis)	† HARRIS, A.
Soli (Solensis)	† BRIGHT, H. P.
Sozusa in Palaestina (*Sozusenus in Palaestina*)	† AMHERST, F. K.
Strathernia (Stratherniensis)	† JUKES OFM Conv., J. P.
Sufar (Sufaritanus)	† CASEY, P. J.
Tacapae (Tacapitanus)	† BRINDLE, R.
Tamallula (Tamallulensis)	† EMERY, A. J.
Tamalluma (Tamallumensis)	® WALMSLEY, F. J.
Tamiathis (Tamiathitanus o Damiatensis)	
† x PECCI, V. G. R. L. (POPE LEO XIII)	
Thagora (Thagorensis)	† CAHILL, J. B.
Thala (Thalensis)	® CROWLEY, J. P.
Theudalis (Theudalensis)	† WHEELER, W. G.
Tiberias (Tiberiensis)	† GRAHAM, C. M.
Tigias (Tigiensis)	† BECK AA, G. A.
Tinis in Proconsulari (Tinisensis in Proconsulari)	† MOVERLEY, G.
Tipasa in Numidia (Tipasitanus in Numidia)	† GRAHAM, H. G.
Tlos (Tloënsis)	† BROWN, G. H.
Trachis (Trachonensis)	† BRIGGS, J.
Trapezus (Trapezuntinus)	† ERRINGTON, G.
Trecalae (Trecalitanus)	† HENDERSON, C. J.
Trocmades (Trocmadianus)	† MAGUIRE, J. A.
Tulana (Tulanensis)	® O'DONOGHUE, P.

Tunnuna (Tunnunensis)	ROBSON, S.
Tyrus (Tyrensis)	† x della GENGA, A. S. (POPE LEO XII)
Usula (Usulensis)	† CAMERON, E. H.*
Vagrauta (Vagrautensis)	† BURKE, G. I.
Valentiniana (Valentinianensis)	® PARGETER, P.
Verinopolis (Verinopolitanus)	† HENDREN OSF, J. W. F.
Voli (Volitanus)	® DEVINE, J.
Westminster (Vestmonasteriensis)	† GRIFFITHS OSB, M. A.**
Xanthus (Xanthiensis)	† HEIM, B. B.
Zabi (Zabensis)	† HALSALL, J. F.
Zarna (Zarnensis)	LONGLEY, B.
Zygris (Zygritanus)	† HRYNCHYSHYN CSsR, M.

Titular Sees: 163

NOTES

*   **EWEN HUGH CAMERON**: nominated 13 November 1917 titular Bishop of *Usula* and coadjutor Bishop of Argyll and the Isles but declined the appointment 20 November 1917.

**   **MICHAEL AMBROSE GRIFFITHS** OSB: resigned 5 April 1984 as Abbot of the Abbey Church of St Laurence, Ampleforth, York and appointed titular Abbot of *Westminster*.

INDEX OF CARDINAL TITLES

† + WISEMAN, N. P. S.

Santi Quattro Coronati

† x della CHIESA, G. P. G-B. (POPE BENEDICT XV)

Santissimo Redentore e Sant'Alfonso in Via Merulana   + NICHOLS, V. G.

San Roberto Bellarmino   x BERGOGLIO **SJ**, J. M. (POPE FRANCIS)

Santi Silvestro e Martino ai Monti

† x MONTINI, G-B. E. A. M. (POPE BL. PAUL VI)

† x RATTI, A. D. A. (POPE PIUS XI)

San Silvestro in Capite   † + HEENAN, J. C.

† + HUME, G. B.

Santa Susanna   † + HINSLEY, A.

Velletri Segni   ® x RATZINGER, J. A. (POPE BENEDICT XVI)

Cardinal Titles: 28

NOTES

*   KEITH MICHAEL PATRICK O'BRIEN: resigned 20
March 2015 the rights and privileges of the Cardinal-Priest of Santi
Gioacchino ed Anna al Tuscolano.

INDEX OF BISHOPS

† ALEXANDER, Mervyn A. N. (1925–2010 • VIII. Clifton)

† ALLEN, Samuel W. (1844–1908 • IV. Shrewsbury)

† AMHERST, Francis K. (1819–1882 • II. Northampton)

† AMIGO, Peter E. (1864–1949 • VI. Southwark)

ARNOLD, John S. K. (1953– • XI. Salford)

† BAGSHAWE CO, Edward G. (1829–1915 • III. Nottingham)

® BARBARITO, Luigi (1922– • VI. Apostolic Nunciature)

† BARRETT, John P. (1878–1946 • V. Plymouth)

† BECK AA, George A. (1904–1978 • VI. Liverpool)

† BENNETT, George H. (1875–1946 • V. Aberdeen)

x BERGOGLIO SJ, Jorge M. (1936– • POPE FRANCIS)

† BEWICK, John W. (1824–1886 • III. Hexham and Newcastle)

† BIDWELL, Manuel J. (1872–1930 • IV.(d) Westminster)

† BILSBORROW OSB, J. Romanus (1862–1931 • I. Cardiff)

† BILSBORROW, John (1836–1903 • III. Salford)

† BLACK, James (1894–1968 • I. Paisley)

† + BOURNE, Francis A. (1861–1935 • IV. Westminster)

® BOWEN, Michael G. (1930– • VIII. Southwark)

® BRAIN, Terence J. (1938– • X. Salford)

† BREWER, John (Jack) (1929–2000 • IV. Lancaster)

† BRIGGS, John (1788–1861 • I. Beverley)

† BRIGHT, Humphrey P. (1903–1964 • III.(b) Birmingham)

BRIGNALL, Peter M. (1953– • III. Wrexham)

† BRINDLE, Robert (1837–1916 • IV. Nottingham)

† BROWN, George H. (1786–1856 • I. Liverpool)

† BROWN, James (1812–1881 • I. Shrewsbury)

† BROWN OSB, T. Joseph (1798–1880 • I. Newport and Menevia)

† BROWN, William F. (1862–1951 • VI.(a) Southwark)

† BROWNLOW, William R. B. (1830–1901 • IV. Clifton)

†CE BRUNNER, George (1889–1969 • III. Middlesbrough)

®   BUDD, H. Christopher (1937– • VIII. Plymouth)

†   BURGESS OSB, T. Lawrence (1791–1854 • II. Clifton)

†   BURKE, Geoffrey I. (1913–1999 • VIII.(a) Salford)

     BURNETTE, Kurt R. (1955– • I. Bishops Around the World)

     BURNS SM, Thomas M. (1944– • XI. Menevia)

†   BURTON, George C. A. (1852–1931 • V. Clifton)

†CE   BUTLER OSB, B. E. Christopher (1902–1986 • VIII.(b) Westminster)

†   BUTT, John B. (1826–1899 • IV. Southwark)

†   BUTT, Joseph (1869–1944 • IV.(c) Westminster)

     BYRNE CO, Robert (1956– • IX.(a) Birmingham)

†   CAHILL, John B. (1841–1910 • II. Portsmouth)

†   CAMERON, E. Hugh (1876–1931 • II.(a) Argyll and the Isles (*nominated*))

†   CAMPBELL, Donald A. (1894–1963 • IV. Glasgow)

     CAMPBELL OSA, Michael G. (1941– • VI. Lancaster)

†   x CAPPELLARI OSB, B. A. Mauro (1765-1846 • POPE GREGORY XVI)

†   CARDINALE, Igino E. (1916–1983 • III. Apostolic Nunciature)

†   CARROLL, John (1838–1897 • III. Shrewsbury)

†   CARY-ELWES, Dudley C. (1868–1932 • V. Northampton)

†   CASARTELLI, Louis C. (1852–1925 • IV. Salford)

†   CASEY, Patrick J. (1913–1999 • V. Brentwood)

†   CASHMAN, David J. (1912–1971 • I. Arundel and Brighton)

†   x CASTIGLIONI, Francesco S. M. F. (1761-1830 • POPE PIUS VIII)

†   CHADWICK, James (1813–1882 • II. Hexham and Newcastle)

†   x CHIARAMONTI OSB, B. N. M. L. Gregorio (1742-1823 • POPE PIUS VII)

†   CHISHOLM, Aeneas (1836–1918 • IV. Aberdeen)

     CHOMNYCKY OSBM, Paul P. (1954– • IV. Ukrainians)

†   CLARK, Alan C. (1919–2002 • I. East Anglia)

†   CLARKE, John M. (1893–1963 • II.(a) Bishopric of the Forces)

†   CLEARY, Joseph F. (1912–1991 • V.(a) Birmingham)

†   CLIFFORD, William H. J. (1823–1893 • III. Clifton)

†   COFFIN CSsR, Robert A. (1819–1885 • III. Southwark)

†   COLLINS, Richard (1857–1924 • VI. Hexham and Newcastle)

®   CONRY, Kieran T. (1951– • IV. Arundel and Brighton)

®   CONTI, Mario J. (1934– • VII. Glasgow)

†	CORNTHWAITE, Robert (1818–1890 • I. Leeds)	
†	COTTER, William T. (1866–1940 • III. Portsmouth)	
†	COUVE DE MURVILLE, Maurice N. L. (1929–2007 • VII. Birmingham)	
†	COWDEROY, Cyril C. (1905–1976 • VII. Southwark)	
†	COWGILL, Joseph R. (1860–1936 • III. Leeds)	
†	CRAVEN, George L. (1884–1967 • VI.(a) Westminster)	
®	CROWLEY, John P. (1941– • VI. Middlesbrough)	
†	CUNNINGHAM, James (1910–1974 • IX. Hexham and Newcastle)	
®	CUNNINGHAM, John (1938– • VII. Galloway)	
	CUNNINGHAM, Séamus (1942– • XIII. Hexham and Newcastle)	
	CUSHLEY, Leo W. (1961– • VIII. St Andrews and Edinburgh)	
†	DANELL, James (1821–1881 • II. Southwark)	
	DAVIES, Mark (1959– • XI. Shrewsbury)	
†	x DELLA CHIESA, Giacomo P. G-B. (1854–1922 • POPE BENEDICT XV)	
†	x DELLA GENGA, Annibale S. (1760-1829 • POPE LEO XII)	
®	DEVINE, Joseph (1937– • IV. Motherwell)	
†	DEY, James (1869–1946 • II. Bishopric of the Forces)	
†	DOBSON, Robert (1867–1942 • II.(a) Liverpool)	
†	DOUBLEDAY, Arthur H. (1865–1951 • II. Brentwood)	
†	DOUGLAS, Edward W. (1901–1967 • I. Motherwell)	
†	DOWNEY, Richard J. (1881–1953 • III. Liverpool)	
	DOYLE, Peter J. H. (1944– • XII. Northampton)	
	DRAINEY, Terence P. (1949– • VII. Middlesbrough)	
†	DUNN, Kevin J. (1950–2008 • XII. Hexham and Newcastle)	
	DUNN, Patrick J. (1950– • II. Bishops Around the World)	
†	DUNN, Thomas (1870–1931 • V. Nottingham)	
†	DWYER, George P. (1908–1987 • VI. Birmingham)	
	EGAN, Philip A. (1955– • VIII. Portsmouth)	
†	ELLIS, Edward (1899–1979 • VII. Nottingham)	
†	EMERY, Anthony J. (1918–1988 • VI. Portsmouth)	
†	ENRICI, Domenico (1909–1997 • IV. Apostolic Nunciature)	
CE	ENTWISTLE, Harry (1940– • III. Bishops Around the World)	
†	ERRINGTON, George (1804–1886 • I. Plymouth)	
†	EVANS, Michael C. (1951–2011 • III. East Anglia)	
†	EYRE, Charles P. (1817–1902 • I. Glasgow)	
†	FENTON, Patrick (1837–1918 • IV.(a) Westminster)	

®   FITZGERALD **MAfr**, Michael L. (1937– • IV. Bishops Around the World)

†   FLYNN, Thomas E. (1880–1961 • II. Lancaster)

†   FOLEY, Brian C. (1910–1999 • III. Lancaster)

†   FOX, Langton D. (1917–1997 • VI. Menevia)

†   FOYLAN, Michael (1907–1976 • VIII. Aberdeen)

†   FRASER, Robert (1858–1914 • IV. Dunkeld)

     GALLAGHER, Paul R. (1954– • V. Bishops Around the World)

CE   GILBERT **OSB**, E. Hugh (1952– • XI. Aberdeen)

†   GLANCEY, Michael F. (1854–1925 • II.(a) Birmingham)

†   + GODFREY, William (1889–1963 • VII. Westminster)

†   GORDON, William (1831–1911 • II. Leeds)

†   GOSS, Alexander (1814–1872 • II. Liverpool)

†   GRAHAM, Charles M. (1834–1912 • III. Plymouth)

†   GRAHAM, Henry G. (1874–1959 • IV.(a) St Andrews and Edinburgh)

†   GRANT, Charles A. (1906–1989 • VIII. Northampton)

†   GRANT, Colin C. (1832–1889 • II. Aberdeen)

†   GRANT, Kenneth (1900–1959 • V. Argyll and the Isles)

†   GRANT, Thomas (1816–1870 • I. Southwark)

†   GRASAR, William E. (1913–1982 • VIII. Shrewsbury)

†   + GRAY, Gordon J. (1910–1993 • VI. St Andrews and Edinburgh)

†   GRAY, Joseph (1919–1999 • IX. Shrewsbury)

†   + GRIFFIN, Bernard W. (1899–1956 • VI. Westminster)

†   GRIFFITHS **OSB**, M. Ambrose (1928–2011 • XI. Hexham and Newcastle)

†   GRIMSHAW, Francis E. J. (1901–1965 • V. Birmingham)

†   GUAZZELLI, Victor (1920–2004 • VIII.(c) Westminster)

†   HALSALL, Joseph F. (1902–1958 • III.(a) Liverpool)

†   HANNIGAN, James (1928–1994 • I. Wrexham)

†   HANNON, Daniel J. (1884–1946 • IV. Menevia)

†   HARRIS, Augustine (1917–2007 • V. Middlesbrough)

†   HART, William A. (1904–1992 • VII. Dunkeld)

†   HARVEY, Philip J. B. (1915–2003 • IX.(a) Westminster)

†   HEDLEY **OSB**, J. E. Cuthbert (1837–1915 • II. Newport (and Menevia))

†   + HEENAN, John C. (1905–1975 • VIII. Westminster)

†   HEIM, Bruno B. (1911–2003 • V. Apostolic Nunciature)

†   HENDERSON, Charles J. (1924–2006 • VII.(a) Southwark)

†	HENDREN **OSF**, Joseph W. F. (1791–1866 • I. Nottingham)	
	HENDRICKS, Paul (1956– • IX.(a) Southwark)	
†	HENSHAW, Thomas (1873–1938 • V. Salford)	
	HESKETT **CSsR**, Ralph (1953– • III. Hallam)	
®	HINE, John F. M. (1938– • VIII.(c) Southwark)	
†	+ HINSLEY, Arthur (1865–1943 • V. Westminster)	
†	HITCHEN, Anthony (1930–1988 • VII.(a) Liverpool)	
†	HOGARTH, William (1786–1866 • I. Hexham (and Newcastle))	
†	HOLLAND, Thomas (1908–1999 • VIII. Salford)	
®	HOLLIS, R. F. Crispian (1936– • VII. Portsmouth)	
CE	HOPES, Alan S. (1944– • IV. East Anglia)	
†	HORNYAK **OSBM**, Augustine E. (1919–2003 • II. Ukrainians)	
†	HRYNCHYSHYN **CSsR**, Michel (1929–2012 • II.(a) Ukrainians)	
	HUDSON, Nicholas G. E. (1959– • XI.(b) Westminster)	
†	+ HUME **OSB**, G. Basil (1923–1999 • IX. Westminster)	
†	ILSLEY, Edward (1838–1926 • II. & I. Birmingham)	
®	JABALÉ **OSB**, J. P. Mark (1933– • X. Menevia)	
†	JOHNSON, William A. (1832–1909 • IV.(b) Westminster)	
†	JUKES **OFM Conv.**, John P. (1923–2011 • VIII.(a) Southwark)	
†	KEATING, Frederick W. (1859–1928 • II. Liverpool)	
†	KEATINGE, William L. (1869–1934 • I. Bishopric of the Forces)	
	KEENAN, John (1964– • V. Paisley)	
†	KEILY, John J. (1854–1928 • IV. Plymouth)	
®	KELLY, Patrick A. (1938– • VIII. Liverpool)	
	KENNEY **CP**, L. William (1946– • VIII.(b) Birmingham)	
†	KING, John H. (1880–1965 • IV. Portsmouth)	
†	KNIGHT, Edmund (1827–1905 • II. Shrewsbury)	
®	KONSTANT, David E. (1930– • VIII. Leeds)	
†	KUCHMIAK **CSsR**, Michael (1923–2008 • III. Ukrainians)	
†	LACY, Richard (1841–1929 • I. Middlesbrough)	
	LANG, Declan R. (1950– • IX. Clifton)	
†	LEE, William (1875–1948 • VI. Clifton)	
†	LINDSAY, Hugh (1927–2009 • X. Hexham and Newcastle)	
®	LOGAN, Vincent P. (1941– • VIII. Dunkeld)	
	LONCHYNA **MSU**, Hlib B. S. (1954– • I. Holy Family of London)	
	LONGLEY, Bernard (1955– • IX. Birmingham)	
†	x LUCIANI, Albino (1912–1978 • POPE JOHN PAUL I)	
	LYNCH **SS.CC.**, Patrick K. (1947– • IX.(b) Southwark)	
®	LYSYKANYCH, B. Benjamin (1943– • IV.(a) Ukrainians)	

McALEENAN, Paul (1951– • XI.(c) Westminster)

† McCARTHY, James W. (1853–1943 • III. Galloway)

® McCARTIE, P. Leo (1925– • X. Northampton)

† McCLEAN, John G. (1914–1978 • IV. Middlesbrough)

† McCORMACK, Joseph (1887–1958 • VIII. Hexham and Newcastle)

† McDONALD OSB, A. T. Joseph (1871–1950 • V. St Andrews and Edinburgh)

† MacDONALD, Angus (1844–1900 • III. St Andrews and Edinburgh)

† MacDONALD CSsR, Hugh (1841–1898 • III. Aberdeen)

† MacDONALD, John (1818–1889 • I. Aberdeen)

® McDONALD, Kevin J. P. (1947– • IX. Southwark)

† MacFARLANE, Angus (1843–1912 • III. Dunkeld)

McGEE, Brian T. (1965– • XI. Argyll and the Isles)

† McGEE, Joseph M. (1904–1983 • V. Galloway)

† McGILL PSS, Stephen (1912–2005 • II. Paisley)

McGOUGH, David C. (1944– • VIII.(a) Birmingham)

† McGRATH, Michael J. (1882–1961 • III. Cardiff)

† McGUINNESS, James J. (1925–2007 • VIII. Nottingham)

† McINTYRE, John (1855–1934 • II. Birmingham)

McKINNEY, Patrick J. (1954– • X. Nottingham)

† MACKINTOSH, Donald A. (1844–1919 • II.(a) Glasgow)

† MACKINTOSH, Donald (1877–1943 • III. Glasgow)

† McLACHLAN, John (1826–1893 • I. Galloway)

McMAHON OP, Malcolm P. (1949– • IX. Liverpool)

® McMAHON, Thomas (1936– • VI. Brentwood)

† McNULTY, John F. (1879–1943 • VI. Nottingham)

McPARTLAND SMA, Michael B. (1939– • VII. Bishops Around the World)

† MACPHERSON, Colin A. (1917–1990 • VII. Argyll and the Isles)

† MAGUIRE, James (1882–1944 • V.(a) Dunkeld)

† MAGUIRE, John A. (1851–1920 • II. Glasgow)

† MAHON MHM, Gerald T. (1922–1992 • VIII.(d) Westminster)

® MALONE, Vincent (1931– • VII.(d) Liverpool)

†CE + MANNING, Henry E. (1807–1892 • II. Westminster)

† MARSHALL, Henry V. (1884–1955 • VI. Salford)

† MARTIN, Donald (1873–1938 • III. Argyll and the Isles)

† x MASTAI-FERRETTI, Giovanni M. (1792–1878 • POPE BL. PIUS IX)

†   MASTERSON, Joseph (1899–1953 • IV. Birmingham)

†   MATHESON, John A. (1901–1950 • VI. Aberdeen)

†   MATHEW, David J. (1902–1975 • III. Bishopric of the Forces)

†   MELLON, William H. (1877–1952 • IV. Galloway)

     MENNINI, Antonio (1947– • IX. Apostolic Nunciature)

†   MONAGHAN, James (1914–1994 • VI.(a) St Andrews and Edinburgh)

®   MONE, John A. (1929– • III. Paisley)

†   x MONTINI, Giovanni-Battista E. A. M. (1897–1978 • POPE BL. PAUL VI)

®   MORAN, Peter A. (1935– • X. Aberdeen)

†   MORIARTY, Ambrose J. (1870–1949 • VI. Shrewsbury)

†   MOSTYN, Francis E. J. (1860–1939 • II. Cardiff)

     MOTH, C. P. Richard (1958– • V. Arundel and Brighton)

†   MOVERLEY, Gerald (1922–1996 • I. Hallam)

®   MULLINS, Daniel J. (1929– • IX. Menevia)

†   MURPHY, John A. (1905–1995 • IV. Cardiff)

®   + MURPHY-O'CONNOR, Cormac (1932– • X. Westminster)

†   MURRAY, Ian (1932–2016 • IX. Argyll and the Isles)

†   MYERS, Edward (1875–1956 • IV.(e) Westminster)

CE   NEWTON, Keith (1952– • I. Our Lady of Walsingham)

     + NICHOLS, Vincent G. (1945– • XI. Westminster)

®   NOBLE, Brian M. (1936– • X. Shrewsbury)

     NOLAN, William (1964– • VIII. Galloway)

†   O'BRIEN, James J. (1930–2007 • IX.(c) Westminster)

®   + O'BRIEN, Keith M. P. (1938– • VII. St Andrews and Edinburgh)

†   O'BRIEN, T. Kevin (1923–2004 • V.(a) Middlesbrough)

†   O'CALLAGHAN, Henry (1827–1904 • IV. Hexham and Newcastle)

†   O'CONNOR, Kevin (1929–1993 • VII.(b) Liverpool)

®   O'DONOGHUE, Patrick (1934– • V. Lancaster)

†   O'HARA, Gerald P. A. (1895–1963 • II. Apostolic Nunciature)

†   O'REILLY, Bernard (1824–1894 • III. Liverpool)

     O'TOOLE, Mark (1963– • IX. Plymouth)

†   x PACELLI, Eugenio M. G. G. (1876–1958 • POPE VEN. PIUS XII)

®   PARGETER, Philip (1933– • VII.(b) Birmingham)

†   PARKER, Thomas L. (1887–1975 • VII. Northampton)

†CE   PATTERSON, James L. (1822–1902 • II.(b) Westminster)

†   PEARSON, Thomas B. (1907–1987 • II.(a) Lancaster)

†   PEARSON OSB, T. Wulstan (1870–1938 • I. Lancaster)

†   x PECCI, Vincenzo G. R. L. (1810–1903 • POPE LEO XIII)

†   PETIT, John E. (1895–1973 • V. Menevia)

†CE   POSKITT, Henry J. (1888–1950 • IV. Leeds)

†   PRESTON, Richard (1856–1905 • V.(a) Hexham and Newcastle)

®   PUENTE BUCES, Pablo (1931– • VII. Apostolic Nunciature)

†   RAFFERTY, Kevin L. (1933–1996 • VII.(a) St Andrews and Edinburgh)

†   x RATTI, Ambrogio D. A. (1857–1939 • POPE PIUS XI)

®   x RATZINGER, Joseph A. (1927– • POPE BENEDICT XVI)

®   RAWSTHORNE, John A. (1936– • II. Hallam)

®   REGAN, Edwin (1935– • II. Wrexham)

†   RENFREW, Charles M. (1929–1992 • VI.(b) Glasgow)

†   RESTIEAUX, Cyril E. (1910–1996 • VII. Plymouth)

†   RIDDELL, Arthur G. (1836–1907 • III. Northampton)

†   RIGG, George (1814–1887 • I. Dunkeld)

CE   ROBSON, Stephen (1951– • IX. Dunkeld)

      ROCHE, Arthur (1950– • VIII. Around the World)

†   x RONCALLI, Angelo G. (1881–1963 • POPE ST JOHN XXIII)

†   ROSKELL, Richard B. (1817–1883 • II. Nottingham)

†   RUDDERHAM, Joseph E. (1899–1979 • VII. Clifton)

†   SAINZ MUÑOZ, Faustino (1937–2012 • VIII. Apostolic Nunciature)

†   x SARTO, Giuseppe M. (1835–1914 • POPE ST PIUS X)

†   SCANLAN, James D. (1899–1976 • V. Glasgow)

      SHERRINGTON, John F. (1958– • XI.(a) Westminster)

†   SHINE, Thomas (1872–1955 • II. Middlesbrough)

†   SINGLETON, Hugh (1851–1934 • V. Shrewsbury)

†   SMITH, George J. (1840–1918 • II. Argyll and the Isles)

†   SMITH, James A. (1841–1928 • IV. St Andrews and Edinburgh)

      SMITH, Peter D. G. (1943– • X. Southwark)

†   SMITH, William (1819–1892 • II. St Andrews and Edinburgh)

      STACK, George (1946– • VII. Cardiff)

†CE   STANLEY, A. Charles (1843–1928 • III.(b) Westminster)

CE   STOCK, Marcus N. (1961– • X. Leeds)

†   STRAIN, John M. (1810–1883 • I. St Andrews and Edinburgh)

†   SWINDLEHURST, Owen F. (1928–1995 • X.(a) Hexham and Newcastle)

      TARTAGLIA, Philip (1951– • VIII. Glasgow)

®	TAYLOR, Maurice (1926– • VI. Galloway)
†	THOMAS, Francis G. (1930–1988 • IX. Northampton)
†	THOMSON, Francis A. S. W. (1917–1987 • III. Motherwell)
†	THORMAN, Joseph (1871–1936 • VII. Hexham and Newcastle)
†	TICKLE, Gerard (Jock) W. (1909–1994 • IV. Bishopric of the Forces)
	TOAL, Joseph A. (1956– • V. Motherwell)
†	TONER, John (1857–1949 • V. Dunkeld)
®	TRIPP, Howard G. (1927– • VIII.(b) Southwark)
†	TURNER, William (1799–1872 • I. Salford)
†	TURNER, William (1844–1914 • II. Galloway)
†	ULLATHORNE OSB, W. Bernard (1806–1889 • I. Birmingham)
†	VAUGHAN, Francis J. (1877–1935 • II. Menevia)
†	+ VAUGHAN, Herbert A. H. (1832–1903 • III. Westminster)
†	VAUGHAN, John S. (1853–1925 • IV.(a) Salford)
†	VAUGHAN, William (1814–1902 • II. Plymouth)
†	VIRTUE (VERTUE), John (1826–1900 • I. Portsmouth)
†	WALL, Bernard P. (1894–1976 • IV. Brentwood)
®	WALMSLEY, Francis J. (1926– • V. Bishopric of the Forces)
†	WALSH MAfr, Francis P. (1901–1974 • VII. Aberdeen)
†	WARD, Bernard F. N. (1857–1920 • I. Brentwood)
†	WARD, James (1905–1973 • IV.(a) Glasgow)
†	WARD OFM Cap., John A. (1929–2007 • V. Cardiff)
†	WAREING, William (1791–1865 • I. Northampton)
†	WEATHERS, William (1814–1895 • II.(a) Westminster)
†CE	WHEELER, William G. (1910–1998 • VII. Leeds)
†	WHITESIDE, Thomas (1857–1921 • IV. & I. Liverpool)
†	WILKINSON, Thomas W. (1825–1909 • V. Hexham and Newcastle)
	WILLIAMS SM, Alan (1951– • VII. Brentwood)
	WILLIAMS, Thomas A. (1948– • XI.(a) Liverpool)
†	WILLIAMS, Thomas L. (1877–1946 • III. Birmingham)
CE	WILSON, John (1968– • XI.(d) Westminster)
†	+ WINNING, Thomas J. (1925–2001 • VI. Glasgow)
†	+ WISEMAN, Nicholas P. S. (1802–1865 • I. Westminster)
†	x WOJTYŁA, Karol J. (1920–2005 • POPE ST JOHN PAUL II)
†	WORLOCK, Derek J. H. (1920–1996 • X. Liverpool)
†	WRIGHT, Roderick (1940–2005 • VIII. Argyll and the Isles)
†	YOUENS SMA, Laurence W. (1872–1939 • VI. Northampton)

KEY TO SYMBOLS

	Bishops: . . . . _318 of which:_
	Active: . . . . _51_
ST	Saint: . . . . _3_
BL.	Beatified: . . . . _2_
V.	Venerable: . . . . _1_
x	Pope: . . . . _16_
+	Cardinal: . . . . _14_
®	Retired: . . . . _36_
CE	Former C. of E.: . . . . _14_
Mgr	Monsignor: . . . . _6_
†	Deceased: . . . . _231_
	Apost. Admin.: . . . . _28_
	Religious Orders: . . . . _39_

CPSIA information can be obtained
at www.ICGtesting.com
Printed in the USA
LVOW06*0407040416

482040LV00017B/137/P